World Economics Association
Book Series
Volume 11

I0125493

Trumponomics
Causes and Consequences

Titles produced by the World Economics Association & College Publications

Volume 1:
The Economics Curriculum. Towards a Radical Reformation. Maria Alejandra Madi and Jack Reardon, eds.
Volume 2:
Finance as Warfare. Michael Hudson
Volume 3:
Developing an Economics for the Post-crisis World. Steve Keen
Volume 4:
On the Use and Misuse of Theories and Models in Mainstream Economics. Lars Pålsson Syll
Volume 5:
Green Capitalism. The God that Failed. Richard Smith
Volume 6:
40 Critical Pointers for Students of Economics. Stuart Birks
Volume 7:
The European Crisis. Victor Beker and Beniamino Moro, eds.
Volume 8:
A Philosophical Framework for Rethinking Theoretical Economics and Philosophy of Economics. Gustavo Marqués
Volume 9:
Narrative Fixation in Economics. Edward Fullbrook
Volume 10:
Ideas Towards a New International Financial Architecture. Oscar Ugarteche, Alicia Payana and Maria Alejandra Madi, eds
Volume 11:
Trumponomics. Causes and Consequences. Edward Fullbrook and Jamie Morgan, eds.

The **World Economics Association (WEA)** was launched on May 16, 2011. Already over 13,000 economists and related scholars have joined. This phenomenal success has come about because the WEA fills a huge gap in the international community of economists – the absence of a professional organization which is truly international and pluralist.

The World Economics Association seeks to increase the relevance, breadth and depth of economic thought. Its key qualities are worldwide membership and governance, and inclusiveness with respect to: (a) the variety of theoretical perspectives; (b) the range of human activities and issues which fall within the broad domain of economics; and (c) the study of the world's diverse economies.

The Association's activities centre on the development, promotion and diffusion of economic research and knowledge and on illuminating their social character.

The WEA publishes 20+ books a year, three open-access journals (*Economic Thought, World Economic Review* and *Real-World Economics Review*), a bi-monthly newsletter, blogs, holds global online conferences, runs a textbook commentaries project and an eBook library.

www.worldeconomicsassociation.org

Trumponomics
Causes and Consequences

Edited by
Edward Fullbrook
and
Jamie Morgan

ISBN 978-1-84890-242-8 print
ISBN 978-1-911156-35-2 eBook-PDF

Published by College Publications (London) on behalf of the World Economics Association (Bristol)

http://www.worldeconomicsassociation.org
http://www.collegepublications.co.uk

Cover design by Laraine Welch
Printed by Lightning Source, Milton Keynes, UK

Contents

Introduction

Edward Fullbrook and Jamie Morgan

Two things seem generally agreed about Donald Trump's election as President of the United States: it is, for good or for bad, potentially a major historical turning point and its most important determinant was the economic reality experienced today by the majority of Americans. Given that over recent decades that reality came into being through economic polices largely designed by the economics profession, it seemed to us imperative that economists come together in an open forum – one not dominated by a particular school or ideology – to share their insights not only with other economists but also with a wider intellectual audience.

The essays collected here provide important insights and analysis from some of the most respected names in their fields. The title of this collection is *Trumponomics: Causes and Consequences,* but the essays range further than this might imply. The contributors have a great deal to say about economy, but are not hidebound by the narrow strictures of much of contemporary economics. This is not a set of essays confirming the obvious through abstruse mathematics. Instead, the essays set out the many socio-economic factors that help to account for the appeal of Trump, the limits and tensions of the policy tendencies articulated by Trump, and the general context of failure of economics as theory and practice that neither prevented the socio-economic factors nor lead to reasonable alternatives now.

Amongst the more general essays, Pressman, Neil, and Wray establish that Trump was a beneficiary of growing inequality in the US. As some also note, the Democrats have become more concerned with cultural conflict than economic benefits to what were once their core voters. For Hudson, Trump is Obama's legacy, whilst Mayhew introduces a note of caution, since not all who voted for Trump were the most economically deprived and desperate, and there is a danger that one denigrates a stereotypical Trump voter to the detriment of genuine understanding of their concerns. The longstanding

1

theory of Polanyi figures significantly here, as it does also for Pettifor. For Ruccio, class provides the underlying commonality. Nelson, meanwhile, provides a stark reminder just how oppositional Trump is in cultural terms when one speaks of the positives of gender analysis. Feiner pursues the dark side of the same in terms of quasi-religious fundamentalism, and Goodwin articulates something similar, locating Trump as a response to twenty-first century trauma (in turn calling forth yet more trauma).

This manufactured sense of loss that overlays genuine concern is a theme that Patomäki and Gills take up in terms of the US role in the world economy. The persistent myth of lost hegemony has consequences for domestic US politics and how the US projects itself in the world. Trump's "make America great again" is the latest articulation of this. Wade provides further general theoretical context to make sense of Trump on trade. The history of globalization has been heavily influenced by comparative trade theory and dubious claims made for the benefits of free movement of goods, labour and capital. Trump's opposition to free trade may attract the pejoratives of protectionism, but speaks also to the possibility of a more enlightened cooperative internationalism, where states take back some policy power space from a situation that benefits corporations and monopoly. Ironically, as Locke points out, Trump is more in the tradition of US corporate behaviour than its more productive capital investment-oriented varieties typified in some other countries. In any case, comparative advantage pays little attention to the realities of winners and losers in real systems. For Sapir, Trump on trade represents a great reversal and this may not in the end be all bad, since trade liberalization has various consequences – notably for poorer nations, including their democratic characteristics. Ghosh reminds us that Trump, of course, is not exactly a harbinger of enlightenment, and so Trump on trade will likely have adverse immediate consequences for developing countries. Puyana takes up the tensions in terms of Mexico's fractious relationship with the US, and Kagarlitsky provides a useful reminder that every threat is also an opportunity. Genuine social change requires viable alternatives to Trump.

However, the question of alternatives presupposes proper analysis of the sources of ideational constraint. This returns us to the questions, what is being learned and on what basis? But it does so first in terms of what Trump

2

is not learning, and so refusing. Though Wray notes he was briefly approached by an advisor claiming to represent Trump, it seems clear that Trumponomics has not turned out to be sympathetic to Post-Keynesian theory, with its critique of financialisation, debt deflation dynamics, money creation fallacies and regressive austerity politics. Nor has it proved sympathetic to ecological economics. Daly provides a concise critique of the problems of the latter, whilst Galbraith skewers the former in terms of current developments in central bank policy. For Galbraith, interest rate policy is liable to provide a break on productive investment and channel capital into the finance and property sectors (stoking asset bubbles). Bank policy is just one factor among many that affect key aspects of Trump's goals and pledges. As Kelton notes, the multiple dynamics of Trump's approach may look superficially Keynesian but actually express versions of Reaganomics, and will likely, via tax cut effects in particular, create short-term unstable growth with greater levels of inequality. Some of that growth, as both Baker and Tcherneva note, will draw in new labour, increasing the participation rate. However, as Tcherneva also argues, the long-term effects on employment are questionable, and the underlying goal of Trumponomics to create 25 million new jobs over ten years is actually around trend and not especially ambitious.

We have by no means made mention of all the contributions here, since there are nearly 30. What this brief introduction is intended to convey is the breadth and depth of those contributions. Trump positioned himself as the answer to all questions, but everything he does seems to beg more questions. With future history in mind, this collection is a good place to start in looking for intelligent answers.

Economic policy in the Trump era

Dean Baker [Center for Economic and Policy Research, Washington, DC, USA]

Introduction

The world looks pretty scary with Donald Trump in the White House and Republicans controlling both houses of Congress, so let's start with a positive side to this picture. As long as a Democrat held the presidency, the Republicans in Congress were devout deficit hawks. Now that they are in control, the Republicans are likely to be less devoted to deficit reduction. This certainly was true in both the Reagan and Bush II presidencies. In both cases Republicans were content to see deficits explode. It is reasonable to believe that they will again be happy to sacrifice their commitment to deficit reduction to the greater cause of reducing taxes for the wealthy.

While giving tax cuts to rich people is hardly the best way to boost the economy, and efforts to reduce social spending to make up the shortfall will have to be resisted, the effect of tax cuts will undoubtedly be to boost demand. If the Fed doesn't act aggressively to counter this stimulus, we are likely to see gains in employment with considerable benefits to large segments of the working class.

There was a shift of almost 4.5 percentage points of corporate income from labor to capital as a result of the weak labor market in the 2008-2009 recession. This shift began in the housing bubble years, but that was largely a matter of accounting. Profits on junk loans were booked in the bubble years, the losses showed up in 2008 and 2009 when homeowners stopped making payments. For this reason, there is little reason to believe there would have been a shift against workers without the Great Recession.

The tightening of the labor market in 2015 and 2016 has reversed more than half of this upward redistribution, but reversing the rest will require continued tightening of the labor market. The additional deficit spending associated with Republican tax cuts will likely accomplish this goal.

This is a huge deal. Not only does a tighter labor market mean more people will have jobs, it will disproportionately help the most disadvantaged. The unemployment rate for African Americans is typically twice the unemployment rate for whites. The unemployment rate for Hispanics is generally one and a half times the rate for whites. And for African American teens the ratio is typically six to one.

The wage gains from a tight labor market disproportionately go to those at the bottom end of the wage distribution. The low unemployment years from 1996 to 2001 were the only period since the early 1970s in which workers at the middle and the bottom end of the wage distribution saw consistent wage gains. During these years even hotels and fast food restaurants had to compete for workers. Some McDonalds offered bonuses to workers bringing in friends as new workers and suburban businesses arranged private bus service to bring in workers from the inner city every morning. In short, a tight labor market can do a great deal of good.[1]

It is also important to realize that there can be a lasting dividend from getting more people employed now. The employment to population ratio (EPOP) for prime age workers (ages 25-54) is still down by two full percentage points from its pre-recession level and by almost four percentage points from its 2000 peak. The mainstream of the economic profession is prepared to accept this falloff as just a fact of nature. For some reason millions of prime age workers no longer have the skills and/or desire to work. (It is worth noting that virtually no one predicted the falloff in prime age employment either before the 2001 recession or the 2008-2009 recession.)

Given the importance of authority in economic policy debates, as opposed to logic and evidence, it is not possible to win this debate against the mainstream of the profession. However, it is possible for the economy to win the debate with the mainstream of the economics profession. If the EPOP for prime age workers were to rise two percentage points back to its pre-

---

[1] The impact of low unemployment rates on the labor market is discussed at length in Baker and Bernstein (2013).

recession level, without a noticeable uptick in the inflation rate, or even better four percentage points back to 2000 levels, then it will be difficult for even mainstream economists to claim it is not possible.

This is exactly what happened in the late 1990s. In the early and mid-1990s it was virtually a matter of absolute faith that the unemployment rate could not fall much below 6.0 percent without triggering an inflationary spiral. Thankfully, then Federal Reserve Board Chair Alan Greenspan was not a mainstream economist. He argued with his colleagues that there was little evidence of inflationary pressure and therefore no reason to raise interest rates and slow the economy. The Fed allowed the unemployment rate to fall below 5.0 percent in 1997 and then reach 4.0 percent as a year-round average in 2000. And there was no noticeable uptick in the rate of inflation.

As a result of this experience, the profession has to discard its 6.0 percent floor on the unemployment rate. The Congressional Budget Office (CBO) and other official forecasters accepted that the unemployment rate could reach levels near 4.0 percent without accelerating inflation. This created a new benchmark for economic policy that allows for far lower unemployment rates than the early 1990s benchmark. We would not have seen this lower benchmark if the Fed has followed the textbook, and the urging of many members of the Open Market Committee, and raised interest rates enough to prevent the drop in the unemployment rate in the second half of the decade.

In this respect, if the demand boost from Trump's policies is not offset by overly restrictive Federal Reserve Board policies, we will have the opportunity to prove that the EPOP can go higher than the mainstream of the economic profession now accepts. This can give us the facts on the ground we need to win the argument on the maximum obtainable EPOP.

Defense on the Affordable Care Act and other social programs

The Republicans have made clear their desire to go after the countries' social programs, targeting not only the smaller ones designed to protect the poor, but also Social Security, Medicare, and the Affordable Care Act (ACA).

These programs make a huge difference in the lives of tens of millions of people. There is little justification for privatizing or cutting these programs. The United States is an outlier in the lack of generosity of its anti-poverty programs and its protections for middle class workers and retirees. These programs are generally well-run, with administrative costs that are far lower than private sector alternatives, and relatively little fraud.

The fact that so many people are dependent on these programs hugely increases the likelihood that they can be protected. It appears that the ACA is first on the Republicans' agenda. Twenty million people are currently getting insurance as a result of the ACA. These people and their family members provide an enormous base of opposition to the elimination of the ACA. For these people, the potential loss of insurance is very concrete; this is not some hypothetical that we have to convince them to accept.

It is also important to realize that the people who are getting insurance through the ACA are constantly changing. Five million people lose or leave their jobs every month. Many of these people are losing employer-provided insurance along with their jobs. These people may benefit from being able to get insurance through the exchanges for six months or a year, but then may be back on an employer-provided plan.

The public appreciates the new freedom allowed by the ACA even if most policy types have not yet noticed it. Voluntary part-time employment is up by more than 2.4 million since the ACA took effect in 2014, with especially large rises for young parents and workers just below Medicare age. Involuntary part-time employment has fallen by almost the same amount, leaving little net change in part-time employment.

In short, there are tens of millions of people who understand their stake in protecting the ACA and will likely pressure their members of Congress. There were major protests in support of the ACA even before Donald Trump was inaugurated. If the Republican efforts to repeal the ACA can be derailed, it will make them very shy about going after Social Security and Medicare. It can be expected that they will continue their attacks on anti-poverty programs with the hope of separating out the poor from the middle class, but stopping repeal of the ACA will be a huge victory which can be used to build momentum

Progressive policy in the Trump era: moving to the States

With actions at the national level likely to be largely defensive, the best hope for progressive change is at the state and local level. Fortunately, there are already many efforts already in place which can be built upon.

For example, many state and local governments have already raised their minimum wage well above the $7.25 an hour national rate. In addition, many state and local governments now guarantee workers paid sick days and/or family leave. These efforts can continue to move forward even with Republican control of the federal government.[2] However there are also opportunities at the state and local level to push policies that may more fundamentally challenge the power of the wealthy.

For example, the issue of reducing average work hours or work years can be pressed further with policies like mandating paid vacations and promoting work sharing as an alternative to unemployment benefits. These policies can bring the United States more in line with other wealthy countries, like Germany and the Netherlands, where workers put in twenty percent fewer hours a year on average. Reducing work hours is both a way to improve the quality of life for workers – people should have time to take vacations and be with their families or pursue other interests – and to increase the bargaining power of workers. While the trade-off between reduced work hours and increased employment will never be exactly one to one (i.e. a 10.0 percent reduction in average hours will not lead to a 10.0 percent increase in

---

[2] An important caution is that these efforts can go too far. At some point, a high enough minimum wage will create enough job loss that the net effect on the low wage labor market is negative. The additional increment to hourly pay will not offset the reduction in hours worked as result of the pay increase, leaving low wage workers on average worse off. It is important not to press increases in the minimum wage to this level in places where the politics might allow it. Not only will an excessive minimum wage be a bad story for the low wage workers immediately affected, it will also be held up as an example of the folly of pushing for higher minimum wages more generally. That could be a serious setback for efforts to raise wages for low-paid workers.

employment), shorter work years will in general lead to more jobs. Mandating various forms of paid leave, including paid vacation, is entirely within the power of state governments.

Similarly, states have the authority they need to promote work sharing as an alternative to layoffs when companies see reduced demand for labor. As it stands more than half the states, including large states like California and New York, already have work sharing programs as part of their unemployment insurance systems. Work sharing policies can be an effective way to combat unemployment. In the recession, Germany's downturn was steeper than in the United States, yet its unemployment rate actually fell. The take up on existing state work sharing programs is extremely low because many employers don't know they exist. Also, many of the programs are overly bureaucratic with rules badly in need of modernization.

Another way that states can improve the labor market for its workers is by ending dismissal at will, at least for longer-term employees. Montana already prohibits dismissal without cause for workers who have been on the job for more than six months. This sort of protection makes workers more secure in their employment and can also facilitate union organizing since it would be more difficult to dismiss workers involved in an organizing drive.

States could also require severance pay in order to discourage companies from simply laying off longer term workers and moving operations overseas. For example, if companies had to pay two weeks of severance pay for each year of employment, a worker who had been on the job for twenty years would be entitled to forty weeks of severance pay. This would provide a substantial financial cushion to a longer term worker facing the loss of their job. More importantly it would change the equation for employers. If they knew they would have to pay a substantial price for dismissing workers they would have more incentive to keep them employed. This would encourage them to modernize facilities and upgrade workers' skills, since this would be preferable to large severance payments for simply getting rid of them.

Severance pay can be set at levels that are too high and discourage hiring and investment, but there is a long way between zero and this point. Germany, which has substantial severance pay requirements, has an unemployment rate of just 4.1 percent. States where progressives have a voice can make steps towards providing more secure unemployment without worrying about massive capital flight.

Reforming health care

Progressives have generally focused their efforts on health care reform at the federal level, which is where many of the key policy decisions are made, however there are steps that can be taken at the state level. Health care is an area where the market has been structured to create enormous rents for doctors, drug companies, and insurers. There are ways to undermine these rents for the benefit of the people in a state taking progressive measures.

One route is to take advantage of the lower cost health care available in other countries. While it doesn't make sense to go to Germany, Canada, or Thailand for a check-up or emergency care, there are many expensive surgical procedures that are done on a non-emergency basis, where there can be enormous savings from having them performed outside of the United States. In some cases the cost difference can be an order of magnitude, with high quality facilities in hospitals in India or Thailand performing procedures costing $100,000 to $200,000 in the United States for a tenth of the price. The gap can allow for enormous savings even after paying for the travel of the patient and family members and a stay overseas for a period of recovery.

By facilitating this travel for medical care states can both directly save money for themselves on programs like Medicaid and for their residents on their health care. At the same time, they will be calling attention to the fact that health care costs in the United States are out of line with the rest of the world, not because we get better care, but because we allow providers to gouge the public.

To facilitate this sort of travel states would need to first assure the quality of care in overseas facilities. In Western Europe and other areas with strong regulatory systems, states should be able to accept the foreign countries' certification. In developing countries, with facilities of uneven quality, it would be necessary to have some independent review process. There are currently international accreditation systems, but their integrity is questionable. In principle it should be possible to support a system that could ensure that patients will be getting high quality care. Developing countries would benefit from having patients from the United States and other wealthy countries, so they should be willing to share in the cost of setting up a strong accreditation system.[3]

The other way in which states can facilitate medical travel is by setting up a clear system of legal liability so that patients will be compensated for damages from improper care. Patients will not be likely to risk their health in another country unless they can have assurances that the care is of high quality and that there is legal redress in the event that something goes wrong. Rules for medical malpractice are largely set at the state level so it should be entirely feasible for a state to put in place rules whereby an intermediary arranging medical travel would be legally responsible for any complications that may result from improper care.

The United States pays its doctors more than twice as much on average as doctors in other wealthy countries. This is the result of both protectionist measures internationally and licensing restrictions domestically. On the international side, doctors are prohibited from practicing in the United States unless they complete a U.S. residency program. Obviously there are hundreds of thousands of very competent doctors in Europe and elsewhere who are excluded from practicing medicine by this measure. While this protectionist measure may cost the country as much as $100 billion a year in higher health care costs, it is almost never mentioned by "free traders", which says an enormous amount about the sincerity of their commitment to free trade.

---

[3] There is an issue that patients from rich countries could be pulling resources away from people in the developing world. This can be offset by a tax on medical travel which is used to train more doctors and medical personal in the developing country. An individual state cannot guarantee that a developing country will tax medical travel and use the proceeds to improve health care, but on the other hand, if a government is not committed to providing health care to its population, the presence of foreigners using its health care system is likely to have little consequence for the ability of its people to get care.

States cannot overturn this federal regulation, but they can try to work around it. Missouri, Kansas, and Arkansas have all passed laws allowing physicians who have not been accepted to a residency program to practice under the supervision of another physician. Programs like this can be expanded to allow more doctors to practice, putting downward pressure on their pay. States can also be aggressive in expanding the range of practice of nurse practitioners and physicians' assistants. In addition to reducing the cost of care, this will also provide good paying jobs to workers somewhat below the top 2-3 percent inhabited by doctors.

There should also be as much effort as possible to take the control of health care standards away from people who have a direct financial stake. In the United States two thirds of physicians are specialists, which in other wealthy countries only one-third are specialists. This means that general practitioners perform many diagnoses and procedures in other countries that are typically done by specialists in the United States. There is little evidence that this greater use of specialists typically results in better outcomes. Doctors should not be the ones setting the standards of care. It would be best if these standards are set by other health care professionals without a direct financial stake. This will be increasingly important as technology is likely to facilitate diagnoses by less highly trained (and paid) health care professionals.

There is also an enormous amount to be saved from avoiding patent protected drug prices in the United States. The country currently spends $430 billion on prescription drugs. These drugs would likely cost around $60 billion in a free market. In the case of very expensive drugs, like the hepatitis C drug Sovaldi, the ratio of the protected price to the free market price can easily be more than 100 to 1. (The list price of Sovaldi in the United States is $84,000, while a high quality generic is available in India for less than $200.) While states cannot directly get around patent monopolies they can make it easier for their residents to circumvent them. One way would be to keep a list of reliable suppliers in other countries from which residents could order drugs.[4] For patients on Medicaid or other state health insurance programs, they can even offer to share the savings with the beneficiary. Also in the

---

[4] While the legal status of importing drugs is not entirely clear, the government has generally allowed individuals to import drugs for personal use.

case of very expensive drugs, which can cost well over $100,000 for a treatment, states can offer to allow beneficiaries to travel to take advantage of lower cost drugs and share in the savings. The point of this policy is both to save money and to drive home how drug companies have taken advantage of government imposed monopolies to get rich at the expense of the rest of society.

Corporate governance

Another area that can be addressed at the state level is the corruption of the corporate governance process. As it currently stands the rules of corporate governance allow CEOs and other top management to effectively rip-off shareholders by giving themselves exorbitant salaries. The ostensible check on CEO pay is the corporations' boards of directors, but these directors almost invariably hold more allegiance to top management than the shareholders they are supposed to represent.[5]

Contrary to what the many self-proclaimed supporters of free markets would have us believe, the rules of corporate governance are determined by the government, not the free market. Companies are incorporated at the state level, which means that states can change rules of incorporation to structure them to be more favorable to shareholders. As it stands now, the bulk of shares are voted by asset managers like BlackRock. These asset managers almost always support management in their choice of directors as well as other issues put up for a vote by shareholders.

State governments could take away these proxy votes and require that corporations only count votes from shares that are directly cast by shareholders. This would make it far easier for a limited number of investors to organize to get rid of directors that are not doing their jobs. It would also make it easier for shareholders to act directly to hold down CEO pay. One way to further this process would be to attach some consequence to currently non-binding "Say on Pay" votes required by the Dodd-Frank Act.

---

[5] More than 99 percent of directors that stand for re-election win.

Under this law, shareholders have the opportunity to vote down the pay package for CEOs at regular intervals. There is no direct consequence of the package being voted down, except as a reprimand to directors for allowing an excessive package. States could alter this, for example, by putting into law that directors lose their pay if a "Say on Pay" package is defeated. While less than 3.0 percent of pay packages currently go down to defeat, this risk is likely to make directors more cautious in awarding high CEO pay. Ideally, this would set in motion a downward spiral in which directors feel the need to make sure that the pay of their CEO does not rank among the highest in the industry, in order to reduce the risk of losing their pay for the year.

Of course many corporations could just opt to re-incorporate in a different state, but this would require CEOs to effectively say that they are scared of letting shareholders have a voice in running the company that they are supposed to own. It would also call attention to the fact that it is not the market that gives CEOs annual salaries in the tens of millions, but rather the corruption of the corporate governance process. Furthermore, there would be relatively little consequence for corporations deciding to re-incorporate elsewhere. The fees for incorporation are a drop in the bucket for most states (Delaware is the major exception).

States could also decide to directly put some downward pressure on the pay of CEOs in the non-profit sector. The explosion of CEO pay in the corporate sector has put upward pressure on the pay of CEOs in universities, non-profit hospitals, and private charities and foundations. The pay of top executives in these areas is directly subsidized by taxpayers through their special tax treatment. Most of the tax subsidy comes from the deductibility of charitable contributions on federal income taxes. For high end earners, this amounts to a 40 percent subsidy. States typically also allow a deduction from state income taxes, as well as special treatment on sales and property taxes.

There is no reason states could not impose a cap on pay as a condition for receiving this subsidy. The president of the United States gets paid $400,000 a year. It seems reasonable to set a comparable cap for pay at institutions benefitting from special tax treatment. This cap would not in any way be limiting what non-profits pay their top executives, it would just limit what they could pay and still receive a subsidy from taxpayers. In addition to putting downward pressure on the pay at the top, caps of this sort would call attention to another way in which taxpayers are subsidizing the salaries of the most highly paid people in the country.

The financial sector

While the federal government must take responsibility for reining in the worst abuses in the financial sector, there are many areas where progress can be made at the state level. First, and most obviously, states have the power to curb many of the worst abuses of the financial industry in dealing with consumers. This includes abuses in the issuance and servicing of loans, excessive fees associated with bank overdrafts and credit card late fees, and fees associated with 401(k)s and other savings vehicles.

This essentially means strong regulatory agencies that are empowered to ban hidden fees and put caps on the size of these charges. In the case of retirement accounts, states can allow workers to buy into accounts that piggy back on the state employee retirement accounts, as Illinois and California have already done.[6] The savings on fees, which can be more than 1.0 percentage point a year, can add tens of thousands of dollars to the retirement savings of middle class workers. Similarly, many state pension funds pay excessive fees to private equity companies and hedge funds. The managers of these funds are among the richest people in the country. States should carefully scrutinize these contracts to ensure that pension funds only pay fees that are commensurate with higher than normal returns. Full public disclosure of fees and returns are an important step in this direction. This will both put a check on inequality and save pension funds money.

Finally, states that don't have major financial exchanges (i.e. everyone except, New York, New Jersey, and Illinois) can tax some financial transactions; specifically they can impose a tax on the transfer of mortgages issued on property within state boundaries. A modest tax on mortgage

---

[6] Illinois already has a plan in place under which workers without 401(k)s at their workplace will contribute 2.0 percent of their pay to a plan administered by the state, unless they choose not to. California has a similar plan set to go into place in 2020.

transfers (e.g. 0.1 to 0.25 percent) can be a substantial source of revenue as well as disincentive to excessive shuffling of mortgages. Issuers that have a good reason to transfer a mortgage will not be discouraged from doing so from a tax of this size.

The impact on homebuyers will be modest even if it is assumed that the tax is fully passed on in the cost of the mortgage. (A 0.1 percent tax would be equivalent to an increase of 1 basis point or 0.01 percentage point, on a mortgage that is transferred once over a ten-year life.) Perhaps more importantly, this sort of measure could be a way of familiarizing the public with the idea of financial transactions taxes and driving home the fact that they are not inconsistent with well-functioning financial markets.

In a similar vein, state and local governments can impose a tax on vacant properties. This is another good way to raise revenue by providing a disincentive to speculate on property. This is a tax that should involve relatively low administrative costs, since governments already have recorded an assessed value for most properties, so the vacancy tax would simply involve an additional tax (e.g. 1.0 percent) on property that sit idle for longer than six months or some other period. This gives owners an incentive to either lower rents or to sell their property. This is a tax where even efforts at evasion have the desired effect of making it more costly to leave a property unused.

The City of Vancouver imposed a vacancy tax in the summer of 2016 to curb speculation in its housing bubble. While it is too early to say anything definitive about the impact, house prices have been falling there in recent months.

Artistic freedom vouchers

Copyrights are another area in which progressives can look to challenge policies that have fostered the upward redistribution of income over the last four decades. While state and local governments cannot reverse laws on copyright that are written at the federal level, and locked in through various international agreements, they can seek to promote work that is funded outside the copyright monopoly system.

There are a variety of ways they can look to do this. Perhaps the simplest is through the direct commissioning of college textbooks that could be made available on an open source basis, at least to students in the state. The logic here is fairly straightforward. Rather than having tens of thousands of students pay the copyright protected fee for use of a textbook, a state could commission academics in the relevant fields to produce a book for the use of the students in the state. It would be important that the process be controlled by experts in the relevant field to limit the possibility of political influence. Also, there would be no requirement that the texts produced be used by classes at the state's schools, it would simply be an option where the benefit would be that the textbook would be available at zero cost on-line or for the cost of printing a hard copy.

For a large state like California this would almost certainly provide huge savings. It would likely still save money in smaller states, especially if they acted cooperatively. The availability of open source textbooks would also have the advantage that a professor would be able to freely mix sections from different texts without imposing large costs on students.

States and/or local governments could also look to directly challenge the copyright system by establishing an alternative funding mechanism for creative work. A route that I have suggested elsewhere is an "artistic freedom voucher".[7] Under this system, every resident of a state or city would effectively be given a refundable tax credit, like the earned income tax credit, of a modest amount to support creative work.[8] The *quid pro quo* for accepting this money is that the creative worker would be ineligible for copyright protection for a period of time (e.g. 3 years) after the received the funding.

This could support a vast amount of creative work, such as books, music, and movies, all of which would be in the public domain. The problem from

---

[7] See Baker, 2016, chapter 5.
[8] The city of Seattle recently passed a policy along these lines, providing $100 to every registered voter to support candidates in local elections.

the standpoint of a state or city going this route, as opposed to a larger body like the federal government, is the classic free rider problem. A state or city that opted to do this would be financing the creation of material that could be enjoyed by people everywhere in the world at zero cost.

Nonetheless, it is possible that the finances could still work. The availability of the funding would be an enormous draw to creative workers, especially if there was a residency rule, for example that a creative worker had to be physically present for eight or nine months a year to be eligible to get funds through the system. Suppose a mid-sized city with 500,000 people made $100 available to each person for this purpose. If 60 percent were spent, this would come to $30 million. That would likely be sufficient to draw many creative workers to compete for this funding.

In order to improve their reputation among the residents, and to generate income, these workers would likely be performing live music, staging plays, offering writers' workshops and doing other activities that would command an audience. A city could quite possibly earn back considerably more money in tourist revenue from people attracted by the influx of creative workers than what it paid out in the vouchers. Of course this sort of experiment could be made easier if an innovative foundation were prepared to share in the costs for the first few years.

This is the sort of policy that could help push the country off the path of copyright supported work and instead on a path that promotes openly available material. This is almost a much more efficient route and one that it is likely to promote a much more diverse range of creative work. It is also likely to lead to less inequality since we would probably not see a few mega stars commanding the bulk of the income going to creative workers, along with the many intermediaries who get rich under the current system.

Conclusion: policy at the state level can create facts on the ground to reorder thinking

The debate on economic policy in the United States and elsewhere is typically framed as one between conservatives who like the market and progressives who favor a large role for government. This is both wrong and wrong in a way that hugely favors conservatives. Conservatives are entirely happy to have a large role for government in structuring the market; they just don't like big government programs that benefit the poor and middle class. Over the last four decades they have promoted a range of government policies aimed at restructuring the market in ways that redistribute income upward.

Progressive policy should focus on creating alternative structures that reverse the upward redistribution of the last four decades. While the likelihood for much progress in this direction at the national level during the Trump administration seems minimal, there will be opportunities in states where progressives still have substantial political power.

This discussion has outlined a number of areas, such as challenging patent and copyright monopolies, reversing protectionist measures that inflate doctors' pay, and altering a corrupt corporate governance process that allows CEOs and top management to rip off their companies. In each case the proposals should both directly benefit the people of the state or city adopting them, while undermining the ideology that the market, as opposed to conscious policy choices, has led to the massive upward redistribution of the last four decades.

Reversing this upward redistribution and pushing policies that ensure everyone a decent quality of life is a massive long-term project. The first step is getting a clear idea of where we are trying to go.

References

Baker, Dean, 2016. *Rigged: How Globalization and the Rules of the Modern Economy Were Structured to Make the Rich Richer*. Washington, DC: Center for Economic and Policy Research.

Baker, Dean and Jared Bernstein, 2013. *Getting Back to Full Employment: A Better Bargain for Working People*. Washington, DC: Center for Economic and Policy Research.

Major miscalculations: globalization, economic pain, social dislocation and the rise of Trump

William Neil [Frostburg, MD, USA]

Introduction

The election of Donald Trump has come as a shock to many around the world, and in the United States as well, especially so for the cautious centrists of the Democratic Party, and surely too for its many free-trading Globalization supporters who happen to be professional economists.

Perhaps we shouldn't be so surprised. It hasn't been terribly hard, in retrospect, to fit President Trump into the prevailing political winds in Western Europe over the past decade or so, or longer: the decline of the social democratic left and the rise of the nationalist right, set against a background of economic stagnation and, for the "periphery", especially Greece, even worse, Great Depression conditions. There is no better way to illustrate the prevailing winds in Europe than to recall that Yanis Varoufakis', James Galbraith's and Stuart Holland's "Modest Proposal" of July, 2013, a wonky "New Deal" essay, containing a bundle of tools to fiscally support that suffering periphery, yet modestly designed to rely entirely upon existing mechanisms and funds, was roundly rejected. It was rejected by the complex and contradictory reality of supposedly "social democratic" Germany, perhaps better expressed as a slowly eroding social democracy for Germans only, with the mindset of German central bankers universalized in the European Union's troika of key institutions.

And we must not leave out the "cultural" side in Europe, the stark realities of recent horrific acts of Islamic Fundamentalist terrorism in multiple countries, the press of immigrants driven westward by failed states, Western globalizing and meddling in the Middle East, and a combination of all four factors in Africa. This intensification of cultural troubles had been primed for decades before that by the two tier citizenship system designed to manage the cheaper labor imported from various nations to the east. Pity and praise the nautical humanitarians of the West who are pulling the current refugees, and the bodies, out of the Mediterranean Sea. Migrations such as these, free or forced, would pose challenges, cultural and economic, to even healthily growing economies, but that is hardly the context today.

Instead, we have the "Elephant Chart" of economist Branko Milanovic making the rounds of Wall Street investors in the summer of 2016, displaying via an elephant-shaped graph the winners and losers in the new global distribution of income, 1988–2008.

Western Europeans may have been used to thinking of "cultural reactions" to modernity as a phenomenon limited to the United States (and the Middle East). And indeed, the rise of its Religious Right in the 1970s and its marriage of religious fundamentalism to "market fundamentalism" in the succeeding decades, a union which found a mostly happy home in the Republican Party, was a uniquely American "melding". The union gave rise to the home base and all that has been meant by our infamous "culture wars".

This marriage has its contradictions, however, between its fundamentalist, evangelical religious base and its free market business community. It requires a grand intellectual fog to obscure the fact that the "manic" pace of technological change, the heart of capitalism's Creative Destruction, will also disrupt the moral universe behind the existing social structure, perhaps no better illustrated than the gap between a New York real estate mogul's lifestyle and the conservative Christians who endorsed him in exchange for key "cultural" policy pledges. The late Sheldon Wolin (1922-2015) wrote of these contradictions in 1980, evaluating the Reagan coalition:

> "The destruction of traditional values is also the condition for the innovating economy to operate freely. The modernizing economy is voracious, not only of natural resources, but of the traditional human resources summed in traditions:

resources of skill, craftsmanship, domesticity, personal ties, and common morality."

Yet much of the same American ground of cultural reaction can be found, with proper continental adjustments, in the work of French author Michel Houellebecq, beginning with his 1998 novel *The Elementary Particles*, and called to the attention of American readers in April, 2015 via a review of his new novel, *Soumission*, which had been sweeping France up in a grand national identity controversy, about the book's plot: the election of a Muslim French President. In the *New York Review of Books* Mark Lilla has a complex take on what it means; ours is that out of "late" Western civilization's "decadence" and fragmentation comes a yearning for moral order and discipline from a powerful leader.

That's not so different than the conclusion of David Harvey's brilliant 1990 summary of the vast Western cultural confusions towards the end of his book *The Condition of Postmodernity: An Enquiry into the Origins of Cultural Change*. Harvey is one of the most gifted writers about late modern capitalism, and Globalization, winning praise even from the *Financial Times* for his 2010 book *The Enigma of Capital*. Harvey's traditional yet sophisticated Marxism had been strained by the babble of controversies emerging in the art world and college English departments, substitutes for real world debates inside the declining left. Here he comments on the bafflement visited on Western intellects by the "deconstructionists"; the note, "Trump, 2015", at the bottom of the page must have been written in the late fall of that year:

> "...deconstructionism ended up, in spite of the best intentions of its more radical practitioners, by reducing knowledge and meaning to a rubble of signifiers. It thereby produced a condition of nihilism that prepared the ground for *the re-emergence of a charismatic politics* and even more simplistic propositions than those which were deconstructed."

Harvey has understood what too few conventional economists and globalizers have not: that technological change, the "Creative Destruction" at the heart of the process of capitalism's Globalization, largely American driven, is a very Janus-faced force: unifying through its vast new nation-spanning supply chains, yet threatening cultural chaos and fragmentation by its micro-specialization, and destroying any sense of predictable careers and employment stability, as Richard Sennett so eloquently reminded us in his 1998 book *The Corrosion of Character: The Personal Consequences of Work in the New Capitalism.* His closing sentence was a haunting warning of pending troubles in Neoliberalism: "But I do know a regime which provides human beings no deep reasons to care about one another cannot long preserve its legitimacy."

Almost 20 years later, the cracks in that system are growing wider.

Both Harvey and Sennett were preceded by historian Carl Schorske's 1980 book, *Fin-De-Siecle Vienna: Politics and Culture*, which Harvey cites early in *The Condition*, quoting Schorske as to Vienna's "ruthless centrifuge of change" and noting that "not only the producers of culture, but also its analysts and critics fell victim to the fragmentation".

What Harvey did not cite, however, was a later chapter in Schorske's prescient, depressing book, Chapter Three, "Politics in a New Key: An Austrian Trio". Schorske is talking about the rise of a new "visceral" politics in the persons of Georg Von Schonerer, Karl Lueger and yes, even Theodor Herzl. The worst of these, the eventual anti-Semitic Mayor of Vienna, was Karl Lueger, but all had been rising inside the growing nationalisms bubbling up in the twilight years of the Austro-Hungarian Empire, 1890-1914.

Schorske sees something else, in "each of these political artists..." – that they "grasped a social-psychological reality which the liberals could not see. Each expressed in politics a rebellion against reason and law which soon became more widespread." And in Karl Lueger's climb, and his vicious rhetoric, Schorske foretells something more, a "dress rehearsal" for what would follow in Germany, 1919-1933. To be more precise, and useful for contemporary problems, what the cautious, rational, incremental (economically laissez-faire believers, classical liberals in Polanyi's sense, ancestors of today's Neoliberals) liberals could not grasp was that social strains and the rise of mass politics had opened up a new, emotionally charged pathway of communication between political leaders and citizens. It leaves us still with the unanswered, haunting question for the left: why is the political right able to exploit this pathway, but not the left, the National Socialists in Germany in the 1930s, but not the older SPD, the Social Democratic Party of Germany?

Before Bernie Sanders, perhaps the last time the left in America was infused with emotion, as well as the participation of a good part of rural Protestantism, was in the 1896 campaign of William Jennings Bryan.

If there is any common denominator to the commentary in America, before and after the election, it is the worry that our politics may never be the same again. More specifically, the recognition was that Trump had driven through so many conventional barriers against personal invective, the overt demonizing of multiple "others" – feminists, Hispanic immigrants, blacks, the handicapped, the press itself, now the courts, indeed, most of what has been building during decades of the Culture Wars between the Left and the Right – that it left half of the nation or more wondering whether political decency, and civility, could be restored.

President Trump cannot be understood along any one plane of analysis. There is much going on in the world and inside the United States which prevents easy unitary explanation. That is why both the cultural and the economic dynamics, and their interactions, are important. Trump's campaign displayed both directions about equally, with his emphasis on white, blue collar de-industrialized workers in the old rustbelt cities of the upper Mid-West seeming to have given him the edge in the Electoral College. (Wesley Yang's piece in *Harper's* magazine, "American Nightmare," and Mike Davis' in *Jacobin*, "The Great God Trump and the White Working Class" are particularly insightful.)

Yet that already shockingly divided Electoral College map tells us something few have mentioned: it was exactly the map, and results, which George Wallace was seeking in 1968, and 1972, but could not achieve. It was sought by others too, pushing towards the eventual Republican Right achievement under Ronald Reagan, expressed by advisor Richard Wirthlin in a 1980 campaign memo:

"...the goal was to break up the coalition that had supported the Democratic Party throughout the post-war years by winning the votes of 'Southern white protestants, blue collar workers in the industrial states, urban ethnics, and rural voters'."

We have held, for a number of years now, two competing narratives about the course of American political economy over the years. One is focused on the decade of the 1850s which led to the American Civil War, when the visions for the country could not be reconciled even by the American genius for legislative compromise; the other narrative is more international in focus, the unhappy ending to what is viewed as the first great age of Globalization, the long 19th century, which Karl Polanyi tells us did not end finally until the collapse of fascism in 1945.

That first narrative, leading to the American Civil war, has its themes, unfortunately, appearing in a still running act, which can be summarized, at some risk, under the contemporary heading of the "Southernization of American Politics".

The second narrative is captured in Karl Polanyi's *The Great Transformation: The Political and Economic Origins of Our Time* (1944). In seeking to understand the rise of fascism in the 1930s, Polanyi tells us to look back to the classical economists whose work paved the way for the Industrial Revolution in Britain, and the near religious intensity with which their free markets were urged upon first Britain, and then the whole world during that long 19th century.

Behind both narratives, the defeat of the slavery south in 1865, and the collapse of capitalism in the West, 1929-1932, lies a story of intense economic pain, without which what followed is not fully comprehensible. And that story of economic pain and social dislocation also applies to the very founding of modern capitalism and its "Creative Destruction", 1790-1850, and especially the terrible decade of the 1840s.

In very important ways then, understanding what is happening in Western Europe today, and grasping the motor force behind the election of Donald

Trump becomes an exercise in understanding, and measuring, economic and social pain. Surely their importance must be highlighted, given the dynamics of the American Presidential campaign. That campaign saw both Secretary Clinton and President Obama touting the success of his policies to tame the Great Recession of 2008-2009, and the good basic numbers of low unemployment and low inflation, and the determined, somewhat defensive assertion that "America never stopped being great." This was in sharp contrast with Donald Trump's relentless portrait of a country in deep economic pain, and his pledge to "Make America Great Again", to bring back the lost industrial jobs, rework the terrible "trade deals", and much more. Senator Bernie Sanders' strong challenge to Secretary Clinton in the Democratic primary shared several of the major economic themes of the Trump campaign, but little else – except the challenge to the party establishment.

There are endless takes on what finally turned the election for Trump. Perhaps Naomi Klein of "Capitalism vs. the Climate" essay fame summed it up most succinctly on November 9, the day after the election:

> "It was the Democrats' embrace of neoliberalism that won it
> for Trump... Trump's message was: 'All is hell.' Clinton
> answered: 'All is well.' But it's not well – far from it."

We now turn to that pain, globally and in Western Europe, and then to a closer look at it in America.

Warnings: a world of economic hurt and social disruption

For a world overview, let us visit briefly with former banker and prolific author Satyajit Das, whose most recent book was renamed, for the American market, *The Age of Stagnation: Why Perpetual Growth is Unattainable and the Global Economy is in Peril* (2016). In some ways it marches step-by-step along with Robert Gordon's much quoted *The Rise and Fall of American Growth: The U.S. Standard of Living Since the Civil War*, also published in 2016. Das recognizes Gordon's now famous "headwinds" slowing the growth in US productivity: demographics, declining educational attainments, rising inequality, the effects of globalization, environmental costs, and the debt overhang. These headwinds are the basis for Gordon's alarming projection of just a 0.2% growth rate, lower even than the "modest 1.8 percent of 1987-2007".

Das presents a remarkable range of citations and information. Lest his readers wallow for too long in the dismal predictions of Gordon, he cheers them up by noting that John Steinbeck, in *Grapes of Wrath* (1939), observed that "'when the monster stops growing, it dies. It can't stay one size'". Lest he sound too uncritical in lamenting the growth stagnation, though, he consoles environmentalists with Edward Abbey's "warning: 'growth for the sake of growth is the ideology of a cancer cell'."

Although to the best of our knowledge it didn't get cited during the Trump campaign, India has been, for more than a decade, building a 2,100 mile wall along its border with Bangladesh, with two purposes, says Das: to keep out "illegal immigrants," and "future Bangladeshi climate refugees".

Das has a powerful summary sense of where the world is poised, with slow growth and limited investment opportunities straight-jacketing most of the globe, India perhaps excepted, but not yet large enough to make up for China's slowing. There is no certain economic crisis looming, although we have repeatedly written that no major nation has ever industrialized without a major disruption, China being the sole exception – so far. Here is Das' warning:

> "A new crisis will be like a virulent infection attacking a body whose immune system is already compromised... Large complex systems operate at the boundary between order and disorder. They can appear to be stable, but a sudden or small change can initiate a phase transition, which triggers a massive failure."

It is very difficult, given the rise of the nationalist Right in Europe, and Trump's election, not to go back and visit some of the best early warnings about the very mixed effects of Globalization. What comes to mind are William Greider's 1997 book, *One World, Ready or Not: The Manic Logic of*

Global Capitalism, and John Gray's *False Dawn: The Delusions of Global Capitalism*, which came out one year later. It is significant to note the timing: both coming close to the high tide of American confidence in the Washington Consensus and the brief Clintonian golden years of 1997-1999, and the crisis solving skills of the Committee to Save the World: Alan Greenspan, Robert Rubin, and Larry Summers.

The striking thing about both these books is that they got most of what happened since 1997 right, about 75% of the major trends by our estimate: the coming financial crises starting in Thailand in 1997, and their spread, due to rapid flows of unregulated speculative capital; the massive occupational disruptions occurring in the global economic pecking order, and inside nations themselves; the logic of the pushback being towards the rise of economic nationalism, already foretold in the bending of American (and Western) free-trade notions, illusions, to the benefit of the Asian exporting powerhouses, first Japan and then China – nations which have invented their own rules of the game.

There is a lot of wisdom in each of these books, and they merit a careful re-reading by both professional economists and thoughtful citizens today. Both also credit Karl Polanyi's insights into the unravelling of the last age of Globalization, and how the major dilemmas of the 1930s are back upon us again, with the basics of Neoliberalism not far removed from the straightjacket of the gold standard which bedeviled the West's response to the events of 1929-1932.

In particular, John Gray, a witness to the ideological excesses of Margaret Thatcher's conservative government, stresses the human need for security, especially economic security, a certain heresy when one reflects upon the very core premises of today's economic world. That's a world of constantly re- inventing one's career until the day one dies – and the strong inclination of upper middle class economists and the professionalized meritocracy of the Democratic Party in the United States to solve all the economic problems of inequality via the individual's climb through ever higher educational ladders. As author Thomas Frank has noted acidly: "Meritocracy destroys Solidarity". Gray also was very pessimistic about the future of Social Democracy under the pressures of Globalization, the mobility of capital

28

having robbed governments of the tools they had used to combat, in some places at least, the crisis of the Great Depression. That's certainly the way the world looked to Bill Clinton's eyes, and the Committee to Save the World's too, in the late 1990s. And that's certainly the way it appears to the Republican Right today; but the consistency of Trump's views, much less plans, on that issue, are an open question.

Do not take our words for it; please consider a few brief passages from each author, selected for contemporary relevance. From William Greider's *One World, Ready or Not*; we start with a quote from the old corporate guru Peter F. Drucker, whom Greider believes got the drift of the times – exactly upside down. It thus reminded us of the 2016 election stance of President Obama and Hillary Clinton: "All is well... thanks to us."

> "The extreme social transformations of this century have caused hardly any stir. They have proceeded with a minimum of friction, a minimum of upheavals... Indeed, if this century proves one thing, it is the futility of politics..." Drucker wrote.

> (Greider now): "The global economy divides every society into new camps of conflicting economic interests. It undermines every nation's ability to maintain social cohesion. It mocks the assumption of shared political values that supposedly unite people in the nation-state. That is the fundamental reason politics has become so muddled in the leading capitalist democracies. In recent years voters have turned on established parties and leaders, sometimes quite brutally, in the United States, Canada, Italy, France, Sweden and Japan, to name the most spectacular cases. Nor is there any ideological consistency to these voter rebellions...What exactly is the national interest in these new circumstances? No elected government in the richest countries, neither right nor left, has produced a definition that convinces its own electorate...

The nationalist strand of capitalism, articulated by such eccentric figures as Italy's Silvio Berlusconi or the populist billionaire from Texas, Ross Perot, or the Anglo-French tycoon James Goldsmith, wants to defend the home country first. Some of the nationalist strands are frankly protectionist, but patriotic capitalists constitute an important storm warning for politicians in the advanced societies. Rising nationalist emotions range from the ill-focused anxieties of the American middle-class to the darker, racist fantasies of neofascism that are gaining political voice across the nations of Europe and in some quarters of America."

And now from John Gray's *False Dawn*:

"New technologies make full employment policies of the traditional sort unworkable. The effect of information technologies is to throw the social division of labour into a flux. Many occupations are disappearing and all jobs are less secure. The division of labor in society is now less stable than it has been since the Industrial Revolution... The regime of laissez-faire is bound to trigger counter-movements which reject its constraints. Such movements – whether populist and xenophobic, fundamentalist or neo-communist – can achieve few of their goals; but they can still rattle to pieces the brittle structures that support global-laissez faire... Is a late modern anarchy our historical fate?

The corrosion of bourgeois life through increased job insecurity is at the heart of disordered capitalism... the result is a re-proletarianization of much of the industrial working class and the de-bourgeoisification of what remains of the former middle classes. The free market seems set to achieve what socialism was never able to accomplish – euthanasia of bourgeois life... How can families meet for meals when both parents work on shifts? What becomes of families when the job market pulls parents apart?

America... is a country riven by class conflicts, fundamentalist movements and low-intensity race wars. Political solutions to these ills presuppose reform of the free market. It is doubtful whether such reform is a real political possibility in America today... issues of economic justice can arise only on the farther fringes of political life. Ross Perot, Ralph Nader and Pat Buchanan all traded on popular distrust of political elites... It may be a portent for the future that only in the 1996 campaign of Pat Buchanan did issues of economic justice make a significant impact on mainstream American political life. Buchanan fused issues of economic fairness with a fundamentalist culture-war and nativist hostility to the rest of the world."

Let us now turn to a crucial question: what was the level of economic pain driving the political insurgency of Senator Bernie Sanders, and the successful campaign of Donald Trump?

America's hidden pains

We begin with some gross numbers from Das' *Age of Stagnation*: the loss of wealth from the Great Recession of 2008-2009. Citing the work of three economists at the Federal Reserve Bank of Dallas (Tyler Atkinson, David Luttrell and Harvey Rosenblum), the figures they put on the loss to the U.S. economy come to 6-14 trillion dollars, "equivalent to U.S. $50,000 to U.S. $120,000 for every American household, or 40-90% of one year's economic output". We've seen figures of family distress ranging from $20,000-$60,000, largely representing losses in the stock market, which seem on target from direct personal experience. The other factor driving towards a more lasting economic pain are those who lost enough in straight financial terms to forestall market re-entry, matched with a psychological aversion to ever trusting it again. Additionally, pension fund retirement viability was affected by the same dynamics. These factors must be considered, as difficult as they are to quantify, to qualify the otherwise impressive performance after 2010 in the financial markets, they being supported by all the permutations known as Quantitative Easing, American and European versions.

Trumponomics: Causes And Consequences

In the fall of 2015, and in many ways now seeming to be an overlooked clue as to what was about to unfold in the election of 2016, Nobel prize winning economist Angus Deaton and his wife Anne Case (both of Princeton University) caused a sensation in the news. It was because of their research findings disclosing a dramatic rise in the death rates, by 22%, among whites 45-54 years old, among those who only had a high school degree. The dramatic mortality increase occurred in the years 1999-2014. According to the coverage and commentary in the *New York Times*, this dramatic increase in mortality rates wasn't caused by the usual suspects – heart disease and diabetes – but by "an epidemic of suicides and afflictions stemming from substance abuse: alcoholic liver disease and overdoes of heroin and prescription opioids". Professor Deaton declared that "Only HIV/AIDS in contemporary times has done anything like this..."

Additional commentary in the *Times'* article, by Dartmouth College economists Ellen Meara and Jonathan S. Skinner, put the findings in further relevant context for our purposes here:

> "The least educated also had the most financial distress... in the period examined by Dr. Deaton and Dr. Case, the inflation-adjusted income for households headed by a high school graduate fell by 19 percent."

On the trail of further hidden economic distress, the Federal Reserve itself has been conducting surveys since 2013 entitled "Report on the Economic Well-Being of U.S. Households". The most reported finding of these surveys, contained in the formal reports issued now annually by the Board of Governors, was that nearly half of the respondents, 47%, "said they either could not cover an emergency expense costing $400, or would cover it by selling something or borrowing money". In other words, almost half of American households have no personal savings or personal financial "safety net".

As reported in an *Atlantic* magazine article by Neal Gabler in the spring of 2016, in the heat of presidential campaigning, "The Secret Shame of Middle-Class Americans", the distress goes beyond the inability to meet small financial emergencies of $400-$1,000, the range covered by the Federal

Reserve surveys. Gabler introduces the research of Edward Wolff, an economist at New York University who has found that "median net worth (family net worth) has declined steeply in the past generation – down 85.3 percent from 1983 to 2013 for the bottom quintile, and down 63.5 percent for the second-lowest quintile, and down 25.8 percent for the third, or middle, quintile."

So we are getting closer now, much closer, to answering two of our key questions: how much economic pain is "out there" in America, and how do we explain the divergence between the good "formal" economic numbers of low unemployment (under 5%) and very low inflation (2.5% average for 2016) touted by the President and his "heir apparent," Secretary Clinton, and those remarkable pre-election poll numbers showing 70% or more Americans feel the nation is on "the wrong track". Economist Wolff, from NYU, summarizes the crux of the matter this way: "… the typical American family is in 'desperate straits'."

This would be bad enough, the precarious imbalance in American household finances, which must be coupled with what William Greider and John Gray have told us is also a permanent sense of precarious employment and career uncertainty, the result of nearly four decades upheavals in production and distribution methods, and labor markets world-wide. But we have also called attention to the role of cultural upheaval in our search for the reasons underlying the triumph of Trump in 2016. While economists are likely to have a strong inclination to keep the two strands of reasoning quite separate, our contemporary dilemmas and a fuller interdisciplinary methodology calls us to inquiries resting on a broader foundation.

What we have in mind is what author and TED talk guest speaker Hannah Rosin explored in her book and lectures under the title *The End of Men: And the Rise of Women* (2012). The essence of her argument is that women are eclipsing men in educational attainment, in the ranks of middle management, and in founding new businesses, relying in part on their "traditional" interpersonal skills and sensitivities. We should note, as she does, that this does not mean the end to the glass ceiling still firmly in place for most of the highest institutional perches of the 1%. After all, Satyajit Das, wearing his financial journalist hat for us now, reports that women make up only about

20% of the attendees at Davos, such as it is: the actual historical location, full of ironic portent, for the setting of Thomas Mann's novel, *The Magic Mountain* (1924).

The ground covered by Rosin, a skillful public speaker, seems pretty solid; unfortunately for men, this substantial rise and improvement for the freedom and careers open to women, has come at a time when the traditional careers for men in the declining industrial economy have had the bottom fall out. Thus the dramatic shifting in gender roles which has continued from its start in the 1960s, also covers the decades of demise for blue collar workers, especially in the 1970s, as documented by Judith Stein's *Pivotal Decade: How the United States Traded Factories for Finance in the Seventies* (2010) and Jefferson Cowie's *Stayin' Alive: The 1970s and the Last Days of the Working Class* (also 2010).

These books describe, in painful detail, the initial shifts inside the Democratic Party away from labor's hopeful agenda for a new New Deal as portrayed through the fumbling of the Carter administration, thoroughly unenthused about Labor Law reform, Industrial Policy and Full Employment guarantees, and also Health Care reform. Instead, the new directions were disclosed by mighty efforts for de-regulation of the airline and trucking industries and the decidedly non-nationalist effort to cede the Panama Canal back to Panama. We shall say no more about these complex matters, other than to suggest the dynamics from a very likely scenario: of a husband coming home with a plant closing notice only to find that his wife has received a Small Business Administration loan to open a thrift shop on Main Street in Youngstown, Ohio.

Youngstown, Ohio was ground zero for the disaster which befell the entire Mahoning Valley: the demise of the steel industry, the shedding of 50,000 jobs, 1975-1985. George Packer, in his 2013 account *The Unwinding: An Inner History of the New America*, tells us that

> "if the institutions and the people who led them had understood what was about to happen to Youngstown, and then to the wider region, they might have worked out a

34

policy to manage deindustrialization instead of simply allowing it to happen."

Instead,

"between 1979 and 1980, bankruptcies in Youngstown doubled, and in 1982, unemployment in the Mahoning Valley reached almost 22 percent – the highest anywhere in the country."

Revealingly, Packer tells of the rise and fall of Youngstown through the story of a black woman's "survivor's tale", a struggle and eventual career success built out of the rubble of her home town. Yet the meaning for the entire country heading into the heart of the Reagan years was crystalized by a former auto worker turned college professor, John Russo, who eulogized the disaster with the epitaph: "The idea that this was systemic didn't occur." That sentence was written despite the fine attempt of Barry Bluestone and Bennett Harrison to do precisely that: see deindustrialization as a systemic national economic problem, in their 1982 book, *The Deindustrialization of America.*

The "Southernization" of American politics

There remains one important task in understanding the triumph of Trump, however short lived it might turn out to be, and that is to more fully explore all the meanings suggested, and implied, by the phrase "The Southernization of American Politics". This may seem at first strange, the connection between the long standing regional "outcast" of American life, and the successful billionaire entrepreneur from the world's most sophisticated real-estate market, New York City. But let us try to make that connection for you, and also to re-emphasize one of the main themes of this short essay: that action and reaction in the political economy often depends on the level of pain and disruption that sets "the double-movement" in motion.

We rely upon the guidance of a little known, new work by Professor Glenn Feldman of the University of Alabama called *The Great Melding: War, the Dixiecrat Rebellion, and the Southern Model for America's New*

Conservatism (2015), which in turn built upon the prior work of Dan Carter's *The Politics of Rage: George Wallace, the Origins of the New Conservatism, and the Transformation of American Politics* (1995).

Perhaps it will help to consider the transition suggested by this biographical sequence: John C. Calhoun, Strom Thurmond, George Wallace, Richard Nixon, Ross Perot, Sarah Palin and finally, Donald Trump.

This is our vastly compressed version of Feldman's longer tale, of how the South went from being solidly Democratic to solidly Republican Right in approximately 170 years, from 1840 to 2015, or slightly less, since the book opens with a jarring biography of violence from the post- Civil War Reconstruction days. We supply our own spotlight on the level of economic pain as a driver, as the seed bed for future ideological intensity.

The South at the end of the American Civil War in 1865 was a demoralized, economically prostate and federally occupied territory. It never had much industry, but what it had was ruined, as was a good part of its plantation based agricultural life. What comes into view for contemporary minds would be the images of Nazi Germany, the ruins from the spring of 1945. (Rather than the images from 1939's *Gone with the Wind*.) Despite the military defeat, and the temporary demoralization of the planter class, the urgent, promethean task of the Southern economic elite was to evict the occupiers, re-invent racial control with new mechanisms that did not rely upon formal slavery, and to eventually present an inviting new investment opportunity for northern capital, all key pathways leading to "the New South".

Just outlining the situation does not conjure up the intensity of the tasks. Feldman does, though, right up front, by shocking the reader with the sheer physical brutality visited upon the newly freed slaves and any allies they might have – Southern or from the hated North. The tools to do so were the whip, the knife, the noose at the end of the rope, and bullets. And the main ingredient in the bubbling emotional cauldron that fueled the reaction against Reconstruction was a blind fury against all things Federal, especially the federal government.

After physical control had been secured by terrors both Roman and Medieval in nature, there came the tenant farming and sharecropping systems for both the former slaves and the bottom rungs of hapless white society. But that was not all: for those who even placed one foot beyond the new lines of white oligarchical authority, there was the prison lease system: a state sponsored form of privatization for mining, agricultural plantations and timber harvesting which turned the control and rate of pay over entirely to brutal entrepreneurs who had a direct and naked interest in horrible housing, miserable food and relentless hours of the most killing forms of labor. The expected life span for many prisoners, mainly young black men, was less than ten years: worse than slavery. The physical punishments were beyond modern belief. White men and women also formed a small subset of this barely acknowledge but widespread system, and of course, under these circumstances, since the cells were shared, children were born into the nightmare. *Cool Hand Luke*, by comparison, was a deeply sanitized modern movie version, appearing in 1967.

Remarkably, however, once this system had been firmly established, the brutal and cunning leaders who had set it up moderated their conduct, and their tone, the first great "melding". They needed to do so both to attract northern financing, and to make sure the federal government did not again threaten to investigate the monstrosity of illusion that they had built. Thus the myth of "cordial and beneficent" racial relations which could not be understood, and only be upset by outsiders. It took outrageous "Sophistic Pruning" and "Smoke and Mirrors" methods to distract from the realities, and to try to conceal the fault lines: the potential alliance between poor whites and blacks, and the always raw racial realities. We can get a hint of the great intensities behind this system of control by remembering the early speeches of George Wallace, especially his Gubernatorial Inaugural Address in 1963, the famous lines "segregation now... segregation tomorrow... segregation forever". The speech was written by a Klansman, Asa Carter, and the intensity was genuine, a politician's Holy Grail of authenticity on the part of Wallace, a former collegiate boxing star. Looming over their shoulders was the advancing federal juggernaut, of the Justice Department's lawyers, and if necessary again, the 82nd and 101st Airborne divisions.

Lest this account seem too fantastic to accept at face value, we invite readers to visit historian Rick Perlstein's essay – "Peter's Choice" – about how a college student in an honor's seminar in Oklahoma justified his support for Trump via the South's old recycled tale of Federal travesty during Reconstruction, still on strong legs far from home and in the fall of 2016, no less.

The Second Great Melding, Feldman tells us, did not take place until that fateful decade for Keynesianism, American Labor, and the faltering New Deal shaped Democratic Party: the 1970s. It was the melding of the rising American religious Fundamentalists (and more complexly, the Evangelicals), who were very worried about alleged American moral decline, adverse Supreme Court decisions on prayer in the schools, abortion, and tax exemption for private religious schools... and the dawning recognition that an alliance was possible with the higher stratospheres of American business, then suffering from declining profit rates, foreign competition and over-regulation.

It is best to let Feldman summarize these permutations for us, how a transformed South became the template for a transformed Republican Party, where the ideological goal posts had not just been shifted, but also the "fifty-yard line" itself:

> "Character, values, religion, and patriotism would become something that could be termed 'The New Racism,' condemning a whole set of 'New Negroes' to the fingers of southern society: feminists, the environmentally conscious, intellectuals, liberals, the secular, those who questioned war or unlimited military spending... the conservative orthodoxy would be a self-satisfying type, soothing to its beneficiaries, with all the nineteenth century platitudes about deserving thrift, superior ingenuity, work ethic, and the entrepreneurial spirit – yet with race securely in place as its vital subtext, and Calvinistic exclusivity openly preached. Despite the veneer and the ceaseless chatter about 'givers' and 'takers,' and the love of 'producers,' the new Republican orthodoxy would be just as narrow, just as exclusionary, and just as

unleavened as the old southern Democratic conservatism had been…

During this period, southern conservatives were hard at work perfecting the techniques of mass distortion that lent themselves to a politics that compelled loyalty based on emotion and gut-level appeal rather than rational thought and reality-based analyses of policy. The liberal alternative – so dependent on rationality, shades of grey, complex argument, and critical thought – didn't stand a chance."

If that seems a bit too much to take in via one breadth, just reflect upon poor Michael Dukakis' fate in the Presidential campaign of 1988 when he was asked in a televised debate how he would respond if his wife had just been raped by a criminal like Willie Horton… and then reflect also a bit upon the career and background of the late Lee Atwater, political attack dog extraordinaire.

Conclusion

The main thrust of this essay has been to emphasize the miscalculations Neoliberalism has made in the West in two major respects: underestimating the economic pain visited upon its middle and working classes due to de-industrialization, and also underestimating the impacts from the uncertainty surrounding the *remaining* jobs – the loss of predictable careers.

While Donald Trump has skillfully mobilized these pains, it is not clear he has come up with a coherent economic policy to correct them. He has no "mandate", having lost the popular vote soundly, and his working class success was a matter of a few hundred thousand votes scattered across key states, not tens of millions "converted" across the country.

Where we can find economic coherence, it follows the likely tax cutting and militarized Keynesianism of the Reagan years, which will not reach those in the bottom rungs of the economic system. In mid-February, a month into his first hundred days, his economic policies have not even been broached in Congress; the infrastructure program is without form or substance.

There are enormous strains that comes with the Trump package: his alliances with the Religious Right and the shadowy world of the Alt-Right. It is not clear at all that he can maintain peace among the major forces in the Republican Party, much less the nation, and it will be very difficult to construct a new "nationalism" if he has lost the confidence of American international corporations and the national security state.

The great tragedy is this: a more vigorous form of social democracy would seem to produce the best of both worlds, keeping the international trading system largely intact and recycling the wealth which has gone upward to the 1% *downward into job programs*, guaranteed jobs even, for all the useful work that needs to be done.

However, given the existing economic ideology in the West, as we noted in the case of Germany towards the periphery, and because of the intense anti-governmental obsessions from the "Southernization" of American politics, the tools needed to reintegrate the working class into the broader economy, and give the middle class a greater sense of security, have been cruelly undercut. And it is not clear that Donald Trump himself would understand, or agree with, a word of what we have just written.

Nonetheless, the Neoliberal influenced Democrats have failed to connect emotionally with those hurting the most, and the party is facing a sea of red conservative voters in the South and much of rural America, and they have lost control of state house after state house.

The economic mainstream bears some responsibility for this, as the reaction of four of its "stars" indicated when they jumped all over an economist in February of 2016 for being "irresponsible" for running the numbers of Bernie Sanders' economic policy proposals, and finding good outcomes.

William Greider perhaps put it best in the final chapter of *One World Ready or Not*: "…modern economists have become the 'thought police' in advanced societies, as futurist Hazel Henderson observed." And their rigidity, especially in forbidding New Deal type interventions into labor markets, have helped make the looming disaster of Donald Trump possible. We haven't changed our mind over the past year: America looks ungovernable right now and it will be surprising if Trump can survive four years.

We will close with two personal recollections from 2015-2016. One came from a Rush Limbaugh broadcast, where the famous conservative broadcaster was lamenting the left-liberal war on "producers", via the efforts to stop global warming. Limbaugh said that no benign Creator could ever allow the alleged coming catastrophes of global warming to actually happen, since they were the fruits of His own creations' inventive, industrious genius, of people bettering their lives. No complexities, contradictions or limits here, to be sure.

The second occurred on a beautiful late summer evening's walk under a spectacularly colored sky with high cirrus clouds and jet vapor trails blended together. We had passed fellow citizens in Western Maryland looking up at what we thought was the same view, and commented to them about it. In return, they said there was more going on than nature's artistry: those jet contrails were spewing toxic fumes and infectious biological agents, a joint enterprise in perfidy by the airlines and the federal government to harm the good citizens. Looking up the plot online when arriving home, sure enough, that was the outline of things to come.

After that revelation, much of what has happened in the realm of political economy seemed to fall into place. Or into a bottomless pit. History has given us more than a few previews on the possibilities, but not yet, hopefully, the inevitabilities.

PS **Disclosure**: this writer was a Bernie Sanders supporter in 2016.

References

Atwater, Lee. Biography at Wikipedia. https://en.wikipedia.org/wiki/Lee_Atwater

BillofRights. "Citizens: If James Galbraith and Bill Black don't have any 'standing,' where does that leave you?" *Daily Kos*, February 23, 2016. http://www.dailykos.com/story/2016/02/23/1489977/-Citizens-If-James-Galbraith-and-Bill-Black-don-t-have-any-standing-where-does-that-leave-you

Block, Fred; Somers, Margaret R. *The Power of Market Fundamentalism: Karl Polanyi's Critique*. Cambridge, MA: Harvard University Press, 2014

Bluestone, Barry; Harrison, Bennett. *The Deindustrialization of America*. New York, NY: Basic Books, 1982.

Carter, Dan T. *The Politics of Rage: George Wallace, The Origins of the New Conservatism, and the Transformation of American Politics*. New York, NY: Simon & Schuster, 1995.

Cowie, Jefferson. *Stayin' Alive: the 1970s and the Last Days of the Working Class*. New York, NY: The New Press, 2010.

Das, Satyajit. *The Age of Stagnation: Why Perpetual Growth is Unattainable and the Global Economy is in Peril*. Amherst, NY: Prometheus Books, 2016.

Das, Satyajit. "This year's World Economic Forum in Davos will focus on the threat of right-wing populism for the first time ever." *The Independent*, January, 2017. http://www.independent.co.uk/voices/davos-world-economic-forum-wef-celebrities-right-wing-populism-first-time-a7528086.html

Feldman, Glenn. *The Great Melding: War, the Dixiecrat Rebellion, and the Southern Model for America's New Conservatism*. Tuscaloosa, AL: University of Alabama Press, 2015.

Frank, Thomas. *Listen Liberal: Or, Whatever Happened to the Party of the People*. New York, NY: Henry Holt and Company, 2016.

Fritzsche, Peter. *Rehearsals for Fascism: Populism and Political Mobilization in Weimar Germany*. New York, NY: Oxford University Press, 1990.

Davis, Mike. "The Great God Trump and the White Working Class." *Jacobin*, February 7, 2017. https://www.jacobinmag.com/2017/02/the-great-god-trump-and-the-white-working-class/?setAuth=63e2fa5ae2f60aa03a7b9fd42d011179

Dukakis, Michael. Biography at Wikipedia. https://en.wikipedia.org/wiki/Michael_Dukakis

Gabler, Neil. "The Secret Shame of Middle-Class Americans." *The Atlantic*, May, 2016. https://www.theatlantic.com/magazine/archive/2016/05/my-secret-shame/476415/

Gordon, Robert J. *The Rise and Fall of American Growth: The U.S. Standard of Living Since the Civil War*. Princeton, NJ: Princeton University Press, 2016

Gray, John. *False Dawn: The Delusions of Global Capitalism*. New York, NY: The New Press, 1998.

Greider, William. *One World, Ready or Not: The Manic Logic of Global Capitalism*. New York, NY: Simon & Schuster, 1997.

Harvey, David. *The Condition of Postmodernity: An Enquiry into the Origins of Cultural Change*. Malden, MA: Blackwell Publishers Ltd., 1990.

Harvey, David. *The Enigma of Capital and the Crisis of Capitalism*. New York, NY: Oxford University Press, 2010.

Houellebecq, Michel. *The Elementary Particles*. New York, NY: Vintage Books, 2000.

Kawa, Luke. "Get Ready to See This Globalization 'Elephant Chart' Over and Over Again." *Bloomberg Markets*, June 27, 2016. https://www.bloomberg.com/news/articles/2016-06-27/get-ready-to-see-this-globalization-elephant-chart-over-and-over-again

Klein, Naomi. "It was the Democrats' embrace of neoliberalism that won it for Trump." *The Guardian*, November 9, 2016. https://www.theguardian.com/commentisfree/2016/nov/09/rise-of-the-davos-class-sealed-americas-fate

Klein, Naomi. "Capitalism vs. The Climate." The Nation, November 9, 2011. https://www.thenation.com/article/capitalism-vs-climate/

Kolata, Gina. "Death Rates Rising for Middle-Aged White Americans, Study Finds." *New York Times*, November 2, 2015. https://www.nytimes.com/2015/11/03/health/death-rates-rising-for-middle-aged-white-americans-study-finds.html?_r=0

Lilla, Mark. "Slouching Toward Mecca." *New York Review of Books*, April 2, 2015, Volume LXII, Number 6, Pages 41-43.

Packer, George. *The Unwinding: An Inner History of the New America*. New York, NY: Farrar, Straus and Giroux, 2013

Perlstein, Rick. "Peter's Choice." *Mother Jones*, Jan/Feb.2017. http://www.motherjones.com/politics/2017/01/donald-trump-2016-election-oklahoma-working-class

Phillips-Fein, Kim. *Invisible Hands: The Making of the Conservative Movement from the New Deal to Reagan*. New York, NY: W. W. Norton & Company Ltd., 2009

Polanyi, Karl. *The Great Transformation: The Political and Economic Origins of our Time*. Boston, MA: Beacon Press, 2001.

Rosin, Hannah. "Keynote Address: Evaluating Claims About 'The End of Men,'" Boston University School of Law, October 12, 2012: https://www.youtube.com/watch?v=CnBbAh2yYyA&t=20s

Schorske, Carl E. *Fin-De-Siecle Vienna: Politics and Culture*. New York, NY: Vintage Books, 1980

Sennett, Richard. *The Corrosion of Character: The Personal Consequences of Work in the New Capitalism.* New York, NY: W. W. Norton & Company Inc., 1998.

Stein, Judith. *Pivotal Decade: How the United States Traded Factories for Finance in the Seventies.* New Haven, CT: Yale University Press, 2010.

Varoufakis,Yanis; Holland, Stuart; Galbraith, James K. "A Modest Proposal for Resolving the Eurozone Crisis, Version 4.0." July, 2013.
https://varoufakis.files.wordpress.com/2013/07/a-modest-proposal-for-resolving-the-eurozone-crisis-version-4-0-final1.pdf

Yang, Wesley. "American Nightmare." *Harpers*, February, 2017.
http://harpers.org/archive/2017/02/trump-a-resisters-guide/3/

Trumponomics and the developing world

Jayati Ghosh [Jawaharlal Nehru University, New Delhi, India]

So now we know: unlike many other politicians, President Trump will indeed do (or try to do) many of the things he promised or threatened to do before he was elected. Internally, he is apparently seeking to bring back a 21st-century version of Reaganomics: a combination of rising fiscal deficits resulting from lower taxes (especially on the rich) and more public spending on the military and on physical infrastructure, with higher interest rates delivered by the US Federal Reserve. He will deregulate private activity further and reduce various protections for labour and the environment that he believes constrain investment. He sought (unsuccessfully) to replace the Affordable Care Act or Obamacare, albeit with little clarity on what to replace it with, and seeks to reduce public spending on various social programmes. All this is supposed to create a domestic boom led by private investment, that is presumably to be financed once again by foreigners willing to pour their savings into US financial assets, particularly Treasury Bills. And some have predicted that such a US boom will once again pull the world economy along through the increased demand it will generate for the rest of the world's exports.

Externally, he has already moved the US out of some committed trade deals like the Trans Pacific Partnership and showed a propensity to undermine the World Trade Organisation if it does not work in a way that he perceives to serve US interests. His administration is already promising protectionist measures and looking at ways to impose unilateral sanctions against other WTO members. He is seeking to reduce immigration by deporting some who have already made it inside the US, and to place significant curbs on future immigration as well as on short-term movement for service delivery, through H1-B visas. He will try to build a wall on the Mexican border and raise tariffs on imports coming from other countries: most symbolically Mexico and China, but also potentially developing countries in general. He will reduce US spending on and engagement with international organisations like the

United Nations and probably ignore US pledges and commitments to treaties that seek to address global warming and related issues.

His foreign policy is at present a confused mixture of aggressive bullying and personal support for other aggressive bullies elsewhere, but it is safe to assume that ultimately there will be more continuity than real change in this matter. Given the complete mess that US foreign policy has created in the world over the last few decades, that continuity is not necessarily very good for the rest of the world. Such change as does occur is likely to be adverse for progressive people in his country and across the world: it is not just Palestinians and those fighting against authoritarianism in Turkey, Egypt, India and the Philippines who have cause for worry, but people everywhere who are concerned about preserving and enlarging democratic rights. If there is one agenda that is now much more likely to be trampled upon globally, it is that of human rights.

But how much of this agenda can Mr Trump actually achieve? And how much of this is self-contradictory, in that movement in one direction will generate changes that affect other parts of the agenda or the goals? The declarations sound disruptive, but how much difference will all this sound and fury make in material terms? The answers to these questions are crucial not only for citizens of the US. They matter hugely for the rest of the world and developing countries in particular, because the US economy still remains dominant and affects global demand directly and indirectly, and because the continuing significance of the US dollar as the main global reserve currency affects both financial and real flows across countries.

It is probably over-optimistic and even misplaced to believe belief that Trumponomics can generate a boom in the US and thereby in the rest of the world, along the same lines as the Reagan boom. It is not just that the world economy is different from three and a half decades ago and that global capitalism has altered in significant ways; it is also that much of what he proposes is unlikely to work out as planned, given the political economy forces in the USA at the moment and the contradictory nature of the various impulses in his administration.

It is not just the failure of his attempt at health reform that generates more scepticism about any future possible successes. It is also the internal contradictions in his policy proposals. Consider the issue of whether President Trump will actually deliver in terms of generating a new boom with sustained medium-term growth of activity and employment. The basis for this is supposed to be the perception that increased public spending and lower tax rates will provide a fiscal stimulus to boost the economy, even if it does at the same time increase inequality and disproportionately favour the rich. But the second outcome is far more likely than the first. As of now, the precise tax proposals that the Trump administration itself favours are not known; but the version being pushed by the Republicans in Congress led by Paul Ryan is supposedly "revenue neutral", in that it balances tax cuts in some sectors and categories with reduction of deductions in the same or others. The overall macroeconomic benefit of this would obviously be limited, although it may well imply a further redistributive shift away from working and middle class families in favour of the country's corporations and rich individuals.

In any case, tax cuts alone are known to have limited impact – even the IMF has recently estimated that the multiplier effects of tax cuts generally tend to be much lower than increased public spending, regardless of the beneficiaries of such cuts. Reagan's strategy "worked" in the 1980s because of the massive increases in military spending that generated new investment by the military-industrial complex, which in turn had spillover effects in other sectors and in terms of technological change. But it is not at all clear that Mr Trump is actually planning such significant increases in government expenditure. The big increases in military spending in his proposed budget are counterbalanced by equivalent cuts in other spending, particularly spending on social programmes. And even these increases may be diminished by the Congressional process.

Much of what Trump has talked about as public investment actually comes in the category of "Public Private Partnerships" (PPPs), in which the government does not invest directly, but underwrites a significant part of the private investment or enables the securing of cheap loans for private investment. There is good reason why this strategy has had such a bad press recently: most countries that have relied heavily on it have found that the actual levels of investment turn out to be much lower than anticipated or planned for, while the fiscal costs tend to be much higher and more prolonged, because the user charges that would cover costs typically turn out to be so high that they are politically impossible to enforce. In other words, these PPPs in most cases have not delivered in terms of actually providing the required physical infrastructure. So a heavy reliance on PPPs may suit several of Mr Trump's cronies and those (including in real estate, a sector of particular personal interest to the US President) who would benefit from certain infrastructure investments, but they are unlikely to generate the kind of increase in investment rates that is being apparently being anticipated by the over-enthusiastic stock markets.

In any case, another political reality that President Trump will have to contend with is the continued presence of the Tea Party as a major lobby affecting both Congress and government functioning. In a peculiar way, the Republicans now seem to have tied their own hands because of the political predilections they created when in opposition. This group is so viscerally opposed to any increases in deficits that any real change in fiscal stance towards a more expansionary role would have to be achieved through subterfuge, if at all it is to occur. This political constraint has not appeared so clearly yet, but it definitely still exists, especially as so many Republican Senators and Representatives have been elected on precisely such a platform.

So the fiscal expansion that has been so eagerly anticipated (not just in the US but even globally) on the basis of the declarations of the US President is not likely to be all that significant. And it will come in combination with a monetary policy "shock" in the form of higher interest rates, in an economy that has grown used to near-zero interest rates for nearly a decade now. This could well attract mobile capital back to the US – and thereby cause different degrees of discomfort or crisis in many emerging markets – but that in turn will cause an appreciation of the US dollar, which too must affect profitability in the tradeables sector. In purely macroeconomic terms, it is hard to see how this combination can deliver significantly higher economic growth or employment.

What then of the other strategies, the physical and trade walls both designed to protect US residents from the depredations of foreigners? The infamous wall along the Mexican border has already overrun cost expectations even before work on it has started, from Trump's original estimate of $10 billion to around $15-20 billion or even more now. But while that may seem expensive for an ugly and offensive piece of landscaping, if it is seen only as a Keynesian stimulus, it would not amount to very much. And the economic effects of that spending for the US would in any case be questionable, since reports suggest that Mexican workers (both legal and illegal) are far more likely to be employed in the work of building it.

The other wall – the imposition of high punitive tariffs on goods coming from Mexico and China, as well as from other countries seen as "threats" to US production – may well get a few dramatic and highly symbolic gestures in its direction, and may mess up trade relations for a while. How serious and sustained this attempt at protectionist nationalism in trade terms will be is not yet clear, but certainly it will be less emphatic than the cronyism that is already so evident. It is more than likely that the President's basic and well-known instinct for pushing business and profit, irrespective of the impact on workers or consumers, will win over the protectionist rhetoric that helped him get elected. In any case, punitive tariffs against one set of countries would simply divert trade rather than generate local production. Wider protection, sufficient to really alter the trade balance, is not really on the cards. But for well-known reasons, it would do very little to bring manufacturing jobs "back" to the US, and technological changes will continue to erode the employment possibilities of such production at an ever-increasing pace. So the workers and other non-traditional voters who installed Trump in his current position are unlikely to get even some of the benefits they expect, regardless of statements to the contrary. Instead, they are more likely to experience a worsening of material conditions because of spending cuts and other changes in institutional conditions that reduce their entitlements.

Mr Trump's policy stance will, however, mean that the United States – which has been providing less and less of a positive demand stimulus to the rest of the world economy ever since the Global Financial crisis – will continue to shrink its import demand and add to the forces that are making global trade decelerate and even decline.

Trumponomics: Causes And Consequences

What does all this mean for developing countries? First, that those who are worried are right to be worried, but perhaps not for the reasons most commonly cited, such as the threat of trade protectionism. Rather, Mr Trump presents a disruptive force in an already febrile and volatile global economic environment, which is weakened not by his election, but because global capitalism had clearly reached the limits of pushing that particular strategy of accumulation. This was increasingly evident in the "secular stagnation" that seemed impervious to massive injections of liquidity and near zero or even negative interest rates, and in economic trajectories that no longer seem to generate stable and regular employment. In turn, the disruption that Mr Trump generates in turn is only partly because of his actions, and probably even more because of the very impact that his statements and the surrounding chatter have on expectations, both in financial markets and in real economic activities.

The most immediate likely concern is that of capital leaving emerging markets once US interest rates are raised, and the potentially disorderly situations this can create. Developing countries have already experienced this several times in the past decade, and have learnt the hard way that policy decisions taken and economic processes in the US are far more significant in determining capital inflows and outflows from their own countries than any measures taken within. The resulting volatility is likely to be compounded by further financial deregulation that will spread from the US to other countries. Since the already inadequate re-regulation of finance that occurred after 2008 in the US is on its way to being dismantled, this will create pressures for associated deregulation even in other developed countries, and add to similar tendencies in emerging markets. This is doubly dangerous for many "emerging markets" because many of them had responded to the global crisis by allowing massively leveraged expansion, and much of that is currently in the process of winding down. Asset markets – particularly of land and real estate – are experiencing a downswing in most countries, rendering them especially vulnerable to financial crises that could originate from an initial outflow of capital to the US.

Obviously, this would be exacerbated by the disruptive impact on global trade that several proposals of the Trump administration are likely to have. The ongoing slowdown in international trade is likely to get worse, and also more uncertain with the unpredictability of US moves. Conflicting signals coming from different elements of the US Government, and even from its leader over time, only add to confusion and reduce the incentive for even medium terms investment in tradeable sectors. Export of commodities from South to North, which powered the expansion of some economies and provided much cheaper goods to consumers in the North, is unlikely to be an engine of growth in the immediate future. This sounds like bad news for many developing countries, and will be so in the short term, but it need not be so bad if it forces a different approach from one that focusses on exports to the North (and therefore treats wages only as a cost), to one that looks at potential in domestic markets and regional arrangements (and therefore treats wages also as an important source of demand).

Certainly, no tears should be shed for the Trans Pacific Partnership. It was a bad deal, that did little to enhance desirable trade; instead it provided inordinate power to corporations, through stringent and unwarranted acceptance of tight intellectual property rights monopolies, reducing possibilities of public regulation in the interests of workers, the environment and the health and other human rights of citizens; and allowing investor-state dispute settlement in wide-ranging cases. These would definitely have harmed workers and consumers in all the member countries. Developing countries that had put so many eggs into that particular basket will now be forced to think more creatively about both trade and policy options, which would not be an adverse outcome. The danger is that – despite the breakdown of this agreement – such deregulation and greater power to corporations will be granted anyway by the Trump administration, and sheer competitive pressure will then force governments across the world to fall in line. Avoiding this worst-of-all-worlds scenario will require constant public vigilance and mobilisation in all countries.

Similarly, financial markets will definitely be more unstable and volatile, and countries across the world may well have to brace themselves for another round of financial crises. This time, the implications may be worse because of the difficulty of using the same old solutions of large publicly funded bailouts to rescue banks and other financial institutions. The global race to environmental destruction pushed by further deregulation in the US and egged on by international competition in trade and investment, will also have to fought with public pressure in all countries.

Another concern for developing economies comes not from the economic policies of the Trump administration but from its foreign policies. Clearly, those who in the period prior to the election had seen Hillary Clinton as a greater threat to global security than Trump because of the extreme hawkish position on Russia had got it wrong. President Trump has assembled some of the most hawkish of military characters in his team, including those who were proponents of the Karl Rove version of "the new American century" under George Bush, and has already engaged in one military operation (however botched) and proposed others in the Middle East. His attitude to Russia may be confused, but that to China is more definitively aggressive. Global conflagrations need not start with direct engagements between the great powers; rather through history they have begun with more minor conflicts that explode out of proportion as the big powers get drawn in. Such possibilities are hugely possible with this US administration, and once again the danger for developing countries is that the wars will be fought on our territories and between our peoples. The propagation by the current US government of a sullen, petty-minded pseudo-nationalism is already finding echoes in too many other governments, including in the developing world where this attitude also similarly involves the suppression of any kind of domestic dissent. This is not just bad for internationalist co-operation and for democratic space within countries: it also affects economic flows and processes between countries and therefore within them.

So is it all bad news, with the gloom and doom justified? Not entirely. Periods of disruption are unpleasant and do throw up all sorts of outcomes, often mostly bad. But they are all periods when the older certainties are thrown aside, and some of these deserve to be discarded. The belief in "free" trade and globalised capital being all that is required for development was always wrong, but now it simply cannot be entertained. This must force more creative thinking about economic strategies in different parts of the world. Such thinking about economic strategies will have to come out of both the intellectual and the institutional straitjackets into which they had been put over the past decades. The confusion and disarray in the multilateral economic organisations that will definitely come about during this US administration and the resulting free-for-all in global economic architecture are certainly likely to reduce the possibilities of international co-operation significantly. But they may also open up policy spaces for developing countries seeking to change their position in the international division of labour, and generate more possibilities for autonomous industrialisation and development. This is not going to be easy, and obviously requires changing political economy configurations in many countries – but then, through history, the various paths to progress have never run smooth.

Nature abhors a vacuum: sex, emotion, loyalty and the rise of illiberal economics

Julie A. Nelson [University of Massachusetts, Boston, USA]

I was just as stunned, initially, as many of my fellow American by the results of the 2016 presidential election. I could see reasons why people might vote for "change" over more mainstream political leadership, especially given that both parties have been quite cozy with Wall Street and have failed to address the wage stagnation affecting the bulk of the population. But I thought that any reasonable person would be revolted by the narcissistic, juvenile, bullying, lying behavior of the Republican candidate, and realize that he was clearly unfit for office. As an economist, I was taken aback by the variously kleptocratic and fantastical aspects of Trump's intended economic directions. As a feminist and ecological economist, I was especially appalled by Trump's braggadocious pussy-grabbing and climate-change-denying. While, according to the popular vote, a majority of voters saw Trump this way, my assumptions clearly did not apply to a substantial and vocal minority.

On further reading, conversing, and reflection, however, I've come to think that the causes of this disastrous event are not unrelated to something that I've been writing about for a long time: the inadequacies of the mainstream neoclassical economics orthodoxy. Mainstream economics and liberal political philosophy have in common a particular story about human beings and how we relate to each other in society. Both have emphasized individuality, reason, freedom, and a marketplace or public sphere in which agent-citizens interact, at somewhat of a distance, as peers and equals.[1] Both have, correspondingly, neglected much about what makes us human,

---

[1] See (Meagher and Nelson, 2004). An assumption of at least relative equality is implicit in the model of optimizing agents and unfettered competitive markets that lies at the core of mainstream economics. The idea that market activities lead to welfare-maximizing outcomes is only even mildly plausible if one also assumes that everyone has an endowment of resources sufficient to make life – and choice-making – possible.

and about how we evolved as social beings. My serious mistake was in thinking that we, as a discipline and a society, might be able to move past this one-sided view in a positive direction.

So this essay will be largely a personal reflection, drawing on my own past work. I will highlight the vacant spaces and weak spots in mainstream economic and political analysis that Trump and his handlers were able to so thoroughly exploit. And, I hope, I will give some small gleam of hope about how we might prevent a new Dark Age.

The void in neoclassical orthodoxy

Since the 1990s, I and some other feminist economists have been pointing out that the mainstream discipline of economics has a profoundly masculinist bias. That is, aspects of human nature, experience, and behavior that fit a culturally "macho" mold have been emphasized and elevated, while those that are culturally associated with a lesser-valued femininity have been ignored.

The neoclassical orthodoxy focuses on markets and perhaps the public sphere, but categorizes families and unpaid work as "non-economic". The discipline adheres to exaggerated notions of (strictly logical) reason, while neglecting emotion and embodiment. It sees the economy in terms of autonomous agents, while glossing over all connection, dependency, and interdependency. It elevates self-interest, considering an interest in the well-being of others to be an anomalous and largely unnecessary trait. It defines objective "rigor" in terms of detachment and abstraction, treating normative or moral concerns as overly subjective, and assuming they can be safely denied or excluded. It elevates mathematical proof and fine-tuned econometric methods while downplaying detailed, concrete observation and good, verbal narratives.

These are all legacies of particular, and peculiar, Enlightenment notions of human nature and of science. Susan Bordo wrote,

"The Cartesian 'masculinization of thought', is one intellectual 'moment' of an acute historical flight from the feminine, from the memory of union with the maternal world, and a rejection of all values associated with it" (Bordo, 1987, p. 9).

James Hillman has written,

"The specific consciousness we call scientific, Western and modern is the long sharpened tool of the masculine mind that has discarded parts of its own substance, calling it 'Eve,' 'female' and 'inferior'" (quoted in Bordo, 1986, p. 441).

The counterpoint to "rational man", Elizabeth Fee has pointed out, is

"woman [who] provides his connection with nature; she is the mediating force between man and nature, a reminder of his childhood, a reminder of the body, and a reminder of sexuality, passion, and human connectedness" (Fee, 1983, p. 12).

While other schools of economics that share the pluralist umbrella have pointed out the limitations of various orthodox assumptions, I believe that feminist economics has made a unique contribution in pointing out the systematic – and unremittingly gender-biased – nature of the assumptions and exclusions made by the orthodoxy.

Of course, recognition of the gender biases in the profession is only a first step. Some would try to reassert that "masculine is good". Others, doing what I call "feminine" economics, try to simply turn the tables: disavowing competition and self-interest, for example, they call for a discipline – and society – founded exclusively on cooperation and altruism. To me, that is still playing with half a deck. The variant of feminist economics that I have propounded seeks to go further. I have wanted to think past the dualism, to think about characteristics we all – men and women both – share, and to explore how one-sided views of any kind tend to create traps.

Julie A. Nelson

Recognizing connection and emotion

Take, for example, the notions of autonomy and dependence. In classical liberal political thought as in economics, the citizen-agent is self-determining, self-sufficient, and ready for active participation in the polity or the market. If you asked where women were in this model, up until perhaps the 1960s, you would be told that women were "dependents" of their husbands or fathers. As it was once stated in British common law, in marriage "the two become one, and the one is the husband". Yet no one – child or adult, man or woman – is ever really self-sufficient. The attainments of "self-made men" are always dependent on the invisible services of mothers, wives, and others. We have called this the myth of the "separative self". The idea that women magically dissolve into subservient roles we labeled the myth of the "soluble self".[2] Getting beyond these myths, we can recognize that we are all, always, both individuated – distinguishable from those around us – and thoroughly connected, though our social and material constitution.

I proposed a "gender-value compass", shown in Figure 1 to illustrate this point. The top two cells show a positive complementarity: The recognition that we are all individuals-in-relation. The M+ to F– diagonal shows our usual, dualistic way of looking at things, e.g., superior masculine individuality versus the invisibility of women. Yet the M– cell shows what actually happens if we emphasize "masculinity" alone, as the F– cell likewise demonstrates for "femininity" alone.

Figure 1 The gender/value compass for individuality and relation

M+	F+
individual	related
M–	F–
separative	soluble

---

[2] This analysis was introduced to feminist economics by Paula England (1993, 2003) and myself (1992), both of us drawing in turn on the work of theologian Catherine Keller (1986).

Going one step further in this analysis – before we turn back to looking at Trumponomics – one can use this diagram to think about a variety of possible human relations.[3]

Three fatally partial – if not outright negative – images are based on the bottom half of the compass:

- *Separative-separative (arm's length):* When separative selves interact with other separative selves, such interactions must be purely external. This is the fundamental story about the nature and interactions of "citizens" in liberal politics and "agents" in neoclassical models of markets. This image appeals (only) to desires for self-preservation, self-sufficiency, and individual autonomy. Society, in this view, is only an agglomeration of individuals, perhaps bound by a freely entered "social contract" modeled on idealized market contracts.

- *Soluble-soluble (merger):* When soluble selves interact with other soluble selves, the image is of complete merger. Less noticed, this is the implicit assumption about the interior of an entity, when talking about "nations", "firms" or "households" as if they were, themselves, individual agents. At a political and emotional level, being "part of a movement" gives one a sense of identity with something larger than oneself, appealing to the human need to belong. Solubility has other attractive features as well: it absolves one of some of the burdens of individual moral responsibility, and allows one to feel virtuous about one's altruism and self-sacrifice.

- *Separative-soluble (domination):* When a separative self interacts with one or more soluble selves, the result is a strict hierarchy. The soluble selves take orders from and support (albeit invisibly) the separative self, who is perceived as autonomous, active, and in control. The separative side offers those who take on its role feelings of great power, while people who put a high value on loyalty, obedience, and sacrifice may find some sense of meaning in life through the self-abnegating service and hero-worship involved in the corresponding role of solubility.

---

[3] I introduced this typology in Nelson (2006). However, I elaborate more here about their emotional and political dimensions.

But the top half of the diagram reminds us that more authentic, fuller, individuals-in-relation ways of being, are also possible:

- *Mutuality:* When individuals-in-relation treat each other with respect and consideration, so that the relation is supportive of the positive formative process of each. This has two important sub-types:

    o *Symmetric mutuality:* mutuality between similarly-situated persons. Relations among equals do not need to be purely external and arms-length. A richer notion of liberal society imagines that justice, cooperation, vision and community spirit inform and motivate "equal" adults.
    o *Asymmetric mutuality:* mutuality in relations characterized by unequal power, status, ability or resources. In the real world there are adults and children, people with greater abilities and people with lesser, and people with more economic and political resources and people with less. Yet these do not have to be relations of domination. Imagining a "good society" in the face of asymmetry requires valuing good leadership and authentic care, perhaps calling on the metaphor of a nurturing family.

My hope had been that by expanding our liberal economic and political philosophies beyond their hyper-fixation on the individual, we might be able to recognize and analyze the wider variety of more complex relationships that, in fact, play large roles in structuring our society, economy, and civic life. By recognizing the diversity of ways in which we imagine our relationships, I hoped we could become both more knowledgeable and more wise. In particular, I hoped we could become more cognizant of unhealthy relations of domination, and try to replace them with healthy relations of mutuality.

Liberal thinkers may find it relatively easy to imagine respectful, supportive, and warm relations occurring among peers (symmetric mutuality), since this image preserves a basic sense of equality. But relations of care and of responsible leadership (asymmetric mutuality) are equally important – even if they may initially seem to belong to the realms of nature, and of monarchy modeled on a paternalistic family, that Enlightenment thinkers tried to leave behind. I have even suggested, as a counterpoint to a tendency to associate relationships of care exclusively with women, that we revitalize the old notion of "good husbandry" (coming from images of careful tending of crops and animals) to inspire more care on the part of men, and more care within culturally masculine-associated realms including finance and commerce (Nelson, 2016).

I have also argued that, along with freedom and reason, economic analysis and policy needed to take into account the very real human desire for affiliation and capacity for emotion (Nelson, 2004). This is illustrated in Figure 2.

Figure 2 The "gender/value compass" for reason and emotion

rational	emotional
inert	impulsive

Feelings both inform us and motivate our actions. The word "emotion", in fact, comes from Latin roots meaning "out-move". Reason can help us determine what the right thing is to do, but reason alone gives us no impetus to actually do it (Damasio, 1994).

In *Ecological Economics* in 2013 (Nelson, 2013), I wrote that I hoped that we could move away from one-sided 17th- and 18th-century notions, which I called "Enlightenment Beta" to a full-fledged, more inclusive and useful "Enlightenment 2.0". Enlightenment 2.0 would build narratives that appeal to profoundly human moral drivers including community, loyalty, and the sense of being part of something much larger than oneself, as well as respect for the individual. It would be geared towards action, not just analysis, and towards building resilience in worst and uncertain cases, not just efficiency in best cases and in a known, predictable world. I had hoped that we could, by developing a more adequate discipline of economics, contribute to a more just and sustainable society. Recently, I have argued that fear of fear – an emotion thought of as especially "unmanly" – is both biasing our empirical research (Nelson, 2014) and playing a role in our inability, as a society, to address climate change (Nelson, 2015).

We have been, by and large, repressing of all notions of connection and emotion with our Enlightenment Beta notions of economic and political life. I hoped that we could incorporate these in a good way and grow more wise, loving, and hopeful.

The rise of Trumpism

But we did not. This left a vacuum.

Various scholarly commentators have been pointed out this hole, and how Trump filled it. Linguist George Lakoff has for many years chastised Democrats for running campaigns that largely appeal only to voters' reason, while neglecting to hit hard on values, emotions, and powerful language and narrative (Lakoff, 2004, Lakoff, 2016). He explains the rise of Trump in terms of emotional appeals to a metaphorical understanding of the nation as a "strict father family", to the idea of a well-ordered hierarchy, and to hero worship. Sociologist Arlie Hochschild's extensive fieldwork among Tea Party supporters in environmentally poisoned areas of Louisiana revealed strong values related to loyalty, sacrifice, family, community, and church. Being a Trump supporter offered the opportunity of belonging to a movement, and a "giddy" sense of emotional release from the constraints of being "politically correct" (Hochschild, 2016, pp. 228, 234). The "deep story" by which people understood their lives pictured government – not in a classically liberal way as being the result of a social contract, or in a richer liberal way of embodying community – but (a la "free market economics") as a domineering force stealing their money and their freedoms (Hochschild, 2016, p. Chap. 9). Psychologists Jonathan Haidt (Haidt, 2012) and Joshua Green (Greene, 2013) have likewise noted the diversity of deep human moral values, which include loyalty and sanctity, and the tendency of liberal rhetoric to appeal to only a narrow, individualist band.

Arguments based on reason and facts alone make little headway when confronted with powerful metaphors, deep stories, and moral intuitions, which in turn may be powerfully supported by habit, stories, and ritual. Taking a longer-term view, author of works on religion Karen Armstrong describes how an exclusive focus on *logos* to the exclusion of *mythos* has created a "void at the heart of modern culture" (Armstrong, 2000, p. 370). *Logos* is the factual, scientific understanding in which "[e]fficiency was the new watchword" (Armstrong, 2005, p. 121). *Mythos*, on the other hand, refers to the spiritual and intuitive ways in which we come to understand the meaning and value of our lives. She writes of how this vacuum has given rise to "numbing despair, a creeping mental paralysis, and a sense of impotence and rage", "fearful and destructive unreason", "destructive mythologies [that] have been narrowly racial, ethnic, denominational and egotistic, and attempt to exalt the self by demonizing the other" and one who "seeks not heroism, but only barren celebrity" (Armstrong, 2005, pp. 122, 129, 136, 143). While Trumpism was not what she was pointing to at the time, it certainly fits her description.

And the discipline which most epitomizes "[e]fficiency as the new watchword" is, of course, economics. While trying to model itself on an image of detached, fact-based *logos*, it in fact has become a powerful though ultimately harmful *mythos*. In the mainstream economic orthodox myth, only *separative-separative* human relationships matter and economic self-interest rules. Feminist economics had attempted to turn the field back towards a richer and more factual basis, by pointing out the importance of power, care, and narratives (Ferber and Nelson, 1993). We made little headway (Ferber and Nelson, 2003). What we have seen, instead, is this void being filled, at a large-scale social and political level, by emotions and connections of a destructive sort: hatred, anger, unreason, and xenophobia. The excesses of neoliberal doctrines have not been superseded by the sort of Enlightenment 2.0 I envisioned, but instead by a raging illiberalism.

Where do we go from here?

The world has, alas, seen the rise of this sort of unreason before. Reason will be one of the tools with which we can address it, but only a weak one unless we leave behind Enlightenment Beta strictures and learn to deal with broader and deeper dimensions of human experience.

Julie A. Nelson

The media bring me daily news of lies, hatred, and fear. As an economist, I still aspire to create knowledge about the economy – about how societies organize themselves to provide for the survival and flourishing of life, or fail to do so. As a feminist economist who has worked on issues of care, I still want to work on the side of love. As an ecological economist who has worked on issues of climate change I still want to work on the side of hope. As a teacher, I still value educating students minds and hearts. As citizens, of the United States or of the earth, we cannot give up.

References

Armstrong, Karen (2000). *The Battle for God*. NY, Alfred A. Knopf.

Armstrong, Karen (2005). *A Short History of Myth*. NY, Canongate.

Bordo, Susan (1986). "The Cartesian Masculinization of Thought." *Signs: Journal of Women in Culture and Society* 11(3): 439-456.

Bordo, Susan (1987). *The Flight to Objectivity*. Albany, State University of New York Press.

Damasio, Antonio R. (1994). *Descartes' Error: Emotion, Reason, and the Human Brain*. New York, G.P. Putnam's Sons.

England, Paula (1993). The separative self: androcentric bias in neoclassical assumptions. *Beyond Economic Man: Feminist Theory and Economics*. M. A. Ferber and J. A. Nelson. Chicago, University of Chicago Press.

England, Paula (2003). Separative and Soluble Selves: Dichotomous Thinking in Economics. *Feminist Economics Today: Beyond Economic Man*. M. A. Ferber and J. A. Nelson. Chicago, University of Chicago Press: 33-59.

Fee, Elizabeth (1983). Women's nature and scientific objectivity. *Women's Nature: Rationalizations of Inequality*. M. Lowe and R. Hubbard. New York, Pergamon Press: 9-27.

Ferber, Marianne A. and Julie A. Nelson, Eds. (1993). *Beyond Economic Man: Feminist Theory and Economics*. Chicago, University of Chicago Press.

Ferber, Marianne A. and Julie A. Nelson, Eds. (2003). *Feminist Economics Today*. Chicago, University of Chicago Press.

Greene, Joshua (2013). *Moral Tribes: Emotion, Reason, and the Gap Between Us and Them*. NY, The Penguin Press.

Haidt, Jonathan (2012). *The Righteous Mind: Why Good People Are Divided by Politics and Religion* NY, Vintage.

Hochschild, Arlie Russell (2016). *Strangers in Their Own Land: Anger and Mourning on the American Right*. NY, The New Press.

Keller, Catherine (1986). *From a Broken Web: Separation, Sexism and Self.* Boston, Beacon Press.

Lakoff, George (2004). *Don't Think of an Elephant! Know Your Values and Frame the Debate*. White River Junction, VT, Chelsea Green.

Lakoff, George (2016). Understanding Trump. *georgelakoff.com* 2/5/2017.

Meagher, Gabrielle and Julie A. Nelson (2004). "Survey Article: Feminism in the Dismal Science." *Journal of Political Philosophy* 12(1): 102-126.

Nelson, Julie A. (1992). "Gender, Metaphor, and the Definition of Economics." *Economics and Philosophy* 8: 103-125.

Nelson, Julie A. (2004). "Freedom, reason, and more: Feminist economics and human development." *Journal of Human Development* 5(3): 309-333.

Nelson, Julie A. (2006). The Relational Firm: A Buddhist and Feminist Analysis. *Business within Limits: Deep Ecology and Buddhist Economics*. L. Zsolnai and K. J. Ims. Oxford, Peter Lang: 195-217.

Nelson, Julie A. (2013). "Ethics and the Economist: What Climate Change Demands of Us." *Ecological Economics* 85(January): 145-154.

Nelson, Julie A. (2014). "The Power of Stereotyping and Confirmation Bias to Overwhelm Accurate Assessment: The Case of Economics, Gender, and Risk Aversion." *Journal of Economic Methodology* 21(3): 211-231.

Nelson, Julie A. (2015). "Fearing fear: Gender and economic discourse." *Mind & Society* 14(1): 129-139.

Nelson, Julie A. (2016). "Husbandry: a (feminist) reclamation of masculine responsibility for care." *Cambridge Journal of Economics* 40(1): 1-15.

Is Trump wrong on trade? A partial defense based on production and employment

Robert H. Wade [London School of Economics and Political Science, UK]

"Free trade assumes that if you throw men out of work in one direction you re-employ them in another. As soon as that link is broken the whole of the free-trade argument breaks down" (J. M. Keynes, evidence to the Macmillan Committee on Finance and Industry, 1930).

Like Gresham's Law, "alternative facts" drive out facts.[1] If the economics profession had not decided long ago that the argument to be made here is wrong, we might not have President Trump.[2] We might not even have the deep cause of his success – the angry, indignant mood infecting swathes of western electorates.

Most of the 63 million Trump voters (47 percent of those who voted) express anger and indignation at elites who have been shredding the bargain on which complex democracies rest. They see those elites as taking a share of income and wealth beyond any plausible measure of social value, squeezing the last cent out of their workers or customers, and seeming to care little for the insecurities thrown up by technology and globalization. Of total employment growth in the US between 2005 and 2015, insecure employment in the categories of independent contractors, on-call workers and workers provided by contracting companies or temp agencies

---

[1] Thanks to Adrian Wood for this sentence and a version of the next one.

[2] Trump also surfed on widespread perception that the political system is illegitimate. The latter perception is substantiated by surveys of thousands of election experts asked to assess the quality of hundreds of elections around the world, whose average put the US as 52nd among 153 countries on "electoral integrity", as reported by the Electoral Integrity Project. Reported in Eduardo Porter, 2017, "Dysfunction in U.S. democracy", *New York Times (International)*, January 5. US voting turnout is one of the lowest in the developed world. In 2016 232 million citizens were legally entitled to vote; only 132 million did so (57%).

accounted for fully 94 percent.[3] Outsourcing of employment plays a big role in what David Weil describes as the "fissuring" of the workplace – depressing wages, magnifying income and wealth inequality, and generating a pervasive sense on the part of those at the wrong end of the fissuring that the world is cheating them, making them angry in return.[4] On top of this, many Trump voters are angry that the government is giving handouts to "shirkers", and sticking them with the tax bill.

They now see themselves as, finally, members of a winning team ("we won, you lost, get used to it!"). They affirm their leader's strikes against pillars of the "establishment" order (including the media and even the judiciary), and they forgive the administration's lies, "alternative facts", authoritarianism, chauvinism, and billionaire composition at the top.[5]

But we should not understand Trump's victory as a *sui generis* case. It fits the larger pattern in the developed world whereby *financial crises* tend to empower the far-Right in their wake. A recent study by Michael Funke and colleagues examines political effects of financial crises in 20 developed countries over the past 140 years and 800 elections. They find:

1) government majorities shrink after a financial crisis, political polarization increases;

---

[3] Lawrence Katz and Alan Krueger, 2016, "The rise and nature of alternative work arrangements in the US, 1995-2015", March 29. By the end of 2015, workers in the authors 'alternative' employment constituted 16 percent of total workers.
[4] David Weil, 2014, *The Fissured Workplace: Why Work Became So Bad For So Many and What Can Be Done To Improve It*, Harvard University Press.
[5] On the billionaire composition, *The Financial Times* reported ("Tillerson in line for $180m if confirmed", 5 January 2017, p.4) that Rex Tillerson, Donald Trump's secretary of state, will be given a payout worth about $180m to sever all financial ties to Exxon Mobil, because before his selection, the Exxon chairman and chief executive was in line to receive about 2 million shares in the oil group, worth about $182 m at today's prices. Mr Tillerson might consider himself hard done by compared to Stephen Schwarzman, the chief executive of Blackstone Group, the leveraged buyout firm, appointed by Mr Trump to be head of the president's business council. Schwarzman was paid $799 million in 2015. On lies and 'alternative facts', G. Grassegger and M. Krogerus, 2017, "The data that turned the world upside down", *Motherboard*, 28 January, at https://motherboard.vice.com/en_us/article/how-our-likes-helped-trump-win argue that they were not shoot-from-the-hip; they were carefully planned and micro-targeted on the basis of Big Data analysis of Facebook and other such data about individuals.

2) policy uncertainty increases;
3) voters tend to be drawn to the far-Right, which typically attributes blame to foreigners or minorities; on average, vote share of far-Right parties increases by 30% after financial crises; these effects are much stronger after financial crises than after 'normal' recessions or macroeconomic shocks that are not financial.[6]

The study suggests that the current wave of electoral support for "populist" leaders and parties in the US and much of Europe is a lagged response to the disruptions of 2008 and the drawn-out Great Recession. One might infer from it a bias for hope that the current far-Right wave will subside... if "normal" growth resumes and/or if governments undertake more pre- and re-distribution. The bias for hope is all the stronger when one remembers that Mr Trump attracted around three million votes less than Hillary Clinton; and that, so far, the far-Right forces in Europe have come close to governmental power only when allied with conventional Center-Right parties.

The elite response to President Trump is of course very different from the mass response. Philip Stephens of the *Financial Times* reports on foreign elite reaction: "A first take from friendly foreign ministries is that Mr Trump's economic nationalism threatens to fracture the open international trade system." This is the climactic sign of "a rogue American president" who "will prove a force for dangerous instability".[7]

Here, without getting into Trumpian specifics, I make a *partial* defense of President Trump's skepticism about the virtues of ever freer trade, ever more economic integration between countries.[8] My bottom line is that "the

---

[6] M. Funke, M. Schularick, C. Trebesch, 2016, "Going to extremes: politics after financial crises, 1870-2014", *European Economic Review*, at
http://www.sciencedirect.com/science/article/pii/S0014292116300587
[7] P. Stephens, 2017, "What the world hears from the White House", *Financial Times*, January 27, p.13.
[8] David Brooks of The New York Times warns that one should not take Trump's policy gestures seriously. "When Trump issues a statement, it may look superficially like a policy statement, but it's usually just a symbolic assault in some dominance-submission male rivalry game... His statements should probably be treated less like policy declarations and more like Snapchat. They exist to win attention at the moment, but then they disappear... The crucial question of the Trump administration

open international trade system" does need adjustment to provide more "policy space" for national governments and regional blocs. "Cooperative internationalism" should be the goal, not the prevailing "integrative globalization" – which relies on multilateral institutions and American hegemony to glue the world together and prescribes that national governments should have no more influence over trade and other cross-border movements than US states or even EU states have over theirs. [9]

I.   The elite globalization consensus

In this context globalization refers to the opening of domestic markets and the integration of global production via multinational corporations (MNCs). More broadly, it refers to movement in the world economy towards "one country", or "deep (not shallow) integration", where nation states have no more influence over flows of goods, services, capital, finance, ideas and people across borders than South Dakota or the other US states have across theirs. Ever since the 1980s leaders of western states – including

---

could be: Who will fill the void left by a leader who is all façade?" David Brooks, 2017. "The Snapchat presidency", *New York Times*, 4 January.

[9] Disclosure: I have a dog in this fight. I worked in the Trade Policy Division of the World Bank in the late 1980s. In the evenings and at weekends I worked on finishing my book, *Governing the Market*, Princeton University Press, 1990, 2004 – a project entirely separate from the Bank. But given my broad knowledge of East Asia the division asked me to write a substantial paper about how East Asian countries had gone about promoting exports. I agreed, but added that I would also have to discuss how they had gone about substituting imports, because export promotion and import substitution were like the two wings of the same bird. Emphatic no, was the response; import substitution could only be mentioned in negatives. Shortly after, I left the Bank for the more honest climate of the US Congress' Office of Technology Assessment. See Wade, 2009, "Reflections: Robert Wade, interviewed by Alex Izurieta", *Development and Change*, v.40, n.6, November, p.1153-1190. See also Wade, 1993, "Managing trade: Taiwan and South Kora as challenges to economics and political science", *Comparative Politics*, 25, 2, January, p.147-168, which gives a more extended economic and political analysis of the trade regime of Taiwan and South Korea than in *Governing the Market*. Also, Wade, 2014, "Current thinking about global trade policy", *Economic and Political Weekly*, XLIX, 6, February 8, p.18-21, gives an account of current thinking about global trade policy (especially in the context of the Sustainable Development Goals), by way of showing how most of UNCTAD (but not the division which produces the *Trade and Development Report*) has been captured by those who give top priority to "trade facilitation", code for almost free trade.

shareholders and top executives of MNCs – have agreed that states, on their own and cooperating (in free trade agreements, and in inter-state organizations like the World Bank, IMF, World Trade Organization, European Union), should push for ever more globalization, more "market access" for their corporations, and less state "intervention" or "regulation" in markets.

Here is Martin Wolf of the *Financial Times*, one of the world's most influential economic commentators:

> "It cannot make sense to fragment the world economy more than it already is but *rather to make the world economy work as if it were the United States, or at least the European Union… The failure of our world is not that there is too much globalization, but that there is too little.* The potential for greater economic integration is barely tapped… Social democrats, classical liberals and democratic conservatives should unite to preserve and improve the liberal global economy against the enemies mustering both outside and inside the gates" (emphasis added).[10]

Here is Renarto Ruggiero, former head of the WTO:

> "trade integration is not just a recipe for growth but *also security and peace*, as history has shown" (emphasis added).

Here is the WTO saying on its website: global integration under WTO and predecessor GATT supervision

> "has been *one of the greatest contributors to economic growth and the relief of poverty in mankind's history*" (emphasis added).

---

[10] M. Wolf, 2004, *Why Globalization Works*, Yale University Press, p.4.

Here is the World Bank summarizing others' research findings, with which it agrees:

> *"openness to international trade, based on largely neutral incentives, was the critical factor in East Asia's rapid growth"* (emphasis added).[11]

The World Bank's Structural Adjustment Loans over the 1980s carried more trade liberalization conditions than those in any other policy domain. The Bank treated trade liberalization as the queen of policies, not just one among many, saying that free trade policy will limit the amount of damage from other government interventions in the market.[12]

The *Financial Times* peppers its editorials about trade protection with negatives like "mercantilist" and "populist", and stresses that any one country benefits from adopting free trade policy even if others do not – because protection amounts to throwing rocks in your own harbor. Apparently the collective interest of any country and of the world at large always favors free trade, because free trade maximizes the size of the pie. Only self-seeking "vested interests" want protection in order to get more of the pie for themselves, at inevitable cost to society.

A big business voice comes from Percy Barnevik, when CEO of the Swedish-Swiss multinational Asea Brown Boveri (ABB):

> "I would define globalization as the freedom of my group to invest where and as long as it wishes, to produce what it wishes, by buying and selling wherever it wishes... while putting up with as little labor laws and social convention constraints as possible." [13]

---

[11] World Bank, 1993, *The East Asian Miracle: Economic Growth and Public Policy*, p. 292.
[12] World Bank, 1989, "Strengthening trade policy reform", Washington DC, Nov 13.
[13] Quoted in J. Gelinas, 2003, *Juggernaut Politics: Understanding Predatory Capitalism*, Zed Books, p. 21

Finally, Bernard Arnault, in 2000, CEO of French luxury group LVMH and 10th richest person on Earth:

> "Businesses, especially international ones, have ever greater resources, and in Europe they have acquired the ability to compete with states... Politicians' real impact on the economic life of a country is more and more limited. Fortunately."[14]

These statements illustrate the tendency for globalization champions to attribute "all good things" to trade and investment integration, including (1) global poverty reduction on an unprecedented scale, (2) East Asia's remarkable economic rise, and (3) global peace and security.

Though they assert causality, the statements are not intended to pass a test of evidence. Their job is to affirm identity: that the speaker or organization is a member of the global elite team which wants capital, goods and services to be able to move freely worldwide between locations and sectors, as the defining feature of desirable globalization, assuming that what is good for the team is good for humanity and the biosphere.

Implicitly or explicitly the claims downplay the value of "policy space" and the value of the solidarity obligations embedded in the idea of "nation", ignoring the employment point made by Keynes in the epigraph. The claims should be understood in the light of Daniel Kahneman's observation, "Declarations of high confidence mainly tell you that an individual has constructed a coherent story in his mind, not necessarily that the story is true".

---

[14] B. Arnault, quoted in Serge Halimi, 2013, "Tyranny of the one per cent", *Le Monde Diplomatique (English),* May 1.

II. Comparative advantage and free trade as the crown jewel of the neoclassical paradigm

Globalization champions draw comfort from neoclassical economic theory, which purports to give a rigorous and "general interest" justification for the policy of free trade in goods and services.[15]

The argument today rests on basically the same theory of comparative advantage as David Ricardo proposed in 1817 – a theory which was static, timeless, abstract, elegant, and which today broadly retains those characteristics (with some theoretical qualifications to do with "increasing returns", which are treated as unimportant for practical policy in the real world). In the following two centuries the theory acquired the status of jewel in the crown of the increasingly dominant neoclassical paradigm.

As Paul Krugman quipped,

> "If there were an Economist's Creed, it would surely contain the affirmations, 'I understand the Principle of Comparative Advantage' and 'I advocate Free Trade.'"[16]

Gregory Mankiw, author of the most widely used textbook in economics, declared,

> "Although economists often disagree on questions of policy, they are united in their support of free trade. Moreover, the central argument for free trade has not changed much in the past two centuries... [E]conomists' opposition to trade restrictions is still based largely on the principle of comparative advantage."[17]

---

[15] Ha-Joon Chang and Ilene Grabel give a measured account of the mainstream theory, its strengths and weaknesses, in *Reclaiming Development: An Alternative Economic Policy Manual*, 2014, Zed Books, London.

[16] Paul Krugman, 1987, "Is free trade passé?", *J. Economic Perspectives* 1 (2) Fall, p. 131.

[17] N. Gregory Mankiw, 2008, *Principles of Economics*, 5th ed., Mason: Thompson, p. 57

Jagdish Bhagwati, celebrated trade economist at Columbia University, put the point more colorfully:

> "Only Neanderthals among the economists now militate against free trade: unfortunately, they will never lack an audience but fortunately, they have little effect presently".[18]

Finally, Douglas Irwin, historian of economic ideas:

> "...one should recognize that free trade commands respect among economists largely because of its continuing theoretical attractiveness" (rooted in the theory of comparative advantage).[19]

Surveys of economists' opinions confirm that there is nothing that economists, especially American economists, agree about more than the virtues of free or almost free trade. For example, a survey of nearly 1,000 economists in five industrialized countries asked them to "generally agree", "agree with provisos", or "generally disagree" with 27 propositions. "Tariffs and import controls lower economic welfare" was the one that elicited most agreement. Seventy nine percent of the American economists and 57 percent of the whole sample said, "generally agree".[20]

III. The argument for free trade policy

The argument boils down to three propositions supporting the conclusion that the institution of free trade is 'right' for each country and the world.

---

[18] Jagdish Bhagwati, 1998, "Free trade: what now?", Keynote address at University of St Gallen, May 25, https://academiccommons.columbia.edu/catalog/ac:123560, p. 8
[19] Douglas Irwin, 1996, *Against the Tide: An Intellectual History of Free Trade,* Princeton University Press, p. 224
[20] B. Frey, W. Pommerehne, F. Schneider, G. Gilbert, 1984, "Consensus and dissensus among economists: an empirical enquiry", *American Economic Review,* 74, 5, pp. 986-94.

1) Free trade leads to production specialization in activities in which the economy holds a "comparative or relative advantage" (not "absolute advantage");
2) This pattern of production specialization yields maximum efficiency of resource allocation among the trading partners, and therefore maximum "welfare" for these trading countries;
3) Economists should recommend policy measures which will result in maximum efficiency (including free trade) and leave it to political choice as to how to distribute the resulting maximum income or consumption.

The basic idea is simple. People want to consume a wider mix than can be produced at home more cheaply than could be imported. Therefore, driven by relative costs, countries tend to export goods whose production makes intensive use of resources or factors (including land, labour, skilled labour, capital) which are abundant nationally, and import goods whose production requires resources scarce nationally. A country with trade barriers blocks this efficiency-enhancing mechanism and imposes higher costs of its consumption mix on its population ("puts rocks in its own harbor"). A country which lowers its trade barriers tends to raise its specialization of production, exports and employment in the resource abundant products, so the returns to the abundant resources tend to rise relative to the returns to the scarcer resources. Ergo, free trade is best for each country and the world, enabling maximum consumption from a given stock of resources.

The argument has more recently been fortified by the fall in "coordination costs" and "information costs" thanks to ICTs (information and communication technologies), as well as production changes that facilitate the unbundling of production into discrete tasks to be done in scattered locations.[21] These developments enable a country to get better access to production, marketing and managerial knowledge than before, and so able to stretch its comparative advantage into the export of products previously out of reach.

---

[21] Adrian Wood, 2017, "Variations in structural change around the world, 1985-2015: patterns, causes, and implications", WIDER Working Paper 2017/34, United Nations University World Institute for Development Economics Research.

In the event that imports of a set of products drive a country's producers out of those products, this is all to the good, because the imports reveal that the products in which the country holds a comparative advantage have changed. Over time in any one economy, as wages and other costs rise, the economy should lose production and jobs in its relatively less productive industries to lower cost economies and gain them in its relatively more productive industries.

It is scarcely an exaggeration to say that *comparative-advantage-driven free trade is the core mechanism by which modern mainstream economics explains the great question, how market capitalism generates human welfare.* Beneficial global integration – moving towards "one economic country" – is the overarching narrative of the past several decades. See the earlier quotes from Ruggerio, Wolf, and the others, and the results of the survey of economists' opinions.

So both specialists and public discourse writ large are confident that, first, the theory of comparative advantage is compelling as an *explanation* of production specialization and trade patterns; second, it is also compelling as the theoretical *justification* for the policy of free trade; and third, the empirical evidence is strong that trade liberalization raises growth rates, and that countries with freer trade have better economic performance than countries with less free trade.

On these grounds believers dismiss those who advocate some degree of trade management with the charge that they are willing to sacrifice the "general interest" (implicitly defined in terms of larger consumption, regardless of employment) in order to protect the interests of narrow interest groups (such as trade unions, or inefficient small and medium enterprises, which typically provide much employment).

IV. Free trade in question: the theory is not robust

At a high level of aggregation the theory of comparative advantage "works", in the sense that global trade patterns are broadly in line with its predictions. Countries with abundant land and scarce skilled labor (Africa) tend to produce and export land-intensive products and import manufactured products, and countries with scarce land and abundant labour (East Asia) tend to produce and export labour-intensive manufactured products and import land-intensive and skill-intensive products.[22]

But this is not the end of the story. The theory's broad consistency with trade patterns does not translate straightforwardly into the policy conclusion that free trade is best for each country and the world. The theory rests on a raft of assumptions so limiting of its domain of applicability as to make one wonder how it could have survived for so long as the crown jewel of economic theory. Here are some of them.[23]

No externalities

The theory assumes no externalities; in other words, assumes that prices reflect true economic value – including the economic cost of environmental damage and the economic gains of one company's innovation for other companies. The theory is driven only by what is included in prices. A country with lax environmental standards will produce and export too much of some goods, because prices do not include environmental damage (deaths from ambient air pollution, for example); and countries with higher environmental standards will import too much relative to prices which do incorporate environmental damage. Less than free trade could benefit both sides. Similarly, free trade can lead to companies producing positive spillovers for other companies being wiped out by foreign competition, because their prices do not reflect their hidden value to others in the same country. Assuming no externalities of course limits all free market theory, not just comparative advantage theory.

---

[22] Adrian Wood, 2017, "Variations in structural change around the world, 1985-2015: patterns, causes, and implications".
[23] This section draws on Ian Fletcher, 2010, *Free Trade Doesn't Work: What Should Replace It and Why*, U.S. Business and Industry Council, Washington DC; and Vishaal Kishore, 2014, *Ricardo's Gauntlet: Economic Fiction and the Flawed Case for Free Trade*, Anthem Press. Thanks to Adrian Wood for comments.

Full employment is sustained

The theory assumes full employment throughout, ignoring "transitional costs" of increased exposure to trade. By assuming full employment, it avoids facing a trade-off between the welfare gains from trade and the welfare losses from unemployment or precariate employment. See Keynes' epigraph. Implicitly, the theory sides with consumers, not with those whose income from labor (rather than capital) might be threatened by unrestrained imports. It is as though the "Walmart effect" of cheap imported consumer goods completely eclipses the employment losses associated with rising imports of manufactures (now amplified by post-2008 fiscal austerity).

The slowness of labour market "adjustment" to trade shocks – and recessions – than assumed in the globalization consensus has been measured by David Autor, David Dorn and Gordon Hanson. They study the effects of "the China shock" that began in the early 1990s in the form of a surge of manufactured exports to the US. They find that,

> "Alongside the heralded consumer benefits of expanded trade are substantial adjustment costs and distribution consequences... *Adjustment in local labor markets is remarkably slow, with wages and labor-force participation rates remaining depressed and unemployment rates remaining elevated for at least a full decade after the China shock commences... At the national level, employment has fallen in U.S. industries more exposed to import competition, as expected, but offsetting employment gains in other industries have yet to materialize.*"[24]

They calculate that about 55 percent of job losses in US manufacturing between 2000 and 2007 was caused by "rising exposure to Chinese import competition", and 33 percent in the earlier period, 1990–2000.[25]

---

[24] David Autor, David Dorn and Gordon Hanson, 2016, "The China shock: learning from labor market adjustment to large changes in trade", NBER WP 21906, January, www.nber.org/papers/w21906, emphasis added.

[25] David Autor, David Dorn and Gordon Hanson, 2013, "The China syndrome: local labor market effects of import competition in the United States", American Economic Review, 103 (6): 2121-68, at 2139.

More evidence on the slowness of labour market adjustment comes from OECD figures on unemployment. As of 2015, eight years after the onset of the global financial crisis in 2007-08, some 44 million people were unemployed and wanting work in the OECD, 37 percent higher than the rate before 2007. The mainstream response prescribes fiscal austerity and job retraining. This is like saying – when 100 dogs are ushered into a room where 95 bones have been hidden and five emerge without a bone – "the five dogs have insufficient bone-finding skills and need more training", rather than the Keynesian response, "there are insufficient bones for the number of dogs".

Rising trade does not drive rising income inequality

The theory of comparative advantage accounts for aggregate (consumption) gains from trade and neglects the distributional consequences. To see the significance of this neglect, take an example from Ian Fletcher.[26] A country lowers trade barriers, then imports more clothes and exports more aircraft, in line with its comparative advantage. Its GDP goes up. For each million dollars of production, clothing requires one white collar worker and nine blue collar workers, aircraft require three white collar workers and seven blue collar workers. So demand for white collar workers goes up, demand for blue collar workers goes down; and their wages move in the same direction. But most workers are blue collar. So most workers face a fall in their employment conditions, even as GDP goes up, thanks to free trade moving the economy closer into line with its comparative advantage. Dani Rodrik calculates that freeing up trade in the US shuffles five dollars to different groups for every one dollar of gain in GDP.[27]

Trade remains balanced

The theory assumes that trade remains balanced between the trade partners.[28] The exchange rate is assumed to adjust so that relative cost

---

[26] Ian Fletcher, 2017, *Free Trade Doesn't Work*, p. 109

[27] Dani Rodrik, 1997, *Has Globalization Gone Too Far?*, Washington: Institute for International Economics, p. 30.

[28] "In trade theory, it is standard to assume that trade is balanced". David Autor, David Dorn and Gordon Hanson, 2016, "The China shock: learning from labor market

differentials (due to differences between countries in their relative factor endowments) are translated into relative price differentials across borders, which lead profit-seeking producers to specialize in line with comparative advantage. If one country's absolutely advantaged goods (think China) start to flood the markets of others (think Brazil), exchange rates will adjust sufficiently to ensure that before long comparative advantage dominates absolute advantage, and trade returns to balance. (Analytically, the adjustment could also occur through wage and price changes. But these are even more implausible in the modern world than exchange rate changes.)

Underlying the invocation of the balancing exchange rate is an assumption that *international trade is basically barter* – producers barter goods among themselves. *Money is simply a neutral medium of exchange, to lower transactions costs.* The assumption rationalizes the discipline separation between "international trade", with its specialists, and "international finance", with its specialists (in exchange rates, payments systems and capital markets), with little communication between the two.

The assumption that international trade is basically barter – and is balanced -- removes a fundamental dynamic of foreign exchange markets, a dynamic which explains why *(1) a trade deficit need not produce an exchange rate devaluation, and (2) the exchange rate change need not restore balanced trade* (no payments surpluses or deficits).

Exchange rates are determined not only by relative flows of goods and services, but also by, often speculative, capital flows unrelated to the financing of trade. Capital flows can and do drive exchange rates far from levels at which trade would balance. They are driven by herd behavior based on "guesses" about how certain "news" will affect the behavior of financial market participants and thereby the direction of asset price movements, on which the speculation builds.[29]

---

adjustment to large changes in trade", NBER WP 21906, January, www.nber.org/papers/w21906, p. 12.

[29] For overview analyses of the global financial system and efforts to "reform" it, see R. H. Wade, 2007, "A new financial architecture?", *New Left Review*, 46, July-August, pp. 113-129; 2008, "Financial regime change?", *New Left Review*, 53, September-October, p.5- 22; Jakob Vestergaard, 2009, *Discipline in the World Economy: International Finance and the End of Liberalism*, Routledge.

So countries with high inflation, high interest rates, and large current account *deficits* can experience currency *appreciation* rather than depreciation (needed to reduce current account deficits), as they become targets for carry trade "investors" (speculators) buying the domestic currency with money borrowed elsewhere at low interest rates.[30]

The *Trade and Development Report 2009*, from the United Nations Conference on Trade and Development (UNCTAD), sums up:

> "The most important lesson of the recent [2008] financial crisis is that financial markets do not 'get the prices right'; they systematically overshoot or undershoot due to centralized information handling, which is quite different from the information collection of normal goods markets. In financial markets, nearly all participants react in a more or less uniform manner to the same set of 'information' or 'news', so that they wind or unwind their exposure to risk almost in unison. *The currency market, in particular, causes results quite different from those envisaged by theory, such as an appreciation of the nominal exchange rate in countries that have high inflation rates over considerable periods of time.*"[31]

Empirically, we know that, since the global liberalization of capital flows in the late 1970s, trade imbalances have persisted for long periods, together with high exchange rate volatility – which can have the effect of jerking economies, and people, around like yo-yos. Yet the theory of comparative advantage assumes that exchange rate adjustment will occur by enough to keep trade balanced.

---

[30] See UNCTAD, *passim, Trade and Development Report* . On Iceland as a case in point, see R. H. Wade and S. Sigurgeirsdottir, 2012, "Iceland's rise, fall, stabilization and beyond", *Cambridge J. Economics*, vol. 36, no. 1, January, 127-144; and R. H. Wade, 2009, "Iceland as Icarus", *Challenge*, 52, 3, May-June, pp. 5-33.
[31] UNCTAD, 2009, *Trade and Development Report 2009*, p. 116, 127, references omitted.

Short-term efficiency gains cause higher long-run growth

The theory of comparative advantage tells how countries can reap efficiency gains by reallocating their *existing* resources by moving to freer trade. It is silent on the effects of the reallocation on long-run growth. If the reallocation results in the country moving out of activities rich in increasing returns to scale, or in technological linkages upstream and downstream, or in productivity gains due to physical proximity (an "industrial ecosystem"), it can harm growth.

Take Ricardo's famous example, showing that both England and Portugal gain by moving towards free trade, resulting in England specializing in textiles and Portugal in wine, consumption of both being higher in both countries than in the absence of trade. That is the end of the comparative advantage story. But of course, now England has the textile industry, with its spillover links to the industry for steam engines and machine tools, which provides England with a platform to enter many other state-of-the-art sectors (stretching its comparative advantage). Portugal has wine, whose technology has not changed for hundreds of years and whose linkages to other sectors are thin. Good for England, bad for Portugal. And in fact, decades before Ricardo wrote, England and Portugal had switched to largely free trade in these products. Portugal's promising textile industry was wiped out, and English (very mobile) capital, including Ricardo's family's, took control of Portugal's vineyards as their owners went into debt with London banks.[32] Portugal fell rapidly into the ranks of Europe's poorest countries. Ricardo knew all this very well. He was an English gentleman, financier and Member of Parliament, and his theory of comparative advantage was a mask for advancing the emerging hegemon's national interest against others'.[33]

---

[32] Ian Fletcher, 2017, *Free Trade Doesn't Work*, p. 114.

[33] For an account of how western states today manage to maintain their dominant position in international economic organizations and steer these organizations to champion the great globalization consensus, see R. H. Wade, 2013, "The art of power maintenance: how western states keep the lead in global organizations", *Challenge*, 56, 1, January-February, pp. 5-39.

V. Globalization in question: the economic evidence is ambiguous

Now to focus more directly on empirical evidence. As noted, during the past several decades globalization – including freer trade and capital mobility – has led to production specialization broadly in line with the theory of comparative advantage. Adrian Wood explains with reference to 1985-2015,

> "In skill-abundant developed countries, manufacturing became more skill-intensive. In land-scarce developing East Asia, labour-intensive manufacturing expanded, especially in China. In land-abundant developing regions, however, manufacturing stagnated or declined, while in land-scarce South Asia manufacturing was held back by low literacy and weak infrastructure."[34]

However, this is a very broad empirical pattern of the factor-intensity of production and exports. The champions of free trade and more globalization make much grander and more normative claims about benefits far exceeding costs. They are inclined to overstate the benefits of free trade and globalization and underestimate the costs (even when confined to material benefits and costs, as in GDP, and especially when extended to employment).

We saw earlier how globalization champions – such as the WTO and the World Bank – tend to attribute "all good things" to rising levels of economic globalization. Recall the World Bank saying, "openness to international trade, based on largely neutral incentives, was the critical factor in East Asia's rapid growth". No ambiguity: "[L]argely neutral incentives... was *the* critical factor" (emphasis added). Nothing in the World Bank study comes close to validating this claim. Also, recall the WTO saying that "global integration... has been one of the greatest contributors to economic growth and the relief of poverty in mankind's history". Not to forget Renarto Ruggiero, former head of the WTO, declaring, "trade integration is not just a recipe for growth but also security and peace, as history has shown."

---

[34] Adrian Wood, 2017, "Variation in structural change around the world, 1985–2015", abstract.

Robert H. Wade

Globalization champions tend to assume that – while globalization certainly brings aggregate benefits larger than costs – sectional interests adversely affected by international competition can successfully lobby the (often predatory) state for less globalization and more protection, at cost to the more diffuse (therefore less organizable) "general or societal interest". So globalization champions dismiss critics as not understanding the theory or as speaking for vested interests.[35]

By way of critique, we can start with Paul Krugman's point: "The first thing you need to know is that almost everyone exaggerates the importance of trade policy."[36] This is a surprise coming from an economist who won the so-called Nobel Prize in Economics[37] for his work on trade theory.

Dani Rodrik affirms that,

> "Countries that have done well in the post-war period are those that have been able to formulate a domestic investment strategy to kick-start growth and those that have had the appropriate institutions to handle external shocks, not those that have relied on reduced barriers to trade and capital flows".[38]

Francisco Rodriguez summarizes literature on the link between openness and growth, and finds that six major measures of openness are only weakly

---

[35] This section draws on Graham Dunkley, 2016, *One World Mania: A Critical Guide to Free Trade, Financialization and Global Integration,* Zed Books.
[36] Paul Krugman, 2015, "TPP at the NABE", *New York Times,* 11 March.
[37] Why "so-called"? See Philip Mirowski, "The neoliberal ersatz Nobel Prize", paper for presentation to conference on The Road from Mont Pelerin II, December 2015. Krugman was honored for showing how the well-known real-world phenomenon of increasing returns could be incorporated into formal trade models, which previously had been driven only by comparative advantage. Remarkable is that this incorporation happened so recently, given that since the early 20th century business leaders competed by building companies big enough to drive down costs through economies of scale and speed sufficiently to establish monopoly positions.
[38] Dani Rodrik, 1999, *The New Global Economy and Developing Countries: Making Openness Work,* Overseas Development Council, Policy Paper 24, Washington DC, p. 93.

if at all correlated with growth (and the causality could go both ways). Also, most growth accelerations are not correlated with trade openings.[39]

Global growth has *fallen* steadily every decade since the 1960s – from over five percent in the 1960s to under three percent over the 2000s. Yet measures of economic integration between national economies show a fairly steady *increase* during these decades.

Many developing countries had their fastest post-World War II growth during their period of "import substitution" with managed trade – which the reigning elite consensus treats as always harmful to the national interest and the global interest. The consensus ignores the mechanism of managed trade in East Asia: the combination of strong encouragement to export certain products and strong encouragement to replace imports in certain other products, complemented by strong encouragement to invest and re-invest within the national territory. The result was that highly managed trade and capital flows (until the 1990s) helped to generate unusually fast and sustained growth, which sucked in rising volumes of imports in the less-protected sectors. The incentive regime restrained imports of (especially luxury) consumer goods while facilitating imports of advanced capital goods. *Closely managed trade went with fast growth of trade.*[40]

Whatever one concludes from these trends, it cannot be that trade liberalization tends to generate faster growth. At most, a step up in trade liberalization could be expected to produce a small, one-off increase in GDP, but there is no evidence that it reliably generates faster growth.

In short, ample evidence is at hand with which to challenge the great globalization consensus. Together with the critique of comparative advantage theory, the evidence suggests we should consider an alternative line of argument to the mainstream's core proposition: namely, the

---

[39] F. Rodriquez, 2007, "Openness and growth: what have we learned?", DESA Working Paper 51, UN, August.

[40] Robert H. Wade, 1990 (2004), *Governing the Market*; Wade, 1993, "Managing trade: Taiwan and South Kora as challenges to economics and political science", *Comparative Politics*, 25, 2, January, pp.147-168; Wade, 1991, "How to protect exports from protection: Taiwan's duty drawback scheme," *The World Economy*, 14(3): 299-309.

aggregate costs of the present level of trade and capital integration outweigh benefits; but sectional interests – especially MNCs and elites vested to international capital – press states for always more openness against the "general interest" (defined not just in terms of consumption but also employment). See the Barnevik and Arnault quotes above. "Free trade agreements" like the North America Free Trade Agreement (NAFTA), and bilateral investment treaties (BITs), are a case in point.

Indeed, a defining moment in the death of "the nation" as an economic and social protection entity in the US came in 1992 with the signing of NAFTA, by which the US, Canada and Mexico took a giant step towards a single economic unit (from "shallow" to "deep integration"). US workers undertook mass protests against it, accurately forecasting large-scale job losses at home, to no avail. Barak Obama, before being elected US president in 2008, declared,

> "... entire cities have been devastated by trade pacts. I don't think NAFTA has been good for America, and I never have."[41]

NAFTA has brought large material gains to shareholders and top executives of US and Canadian MNCs and to their dependent Mexican counterparts. It has also stimulated FDI into Mexico, and manufactured exports from Mexico. But Mexico's growth has been sluggish since the 1990s, behind most other countries in Latin America. Average real wages have fallen to the point where the average real wage in Mexico City is below Shanghai. In a recent poll in Mexico, only 20% of respondents believed that NAFTA had been good for Mexican consumers and businesses. A Mexican economist noted,

> "as a development strategy, it should have led to higher sustained growth, generated well-paid salaries and reduced the gap between Mexico and the United States. It has remained well below what was hoped for."

---

[41] Quoted in S. Thornton, 2008, "Trade pact smolders in fiery campaign", AFR, 31 March, www.afr.com.

Of course, the fault is not all due to NAFTA. The government and the domestic private sector have failed to increase investment in R&D, regulations remain burdensome, and banks have lent less than their Latin American counterparts, leaving small and medium enterprises scrambling for credit.[42]

VI. Globalization in question: the political evidence is ambiguous

The discussion of NAFTA takes us to the political effects of trade liberalization and capital mobility. The core point is that as the dominant private economic agents detached from their domestic markets, shareholders and top executives of MNCs lost the idea of belonging to a nation, the idea of a basic solidarity with their people, including employees – because their sales and profits no longer depended mostly on the domestic market. As Robert Blecker says,

> "Although the US economy has been running large trade deficits that represent net losses of jobs in tradeables industries, US-based corporations have no such large deficits and have profited immensely from their foreign operations."[43]

Western states under strong influence from business lobbies have been unwilling to protect the public from goods and services produced in cheap labor countries; justifying their unwillingness by faith that globalization – specifically, free trade and investment – will benefit "all (hard working) families" in the longer run. [44]

A cartoon in the *New York Times* captures the point obliquely. A private jetplane lands at an airport, the red carpet is rolled out, down the gangplank walks the chief executive, who declares to his companion,

---

[42] A. Ahmed and E. Malkin, 2017, "Mexico doesn't feel like winner in trade deal", *New York Times (International)*, January 6, p. 1.

[43] R. Blecker, 2005, "International economics after Robinson", in B. Gibson (ed), *The Economics of Joan Robinson: A Centennial Celebration*, E. Elgar Publishing, p. 341.

[44] Luiz Carlos Bresser-Pereira, "The political crisis of globalization", http://www.bresserpereira.org.br/view.asp?cod=6723

"Why should my taxes pay for roads and bridges?... When I don't really use them?"

The cartoon illustrates that the rich now have so much income and wealth relative to the rest of the population that they can effectively live in orbits quite separate from those of the large majority, free from the downsides of globalization, and shape public policy to their liking on issues where their preferences diverge from those of the median voter.[45]

Technology, particularly information and communication technology (ICT), probably accounts for a larger part of job losses in western manufacturing than imports from cheap labour sites.[46] But what matters for political effects is perception, and it is easier for those displaced from well-paying manufacturing jobs into low-wage service jobs or no jobs at all to blame foreigners and foreign countries for their hardship than to blame amorphous technology or inanimate robots.

Erosion of the idea of the nation as an economic solidarity entity (continuing since the 1980s) has gone with a second negative effect of globalization, namely, erosion of Center-left parties and movements all over the West. In the face of triumphant globalization ideology the Center-Left has long tried to compete with the Right by (a) adopting similar neoliberal economic policies of deregulation, liberalization, privatization, downplaying "the nation" an economic unit, unlike Trump, while (b) differentiating itself from the Right on "social" (or "moral") issues like abortion, gender equality, and gay rights. The strategy has had limited success, especially since the financial crisis of 2007-08. These "social" issues are not compelling for electoral majorities,

---

[45] Martin Gilens, 2014, *Affluence and Influence: Economic Inequality and Political Power in America*, Princeton University Press. And not to be missed, Keith Olbermann,
https://m.youtube.com/watch?feature=youtu.be&v=gPayKb39Kao

[46] Separating out the causal weight of "globalization" and "technology" on employment, wages and working conditions is difficult because they are so interrelated. Offshoring of manufacturing raises the supply of people seeking employment in service sector jobs, and the spread of information technology makes it easier for companies to outsource many low-skill tasks – running the cafeteria, building maintenance, security, hotel reception – to low-wage subcontractors. See Eduardo Porter, 2017, "How domestic outsourcing hurts workers", *New York Times (International)*, 2 March, p. 10.

whereas core issues of employment, income protection, and social protection, are compelling – yet the Center-Left hardly differs from the well-financed low-tax Right on this terrain.

A third political effect of globalization is that, finding little comfort from the Center-Left, those who feel disadvantaged, even humiliated, as they see all around the wealthy few making huge fortunes and living luxuriously, and as they see the state giving help to minorities and immigrants financed with their taxes, grasp at comfort from people and parties who do speak the language of "the nation", meaning "people like us", and who promise to "support the people, not the elites". Even when they see the billionaire leader appointing many billionaires to his cabinet. We noted earlier that this broad pattern is well-established in elections around the developed world in the wake of financial crises, not specific to the recent US election.

VII. Why have economists been so committed to free trade and globalization?

Why have the large majority of professional economists, especially in the academy and in western-dominated international organizations like the World Bank and IMF, been committed to free trade policy, downplaying theoretical and empirical weaknesses in order to remain so?

The teaching of economics in just about all universities of the western world, and in large parts of the developing world, socializes students into belief in the rightness of the "market" paradigm, and the more "rigorous" the training the more thoroughly socialized they become.[47] The paradigm focuses on price competitiveness – free labor markets, flexible prices, free international trade – as the key to national competitiveness. It treats the market system as "self-organizing", firms being essentially passive except for competing in price. It treats technology as external to production, as something which firms can buy on the market. It has no built-in process of innovation, no conception of an "industrial ecosystem" of firms competing and cooperating

---

[47] As one example, G. Racko, et al., 2017, "Economics education and value change", *Academy of Management Learning and Education*, January.

with each other.[48] With all these things stripped out, the culture of the profession elevates belief in comparative advantage and free trade as the litmus test of competence to be an economist, as the earlier quote from Krugman suggests.

The market paradigm fits the larger "conservative" worldview, which sees the market as 'natural' and the realm of 'freedom', the state as artificial and the realm of coercion (often predatory coercion). This worldview is not just cognitive ("how the world works"), but intensely normative ("how the world should work", "the right order of society").[49] In the market paradigm, the role of government is limited to "correcting market failures"; so state "interventions" in the market have to be carefully justified case by case. Many conservatives do accept the case for taxes to curb some "externalities", such as pollution taxes to discourage private agents from polluting the environment. Some would even favor a carbon-emissions tax, but not emission regulations (as in Obama's Clean Power Plan).[50]

---

[48] The Crash of 2008 and the ensuing Long Recession, and the experience of taking economics undergraduate courses which made no mention of these events, prompted three Manchester University students in 2011 to form the Post-Crash Economics Society to explore how to get a wider range of approaches into the curriculum. The movement has spread to 43 student campaigns in 15 countries. It is unified around the drive to shift economics from a public no-go area, occupied by a tiny minority of the population who speak the profession's language; and around the drive to introduce more critical thinking, more evaluation, into exams – which currently are comprised mostly of multiple-choice questions to be answered on the basis of rote learning repeated under invigilation. The original three students have written a book, reviewed by Aditya Chakrabortty, 2017, "The Econocracy review – how three students caused a global crisis in economics", The Guardian, 9 February, https://www.theguardian.com/books/2017/feb/09/the-econocracy-review-joe-earle-cahal-moran-zach-ward-perkins. See also A. Chakrabortty, 2013, "Mainstream economics is in denial: the world has changed", Guardian, 28 October, at: http://www.theguardian.com/commentisfree/2013/oct/28/mainstream-economics-denial-world-changed
[49] For a discipline so strongly normative, it is paradoxical that economics is an ethics-free zone, lacking relevant teaching, journals, newsletters, conferences or even professional codes (the latter until very recently, and then very partial ones). See G. DeMartino and D. McCloskey (eds.), 2016, The Oxford Handbook of Professional Economic Ethics, Oxford University Press; and E. Fullbrook, 2016, Narrative Fixation in Economics, World Economics Association Books.
[50] M. Feldstein, T. Halstead, N.G. Mankiw, 2017, "A conservative case for climate action", New York Times (International), February 10.

In short, the consensus belief in free trade stems from the wider cognitive and normative belief – inculcated in economics education -- that the key to economic development lies in improving the scope of, and the institutions of, *exchange*. Government should strengthen property rights, foster the rule of law, and do what is necessary to align domestic prices with international prices (which means, free trade); and then, having put the right incentive structure in place, get out of the way, allowing the production structure to emerge as the result of profit-seeking investment decisions by private firms, domestic and foreign equally.

The dominance of the market paradigm has hardly been challenged by the new phase of capitalism associated with the hyper-growth of the financial sector and turbo-charged by ICTs. Money funds and shareholders are pressing companies to give priority to success targets such as profits, dividends, and share prices; and to shift production to cheaper sites offshore, using investable funds at home to buy back shares (to boost share prices), as distinct from invest in R&D and training. Stock markets now tend to reward dividends and share buy-backs, not investment.[51,52]

We see the impacts of the market paradigm in the fracturing of the European Union and Eurozone, gripped by the German and other northwest European countries' conviction that their own economic success is due to their devotion to the market paradigm – flexible costs and prices, small budget deficits, low inflation, and private utilities. They urge the peripheral countries to follow in their footsteps, with fiscal austerity, labour market deregulation, and privatization. They miss the point that their own economic success comes from a very different production and employment system than exists in most of the periphery (Greece, Portugal and southern Italy, for example).[53]

---

[51] William Lazonick, 2014, "Profits without prosperity", *Harvard Business Review,* September; OECD, 2015, *Business and Financial Outlook*, Paris.

[52] For a discussion of how mainstream economists' deep normative commitment to the market paradigm blinded them to the build-up of the causes of the Crash of 2008 and subsequent Great Recession, see R. H. Wade, 2016, "Economists' ethics in the build-up to the Great Recession", chapter 15 in G. DeMartino and D. McCloskey (eds.), *The Oxford Handbook of Professional Economic Ethics*, p.268-292

[53] R. H. Wade, 1982, "Regional policy in a severe international environment: Politics and markets in South Italy," *Pacific Viewpoint*, 23(2), October: 99-126; Wade, 2012, "Greece, breaking the doom loop", *Le Monde Diplomatique* (English), blog, 6 July.

Both the contrast in economic performance within the European Union, and my critique of the globalization agenda, can be understood in terms of the much less favored 'production' paradigm. As Ricardo is the source of the market paradigm, Charles Babbage is the source of the production paradigm, in the form of his 1832 book, *On the Economy of Machinery and Manufacturers.*[54] His successors included Alfred Marshall, Allyn Young, Edith Penrose and George Richardson. It is a fair bet that most economics PhD students in Anglo universities have never heard of these people, let alone read them.[55]

The production paradigm says that the core mechanism of how economies transform (or not) lies in the combination of production capabilities, business organization, and economic governance; or what Michael Best calls the "capability triad".[56] Economies with high capability pivot on a sufficient density of "entrepreneurial" firms which pull basic and applied R&D or production and marketing ideas from MNCs with branches in the economy in question, into innovation in products, processes, organizations, and marketing. These entrepreneurial firms do not emerge by themselves as a natural result of a well-working market. Their own internal capacity development requires a larger ecosystem of finance, skills and S&T partnerships; which depends on trust in social interactions, and therefore physical and/or cultural proximity. The government (national or regional) is the organizer, the steward of the infrastructure needed to support this ecosystem. "Macro stabilization" has a supporting, not driving role. Well-known examples are Boston's Route 128, Silicon Valley, the Third Italy, and Germany's *mittelstand* and similarly organized small and medium enterprises (less than 500 employees) in Austria, Denmark, Finland,

---

[54] Babbage is credited with inventing the mechanical calculator and pushing for the high precision engineering necessary to build such machines, and being one of the first to infer general principles of effective production from close observation, which Ricardo-inspired economists did not do.

[55] On the World Bank's full-on embrace of the market paradigm starting in the 1980s, and move away from helping to boost borrowing countries' production capabilities, including material infrastructure, see R. H. Wade, 2015, "Agenda change in western development organizations: from hard production to soft, timeless, placeless policy", *Lahore J. of Economics*, 20: SE, September, pp. 1-12.

[56] This section draws on Michael Best, forthcoming (2017), *How Growth Happens: The Economics You Were Never Taught*, Princeton University Press.

Netherlands, Switzerland.[57] The most spectacular transformation of all is Singapore, which, like Ireland and Malaysia, aggressively invited in MNCs and also, unlike those cases, carefully developed national capacity to pull more complex production and technology from corporate headquarters to local operating divisions in Singapore and from there to national firms.

From this point of view, the standard argument that: "it is OK, in terms of the national interest, for firms to offshore their 'scale-up' production provided 'start-ups' with their knowledge stay at home" is mistaken, because (a) innovation depends on building on experience of production, "learning while doing", and (b) scale-ups are where the jobs are, not the start-ups.[58]

Germany's economic performance, and in particular its large trade surpluses, comes out of the production system codified in the production paradigm – combined with the longstanding agreement between government, business and labor to hold down wages and domestic demand.

Britain, on the other hand, is a sad case of the costs of following the market paradigm. British manufacturing (with exceptions) was slow (compared to northwest Europe) to introduce interchangeable parts, a culture of "continuous improvement", profit-sharing reward incentives, team-based

---

[57] For the role of US government agencies in forming innovation-focused networks of competing and cooperating firms, see R.H. Wade, forthcoming (2017), "The American paradox: ideology of free markets and practice of directional thrust", *Cambridge J. Economics.*

[58] See Andrew Grove, 2010, "Andy Grove: how American can create jobs", BloombergBusinessweek, July 1. https://www.bloomberg.com/news/articles/2010-07-01/andy-grove-how-america-can-create-jobs. Grove was co-founder and CEO of Intel. He says, "As happened with batteries, abandoning today's 'commodity' manufacturing can lock you out of tomorrow's emerging industry... Our fundamental economic belief, which we have elevated from a conviction based on observation to an unquestioned truism, is that the free market is the best of all economic systems – the freer the better... [Evidence that this is not true] stares at us from the performance of several Asian countries in the past few decades. These countries seem to understand that job creation must be the No. 1 objective of state economic policy. The government plays a strategic role in setting the priorities and arraying the forces and organization necessary to achieve this goal. In a thorough study of the industrial development of East Asia, Robert Wade of the London School of Economics found that these economies turned in precedent-shattering economic performance over the '70s and '80s in large part because of the effective involvement of the government in targeting growth of manufacturing industries."

multi-skilled work organization, minimal separation between managers and workers, and heavy investment in vocational education. Britain remained stuck with piece-rate incentive systems, elaborate job classifications, sharp hierarchical separation between managers and workers, even as its manufacturing firms lost more and more market share.[59] By way of compensation, the government undertook ad hoc industrial policy with subsidies, tax concessions and material infrastructure driven not by a national or regional strategy but by electoral calculation and intense lobbying in the shadows.

British-owned road car manufacturers were wiped out by foreign firms assembling in Britain – which imported two thirds of their parts and components in place of domestic production. The British government did little to encourage them to deepen their production in Britain, saying, in the spirit of the market paradigm, "If they can get cheaper parts elsewhere, then they should do it". The Japanese, Korean and Taiwanese governments would have had a more developmental mindset.

Britain's low level of output per hour productivity relative to its peers (a bit over three quarters of the US, German and French levels, about the same as Italy, and stagnant since 2007) has been the subject of much research and anguished commentary. The conclusions typically point to: (1) poor infrastructure (rated by the OECD as second worst in the G7); (2) low investment in R&D (at 1.7 percent of GDP in private and public R&D, well below the OECD average, let alone the leaders on over 3 percent of GDP); and (3) a relatively unskilled population, which cannot drive productivity forward.[60]

Strangely overlooked as causes of Britain's low productivity are: (4) British companies have for two centuries invested relatively heavily overseas compared to at home (the opposite in Germany, Japan, South Korea). (5) The economy has become dominated by finance, with its demands that

---

[59] See the dramatic contrasts between organization in a British-owned factory in Britain and a Japanese-owned one making similar products, in Ronald Dore, 1973, *British Factory-Japanese Factory: The Origins of National Diversity in Industrial Relations,* George Allen & Unwin, London.

[60] Martin Wolf, 2017, "The productivity challenge to the British economy", *Financial Times,* January 27.

British companies give priority to success targets such as profits, dividends, and share prices; and use investable funds at home to buy back shares so as to boost share prices. Finance has also had a backwash effect on the "real" economy, attracting highly skilled people to work in finance by offering remuneration many times that available elsewhere. (6) Britain's captains of industry and its financial magnates are zealous champions of the market paradigm. So they rubbished the government's green paper on industrial strategy published in early 2017, saying that the solution to lagging productivity is not "industrial strategy" but cuts in regulations – even though OECD measures show that Britain's labor and product market regulation is low and about the same as in the US.[61]

Emphasising the costs of the last three points would challenge the core of the market paradigm in a way that emphasizing the first three does not. Meanwhile, all the attention is on the costs of Brexit, which will be small compared to the loss from low productivity.

VIII. Conclusion

It may be that,

> "President Trump, animated by private motives as yet undisclosed, wants to bring about a Russian-American axis that would enfeeble Nato, destroy the European Union and dominate a continent reduced to politically dysfunctional national fragments... Operating under the 'America First' rubric, Donald Trump has instantly turned the US into a rogue state. Internationally agreed rules on trade, territories, refugees, climate and disarmament are, it seems, to be treated as no longer binding on America."[62]

---

[61] Nicholas Oulton, 2017, "Productivity puzzle meets delusions of adequacy", letter, *Financial Times*, February 8.
[62] Joseph O'Neill, 2017, "The case for putting Brexit on hold", *Guardian*, February 10, p. 29.

The problem is that branding Trump "populist" goes with knee-jerk condemnation of everything he favors. Here is Philip Stephens of the *Financial Times*: "No one should pretend, though, that the populists have the answers. Protectionism impoverishes everyone."[63] As in all the *Financial Times'* commentary, he leaves "protectionism" completely unbounded, his blanket condemnation inviting the reader to suppose it means something close to autarky – an obviously stupid trade regime.

I have used Trump's skepticism about free trade as an excuse for questioning the crown jewel status of the theory of comparative advantage and the said-to-be-rigorously derived-and-empirically-well-supported policy of free trade as best for each country and for the world. The reigning belief that all countries should practice free or almost free trade, and that the purpose of "free trade agreements" and international organizations like the WTO is to move public policy towards freer trade – and deeper economic integration more generally – can be challenged on several grounds set out in sections IV–VI, not repeated here.

The standard response to these challenges is:

> "Policy must target the problems directly, and not use protection. The trade-off between free trade and employment must be handled by more social protection and more skill training, while keeping (or moving to) free trade and deep integration. This is best for all."

But what if these policy responses are barely forthcoming? Moneyed politics works strongly against them, as we see in the US's threadbare social protection system.

The British government gives another example. Soon after Theresa May became the Prime Minister of the Conservative government in mid 2016 she declared to the Conservative Party conference,

---

[63] Philip Stephens, 2017, "Why the liberal order is worth saving", *Financial Times*, 10 February, p. 11.

"Our economy should work for everyone, but if your pay has stagnated for several years in a row and fixed items of spending keep going up, it doesn't feel like it's working for you."

She was right. But her government inherited – and crucially, maintained – tax and benefit plans which have the opposite effect; which give substantial tax cuts to the relatively well-off, and give substantial benefits cuts to those of working age. As Martin Wolf says,

"The government has decided to give greater priority to... the better off than to the relatively worse off."[64]

In short, making a level playing field does not ensure that the players turn up to play. Creating effective institutions of exchange in conditions of free trade does not tilt the production-business organization-economic governance capability triad towards innovation and expansion of higher value-added activities. The government can play a crucial role in securing the latter, including by managing trade as part of a larger investment strategy. But first we have to dispense with the saturated scorn with which managed trade is dismissed as "protectionism".

All inter-state agreements imply some sacrifice of national autonomy. Agreements on health, environment, human rights, refugees, development, tax evasion, minimum top marginal tax thresholds and the like, have a high potential for mutual gains between the signatory states; they should be encouraged in the spirit of "cooperative internationalism". Liberalization agreements on trade, investment, capital mobility and other domains of economics and finance typically have far-reaching, more ambivalent effects on the structures of production, employment and income distribution in which national populations live. They express the spirit of "integrative globalization", which encourages governments to improve the conditions for markets in their country, remove limits on cross-border economic flows, and let the production and employment structures develop as they will on the

---

[64] Martin Wolf, 2017, "May's policies make a mockery of her rhetoric", *Financial Times*, February 10, p. 11.

basis of private profit-seeking competition between domestic and foreign firms equally.[65]

Free trade is the sensible rule of thumb most of the time in most sectors. It is sensible because the efficiency gains are often real, even if the theory of comparative advantage over- generalizes them; and it is a simpler rule for any state and for inter-state agreements than rules for managed trade. But the argument made here about production and employment, in the context of economic growth rather than static resource efficiency, suggests that inter-state agreements, including the rules of the WTO, should be revised to permit more government "leadership" and "followership" of the market – sometimes by leading the production structure into activities the private sector would not undertake on its own, sometimes by making bets on initiatives already underway in the private sector to assist those initiatives to scale up.[66] This contrasts with the current situation, in which the WTO restricts the use of instruments relevant to developing countries' efforts to upgrade the national production structure – including tariffs, non-tariff barriers, and direct industry subsidies – while allowing instruments relevant to advanced countries' efforts to grow new activities on the world frontier, such as R&D subsidies. The WTO is, put crudely, an industrial upgrading device for advanced countries, an industrial downgrading device for developing countries.[67] President Trump surely does not intend his skepticism of free trade to benefit developing countries, but it gives the potential for others to modify international rules towards more "policy space".

---

[65] I take "cooperative internationalism" and "integrative globalization" from Dunkley, 2016, *One World Mania*.

[66] R.H. Wade, 1990, "Industrial policy in East Asia: does it lead or follow the market?", chapter 9 in G. Gereffi and D. Wyman (eds.), *Manufacturing Miracles: Paths of Industrialization in Latin America and East Asia*, Princeton University Press.

[67] R.H. Wade, 2003, "What development strategies are viable for developing countries? The World Trade Organization and the shrinking of 'development space'", *Review of International Political Economy*, 10(4), November, 621-44.

President Trump and free trade

Jacques Sapir [École des Hautes Études en Sciences Sociales, Paris and Moscow School of Economics]

President Donald Trump did not wait until he took office on January 20th, 2017 to start implementing part of his economic program, mainly through protectionist pressures and the calling into question of free trade agreements. Whether it is the Trans-Pacific Partnership agreement, the NAFTA (signed several decades ago with Mexico and Canada), or even a measure calling into question the authority of the WTO, it is a general offensive against the very principle of free trade that we are witnessing. The fact it comes from an administration supposed to be one of the most "pro-business" of recent years is in itself raising a lot of questions. Could the so-called "Trumponomics" surprise us? It is important to understand how this kind of protectionist turn could merge with other projects and above all those concerning infrastructure that were prominent in the then candidate Trump's campaign.[1] What lays in store for the coming months, and how could it shape the future of global trade? These major questions are now on the agenda of all important developed nations.

A paradigm shift?

It is quite significant that free trade is being challenged, here and now, by the United States. Usually challenges come from nations of the South and from leftist or populist leaders. For nearly forty years, the United States had been the driving force in most free trade treaties. This trend was obvious since the XIXth century, and quite prominent in the early Bretton-Woods years. Of course these proposals were well received within the framework of the European Union which developed a notorious love affair with free trade. This

---

[1] Baker D., "The Trump Stimulus and the Money Obama Left on the Table" in http://cepr.net/publications/briefings/testimony/the-trump-stimulus-and-the-money-obama-left-on-the-table

organization shared with the United States the belief that free trade was the way of the future. We have witnessed how the EU, through the European Parliament, gave its blessing to the CETA. This vision, moreover, was rooted in a very ideological conception of the virtues of free trade, supposed to bring peace, or at least the end of conflicts. But the last twenty years have not been encouraging for free-trade advocates. Conflicts were not eliminated and the progress of free trade stopped with the crisis of 2008–2010. The Doha Round has been a resounding failure. This could explain why the turning point taken by the United States under the direction of President Donald Trump, however spectacular it may be, is less astonishing than one might have thought.

Globalization is not, and never was, "happy" whatever various ideologues said. The idea that "sweet commerce", was to be substituted for warlike conflicts, was much propagated. But, in truth, it was only a myth. Still, the warship preceded the merchant ship. The dominant powers have constantly used their strength to open up by force markets and modify the terms of trade as they see fit. The globalization that we have witnessed for nearly 40 years has been in combination with financial globalization, which has taken place with the unraveling of the system inherited from the Bretton Woods agreements in 1973. We are seeing today the result: a generalized march to regression, both economic and social, which strikes first the so-called "rich" countries but also those designated as "emerging" countries. It has led to the overexploitation of natural resources, plunging more than one and a half billion human beings into ecological crises that are getting worse every day. It has caused the destruction of social ties in a large number of countries, and there are also countless masses in the specter of the war of all against all, to the shock of an exaggerated individualism that suggests other regressions.[2]

---

[2] J. Généreux, *La Grande Régression*, Paris, Seuil, 2010.

The great reversal

At the root of this reversal we see the decline in incomes of the lower middle classes and the working class. And this drop is largely due to globalization.[3] The gap between the highest 1% and the lowest 90% has greatly increased since the 1980s as shown in Thomas Piketty's work.[4] This discontinuation was confirmed by another study dating from 2015.[5] This discrepancy is also reflected in the drop-off between the rate of increase in labor productivity and the rate of hourly wages. While the two curves appear almost parallel between 1946 and 1973, which implies that productivity gains have also benefited wage earners and capitalists alike, it is no longer the case after 1973. Since then, wages have increased significantly more slowly than labor productivity, implying that productivity gains have now mainly benefited business and shareholder profits. This situation worsened in the 1990s, obviously as a result of globalization and open borders.[6] This trend, already perceptible before the 2007–2010 crisis,[7] was not reversed by the implementation on anti-crisis policies, to the contrary. This had been one of the major failing of the Obama administration, one that fostered anger among the middle-class and would explain Donald Trump success in the Presidential race. The attack against NAFTA is here both symbolical and quite accurate. NAFTA was (and still is) a quite typical agreement that was thought to help regional integration. It turned out to be a mass-destruction weapon, as far workers incomes are concerned, both in the United States and in Mexico. A recent paper by the director of the CEPR, Mark Weisbrot, clearly establishes NAFTA's cost for Mexico.[8]

---

[3] Bivens J., "Globalization, American Wages, and Inequality" *Economic Policy Institute* Working Paper, Washington DC, 6 Septembre, 2007.
[4] Piketty T. and E. Saez, "Income Inequality in the United States", *Quarterly Journal of Economics*, February 2003 .
[5] Mishel L., Gould E and Bivens J., "Wage stagnations in 9 charts", *Economic Policy Institute*, Washington DC, 6 janvier 2015.
[6] See G. Irvin, "Growing Inequality in the Neo-liberal Heartland," *Post-Autistic Economics Review*, 43 (September 15, 2007), pp. 2–23, http://www.paecon.net/PAEReview/issue43/Irwin43.htm
[7] Sapir J., "Global finance in crisis", *real-world economics review*, issue no. 46, 20 May 2008, pp. 82-101, http://www.paecon.net/PAEReview/issue46/Sapir46.pdf
[8] Weisbrot M., "NAFTA Has Harmed Mexico a Lot More than Any Wall Could Do" in http://cepr.net/publications/op-eds-columns/nafta-has-harmed-mexico-a-lot-more-than-any-wall-could-do

In the United States, this evolution was psychologically fundamental, because it meant the "end" of the American dream for a vast majority of the population. This was marked by the very clear difference between the rates of change in average income, which continued to rise, and the median income[9]. But the United States was not the only country where this situation manifested itself. It should be noted that it is also present in Great Britain, which is not politically without consequences if we look to the BREXIT in this context.[10]

Whatever figures we are given about the sharp drop in the unemployment rate under President Obama, the awful truth is that the labor market is still very weak by many measures. The employment rate for workers aging 25–54 is still 2.0% points below the pre-recession level and 4.0% below the 2000 level.[11] This corresponds to a mass of around 2.5 to 5.0 million missing jobs. Such figures explain clearly the angriness in the lower middle-class, and angriness that was instrumental in Donald Trump's victory. It is therefore clear that free trade has not had the beneficial consequences predicted by mainstream economic theory on the economies and on the workers who live in these economies.

Is free trade the future of humanity?

It is true that the various subsidies and barriers to competition, which are the essence of protectionist policies, have a very bad press today. On both the right and the liberal left, they are taboo. The former French Minister of Economy and now candidate to the French presidential election, M. Emmanuel Macron, speaks loudly of "freeing" the French economy, which is equivalent to saying that we need more competition. The law attached to his name and that he pushed forward when he was minister was about de-regulating some activities. This was done, but results have so far been less than successful. It should also be pointed out that Mr. Macron distinguished

---

[9] US Congress, *State Median Wages and Unemployment Rates*, prepared by the Joint Economic Committee, table released by the US-JEC (June 2008).
[10] Brewer M., A. Goodman, J. Shaw, and L. Sibieta, Poverty and Inequality in Britain: 2006, Institute for Fiscal Studies (London, 2005).
[11] http://cepr.net/publications/briefings/testimony/the-trump-stimulus-and-the-money-obama-left-on-the-table

himself by his support for the very contested treaty between the European Union and Canada, the so-called CETA treaty, a treaty that has been adopted very recently by the European parliament[12] after what could only be described as a nasty joke of a debate. The same viewpoints are expressed by the European Commission, which has reacted vigorously to the statements of Donald Trump. There is obviously a point of consensus here. But this point is built on self-proclaimed evidence.

Prescriptive discourses that seek to extend free trade are based on extremely questionable normative bases[13]. The assumption that competition is ever and everywhere beneficial for all is neither theoretically nor in practice grounded. The first demonstration against this belief in competition came from agricultural economics, through the Hog-cycle theory. But as shown by a careful reading of the founding article written by Mordecai Ezekiel in 1938,[14] we are faced with a problem that goes far beyond the phenomena that allowed its initial identification, the fluctuation of agricultural prices. The analysis of the conditions giving rise to the cobweb mechanism shows a major flaw in the theory of competitive equilibrium. This analysis contains a radical criticism of the normative role accorded to so-called "pure and perfect" competition. It leads to restoring legitimacy to measures restricting the exercise of competition, whether subsidies or limits on entry into certain markets through the presence of quotas or customs duties. It is not without reason that the compilers of an extremely important work on the theory of economic cycles introduced Ezekiel's article into the collection of texts they edited.[15]

Indeed, the term "cobweb" was proposed by Nicholas Kaldor. It should be emphasized that Kaldor was thinking that it was necessary and even mandatory to extract the dynamics of the cobweb from its unique agricultural environment, since we are faced with a general problem affecting the theory of competitive equilibrium as soon as one is in presence of a situation where

---

[12] On February 15th, 2017.
[13] Sapir J., "Retour vers le futur : le protectionnisme est-il notre avenir ?" in *L'Economie Politique*, n°31, 3rd Quarter, 2006.
[14] Ezekiel M, "The Cobweb Theorem", in *Quarterly Journal of Economics* , vol. LII, n°1, 1937-1938, pp. 255-280.
[15] *Readings in Business Cycle Theory - selected by a committee of THE AMERICAN ECONOMIC ASSOCIATION*, Londres, George Allen and Unwin, 1950, pp. 422-442.

"... the adjustments are completely discontinuous".[16] The late Wassili Leontief made quite a similar reflection at the same time. Leontief demonstrated the impossibility of determining a spontaneous mechanism of price and production equilibrium by "pure" competition as soon as supply and demand curves did not correspond precisely to the specifications of the Leon Walras model[17]. Equilibrium then appears as a special case and not as a general case, which was confirmed by more recent work by Sonnensheim and Mantel.[18]

Moreover, if the objective is to avoid or to limit fluctuations, because these can have short- and long-term negative effects on both producers and applicants (in particular for the investment process),[19] the conclusion that can be drawn is that measures suspending competition such as subsidies, quotas or customs duties become useful and legitimate. Gilbert Abraham-Frois and Edmond Berrebi have shown that the introduction of realistic clauses into reasoning (for example, by accepting that the economic agent has a choice between not two but three options) leads to the generalization of situations of instability as long as competition is maintained.[20] Yet while theoretical work since the early 1970s confirms and extends Ezekiel's conclusions about a radical critique of the normative scope of the competitive equilibrium model, one tends to forget the general lesson of his work.

---

[16] N. Kaldor, "A Classificatory Note on the Determinateness of Equilibrium" in *Review of Economic Studies*, Vol. 1, février 1934.
[17] W. Leontief, "Verzögerte Angebotsanpassung und Partielles Gleichgewicht" in *Zeitschrift für Nationalökonomie*, Vienne, Vol. IV, n°5, 1934.
[18] Sonnenscheim H., "Do Walras Identity and Continuity Characterize the class of Excess Demand Functions?" in *Journal of Economic Theory*, vol. 6, 1973, N°2, pp. 345-354. Mantel R., "On the characterization of Aggregate Excess Demand" in *Journal of Economic Theory*, vol. 7, 1974, N°2, pp. 348-353
[19] Malinvaud, E, "Profitability and investment facing uncertain demand", *Document de travail de l'INSEE*, n° 8303, Paris, 1983 ; Idem, "Capital productif, incertitudes et profitabilités", *Document de recherche de l'IME*, Université de Dijon, n°93, 1986.
[20] Abraham-Frois G. and E. Berrebi, *Instabilité, Cycles, Chaos*, Paris, Economica, 1999, pp. 3-4. See also, Guerrien B., *La Théorie Néo-Classique. Bilan et perspective du modèle d'équilibre général*, Economica, Paris, 1989.

Donald Trump's twitter diplomacy

Donald Trump's recent statements, as well as pressures he exerted on large industrial groups with twitter messages, though they may seem somewhat exotic, have revived the question of modern forms of protectionism. In fact, this debate has already taken place. In the 1930s, as a result of the great economic crisis, a number of economists shifted from traditional "free trade" positions to a more protectionist one. John Maynard Keynes was one of those, and certainly the one who exerted the most considerable influence. The text of J.M. Keynes on the necessity of national self-sufficiency was published in June 1933 in the *Yale Review*.[21] It's quite an important paper, as Keynes was in the early 1920s a long-standing supporter of free trade.

Today, as in 1933, the reasons for doubting the value of Free Trade are accumulating. World Bank experts brutally revised downwards their estimates of "gains" from international trade liberalization,[22] even though they were computed without any reference to possible costs. A UNCTAD study showed a few years ago that the WTO "Doha Round" could cost developing countries up to $60 billion when it would bring them only $16 billion.[23] Far from fostering development, the WTO could well have contributed to global poverty. Even foreign direct investment, long regarded as the miracle solution to development, is now under attack.[24] In many countries competition to attract direct foreign investment as clearly negative effects in the social and environmental fields.[25] Very clearly, this is not taken

---

[21] John Maynard Keynes, "National Self-Sufficiency," *The Yale Review*, Vol. 22, no. 4 (June 1933), pp. 755-769.

[22] For a precise analysis: Ackerman F., *The Shrinking Gains from Trade: A Critical Assessment of Doha Round Projections*, Global Development and Environment Institute, Tufts University, WP n° 05-01. See also "Doha Round and Developing Countries: Will the Doha deal do more harm than good" *RIS Policy Brief*, n°22, April 2006, New Delhi.

[23] S. Fernandez de Cordoba and D. Vanzetti, "Now What? Searching for a solution to the WTO Industrial Tariffs Negociations", *Coping with Trade Reform*, CNUCED, Genève, 2005. See table 11.

[24] T.H. Moran, *ForeignDirect Investment and Development, The New Policy Agenda for Developing Countries and Economics in Transition*, Institute for International Economics, Washington D.C., 1998.

[25] Oman, C., *Policy Competition for Foreign Direct Investment*, OCDE, Centre du Développement, Paris, 2000. See also, L. Zarsky, "Stuck in the Mud? Nation-States, Globalization and the Environment" in K.P. Gallagher et J. Wierksman (edits.)

into account in Donald Trump's "America First" logic and was not even present in his reasoning. But its overall consequences for the protection of the environment could prove to be very positive indeed, which, it must be emphasized, would be an amusing paradox.

How has free trade been imposed on people's minds?

The opening of global trade since the 1970s and 1980s had notable effects all across the world.[26] Publications, including those of Dollar in 1992,[27] Ben-David in 1993,[28] Sachs and Warner in 1995,[29] and Edwards in 1998,[30] have sought to link international trade and growth. These years were marked by extremely important changes. There were two major phenomena: the end of Eastern Europe, in the sense of the Council of Mutual Economic Aid (CMEA), and the end of the USSR. In both cases, it was found that the trade flows as recorded have grown strongly. But the mere passage from what was an "internal trade" to an "international trade" resulted in a sharp rise in the latter. Part of the growth in world trade can thus be attributed to a "revelation" effect of trade occurring within other statistical frameworks and not to an actual "creation" of trade. Specialists, the same who intone the credo of globalization, only very rarely mention this problem.

A second cause is subtler but no less important. The increase in international trade flows has been linked to the evolution of these economies during the early years of their transition. In the case of the USSR, for example, a large part of the production of aluminum and steel did not find

---

International Trade and Sustainable development, Earthscan, Londres, 2002, pp. 19-44.

[26] Sapir J., "Le vrai sens du terme. Le libre-échange ou la mise en concurrence entre les Nations" *in* D. Colle (dir), *D'un protectionnisme l'autre. La fin de la mondialisation ?*, Paris, PUF, "Major", 2009.

[27] Dollar D., "Outward-Oriented Developeng Economies Really Do Grow More Rapidly: Evidence From 95 LDC, 1976-1985", *Economic Development and Cultural Change*, 1992, p. 523-554.

[28] Ben-David D., "Equalizing Exchange: Trade Liberalization and Income Convergence", *Quarterly Journal of Economics*, vol. 108, n° 3, 1993.

[29] Sachs J., A. Warner, "Economic Reform and The Process of Global Integration", *Brookings Paper on Economic Activity*, n° 1, 1995, p. 1-118.

[30] S. Edwards, "Opennes, Productivity and Growth: What We Do Really Know?", *Economic Journal*, vol. 108, mars 1998, p. 383-398.

markets within the economy, due to the decline in manufacturing activity. The export of this surplus was immediate, whether it was legal or illegal. Similarly, there has been a phenomenon of substitution of imported products for local production, which has been favored by the sharp exchange rate developments. In this respect, the extremely high figures of international trade in 1994–1997 seem to have been the product of a statistical illusion. It is these figures, recorded over four years that have largely conditioned our vision of growth as linked to international trade. This shows the need to look again to the issue. Were not mainstream economist victims of the old mercantilist fallacy?

Holding the free trade orthodoxy at bay

Various attempts have been made to find a positive correlation between trade and growth. In general, the tests performed give results that are at least very ambiguous. It can be deduced that for some countries openness has had positive results, but not for others. Economic success depends more on the quality of the macroeconomic measures than on the openness.[31] Indeed, countries that have associated protectionist policies with good macroeconomic policies are experiencing growth rates that are much higher than those of the more open countries, which invalidates the primacy of openness.[32] This brings us back to the problem of development, which turns out to be far more complex than what the proponents of generalized free trade are saying. The work of Alice Amsden,[33] Robert Wade[34] and also those regrouped by Helleiner[35] show that in the case of

---

[31] See Ben-David D., "Equalizing Exchange: Trade Liberalization and Income Convergenge", *op. cit.*

[32] See H.-J. Chang, "The Economic Theory of the Developmental State" *in* M. Woo-Cumings (dir.), *The Developmental State*, Ithaca, Cornell University Press, 1999 ; *Kicking away the Ladder: Policies and Institutions for Development in Historical Perspective*, Londres, Anthem Press, 2002.

[33] Voir H.-J. Chang, "The Economic Theory of the Developmental State" *in* M. Woo-Cumings (dir.), *The Developmental State*, Ithaca, Cornell University Press, 1999 ; *Kicking away the Ladder: Policies and Institutions for Development in Historical Perspective*, Londres, Anthem Press, 2002.

[34] R. Wade, *Governing the Market*, Princeton (N. J.), Princeton University Press, 1990.

[35] G. K. Helleiner (dir.), *Trade Policy and Industrialization in Turbulent Times*, Londres, Routledge, 1994.

developing countries the choice of protectionism, combined with genuine national policies of development and industrialization[36] have paid off. Growth rates were far above those of countries that did not made the same choice. Dani Rodrik emphasized the fact that the fastest growing Asian countries had systematically violated the rules of globalization, established and codified by the World Bank and the IMF.[37]

This brings us back to the question of national policies and the problems of the developing state that have re-emerged in the debate over the last few years.[38] This issue is really at the heart of the industrial revival of Asia. In fact, it is these national policies that are the real critical variables for growth and development, not the existence or otherwise of measures to liberalize international trade. But to admit this is to reconsider the role of the State in economic policies and the role of nationalism as an ideology associated with development. Here one touches on powerful taboos of mainstream thought in economics as well as in politics. It looks like free trade ideologues have been moved by their horror of the State and played games with theory, completely disregarding historical experience. And, to their horror, now the developmental State theory could well be politically vindicated by changes President Trump is introducing. This is not to say that Donald Trump is a supporter of the developmental State. He probably even ignores the term and the history of the phenomenon. But by challenging the free trade orthodoxy, he opens a new window of opportunity for policies aiming at creating strong developmental states.

---

[36] Voir C.-C. Lai, "Development Strategies and Growth with Equality. Re-evaluation of Taiwan's Experience", *Rivista Internazionale de Scienze Economiche e Commerciali*, vol. 36, n° 2, 1989, p. 177-191.
[37] D. Rodrik, "What Produces Economic Success?" *in* R. Ffrench-Davis (dir.), *Economic Growth with Equity: Challenges for Latin America*, Londres, Palgrave Macmillan, 2007. See also by the same author, "After Neoliberalism, What? ", *Project Syndicate*, 2002 http://www.project-syndicate.org/commentary/rodrik7
[38] Voir T. Mkandawire, "Thinking About Developmental States in Africa", *Cambridge Journal of Economics*, vol. 25, n° 2, 2001, p. 289-313; B. Fine, "The Developmental State is Dead. Long Live Social Capital?", *Development and Change*, vol. 30, n° 1, 1999, p. 1-19.

A return to reason

It is mainstream wisdom that over the past three decades, international trade has largely driven economic development. This thesis has been popularized by some economists, but on closer inspection appears false. In 2008 and 2009, international trade declined in proportion to the decline in production in the major industrialized countries. Trade, therefore, does not create value by itself, an old error of mercantilists that reappears in the form of the belief in growth driven only by trade. On the contrary, growth in the main countries draws trade. It is therefore necessary to ask whether we have not been faced with an error, at least of an illusion, due to statistics. Indeed, the phenomenon of growth, whether that of gross domestic product (GDP) or that of international trade, could very well be overestimated for various reasons. The possibility of a measurement error may call into question the agreed idea of a direct and mechanical link between the development of international trade and global growth. This requires rethinking the causal links between growth and trade. From that point on, it is the entire ideology that has surrounded the globalization that will be called into question.

The rupture of this cognitive veil then makes it possible to ask other questions. To what extent is globalization responsible for the destruction of the natural environment, which has been accelerating since the late 1980s? This destruction is not simply linked to the multiplication of long-distance transport, to the competition between the West European worker and the Asian worker over the very different social systems that govern their work. However, it is now known that this has had profoundly destabilizing effects on the internal distribution of income. Companies have been relieved of the constraint that, in a relatively closed economy, their wages (which are therefore costs to them) are also decisive for their markets. This emancipation stems from the submission of local economic logics to global ones which can result in significant ecological damage.

The Trans-Pacific Partnership (TPP) agreement, a treaty cancelled by President Trump, is an obvious example of the common misrepresentation of trade agreements in the mainstream media. A document coming from the

Peterson Institute was putting gains for all participants at a very high level.[39] The International Trade Commission criticized figures coming from the Peterson Institute.[40] While the Peterson Institute analysis projected an increase in national income of 0.5% by 2030, which is not really spectacular, the ITC report projected an increase that actually was less than half this size. The ITC report was giving a gain of 0.23% by 2032. To understand what it means we have to understand an increment to the annual growth rate of 0.015%. The ITC projection implies then that *with the TPP* in operation the economy would have a projected gain amounting to roughly one and a half month's GDP. It means then that growth on January 1, 2032 would be at the same level it would be in February 15th 2032 *without* the TPP! But the ITC also was using a CGE model for its computation in spite of considerable criticism against this kind of model.[41] Actually, in other cases, ITC projections have been found seriously overstating growth and seriously off the mark. This has been found in the ITC evaluation of the US-Korea treaty (or KORUS). The ITC evaluation failed also to pick-up the large increase in the trade deficit and failed also to identify what could be the gaining and the losing sectors. The ITC model explicitly ruled out the various ways in which a trade agreement could lead to negative economic outcomes. This is why it is wrong to view the projections from the ITC as a comprehensive or operational assessment of the impact of the TPP. The excluded factors noted above would be difficult to model and the ITC did not try to introduce them into its model.[42] The actual history of divergence between ITC

---

[39] Petri, Peter and Michael Plummer. 2016. "The Economic Effects of the Trans-Pacific Partnership: New Estimates." Washington, D.C.: Peterson Institute for International Economics. Working Paper Series WP16-2.
https://ideas.repec.org/p/iie/wpaper/wp16-2.html
[40] ITC. 2016. "Trans-Pacific Partnership Agreement: Likely Impact on the U.S. Economy and on Specific Industry Sectors." Publication Number 4607. Washington, D.C.: United States International Trade Commission,
https://www.usitc.gov/publications/332/pub4607.pdf
[41] See Ackerman, K. Gallagher, "Computable Abstraction: General Equilibrium Models of Trade and Environment" *in* F. Ackerman, A. Nadal (dir.), *The Flawed Foundations of General Equilibrium: Critical Essays on Economic Theory*, New York/Londres, Routledge, 2004, p. 168-180. For a more general assessment of general equilibrium models, see J. Sapir, *Les Trous noirs de la science économique*, Paris, Albin Michel, 2000, chap. I.
[42] This was however done by researchers from Tufts University : Capaldo, Jeronim and Alex Izurieta. 2016. "Trading Down: Unemployment, Inequality and Other Risks of the Trans-Pacific Partnership Agreement." Medford, MA: Tufts Global

projections of the impact of trade agreements and actual outcomes suggests then that the impact of factors not included in the model is substantially larger than the factors that ITC has incorporated into its analysis.[43] A more sober and realistic evaluation would show that the TPP short and long-term influence would be unfavorable to the US economy and generally speaking to all countries involved in the TPP.

Hence, Donald Trump cancellation of the agreement probably salved workers in related countries, even if it was not the main driver for his action.

Economy and politics

In fact, globalization is synonymous with growth only when it can be based on a national development project, often articulated to a nationalist ideology. Merchant globalization only yields results if one does not play its game but while others do. The case of China is exemplary here, because it is through the combination of a National policy and the openness of development over the last 25 years. But even in this case, the rise of social inequalities and ecological destruction makes the continuation of this model problematic. This is particularly true in the Far East, with other examples like Taiwan and Korea, but can also be seen in Russia since 1999. Actually, the very process of emergence of a multi-polar world is rooted in the birth or re-birth of powerful developmental states that are clashing with equally powerful multinational corporations. Trump's economic policy is an attempt, even if sometimes clumsy and plagued by inconsistencies, to adapt to this new situation.

Thus, far from leading to the overcoming of the nation, globalization is proving to be the new framework for the expression of national policies that generate either domination and destruction of national cadres for the benefit of stronger nations or phenomenal reactions and national development.[44]

Development and Environment Institute. *Working Paper* No. 16-01. http://www.ase.tufts.edu/gdae/Pubs/wp/16-01Capaldo-IzurietaTPP.pdf
[43] Baker D., *The International Trade Commission's Assessment of the Trans-Pacific Partnership : Main Findings and Implications*, CEPR, November 2016.
[44] See, Sapir J., "Retour vers le futur : le protectionnisme est-il notre avenir?", *L'Économie politique*, n° 31, 3ᵉ trimestre, 2006.

Basically, the idea that we would have from the end of the "short 20th century"[45] regained a tendency to integration by trade thus proves to be a myth. This was clearly shown by Paul Bairoch and Richard Kozul-Wright in the systematic study of these flows, which was carried out in 1996 for the United Nations Conference on Trade and Development (UNCTAD).[46] There has never been a "golden age" of globalization, which would have ended with World War I and which would have been followed by a long period of decline, before experiencing a revival since the 1970s. It is indeed the whole idea of a march towards the "global village" which is deeply questioned. This debate has continued in the recent period and its results have been the same. Let us keep, however, for the moment, the image that is provided to us by Rodrik and Rodriguez.[47] The push towards greater openness was not favorable to as many people as possible.[48] It is then of the utmost importance to debunk the fallacy of free trade working for the poor. It never did and never will.

Requiem for free trade?

Economically, free trade is not the best solution and carries risks of crises and increases in inequalities that are considerable. It puts different territories in competition, not on the basis of the human activities deployed in them, but on that of social and fiscal choices themselves very debatable.[49] Trade liberalization has not benefited the poorest countries, as shown by the most recent studies. A comparison of benefits and costs, particularly with regard to the collapse of public investment capacity in health and education

---

[45] Sapir J., *Le Nouveau xxIe Siècle*, Seuil, 2008.

[46] Bairoch P., R. Kozul-Wright, "Globalization Myths: Some Historical Reflections on Integration, Industrialization and Growth in the World Economy", *Discussion Paper*, n° 113, Genève, UNCTAD-OSG, mars 1996.

[47] F. Rodriguez, D. Rodrik, "Trade Policy and Economic Growth: A Skeptics Guide to the Cross-National Evidence", *in* B. Bernanke, K. Rogoff (dir.), *NBER Macroeconomics. Annual 2000*, Cambridge (MA), MIT Press, 2001.

[48] Voir J. Sapir, "Libre-échange, croissance et développement : quelques mythes de l'économie vulgaire" in *Revue du Mauss*, n°30, 2e semestre, La Découverte, 2007, p. 151-171.

[49] Sapir J., voir Ch. 8 et Ch. 9 de D. Colle (edit.), *D'un protectionnisme l'autre – La fin de la mondialisation ?*, Coll. Major, Presses Universitaires de France, Paris, Septembre 2009.

following the collapse of fiscal resources, suggests that the balance is negative.

Politically, free trade is dangerous. It is an attack on democracy and the freedom to choose one's social and economic institutions. By promoting the weakening of state structures, it encourages the rise of communitarianism and cross-border fanaticism, such as Jihadism. Far from being a promise of peace, economic internationalism actually leads us to disaster and to war. The destruction of nation-states in Middle-East, like Iraq, or the attempt to do the same in Syria, whatever criticisms can be made of these states and their leaders (and they are many) led only to a bloody chaos.

Morally, free trade is clearly indefensible. It has no other shores than that of the reduction of all social life to commodity. It establishes as a moral value the social obscenity of the new globalized "class of leisure".[50] The future is thus protectionism. But it is to be understood that protectionism is not autarky. It will first impose itself as a means of avoiding the social and ecological dumping of certain countries as we can see with policies developed inside the EU. It will then take the form of a coherent industrial policy in which the aim will be to stimulate the development of sectors with a strategic role in a development project. This will lead to the redefinition of a global economic policy that may include the regulation of capital flows, in order to rediscover the instruments of economic, political and social sovereignty. The forms of the policy of the future remain to be found and this is a general challenge for all populist leaders who come to power in the world. But its general meaning, however, is not very doubtful.

As we said before, it is an interesting, but rather paradoxical point, that free trade is challenged by Trump who is considered the most pro-business and also the most indifferent to ecological concerns of any President for many years. Beyond the questionable political style of Donald Trump, and its questionable policies too, let us admit that his project is part of the great reversal that I had predicted a few years ago.[51] We do not yet know whether Donald Trump will succeed in articulating a genuine policy of re-

---

[50] See A. Wolfe, "Introduction" in T. Veblen, *The Theory of the Leisure Class*, The Modern Library, New York, 2001 [1899].
[51] Sapir J., *La Démondialisation*, Le Seuil, Paris, 2011.

industrialising his country, a policy that would benefit the largest number of people. We can have serious doubts on that point. At the same time, it is quite obvious that part of the hate he is inspiring right now is coming from his opposition to the "globalist" and free-trade orthodoxy. His administration is already under siege. And the violence of his opponents tells us a lot about what is at stake. But its policy takes into account, unlike what can be seen in the European Union that, for now, the era of free trade is over.

U.S. private capital accumulation and Trump's economic program

Jim Stanford [Centre for Future Work, Sydney Australia, and McMaster University, Hamilton, Canada]

Introduction: what do capitalists actually *do*, anyway?

In its purest form, capitalism is supposed to be an investment-led economic and social system. The owners of private firms invest in expanding their operations, advancing funds to pay for structures, equipment, and materials, as well as initial wages for their employees. This investment, undertaken in expectation of generating a sufficient profit in the future, starts a cycle of income and expenditure that supports a multiplied level of economic activity throughout the economy. Workers are hired to staff these growing businesses, they produce and get paid, and then they spend their incomes on consumption ("spending what they get," in the famous Kaleckian adage). That spending in turn creates additional sales opportunities that motivate further investment and expansion by investing firms. Even though workers are the ones actually producing incremental value-added in this process, they nevertheless depend on the capitalists' willingness to push the "go" button: keeping the machine running with ongoing injections of new investment. Capitalists, in turn, depend on the stimulus provided by their collective actions to underpin a sufficient level of overall demand to ratify and realize their business plans: they "get what they spend". Their capacity to initiate (or not initiate) the whole process gives investing capitalists enormous economic, political, and social power: over workers, who would be economically stranded without the initial stimulus from investment, and over governments (of all stripes) who understand well that the whole system rises or falls with the animal spirits of the investing class. Even in the more complex setting of a modern, mixed capitalist economy (with a significant public sector, foreign linkages, and finance), private business accumulation is undoubtedly the leading engine of capitalist growth and development; the ups and downs of business investment are more closely correlated with the momentum of the overall economy, than any other component of GDP. Investment, in Jorgenson's (2005) words, "is the most important source of economic growth in the G7 nations" (p. 806). Strong investment is also typically associated with other positive outcomes including productivity growth, stronger innovation and structural change, enhanced international competitiveness, and rising wages (Waller and Logan, 2008).[1]

Ironically, heterodox thinkers tend to be more cognizant of the leading role of business investment in driving economic development under capitalism than neoclassical economists – who (in theoretical models, at least) treat investment as a generally passive outcome of the clearing of a market for capital (whether defined as real assets or loanable funds), endowed thanks to the autonomous preferences of savers.[2] In contrast, heterodox writers focus on the autonomy of investment decisions, the range of motivations capitalists consider, the economic independence of investment expenditure (which, in a monetary, demand-constrained system, determines savings, rather than the other way around), and the power relationships and social factors which create the context for profit-driven investment decisions. Modern heterodox economists (such as Graziani, 2003) integrate monetary processes into this story, to explain how the initial willingness of capitalists to invest also leads the creation of credit as well as real production.

However it is explained in economic theory, the fundamentally productive, entrepreneurial role of capitalist investment is essential to the political and social legitimacy of the elites who lead the system – and who own and profit from the bulk of its wealth. Indeed, the thriftiness of the early capitalists, and their willingness to plough their savings back into growth, accumulation, and innovation, is precisely what endeared this dynamic new class to the classical economists. Smith, Ricardo, and their colleagues celebrated the productive leadership of capitalists, and developed policy recommendations which consistently favoured that class accordingly: everything from tariff reduction on imported food (to reduce real wage bills) to the expansive enshrinement of property rights. Anything that granted more money and

---

[1] Delong and Summers (1991) argue that machinery and equipment investment is especially correlated with broader economic performance.

[2] Junankar (2002) provides a useful summary of the core logic of neoclassical investment theory, and its varied empirical applications.

certainty to productive, ambitious investors would be good for the economy, and the rest of society would benefit accordingly. That core idea (albeit perverted by the analytical twists and inconsistencies of neoclassical theory) lives on in the "trickle-down" policy vision which defined neoliberalism from the outset. Neoliberalism was a response to the deceleration of private accumulation after the long postwar boom. That slowdown was due in part to constraints on business imposed by workers, governments, and liberation movements in the former colonies. The goal of neoliberalism was to restore the all-round power and legitimacy of private business; to free companies from the inconveniences of intrusive regulations, pushy unions, and taxes; and to pro-actively create and expand new investment opportunities (through globalization, privatization, and market-creation). The social hardship associated with these policies was always justified on grounds that they would unleash the dynamic impulses of accumulation, to the benefit of workers and others who depend on business investment to play this productive, leading role.

Neoliberalism certainly succeeded in strengthening profit conditions, which have improved substantially in the U.S. and most other developed economies since the 1980s. But the second part of the equation – a restoration of capital accumulation as the driving force of growth and prosperity, with widespread benefits that spread through the rest of society – was never realized. Perhaps it was never actually part of the plan: it can be argued convincingly that neoliberalism has been more interested in re-dividing the pie than growing it, and more interested in controlling growth than unleashing it. But the continued sluggishness of real accumulation (and hence of GDP, employment, and incomes) is a glaring problem for neoliberal legitimacy. Profits have been restored, incomes are flowing more strongly to corporations and their owners, but business investment has weakened under neoliberalism, not strengthened. Measured as a share of GDP, net fixed capital investment in OECD countries (after deprecation) has declined from an average of 12 percent in the 1970s, to just 4 percent since 2010.[3] The U.S. experience has been even worse (as documented below). Years of stagnation and austerity since the global financial crisis have exacerbated the problem, politically as well as economically. The contrast between fat

---

[3] Author's calculations from OECD National Accounts Statistics; unweighted average.

bonuses, strong profits, and luxury consumption at the top, and the continued stagnation of work and living standards for most of society, must inevitably provoke a crisis of legitimacy. After all, it is supposed to be their willingness and capacity to plough economic surplus back into accumulation and innovation that is the *raison d'être* of the capitalist class, and the core engine that drives the system forward. If the wealthy are capturing a larger surplus than ever, but consuming or wasting it rather than reinvesting it,[4] the political stability of the system, in addition to its economic vitality, will be threatened. As Ruccio (2017) puts it succinctly, "The machine is broken."

This makes it all the more ironic that the politician who most successfully mobilized the anger and alienation of the workers and communities who have suffered from stagnation, now promises to repair the top-down logic of the system with more of the same, painful medicine. Donald Trump has certainly placed the failure of business investment at the center of his policy program. Proposals for facilitating, encouraging, and even browbeating business to invest more in America constitute a running and consistent theme throughout his plan. But his ideas for "making America great again" through restored business leadership and investment are not novel at all: he is repeating exactly the same script that has guided neoliberal policy for over three decades – and which has manifestly failed to revitalize private capital investment. Trump's proposals may elicit spurts of new business activity in certain sectors of the U.S. economy – led by petroleum companies taking advantage of his aggressive deregulation of environmental protections, and military contractors lining up for a share of coming defense spending. But that will not restore the general vibrancy of private capital accumulation, growth, and employment on any sustained basis. Trump's program, like other incarnations of trickle-down policy, does not tackle the deeper structural problems which explain the continuing slowdown in business activity, despite enhanced business power and profitability.

This article will first describe and review the deceleration in U.S. business investment over recent decades, and discuss its consequences. It will summarize the major determinants of investment typically emphasized by

---

[4] My estimations suggest that less than one-tenth of the surplus generated in the U.S. economy is reinvested in new capital accumulation; most of the rest is consumed. See Stanford (2015), p.78.

economists. Then it will consider the various elements in Trump's policy platform, investigating the likely effect of each measure (and the program in its entirety) on the pace of capital accumulation. The conclusion will return to the deeper structural problems arising from the economy's broad reliance on profit-seeking investment as the driver of growth and job-creation – structural problems which Trump's program does not begin to address.

The deceleration of U.S. capital accumulation

Empirical evidence confirms that the vitality of U.S. business investment diminished beginning in the late 1970s – and moreover that investment performance has gotten worse, not better, since then. Previous neoliberal policies aimed at restoring profitability, and reducing regulatory and other constraints on business activity, have not helped business investment, and have likely hurt it. This casts immediate doubt on the effectiveness of Trump's plan to do even more of the same.

Figure 1 charts the average annual rate of growth in gross non-residential business fixed capital spending (including structures, machinery and equipment, and intellectual property assets) through the major economic cycles of the postwar era. The figure indicates the average annual growth of real non-residential investment expenditure (adjusted for changes in the prices of capital assets) from cycle peak to peak.[5] During the first three decades after the Second World War, investment grew robustly: at a sustained real rate of around 6 percent per year. This pace of accumulation slowed somewhat in the 1970s expansion – reflecting the uncertainty associated with oil price shocks, and the squeeze on profits from other sources. The "cold bath" of neoliberalism, led by the Volcker interest rate shock, significantly reduced the rate of accumulation – but then investment bounced back to pre-neoliberal growth rates during the long Clinton expansion of the 1990s. That strong investment contributed to strong employment results, and a partial recovery of real wages, during that time.

---

[5] Peak years are selected based on standard NBER dating; see NBER (2017). For simplicity in presentation several shallow cycles experienced between 1945 and 1960 are amalgamated into one long postwar expansion, and the short cycle dated from 1980 through 1981 was incorporated into the previous cycle.

After the turn of the century, however, real capital spending growth decelerated again, despite (or perhaps because of) the heightened financial exuberance of the time (facilitated by Clinton's late-1990s financial deregulations). Since the global financial crisis and the Great Recession, real investment has hardly grown at all: by barely 1 percent per year since 2007. Real U.S. business investment actually declined during 2016, unusually for a non-recessionary setting.

Figure 1

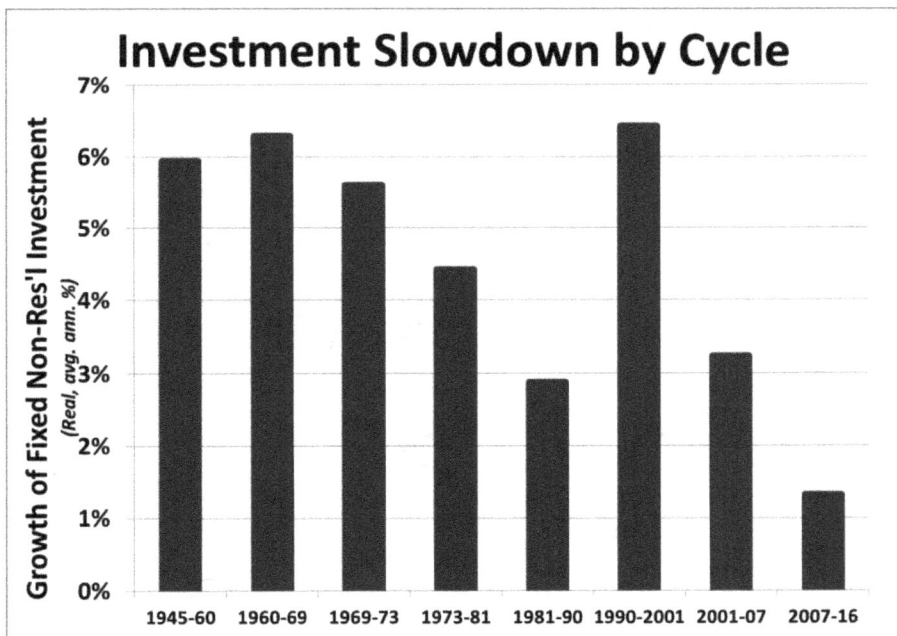

Source: Author's calculations from BEA NIPA data.

Another way to measure the vitality of business investment is as a share of total GDP. This indicates the proportion of current output devoted to business capital spending. This comparison must be conducted in nominal terms (not real), since real measures of business capital spending and overall GDP are deflated with different, non-compatible deflators. Figure 2 illustrates the trend in the investment share since 1980. The top line indicates that gross business non-residential investment has declined by about 2 percentage points of GDP since the onset of neoliberalism. However, gross investment does not take account of the ongoing wear-and-tear of existing capital equipment, which must ultimately be replaced in order to maintain the accumulated capital stock. Depreciation rates on capital assets have increased slightly in recent years because of the faster pace of technical change and the relatively greater importance of shorter-lived machinery (rather than longer-lived structures) in total capital investment. The lower line in Figure 2 indicates that the decline in net investment (after depreciation) has been somewhat steeper than the decline in gross investment: declining by over half, to less than 2 percent of GDP per year on average since 2010. Net accumulation of real capital has been so slow, that both the capital-output ratio and the capital-labour ratio have been declining in the U.S. economy since 2010 – quite counter to the usual view that production is becoming dramatically more capital- and technology-intensive.

Figure 2

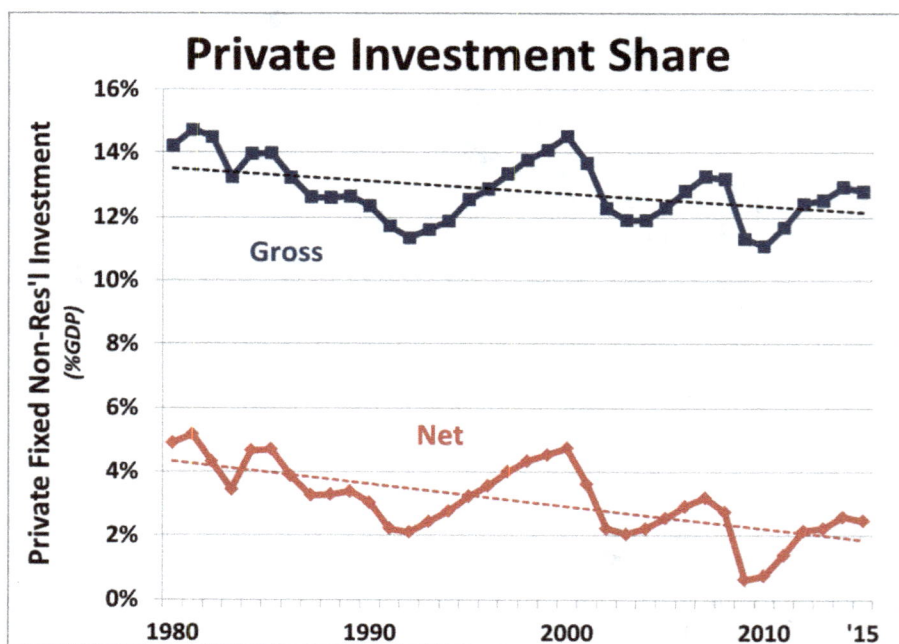

Private Investment Share

Source: Author's calculations from BEA NIPA data; linear trend lines shown.

The sustained slowdown in U.S. business investment has occurred despite a marked improvement in business profitability since the advent of neoliberalism. Figure 3 illustrates the fall and rise of business profits in the U.S. over the postwar era. The measure illustrated is gross operating surplus (before deducting depreciation charges) for private firms; it's the broadest measure of the core profitability of production.[6] Initially robust profits after the war were eroded by many factors (including rising unit labour costs), losing about 8 points of GDP share by the 1970s. Profits were not helped by the recession and "cold bath" of the 1980s, as harsh neoliberal policies were initially implemented. But they began to recover strongly in the 1990s, and have increased steadily since – interrupted only temporarily by the recessions of 2001 and 2008-09. Profit shares since 2010 have been the highest since the early 1950s, accounting for over 30 percent of all GDP, and recouping most of the share lost during the long postwar expansion.[7]

---

[6] This measure includes the profits of small businesses, not just corporate profit, but excludes interest income and rents. Since the investment measures above also include smaller firms, it is appropriate to include their gross surplus in the corresponding measure of profitability. We include depreciation charges in gross profits since they are a non-cash charge; Figure 3 is thus a measure of gross profitability best comparable to measures of gross investment. Finally, the measure illustrated in Figure 3 is before-tax; if we adjusted for the impact of business taxes, then both the decline of profitability in the postwar boom (when taxes were high) and the recovery under neoliberalism (when taxes on capital have been reduced) would be even more apparent. Effective tax rates on corporate profits have declined from an average of 42 percent in the 1970s, to just 29 percent since 2010 (author's calculations from BEA data).
[7] It is interesting (and not coincidental) to note that the U-shape of this profit-share graph closely matches the famous U-shape of top income shares that has been used to illustrate the decline in income inequality during the postwar boom, and its subsequent rebound under neoliberalism; see, for example, Piketty and Saez (2006). Since it is individuals with top incomes who own most business wealth, their personal incomes will automatically parallel the shifts in income distribution between factors.

Figure 3

Profit Share

Source: Author's calculations from BEA NIPA data.

The contrast between rising profitability and falling net investment certainly damages the legitimacy of neoliberal trickle-down policies and politics. But it also highlights a more immediate, economic problem. Private firms are capturing a larger share of current output in the form of gross profit, but reinvesting significantly less than that back into new gross investment. In 2015, for example, the gross operating profit of private firms, after deducting income taxes, was close to $5 trillion. Yet gross private investment in the entire U.S. economy was only $3 trillion. The difference represents a chronic drain on aggregate demand: companies are receiving strong income flows, which are only partially reinvested into new investment projects. The rest may be paid out in dividends (which have increased substantially as a share of GDP[8]), used to buy back shares or participate in other financial schemes,

---

[8] Net dividend payouts have averaged close to 5 percent of U.S. GSP since 2012, a postwar high, and more than twice the average payout of around 2 percent per year from 1950 through 1980 (author's calculations from BEA data).

or simply hoarded. For example, Figure 4 indicates the accumulation of financial assets in the hands of *non-financial* U.S. corporations. Financial holdings by non-financial businesses have increased rapidly under neoliberalism, reflecting both the incentives of financialization (non-financial firms have tried to capture a share of lucrative financial profits), as well as the simple fact that businesses are literally taking in more profits than they know what to do with. After only a temporary fallback during the 2008-09 banking crisis, financial holdings of non-financial corporations began to grow rapidly again – reaching over 100 percent of total GDP for the first time in 2016. Non-financial corporations have been accumulating assets over the last five years at a rate of almost $1 trillion per year, or close to 5 percent of GDP per year, and this constitutes a significant and chronic drag on aggregate demand.

Figure 4

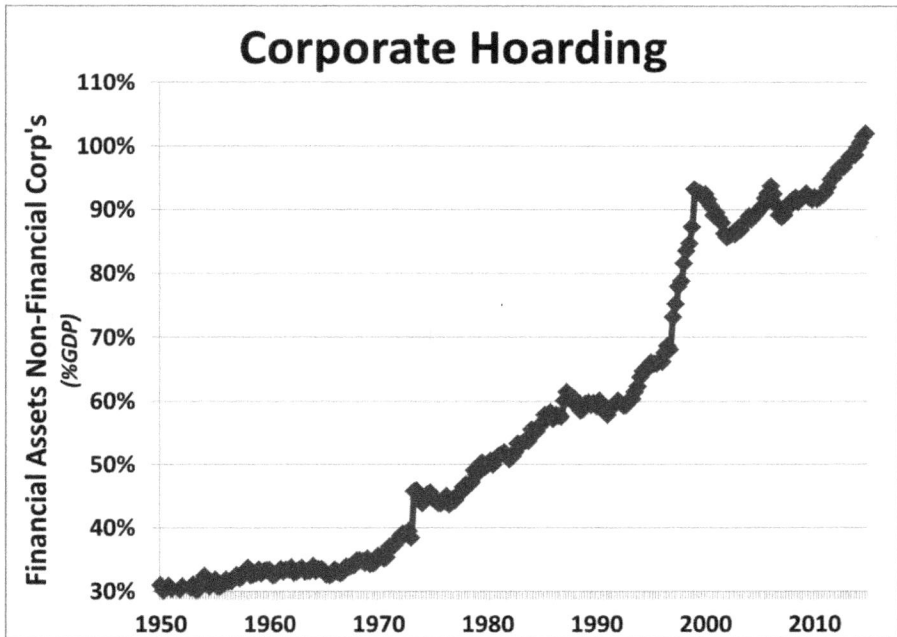

Source: Author's calculations from BEA NIPA data.

In sum, the deceleration of U.S. capital accumulation which became visible in the latter phases of the postwar expansion has not been resolved by the business- and capital-favouring policy measures implemented during three decades of neoliberalism. Redistributive and deregulatory policies have certainly restored the freedom, power, and profitability of U.S. business. But those restored profits have not "trickled down," through renewed business capital spending, into expansionary investments and jobs for the American population in general. Instead, the upward redistribution of income has undermined spending conditions and economic activity: much of the economic surplus is now being consumed by high-income constituencies, or simply hoarded as financial assets, rather than being reinvested in accumulation. This non-investment undermines both short-term demand conditions and the long-run dynamism of the system; it has certainly contributed to the understandable disaffection of a large constituency of American workers and voters, whose real opportunities have diminished under neoliberalism, with no relief in sight. This is the constituency which Trump's campaign successfully mobilized during the election campaign. Will his policy program deliver the promised change in the trajectory of U.S. investment?

The determinants of business capital spending

To judge whether Trump's economic plan will succeed in revitalizing business capital spending in the U.S., it is useful to consider the major determinants of business investment typically emphasized in economic research. A distinction can be made between factors which may influence the overall pace of business investment arising within a particular system, and factors which influence the location of investment. Key factors determining the total volume of forthcoming capital expenditure emphasized in economic research include the following:[9]

- *Current and expected profit*: Current profitability, adjusted for judgments regarding future changes in profit, will motivate investment decisions – both by strengthening the incentive and by providing cash

---

[9] This discussion is adapted from Stanford (2015), Chapter 12.

flow for finance. However the relationship between investment spending and business profits seems to have weakened in OECD countries under neoliberalism.

- **Capacity utilization**: If companies are pushing the limits of their existing capacity, they are more likely to increase investment to meet future demand.

- **Economic growth**: Empirical research shows a strong "accelerator" relationship between growth (which itself is influenced by investment) and further investment.

- **Interest rates**: For investments which must be financed through debt or other external finance, interest rates (and other measures of the cost of capital) will be negatively correlated with investment.

- **Economic, political, and legal stability**: Investing firms must have reasonable confidence about the stability and amenability of broader economic conditions, and the political and legal climate governing business activity.

- **Technology**: The clustering and spread of major innovations is often associated with sustained upswings in capital investment.

In addition to spurring a larger amount of total investment, the Trump program also pledges to relocate more investment decisions toward the U.S. Investment in relatively mobile, tradeable industries (like manufacturing or tradeable services) is most responsive to these location-specific factors, including:

- **Unit labour costs**: Low unit labour costs (considering both compensation and productivity) can be a lure for investment, especially in tradeable industries.

- **Infrastructure**: Firms benefit from high-quality infrastructure (typically paid for by the state) that facilitates their operations – including transportation, utilities, and social infrastructure (like education and training).

- **Supply chain**: In a vertically disintegrated production process, companies require the presence of a reliable network of nearby suppliers for the various materials, inputs, and services required in production.

- **Taxes**: Inter-jurisdictional differentials in business taxes (including corporate income, capital, and value-added taxes) may affect investment location decisions.

- **Transportation costs**: Firms will select locations that minimize total transportation costs, including supply chain logistics and delivery of final products to market.

- **Local market opportunities**: Access to nearby market opportunities may influence investment location, and may also be useful for marketing and political purposes.

- **Trade policy**: Inward foreign investment may be motivated by higher tariff or other trade barriers, which enhance the business case for local production (rather than imports). Alternatively, barrier-free access to other markets might also motivate investment location in some industries.

- **Political and legal risk**: Mobile investment will also depend on perceived stability in the long-run political and legal stability of host jurisdictions.

Some of these determinants of investment are addressed by Trump's program, but many are not; the ability, therefore, of Trump's policies to alter the general course of accumulation is inherently muted by the many factors beyond his control. Moreover, in several cases (such as the importance of strong aggregate demand in motivating capacity additions, and the role of business confidence in unleashing capital spending), it is not at all clear whether Trump's presidency will help or hurt the business case for investing in America.

Donald Trump's plan for investing in America

Given this catalogue of the usual determinants of business investment spending, we will now consider the various elements of Trump's program, to assemble a composite judgment of the likely overall impact on U.S. private capital accumulation. Table 1 summarizes the major planks in Trump's stated program, drawing on his election platform (the "Contract with the American Voter;" Donald J. Trump for President, 2016), and on other policy statements during and after the election.

Table 1 Relevant Trump Policies and their Likely Effects on Investment

Policy	Channel of Effect	Evaluation
Corporate tax cut or reform	Enhance after-tax profits.	Unlikely to reduce rate as much as promised; impact on profits muted by loopholes; impact of higher profits on investment weak; may simply facilitate more corporate hoarding & dividend payouts.
Trade policy: end or alter trade deals, penalize imports	Reduce offshore competition; motivate repatriation of investment.	May slow outward migration of manufacturing investment; uncertainty posed by supply chain disruptions; unlikely to change fundamental pressures of globalization.
Increase infrastructure investment	Stimulate aggregate demand; improve productivity & transportation.	Major new spending (if approved) will accelerate aggregate demand; demand benefits partly offset by tax/user fee plans; focus of new projects may be narrow.
Roll back energy and climate regulations	Open energy investment opportunities; reduce energy costs.	Will allow major energy projects to proceed (eg. pipelines, Alaska drilling); will reduce investments in renewables; energy prices not a major determinant of most investment.

Trumponomics: Causes And Consequences

Policy	Channel of Effect	Evaluation
Financial deregulation	More freedom for financial innovation and speculation.	Measures will enhance financial profits but not real investment; will fuel speculative and housing investments more than real capital.
Monetary policy	Slower demand growth; higher interest costs.	Trump's Fed appointments will reinforce emphasis on financial deregulation; impact on interest rates not clear but likely hawkish.
Labour market and union policy	Reduce unit labour costs, enhance profitability.	Measures will boost profit margins in production but suppress wages and hence aggregate demand; exacerbate household financial instability.
Immigration restrictions	Reduce supply of skilled labour for innovation-intensive businesses.	Technology sectors have been crucial to U.S. innovation and exports; their investments (and even presence) in U.S. will be hurt by restricted talent immigration.
Expand military spending	More profit and investment opportunity for military contractors.	New projects and larger margins will increase defense sector profits and investments.
General aggregate demand	Increased sales, capacity utilization.	New spending and larger deficits (if realized) may support stronger aggregate demand and employment conditions; offset by continued upward redistribution of income, user fees, and cuts in civilian program spending.
General business confidence	Enhance willingness of firms to invest.	Initial stock market rally seemed to indicate business confidence in Trump policy; may be undermined by erratic or unstable actions; enhancing business power may not translate into more business investment.

The centerpiece of Trump's investment program is his proposal to dramatically cut or reform U.S. business taxes. His platform promised to reduce the base corporate rate, from 35 percent to 15 percent,[10] and to establish a new tax rate on repatriated profits from overseas operations of just 10 percent. Discussions within the Republican-led Congress since the election, however, have focused on a GOP proposal for a more radical restructuring of the corporate tax, replacing the standard corporate income tax with a so-called "destination-based cash flow tax" (DBCFT). This new tax would allow companies to fully deduct the immediate cost of new investment (rather than depreciating it gradually over time), and would not tax income on exports (under a "border adjustment" contemplated in the Republican proposal). The final outcome (in terms of both the form of tax, and its rate) will depend on political and budget negotiations over coming months or years; it is unlikely, given the to-and-fro that typifies U.S. budget-making, that the rate would fall by the full amount promised by Trump. Both cutting the existing rate, and shifting the structure of the tax, would certainly enhance the after-tax revenues of U.S. businesses. It should be kept in mind, however, that few companies pay the full 35 percent rate due to various loopholes, exemptions, and carry-forward losses,[11] and hence the impact of reductions in the statutory rate on final profitability will be muted. With its alternative treatment of capital costs (allowing, in essence, immediate and complete write-off of capital investments), the Republican proposal would certainly enhance the tax treatment of new capital spending. However, the lack of responsiveness of U.S. investment to strong profits in recent years, and the accumulation of financial assets by non-financial firms, also suggest limited effects of higher after-tax profitability on investment.

Another high-profile element of Trump's program is his aggressive statements regarding ending or renegotiating international trade agreements, and his threats to impose significant "border taxes" (or tariffs) on imported products. His stated goals are to reduce chronic U.S. trade deficits by limiting imports, and to encourage companies to invest in the U.S.

---

[10] U.S. states also levy their own corporate income taxes, which average around 4% nation-wide.

[11] Since 2010 the average effective rate of corporate income tax paid by U.S. corporations (29.1%) has been 10 full percentage points lower than the combined federal and state statutory rate (over 39%). The effective rate paid by U.S. companies has been comparable to average rates paid in other OECD economies (Hungerford, 2013). Tax avoidance in overseas tax havens has been an especially lucrative form of tax avoidance for U.S. business (Clemente, Blair, and Trokel, 2016).

to produce manufactured goods rather than importing them (especially from Mexico and China, the two countries which receive most of Trump's negative attention[12]). Trump's early success in pressuring specific companies (like Ford Motor Co.) to cancel projects in Mexico, and increase investments in the U.S., might seem to presage a bigger relocation of investment back to the U.S. However, Trump's plan to limit imports is not without risks of its own to U.S. business, including disruptions in established supply chains, and the potential for offsetting actions by U.S. trading partners (and hence the risk of a more generalized "trade war"). Trump's financial and monetary policies (discussed below) are likely to spark appreciation of the U.S. dollar,[13] which will offset some of the gains in relative competitiveness his trade policy changes might accomplish. It is also not clear to what extent Trump's attacks on existing trade agreements and practices will be truly focused on repatriating manufacturing investment and jobs. For example, his trade policy statements have often stressed the need for even stronger patent rights for U.S. businesses (Baker, 2017); to the extent that his trade agenda focuses on those issues (rather than on addressing trade deficits), it will hurt living standards of U.S. workers with no impact on real investment.

Trump pledged during the election to accelerate public infrastructure investments. He proposed a public-private initiative to allocate $1 trillion to infrastructure projects over the next ten years (implying a flow of new spending equal to $100 billion per year). U.S. public capital investment (by all levels of government) equaled close to $650 billion in 2016. The $100 billion per year flow of projects under Trump's program will not be fully incremental (since some supported projects would have occurred anyway), so perhaps the program might boost existing public investment flows by around 10 percent. Public infrastructure spending can "crowd in" private investment via several channels. The immediate spending power of public investment strengthens demand conditions, employment, and incomes, thus

---

[12] It is not coincidental that other countries maintaining large trade surpluses with the U.S. have so far escaped the brunt of Trump's protectionist rhetoric. For example, both Germany's and Japan's bilateral trade surplus with the U.S. were larger in 2016 than Mexico's, and much larger as a share of two-way trade (implying a higher proportionate degree of imbalance). This suggests there are other motivations, including no doubt racialized ones, for Trump's focus on Mexico and China.

[13] Many observers also expect the Republican corporate cash flow tax plan, if implemented, to spark a sustained appreciation in the dollar as well (Gale, 2017).

supporting capital utilization and accelerating private investment. In the long-run, better public infrastructure can enhance private-sector productivity and capabilities, also encouraging faster private investment. Trump's emphasis on public-private partnerships in new infrastructure may directly draw in private capital to these projects. Trump has pledged that the infrastructure program will be "revenue neutral", implying that projects will be funded through new taxes, user fees, or other revenue collections; this would offset the demand-side benefits of the new spending.

The energy industry has been one of the most enthusiastic backers of Trump's program, and it's easy to see why. He targeted environmental regulations for special criticism throughout his campaign, and his cabinet nominations (notably including a known climate change denier as head of the Environmental Protection Agency) confirm that he intends to move quickly in dismantling U.S. environmental protections. He will quickly approve major new energy projects (such as the Keystone and Dakota Access pipelines); open up federal lands (including the Arctic National Wildlife Refuge in Alaska, and other offshore areas in the Arctic and Atlantic oceans) for energy exploration and development; and abolish the Obama administration's Clean Power Plan. Trump's promises to rescue the coal industry (which has faced falling demand, bankruptcies, and massive downsizing, mostly because of factors – like automation in mining and the falling price of natural gas – unrelated to federal environmental laws) were especially potent in several Midwest and Appalachian states during the election. Rolling back environmental rules will indeed facilitate some big-ticket energy investments, more in petroleum than in coal. (Even backtracking on clean power rules can't reverse the rapid switch of electricity generation away from coal that has already occurred.) It is important to keep perspective on the likely scale of the investment response to this aspect of Trump's program: energy and mining investment accounted for under 6 percent of total business fixed capital spending in 2015. So even a dramatic increase in capital spending in this sector won't make a significant difference to total U.S. capital investment. Moreover, backtracking on environmental regulations may forestall significant capital spending that otherwise would have occurred in renewable energy and energy conservation. Much of American business will celebrate Trump's environmental backsliding, but that does not confirm that it will translate into faster investment and growth.

Trumponomics: Causes And Consequences

Contrary to the pro-investment rhetoric evident in other policy areas, Trump's financial and monetary policies seem out of synch with the overarching objective of accelerating real capital accumulation. Never mind his populist self-image, in one of his first acts Trump confirmed his true allegiances by ordering a review of the Dodd-Frank regulations implemented under the Obama administration after the 2008 financial crisis. Weakening restrictions on banks and quasi-banks, which were not very strong to begin with, is a clear sign that Trump is committed to restoring the full power and freedom of the financial class. This implies a return to financial expansion, fragility, and instability. Recent history confirms that financialized exuberance tends to overwhelm the logic of real accumulation, especially when moments of crisis inevitably erupt. Trump's vision of financial deregulation is a recipe for another financial catastrophe, not for faster investment in real capital.

Trump's considerable influence over the future make-up of the U.S. Federal Reserve Board of Governors will reinforce this bias in favor of financial deregulation and financialization. Trump can immediately nominate two vacancies on the seven-member Board, and a third in April when David Tarullo retires. Trump can also nominate a new vice-chair for banking supervision (a post which is currently vacant). Further vacancies on the Board are likely to come open during the next two years, and the Chair, Janet Yellen, must be reappointed or replaced after February, 2018. During the campaign Trump railed regularly against Yellen and the Fed for keeping interest rates "artificially low", supposedly to enhance the Democrats' election prospects. This implies that Trump will nominate new Governors with a more hawkish orientation – although his priorities may change as his own economic and fiscal plan rolls out. There is no doubt, however, that Trump's Fed appointments will be supportive of his general emphasis on reinforcing the power and privilege of the financial industry; given the Fed's various responsibilities for banking supervision, this will be reflected in a lighter regulatory touch. Again, the reassertion of financialized logic as the dominant force in the U.S. economy is likely to undermine real investment and accumulation, not strengthen it.

In labor market policy Trump will also quickly confirm that he is no friend to the dislocated and alienated workers who supported him in key rustbelt states. He will certainly act to further undermine the bargaining power of workers with regulatory changes that suppress wages. Regarding the federal minimum wage, Trump espoused wildly contradictory positions during the election: ranging from increasing it, to freezing it, to abolishing it altogether (handing all authority to individual states to set legislative minimums). His initial nominee for Labor Secretary – fast food magnate Andrew Puzder – was energetically committed to weakening labor protections; this provided a good clue as to Trump's intentions, regardless of Puzder's eventual withdrawal from the nomination. The labor relations community widely expects Trump to push, with support from the Republican Congress, for nation-wide "right-to-work" provisions that would prohibit union security clauses (like dues check-off procedures), thus universalizing the bars to union organizing that already prevail in half the states (Meyerson, 2016). All of this will undermine general wage pressures, labor incomes, and consumer spending. Business will celebrate increased workplace power and profit margins. Again, it is doubtful this will translate into increased investment effort. To the contrary, there is growing macroeconomic evidence that the U.S. economy is wage-led, especially in light of the longer-run stagnation that has characterized aggregate demand conditions since the 2008 crisis (Lavoie and Stockhammer, 2014; Blecker, 2016). This suggests that Trump's wage-suppressing policies will do more harm than good to overall growth and employment; the resulting weakness in domestic demand will probably overwhelm fatter profits in influencing future investment.

Another labor-related policy likely to backfire on investment is the Trump administration's aggressive efforts to curtail immigration. Dynamic clusters of technology-intensive firms in key innovation centers have been a rare bright light in the lackluster performance of U.S. investment and business development in recent years. Trump's initial ham-fisted restrictions on immigration, catering to the populist sentiments that helped him win the election, will shock the business models of those industries. Their capacity to attract leading global scientific and innovation talent to the U.S. will be constrained, and the willingness of international experts to come will be significantly damaged by both the new rules themselves, and the climate of division and scapegoating which they cater to. Public research and innovation activity (including at universities and elsewhere) will also be damaged.

Trumponomics: Causes And Consequences

Trump's bellicose approach to world affairs will also be reflected in his defense spending policies. He has committed to a substantial increase in defense spending, and this will support sales, profits, and future investments for defense contractors. As with his expansive plans for infrastructure investments, the defense spending increases are meant to be "revenue neutral": Trump promises to offset them with equivalent cutbacks in other public programs and spending. In this regard, the net effect of bigger defense budgets on overall demand conditions will likely be negative – since capital-intensive defense programs will provide a smaller boost to total employment and incomes than the same amount of spending being cut from more labor-intensive public programs. Nevertheless, within the defense industry the Trump program will motivate new investment and research. If Trump's aggressive approach to international affairs culminates in actual war, then of course future defense budgets will swell even further. But U.S. spending on other military misadventures in the recent past (such as the long Iraq campaign) was also enormous – and while certain sections of business profited mightily, this did not translate into all-round economic dynamism.

The biggest impact of Trump's policies on business investment may not come from any of the specific policy measures catalogued above. Instead, the most important impacts may be felt indirectly through the effect of Trump's program on the overall vitality of aggregate demand in the U.S. economy, and on the general confidence of the business leaders who must ultimately commit funds to real investment projects. On these counts, the likely impact of Trump's program is contradictory and uncertain. Financial markets had originally interpreted Trump's victory as a sign of an impending boost to demand conditions and inflation. This view was behind the initial post-Trump spurt in U.S. stock market indices, and the corresponding pullback in bond markets (fretting over future inflation and higher interest rates). The common view was that Trump's expansion of infrastructure and defense spending, combined with tax cuts for business and high-income households, would create a larger deficit, faster growth, and higher inflation. It is a painful irony, of course, that a Republican Congress could ratify larger deficits under Trump than those they blocked under the preceding Democratic administration. But a more careful review of Trump's specific proposals suggests that the net impact on final demand of his fiscal plan will be more modest. Both the infrastructure and defense measures are meant to be revenue-neutral – offset by user fees in the former case, and offsetting civilian program cuts in the latter. The demand stimulus arising from corporate and high-income tax cuts is muted by the hoarding of both businesses and wealthy households. And the whole expansion could be thrown into neutral or even reverse by a Federal Reserve Board that is likely to be more hawkish after Trump's appointments. In sum, it seems unlikely that Trump's program will initiate a sustained macroeconomic recovery.

The same mixed judgment is true of his impact on business confidence. True, business elites have celebrated Trump's unapologetic willingness to cut business taxes, dismantle regulations, and suppress wages. Those are core priorities for corporations and the mostly wealthy people who own them. On the other hand, Trump's erratic and contradictory behavior, and the deeper political and legal uncertainty which his tenure could bring (internationally as well as within the U.S.), will spark caution on the part of businesses. If the long upswing in business profits that accompanied the consolidation of neoliberal policy in the U.S. has not elicited a more vibrant investment effort on the part of business, it is not likely that a little icing on the cake delivered by an erratic, authoritarian, and potentially destabilizing leader will somehow open the vaults and get all that capital flowing.

Conclusion: the indolence of late capitalism

The weakness of private business investment in most developed countries through the neoliberal era is difficult to explain on the basis of a standard regression equation. Most of the usual determinants of investment – including profitability, interest rates, and tax and regulatory policies – were aligned in a direction that should have elicited more private investment effort. But the neoliberal recipe delivered less investment, not more. And the failure of accumulated wealth to trickle down creates major economic and political problems for the system and its elites.

For all of Donald Trump's claims of being an "outsider", changing the traditional rules of politics and policy, his economic program is absolutely consistent with the general direction of the trickle-down, neoliberal policies that have already governed the U.S. for almost four decades. Trump will further shift the distribution of income upward to corporations and those who own them. His policies will suppress the incomes and the consumption of workers – including cutting their public services. His regulatory and fiscal priorities will favour investment in expensive, capital-intensive sectors (like energy and defense) that support relatively few jobs, while imposing enormous costs on broader society and the planet. His financial and monetary policies will continue to privilege financial wealth and speculation over real investment and production, undoing even the baby steps taken to rein in finance after the conflagration of 2008. The core logic of his approach is transparent: enhance the wealth and power of business and the wealthy, and they will invest more in America, and everyone will prosper. There is very little novel content in Trump's incarnation of trickle-down policy, and very little reason to believe that it will succeed in revitalizing business investment activity that has chronically disappointed. Outside of bursts of new activity in a couple of targeted sectors (like energy and military industries), there is no reason to expect that the trajectory of U.S. business investment will improve in any sustained fashion under Trump's guidance. Certainly his program cannot recreate the virtuous combination of driving factors that powered the long postwar boom in U.S. capital accumulation: near-full employment, a growing public sector, and strong productivity growth, all of which (for a while) reinforced the vitality of private investment.

Even if the Trump program did succeed in motivating a generalized resurgence in U.S. private business investment, of course, Americans (and others around the world) would have to ask themselves, "At what cost?" A temporary burst in investment in fossil fuel extraction and consumption, achieved by abandoning environmental regulations that were already too weak, is of dubious value when the costs of fossil fuel use are becoming intolerable. Similar questions could be asked about the general strategy of reinforcing profit margins through the suppression of wages and other socially destructive levers, in a country which already experiences more poverty and inequality than any other industrial nation. Business investment is never an end in its own right; it is socially beneficial only to the extent that it underpins job creation, incomes, productivity, and ultimate improvements in living standards. Trying to elicit a bit more investment effort by suppressing living standards a little further, is self-defeating to the ultimate purpose of economic development.

Investment in the U.S., and other advanced industrial countries, is held back by more fundamental problems than corporate tax design or environmental regulations. The fundamental vitality of the profit motive in eliciting accumulation, so celebrated in the early chapters of capitalist history, seems to have dissipated. The owners of businesses are content to consume their wealth, or hoard it, or speculate with it, instead of recycling it via new investments. Ever-more desperate attempts to elicit a bit more investment effort never seem to alter this stagnationist trajectory – with the incredible result today that overall production is actually becoming less capital-intensive, despite "miraculous" technological innovations. Trump is giving the trickle-down theory one more kick at the can, having successfully capitalized on popular discontent with the failures of previous attempts. Progressives must work harder to illuminate the failure of this business-led economic logic, and come up with other visions for financing capital investment, innovation, and job-creation that do not depend on fruitlessly bribing the investing class to actually do the job it is supposed to.

References

Baker, Dean (2017). "What does Donald Trump actually intend to do about trade?," Real-World Economics Review, January 5, https://rwer.wordpress.com/2017/01/05/what-does-donald-trump-actually-intend-to-do-about-trade/#more-27705.

Blecker, Robert A. (2016). "Wage-led versus Profit-led Demand Regimes: The Long and the Short of It," *Review of Keynesian Economics* 4(4), pp. 373-390.

Clemente, Frank, Hunter Blair, and Nick Troket (2016). *How Corporations Rig the Rules to Dodge the Taxes They Owe* (Washington: Economic Policy Institute).

DeLong, Bradford, and Lawrence Summers (1991). "Equipment Investment and Economic Growth," *Quarterly Journal of Economics* 106(2), pp. 445-502.

Donald J. Trump for President (2016). "Donald Trump's Contract with the American Voter," https://assets.donaldjtrump.com/_landings/contract/O-TRU-102316-Contractv02.pdf.

Gale, William G. (2017). "Understanding the Republicans' Corporate Tax Reform" (Washington: Brookings Institution), https://www.brookings.edu/opinions/understanding-the-republicans-corporate-tax-reform/.

Graziani, Augusto (2003). *The Monetary Theory of Production* (Cambridge: Cambridge University Press).

Hungerford, Thomas L. (2013). *Corporate Tax Rates and Economic Growth Since 1947* (Washington: Economic Policy Institute).

Jorgenson, Dale W. (2005). "Accounting for Growth in the Information Age", in Phillipe Aghion and Steven N. Durlauf, eds., Handbook of Economic Growth (Amsterdam: Elsevier).

Junankar, Pramod (2002). "Neoclassical Theories of Investment," in Howard Vane and Brian Snowdon, eds., *Encyclopaedia of Macroeconomics* (Cheltenham: Edward Elgar).

Lavoie, Marc, and Engelbert Stockhammer, eds. (2014). *Wage-Led Growth: An Equitable Strategy for Economic Recovery* (Geneva: International Labour Organization).

Meyerson, Harold (2016). "Donald Trump can Kill the American Union," Washington Post, November 23, https://www.washingtonpost.com/posteverything/wp/2016/11/23/donald-trump-could-kill-the-american-union/?utm_term=.c6b0d675092f.

National Bureau of Economic Research (2017), U.S. Business Cycle Expansions and Contractions, http://www.nber.org/cycles.html.

Piketty, Thomas, and Emmanuel Saez (2006). "The Evolution of Top Incomes: A Historical and International Perspective," NBER Working Paper No. 11955.

Ruccio, David (2017). "The machine is broken," Real-World Economics Review, January 3, https://rwer.wordpress.com/2017/01/03/the-machine-is-broken/.

Stanford, Jim (2015). *Economics for Everyone: A Short Guide to the Economics of Capitalism* (London: Pluto, Second Edition).

Waller, Christian E., and Amanda Logan (2008). *Investing for Widespread, Productive Growth* (Washington: Center for American Progress).

Trumponomics and the "post-hegemonic" world

Barry K. Gills and Heikki Patomäki [University of Helsinki, Finland]

"Turning and turning in the widening gyre
The falcon cannot hear the falconer;
Things fall apart; the centre cannot hold;
Mere anarchy is loosed upon the world,
The blood-dimmed tide is loosed, and everywhere
The ceremony of innocence is drowned;
The best lack all convictions, while the worst
Are full of passionate intensity.
Surely some revelation is at hand."
(William Butler Yeats, "The Second Coming", 1919)

(Note: a Factiva analysis has shown that the "The Second Coming" has been quoted more in the first seven months of 2016 than in any of the preceding 30 years.)

Introduction: taking the "long view": alarm or *déjà vu*?

All models for a world order are contested and historically temporary. They have an origin, a development and apogee. They may become real for a while under particular changing world-historical circumstances, but they have an (inevitable) historical demise or decomposition, giving rise to new configurations in new eras of history. The present international political and economic conjuncture is no exception. The illusion of global systemic stability has once again been shattered. The fragility and vulnerability of the present US-led market-globalist *status quo* is now exposed, naked for all to see. Although the present malaise and growing anticipation of impending global systemic disorder may seem to have arisen suddenly, precipitated by recent developments (e.g. post-Arab spring chaos, the endless euro crisis, conflict in Ukraine, the Brexit vote and especially Donald Trump's election as US president), in reality its root causes are long term and much deeper than surface appearances may reveal. We will argue that the design of the post-WWII "world order" already carried the seeds of the present state of disarray.

The present situation is one of great uncertainty, touching upon the formal institutional arrangements of the post-WWII international system and its rules, norms and principles. It is the acute manifestation of cumulative historical currents of transformation already long at work. So great is the intensity of feelings in the present moment, full of provocation to the established order, that in recent months a new chorus of voices has arisen to defend the still prevailing "order". This is in response to what many now perceive to be a genuine existential threat to the (neo) liberal system of values and practices.[1] These vocal commentators tend to share a sense of urgency, even alarm, and a common fear of impending global disorder. The atmosphere is replete with dire predictions, e.g. of the end of the West itself or at least of its dominance in global political economy. These new systemic defenders typically lament the demise of what they tend to represent as a universally benign, beneficent, and prosperous form of hegemonic order, one designed, lead, and maintained by the power of "The West" and depending pivotally on the role of the United States of America as its leading power.

The provocations to the status quo are perceived to be so great, and the existential threat so imminent, that the self-appointed defenders of the established order react with a tendency to idealize the existing international political and economic relationships, and in Panglossian tones elevate its presumed virtues for humanity onto a higher moral plane. This reaction accords with the basic ideas of hegemonic stability theory (HST), positing that a single hegemonic state is both a necessary and a sufficient condition for an open, liberal world economy. A similar response was evident in the "declinist" literature of the 1970s and 1980s regarding the debate at the time concerning the perceived decline of US global hegemonic power (as so acutely analysed by Strange, 1987; and Grunberg, 1990). However, this was partly, and temporarily, set aside by the end of the Cold War and during the

---

[1] See e.g. the numerous commentaries by intellectual and political elites, distributed by Project Syndicate, such as Fischer, 2017 and Leonard, 2017.

"roaring nineties" (Stiglitz, 2003) and its aftermath. This aftermath finally ended in the global financial crisis of 2008-9. Since then some pundits have started to argue "this time it's real" (e.g. Layne, 2012; for discussion see Wohlforth, 2012). While we concur with HST-theorists that current developments can have tangible negative consequences through the mechanisms and processes of the world economy, we fundamentally disagree about both the causes and nature of this disarray and alternatives to it.

The late Susan Strange (1987, p. 552), a British professor of International Political Economy and self-proclaimed loyal opposition to the US in its role as global hegemon, compared the myth of lost hegemony to the once widely believed idea that German-speaking people came from a distinct Aryan race and to the persistent myth that rhinoceros horn is an aphrodisiac. Strange warned that the persistent myth of lost hegemony can be every bit as dangerous by inducing unashamed self-regarding behaviour. Following Strange, we may argue that as the "hegemon" abandons the hegemonic role defined in terms of common good and asserts its own narrow self-interests, which often involves reliance on double standards, then there are (unintended) consequences for itself and for the world economy as a whole. Double standards can be seen as an act of increasingly narrow power: those who possess the greatest power are able, for a while, to make the rules that others must follow, while the most powerful do not always necessarily follow these rules themselves. Over time, however, double standards erode the legitimacy of those very standards.

In this paper, first we will outline the logic of hegemonic stability theory and expose its vagueness and ambiguities. Second, we will discuss the issue of whether global cooperation is possible "after hegemony", as argued by Robert Keohane in 1984 (Keohane, 2005), one of the original authors of hegemonic stability theory. According to Keohane, while a hegemonic state may facilitate the emergence and development of common institutions, they may well continue to exist and function after hegemony, in a decentralized way through extended, bendable and institutionally ensured tit-for-tat strategies. The obvious problem from this point of view is that if the former hegemon refuses to cooperate, it can lead to a spiral of tit-for-tat retaliations. Third, we will show the limitations of this economistic literature and discuss alternative conceptualizations of hegemony and the politics of global cooperation. Global common good is profoundly contested, in both theory and practice. How it should be seen depends on our factual and normative theories of political economy and peace and security.

Finally, we argue that a dialectical perspective on change and continuity in world history can be a powerful analytical tool for understanding the causes and consequences of the present global conjuncture and potential crises.[2] The appearance of stability and of fixedness in the international "order" is more of an illusion than a reality. From a dialectical point of view, events are understood as multiple layers of the contradictory and complementary, and often inner determination "to which they own their hidden unities, divergent meanings, and possible futures" (Alker, 1996, p. 351). Thus HST, under current historical circumstances, may function to justify, and thus co-generate, President Donald Trump's approach to US trade and security policies. When weaker states are perceived to free ride on the US, in the new US administration's view it is apparently only fair that the US should apply countervailing measures, either to balance its current account or to compel others to pay the costs for the military burden of defending them.

"Hegemonic stability" of the liberal-capitalist world economy is a particular model for a world order, but it is certainly not the only one.[3] World order models in this broad sense constitute those doctrines of practical action and institutional design that exist, reign, cooperate, compete and at times clash in any given geo-historical era. Doctrines codify the lessons learned from previous practices; and doctrinal debates define the geo-historical eras and their characteristic practical and institutional arrangements. Collective learning and the exercise of power (understood as transformative capacity), not least by social movements, determine which doctrines prevail.

---

[2] See the special issue of *Globalizations* on "Dialectics and World Politics", Vol. 11 Number 5, October 2014, edited by Shannon Brincat.
[3] "World order can be conceptualized as a cohesive system of ideas (or world view) mutually or intersubjectively shared by [actors], including those located in different communities across territorial boundaries. This cohesive system of ideas and normative values encompass ideas about political and economic systems, conceptions of religion (and its role in society), ontological and epistemological assumptions, a sense of mission in the world, a conception of the scope of that world, practices of legitimation, and ways of ordering, creating and forgetting history." Alker, Amin, Biersteker and Inoguchi (1996: 9).

Barry K. Gills and Heikki Patomäki

Hegemonic stability theory

HST emerged at a time when the partial collapse of the Bretton Woods system was widely conceived as a sign of crisis in US global leadership. This perception was further reinforced by the catastrophe of the Vietnam War and the rise of the New Left movement. Basically, HST claims that the stability of the world economy is dependent on the benevolent leadership of the hegemonic state. HST was first proposed by economic historian Charles P. Kindleberger (1973) in *The World in Depression 1929-1939*. In the concluding chapter of that work, "An Explanation of the 1929 Depression", Kindleberger suggested a chain of partly contrastive historical analogies between three eras. The first was the era of free trade under British leadership from 1846 (abolition of the Corn Laws) or 1860 (further elimination of tariffs) until 1913.[4] The second was the interwar era of 1919-39, when the US first refused to accept the role of hegemonic leadership and then resorted to the protectionist Smoot-Hawley Tariff Act of 1930 in response to the financial crisis and its consequences. The third was the era of the US (hegemonic) leadership in 1945-71. In addition, the fourth era was beginning in the 1970s, when the US was arguably "beginning to slip" (ibid., p. 307), but which we retrospectively know as the era of neoliberalism or market-globalism (see Harvey, 2005; Steger, 2009; Springer, Birch and MacLeavy 2016). Kindleberger anticipated future tendencies towards protectionism and a diplomatic stalemate between the US and EEC. The next forty years turned out different, but in Kindleberger's historical reading, a stalemate and repression would mean a heightened danger of regressive spiral into war.

These historical analogies were subsequently formulated into a general theory by Stephen D. Krasner (1976), Robert Keohane (1980), Robert Gilpin (1981), and Kindleberger (1981) himself. In Krasner's (1976, p. 318) formulation, the main hypothesis of the theory is that "a hegemonic distribution of potential economic power is likely to result in an open trading

---

[4] Note that Kindleberger fails to account for the turn to neo-imperialism in 1874-1914. Patomäki (2008) presents a different – also more protectionist – picture of the developments in the late 19th and early 20th century. See also Andre Gunder Frank's final posthumously published work, *Reorienting the Nineteenth Century: Global Economy in the Continuing Asian Age*, (Frank 2014) in which the global pattern of capital flows orchestrated under British imperialism plays a central role.

structure" and, more generally, in an open world economy. Krasner qualified his state-power argument by talking about delayed political reactions to changes in patterns of trade and finance and structures of production; the actual effects of gradual economic changes may in some cases become visible only after decades. Moreover, "some catalytic external event seems necessary to move states to dramatic policy initiatives in line with state interests" (1976, p. 341). Policy-choices are thus path-dependent, and states become rather easily locked into the pattern set by their previous choices.

The key assumption underlying the theory of hegemonic stability, however, is that free trade and maximal (global) openness in investments and finance are beneficial to everyone, albeit not equally so, in sharp contrast to many alternative perspectives (such as Rodrik 2001; Unger 2008):

> "Neoclassical trade theory is based upon the assumption that states act to maximize their aggregate economic utility. This leads to the conclusion that maximum global welfare and Pareto optimality are achieved under free trade. While particular countries may better their situations through protectionism, economic theory has generally looked askance at such policies. [...] Neoclassical theory recognizes that trade regulations can also be used to correct domestic distortions and to promote infant industries, but these are exceptions or temporary departures from policy conclusions that lead logically to the support of free trade" (Krasner, 1976, p. 318).

Krasner stressed that the benefits are clearest in the case of large and technologically advanced states and for some small states, but large backward states may in some cases experience excessive costs from trade openness. Krasner's qualifications notwithstanding, in the next step of the development of the theory, liberal international order was bluntly defined as a (global) public good. The global public good was supposed to include the definition and enforcement of property rights, resolution of disputes, stability and security (Gilpin, 1981, p. 16, 30, 34; Gilpin, 1987, pp. 86-7;

Kindleberger, 1981, p. 247).[5] Yet these HST theorists were not united about the nature of what constituted that 'good'. Whereas Kindleberger emphasised moral responsibilities and the need to overcome temporary asymmetries and counter business cycles, Gilpin, by contrast, put forward a more neo-imperialist interpretation:

> "As was the case with premodern empires, the hegemonic powers may be said to supply public goods (security and protection of property rights) in exchange for revenue. The Pax Britannica and Pax Americana, like the Pax Romana, ensured an international system of relative peace and security" (Gilpin, 1981, p. 145).

The theory of hegemonic stability thus depicted 19th century Britain as a model for the late 20th and early 21st century US. The precise ethical and political implications of the theory were somewhat unclear, however. Gilpin presented a gloomy picture of future options. Despite the Cold War bipolar structure being a major stabilising factor, threatened only by the continuous rise of the Soviet Union, Gilpin argued that "the danger of a hegemonic war is very real" (ibid., p. 234). His prescription: a hegemonic or imperial enforcement – i.e. that powerful states should control the "lesser states" – for global security and protection of property rights, has been taken seriously by many US-based scholars, politicians and journalists. Coupled with the assumption of the benevolence of the hegemon and related apologetic narratives, this line of thinking readily lends itself to the conclusion that the US has been assuming an unfair share of sustaining the global public good.[6] Strange (1987, p. 552) expressed the main practical implication of the theory:

---

[5] Note that all these are aspects identified by Hedley Bull (1977) as constitutive of his definition of "order" *per se*, which in turn are exactly the same as David Hume's principles of justice in capitalist market society. The three fundamental rules of Humean justice, namely, stability of possession, transfer by consent, and keeping of promises, are argued to be laws of nature, i.e. universally applicable.

[6] Isabelle Grunberg (1990) argues that the appeal of the theory stems from its mythic structure. The day-to-day dilemmas of the US foreign policy-makers are mixed with American ethnocentrism, assumptions about the benevolence of the US and claims that the "small exploit the rich". Further, the theory accepts uncritically the idea that free trade and security of property rights are public goods.

"[T]he myth of lost hegemony is apt to induce in everybody only pessimism, despair, and the conviction that, in these inauspicious circumstances, the only thing to do is to ignore everyone else and look after your own individual or national interests. Thus, some of the same American contributors to *International Organization* who are personally persuaded of the benefits of more international cooperation and conflict resolution, may paradoxically be contributing to a less cooperative environment by subscribing to and perpetuating the myth of lost American power."

Trump's project to "Make America great again" has deep historical roots. The erosion of the Bretton Woods system triggered the emergence of the US-American myth about lost hegemony and its global consequences. The Bretton Woods system itself was inherently dilemmatic and presupposed a largely disintegrated world economy of the 1940s and its continuous economic domination by the US. The Triffin Dilemma[7] was a direct consequence of the decision reached in Bretton Woods – on the insistence of the US – to make the dollar the currency of world trade, and let creditors retain their surplus and remain passive. The turning point of the early 1970s would not have occurred until much later had Keynes' proposal been implemented in full, and it could have occurred in a very different way (Patomäki, 2008: 185-90). The implication of the HST – that others should be made to pay for the maintenance of the existing "order" and indirectly thereby subsidise the costs on US terms – has paved the way towards the US inclination to become, over time, ever more self-regarding.

---

[7] According to Robert Triffin (1961; see also 1968), if the United States stopped running the balance of payments deficits, the world economy would lose its largest source of additions to reserves. The resulting shortage of liquidity could pull the world economy into a contractionary spiral, leading to instability. If US deficits continued, a steady stream of dollars would continue to stimulate world economic growth. However, excessive US deficits (dollar glut) would erode confidence in the value of the US dollar. Without confidence in the dollar, it would no longer be accepted as the world's reserve currency. The fixed exchange rate system could break down, leading to instability. Triffin's idea was to create new reserve units. These units would not depend on gold or currencies, but would add to the world's total liquidity. Creating such a new reserve would allow the United States to reduce its balance of payments deficits, while still allowing for global economic expansion.

Of the early developers of HST, Kindleberger (1973, p. 308) was open to the alternative of new "international institutions with real authority and sovereignty" to govern the world economy (i.e. an evolutionary path towards a "post-hegemonic" situation, with increased trans-nationalisation of state authority, governing a highly trans-nationalised global economic system). However, he too seems to have ultimately assumed that agenda setting and decision-making must always be hierarchical at least to a degree; i.e. one state must always lead and others must follow.

International cooperation "after hegemony": a reconstructive critique

The assumption underlying HST that a single hegemonic leader is necessary for effective international cooperation (to uphold the existing international institutions of "order" and ensure the stability of the global capitalist economic system) was questioned by Keohane in his 1984 book *After Hegemony: Cooperation and Discord in the World Political Economy*. In this book, Keohane (2005) argues, "it might be possible, after the decline of hegemonic regimes, for most symmetrical patterns of cooperation to evolve after a transitional period of discord".

Keohane uses game theory to show that spontaneous cooperation can emerge even among egoists and in the absence of common government, but "the extent of such cooperation will depend on the existence of international institutions, or international regimes, with particular characteristics" (2005, p. 13). The possibility of effective international cooperation continuing or even blossoming "after hegemony" is reinforced by the complementary nature of hegemony and international regimes. These can both make agreements possible, and facilitate continuing compliance with the rules established in this system of world order. Keohane thus made it clear that in his analysis there is no need to expect a serious historical decline in international cooperation in the 1980s, 1990s or beyond, even as the dominance of the US within the system undergoes gradual decline. The 'system' itself will not collapse into a state of chaos or disorder. On the contrary, there is a real prospect that vital post-war international norms, institutions, and practices will not only continue, but will even be strengthened. This is a condition he refers to as "non-hegemonic cooperation" (Keohane, 2005, p. 79).

Keohane's optimistic account of the development and maintenance of co-operation after hegemony rests, however, on a view of states-as-rational-egoists. He concretely considers instances of international cooperation in fields such as monetary policy and the oil sector, as an iterated prisoner's dilemma (PD) game (following Axelrod, 1984). He extends his analysis to cover the impact of ethics, power, and institutions on international co-operation. According to Keohane, tit-for-tat is the best strategy in an iterated PD-game. However, a large number of players, asymmetric information, moral hazard and irresponsibility often complicates the situation. On the other hand, multiple parallel games in many issue areas, the unequal nature of inter-state relations (in terms of power: only some states really count), and the existence of established international organizations can alleviate these problems.

> "Thus intensive interaction among a few players helps to substitute for, or to supplement, the actions of a hegemon. As a hegemon's power erodes, a gradual shift may take place from hegemonic to non-hegemonic cooperation. Increasingly, incentives to cooperate will depend not only on the hegemon's responses but also on those of other sizeable states. Such a transition may be difficult in practice, since expectations may lag behind reality; but nothing in rational choice analysis renders it impossible" (Keohane, 2005, p. 79).

Keohane has not been alone in envisaging the possibility of future international cooperation without a single hegemon. For instance Oran Young (1989; 1991), although he retains the view of states-as-rational-egoists, has considered various forms of initiative and leadership also in creating new regimes of cooperation, including intellectual leadership. Peter Haas (1989; 1992) goes beyond the state-economism of Keohane and many others[8] and argues that there are transnational communities of experts, who

---

[8] Sonja Amadae (2015) traces the causes of the decline of virtues and common good in the American political system in the rise of rational choice theory and especially

share epistemic standpoints, and who are able to take part in the process of interest and identity formation both within states as well as within the regional or global level, often facilitating cooperation. Moreover, rules and institutional arrangements are important, because they enable and facilitate learning that can, and often does, lead to the convergence of the policies of states. For instance, along the lines of this perspective, John Ikenberry suggests that the origin of the Bretton Woods system should not be seen merely in terms of the "structural" power of the US but also in terms of an epistemic community of British and US economists and policy specialists, which fostered the Anglo-American agreement (Ikenberry, 1992).

The concept of epistemic community is in some ways similar to that of world order (or "world order model"; see footnote 3), but more limited. For Braithwaite and Drahos (2000), the world is already "post-hegemonic" in the sense that while it has been frequently the case that if the US and the EU agree on a particular form of global cooperation and regulatory change, this change gets fostered. However, under certain circumstances the will and initiatives of many other states and NGOs and key individuals have made a difference; and the role of transnational networks and epistemic communities is often decisive. Since Braithwaite and Drahos wrote their book, the role of the BRICS countries has grown, as is evident from the stalemate of the WTO Doha round.

The neo-Gramscians have gone further toward developing a dialectical account of the development of global institutions of cooperation. Robert Cox (1987; 1996), in particular has emphasised that there are always different kinds of social forces involving capabilities for production or destruction; institutional arrangements; and collective understandings.[9] Once created, institutional arrangements "take on their own life" and can "become a battleground for opposing tendencies, or rival institutions may reflect different tendencies". New forms of social existence can emerge, made

---

game theory as exemplified by the Prisoner's Dilemma model. Game theory was used, among other things, for developing nuclear strategies for the US state during the Cold War. Thus it is best seen as *constitutive* of some key state practices rather than as an external explanation of them.

[9] See also the recent special issue of *Globalizations*: "From International Relations to World Civilizations: The Contributions of Robert W Cox", edited by Shannon Brincat, Vol. 13:5, October 2016.

possible by (new) forms of production but also as a response to the consequences of certain modes and relations of production. Novel forms of social existence necessarily imply new collective understandings and systems of knowledge that are constitutive of their existence and often articulated by "organic intellectuals". Consequently, these emergent new actors, groups and collectives can then take part in the struggles within and about certain institutional arrangements, and also within and about those that have to do with the governance of global political economy. Systems are open, change is ubiquitous and everything is historical, although there are patterned processes that enable us to anticipate aspects of the future.[10] The "dialectics of world orders" occurs within existing practical and institutional settings, but they may also contribute to the transformation of these arrangements and settings.

Trumponomics: its possible and likely global consequences

The demise of the Bretton Woods international monetary system in the early 1970s was a consequence of the US unilateral abandonment of US dollar-gold convertibility. The so-called "Nixon shocks" rocketed throughout the world economy, producing profound monetary and economic instability, which arguably persists to the present. Contrary to mythologised accounts of "benevolent" US "hegemony", the actual historical record reveals contradictory policies by the dominant power throughout the post-Bretton Woods era. The present Trump administration's economic and strategic policies represent important continuities and indeed intensification of past US non-cooperation internationally, rather than an abrupt about-face.

---

[10] In his writings from the early 1990s, Cox (1996, pp. 231-2, 311) foresaw remarkably well the possible and likely developments of the next 25 years. He analyzed the neoliberal era in terms of a global Polanyian double movement and contestations among different social forces and world order models. The decline of hegemony in the system "undermines conviction in the legitimacy of the principles upon which the globalization thrust is grounded". Segmented polarization leads to identity politics, where nationalism rises and "Islam, for instance can become a metaphor for Third World revolt against Western capitalist domination". "The other tendency is toward a world of economic blocs", competing for shares in world markets and raw materials. And "a financial crisis is the most likely way in which the existing world order could begin to collapse".

Trump's economic and security policies mostly just radicalise existing US foreign policy practices, although this radicalisation may also involve qualitative changes, for example in US trade policy, where self-regard is now assuming also protectionist forms. Chief White House strategist Steve Bannon, in a 2014 speech, invoked the Italian fascist thinker Julius Evola, saying that "changing the system is not a question of questioning and polemicizing, but of blowing everything up" (Navidi, 2017). This point of view also reflects a new attitude of greater US assertiveness in foreign and security policy. According to former US Secretary of State Madeleine Albright, attending the recent Munich security conference in mid-February 2017, representatives from several countries, including Turkey, Iran, China, and Russia made speeches invoking the theme of a "Post-Western World" (Glasser, 2017). Albright's impression of reactions from other states to the new US foreign policy stance reveals a change of mood, "there was a sense that the bullying approach of the Trump administration was alienating people rather than giving them solace in terms of the fact that we still were a united world." She lamented that at Munich, the US had moved from being the "centre of attention" to becoming "the centre of doubt" (ibid.).

Alongside his intentions to conduct a very large infrastructural investment plan, the US president, in a speech on 24 February 2017 to the Conservative Action Conference, pledged to execute "one of the greatest military build-ups in American history", upgrading all aspects of the US military, both offensive and defensive. First indications of the 2018 federal budget outline by the White House also includes core emphasis on strengthening the US intelligence and national security apparatus, including homeland security and the law enforcement agencies. The commitment by the new administration to a balanced budget approach, however, despite the anticipated large increase in military and security expenditures, means that many other areas of federal spending would undergo very deep cuts, for instance funding for the Environmental Protection Agency, or even the State Department, along with many other federal department budgets and programmes. The Heritage Foundation has apparently initiated discussion circulating on Capitol Hill aiming at cumulative reduction of federal spending of 10.2 trillion US dollars over a ten-year period. However, congressional approval and formal appropriation legislation is necessary for these policy ideas to be translated into reality, and this, given the recent history of deep divisions on fiscal policy issues across the political spectrum in Congress, seems doubtful. If these policies are ever executed in full, this represents nothing less than a radical transformation of the state itself, and a reorientation of its primary roles in both domestic and global contexts.

All this is an example of a process that has become self-reinforcing. Over time, this process has led to pathological learning by reducing collective learning capacity and by hardening, on the whole and over time, the will of the changing US foreign policy makers. Trump's election is a further step in this process. Already in the 1990s and early 2000s there were a large number of US international non-cooperations, including its posture towards ILO conventions, the Law of the Sea Convention, the Convention on Biological Diversity, the Kyoto protocol, the International Criminal Court and the Landmines treaty. At present, there are concerns that the new US administration intends to withdraw or not cooperate with the Paris Agreement on climate change, arguably the single most important global issue for effective international cooperation to address a severe threat to human security. There are rumours circulating in Washington that the US administration is considering withdrawing from the UN Human Rights Council, in part due to alleged "bias against Israel" in that organisation. George Soros, the well-known global financier and promoter of a global open society named the US as "the major obstacle to international cooperation today" already 15 years ago (Soros, 2002, p. 166). Moreover, Soros shared the observation of many that despite the US holding "special responsibility" due to its globally dominant position, the US has "not always sought to abide by the same rules that apply to others" (ibid., p. 167).

The exercise of double standards by the US, and the dogged pursuit of its own national sovereignty and narrow "national interests", contradicts and tends to undermine the course of international cooperation and thus destabilise the world economy (when one is actually applying double standards is of course open to conflicting interpretations). The irony in this historical situation is that the US appears, both past and present, to assume that the "others" will nevertheless continue to abide by the agreed rules, norms and principles, though often it does not do so itself. Future scenarios of global change will now largely pivot upon how all these "others" will respond to changes in US attitudes and actions. Will the US continue to act uncooperatively internationally, and single-mindedly pursue its vision of strengthened "national sovereignty" (at home and abroad)? The consequences of such a course are likely to be highly disruptive, not only for the formal sphere of international cooperation and prospects for future global governance, but for the global economic system as well. A spiral of aggressive actions and retaliatory reactions could be set in motion. The probable long-term consequences of such a pattern are quite well known, as any reading of the first half of the 20th century will reveal (see e.g. Moser, 2016).

There are 2 x 3 different possibilities, some of them more likely than others, as depicted in Table 1. First, there are two possibilities regarding how radical Trump's foreign economic and security policies will turn out to be. It is possible, in principle, that through being forced to make compromises because of checks and balances and multiple interests within the US, and by learning from experiences about the effects of decentralised tit-for-tat sanctions brought about by the international systems of cooperation, Trump will eventually moderate his stance on a number of issues. The full realisation of the stated aims of the Trump administration may require increasingly overt authoritarianism, which in turn is likely to lead to widespread resistance within the US, including in terms of possible efforts to remove President Trump from office. This scenario entails intensifying domestic conflict and ideological polarisation, already arguably rather severe. Such conflict, including in potentially violent forms, could precipitate calls to "restore order", thus reinforcing the trend towards erosion of checks and balances and greater domestic repression of the opposition. However unlikely it may still be, a "civil war" in the US is not anymore an excluded possibility.

Table 1 Six scenarios about the effects of Trumponomics, especially in trade

	Double standards (no retaliation by others)	Limited retaliation targeted to the US	Generalised "beggar-thy-neighbour" policies
Moderate Trump	A	B	
Radical Trump		C	D

Out of the six theoretical possibilities, four seem relevant in practice. Moderate Trump is compatible with (A) double standards or (B) limited retaliation. Radical Trump will either (C) trigger limited and targeted retaliation against the US (the rest of the world will continue to abide by the rules of the WTO and bilateral and regional free trade arrangements amongst themselves) or (D) create a generalizable example to be followed, leading to widespread "beggar-thy-neighbour" policies. B and C mean that the US share of world imports (already down from 17 percent in 2000 to just 12 percent in 2013) and US share of world exports will likely fall further (already down from 12 percent in 2000 to just above 8 percent in 2013).[11] D would provoke, at a minimum, a global recession and, at the maximum, a severe global depression.

The Trump administration has already announced a new foreign trade doctrine, known officially as the "America First Trade Policy" (see the website of the United States Trade Representative for details at: https://ustr.gov/). The United States Trade Representative website describes the aims of this policy as "ensuring that American workers are given a fair shot at competing across the globe... On a level playing field, Americans can compete fairly and win." It is a central policy goal to keep existing companies located within the US and that overall "companies compete to set up manufacturing in the U.S." thus generating new jobs, tax revenues, and prosperity. However, the majority of jobs that have recently been lost within the US economy are arguably as much or possibly more due to automation than to the effects of foreign trade or out-sourcing abroad. The degree to which this new US trade doctrine of "America First" will be neo-protectionist in orientation remains to be seen, but the president has previously indicated that the US could potentially impose unilateral trade tariffs on partners that in its view are not playing fair with the US. This includes signatories to past and future trade agreements with the US who subsequently, in US perception, do not correctly fulfil their obligations under the agreement. According to the president, the US could cancel any trade agreement after a 30-day grace

---

[11] A mere look at the export and import figures would suggest a rapid decline in US competitiveness, but reality is more complicated. For example, Mandel (2012) argues that the decline is mostly due to the changing composition of the products traded internationally (the rest of the world is increasingly trading goods that the US does not produce) and the diminished share of U.S. GDP in global output, i.e. not due to the relative competitiveness of US firms.

period during which the US would seek compliance by their trade partner. During his first few days in office, president Trump used executive powers to order US withdrawal from the Transpacific Trade Partnership agreement (TTP), to the consternation of several key trade partners, including Japan and Australia, who have been supporting the multilateral agreement.

Trade protectionism via tariffs or complicated arrangements of taxation are not the only forms of potential beggar-thy-neighbour policies, of course. Attempts to enhance external competitiveness by means of internal devaluation or tax competition can be equally harmful, albeit in a different way. A number of countries, and the EU as a whole, are keen to increase their competitiveness. The idea is to increase demand for national goods and services in the world markets – at the expense of other countries. World imports and exports cancel out. Although it is not impossible for all countries to simultaneously increase the value of their exports and imports, their overall sum is always zero. The same holds true for investments. There is no aggregate level historical evidence that corporate tax cuts would have increased the overall pool of investments. Rather the opposite seems to be true: investment rates have been declining, at least in the OECD world (if not in expanding economies such as China and India). If corporate tax cuts have a positive effect on the level of real investments in one given country, it will likely do so at the expense of other countries. Combined with measures of austerity (that may appear desirable to budget-balancers in part because of budgetary effects of the tax cuts), these kinds of downward spirals tend to reduce total effective demand regionally and, to a degree, globally. Overt protectionism would come on top of these other measures and strengthen their already significant effects.

In his first presidential address to the joint session of the US Congress, on 28 February, 2017, president Trump outlined the main elements of his administration's new economic policy goals, revealing aspects of his budget proposals for Congressional debate and approval. The main elements of the new economic policy include: a one trillion dollar infrastructural programme (including a 25 billion dollar project to construct the Wall on the border with Mexico); tax reductions for the middle classes (but also for US corporations, and the very wealthy); a big increase in military spending (estimated at 54 billion dollars in the first year; to "rebuild" the US military, and purchase advanced weapons systems); the repeal of Obamacare (with the stated aim of reducing the costs of health insurance); and some general aims to improve childcare provision, women's health, and promote clean air and water. (Politico Magazine 01-03-2017) Whether and to what extent any of the very ambitious spending proposals entailed in this programme will eventually attain full Congressional approval and legislative authorisation remains doubtful, given the fiscal conservatism amongst many Republicans, and scepticism and resistance amongst many Democrats in both houses of Congress.

The Trump administration is also proposing potentially far-reaching financial deregulation, accompanied by major tax cuts for corporations and the richest 1 percent of income earners (one estimate predicts that under Trump's probable tax reform measures, the income of the top 1% of income earners would see their annual income increase by 13.5%, while average earners income would increase by only 1.8% (Navidi, 2017) Financial deregulation would annul the corrective measures and learning concerning reregulation of the financial sector (Mackintosh, 2016) that took place in the wake of the global financial crisis of 2008-9. US financial deregulation enacted now may have the further effect of impeding future global cooperation in this area.[12] On 2 February 2017, president Trump, by executive order, instructed a review of the Dodd-Frank Act, which was enacted during the Obama era to ensure that there would never be another 2008-style financial sector meltdown.

The stated aim is to make US financial companies more competitive – but in all likelihood at the expense of global financial stability. The periodic crises since the late 1970s have been part of a larger boom-bust process. The underlying super-bubble based on credit expansion and financial multiplication has grown in potential for three decades. It has continued to grow after the weak recovery from the global crisis of 2008-9; and it has been gradually assembling conditions for an even bigger crash probably in

---

[12] This is however more complicated than it may first appear. The Trade in Services Agreement (TiSA) is more in line with the ideology of the Trump administration than the TTP or TTIP, and it seems that the US continues to participate in the TiSA negotiations. These negotiations are basically about de-regulation (often amounting to neoliberal re-regulation) and privatization. Trump's review of the Dodd-Frank Act is fully in line with the aims of TiSA.

the late 2010s, at the latest in the early 2020s (an expectation outlined in Patomäki, 2010, pp. 79-80). The Trump administration's financial deregulation policy seems determined to speed up this process, making an early large-scale financial bust more likely. The effects of financial deregulation, combined with other aspects affecting the future stability of respect for the rule of law within the US, may also have the unintended consequence of decreasing the attractiveness of the US economy as an economic "safe haven" globally.

Tax cuts for the rich may also be accompanied by a lax policy toward global tax havens that help firms and companies to avoid taxation, although the economic nationalist side of the Trump administration would also at the same time logically have an interest that companies really do pay tax in the US on their worldwide profits. Be that as it may, financialization and the growing financial super-bubble have contributed to growing inequalities across the world (by increasing r and decreasing g in Piketty's $r > g$), while the growing inequalities have added to the volume of speculation (because the rich tend to consume only a small part of their extra income). For the same reason, tax cuts to the rich have also the lowest fiscal multiplier and weakest stimulating effect on the economy, thus probably aggravating the deficit of the US federal budget. The Fed can of course print more money, but not endlessly without spelling trouble.

In terms of trade policy, only (D) in Table 1 would take the world directly to a situation reminiscent of the early 1930s, while also B and C are steps in the same direction. Moreover, there is another path that may lead to the same outcome as (D). A new major global financial crash during Trump's first term could easily trigger a further worldwide round of growing economic nationalism. It is worth stressing that "the relatively benign international political environment in 2007-2008 compared with the intense security dilemma of the inter-war years were also essential in not making a bad situation worse" (Kirshner, 2014, p. 47). Next time the international political environment will be less benign.

Conclusions: disabling effects and the possibility of transformative praxes

The US now seems set on a course to contribute to creating the conditions for a new era of international discord, leading to the further destabilisation of the (neo)liberal "world order" that it had itself co-designed and upheld, though of course also to project and protect its own advantages, interests, and values on a world scale. The recently intensified historical tendencies of increased oligarchization of wealth and authoritarianization of power are being produced by the system itself, but threaten the stability of liberal democratic culture.[13] Growing popular discontent with the status quo, and the rise of nationalist, populist, and authoritarian ideological and political currents, are symptomatic of rising frustration and popular anger with the established "order" (for a discussion of the two sides of Polanyian double movement, see Patomäki, 2014).

With the anticipated unintended effects of ongoing developments in the US and other parts of the world, historical preparations are now in motion that are likely to produce the next major systemic crisis, or even global catastrophe. These unintended consequences will be deeply disabling, calling into question the prevailing paradigm of (neo)liberal "world order", including its characteristic modes of subjectivity, practices, and institutions. At present, as judged from the impressions of participants at the recent Munich security conference in mid-February 2017, there has emerged "a lack of consensus even on what a liberal order is" (Leonard, 2017). There is a growing perception, and increasing global comment, that the era of Western liberal dominance is now ending, and that a "post-Western" world order is dawning. Power and influence have diffused significantly, through processes of globalization, and economic expansion by "emerging powers",

---

[13] For discussions on how growing inequalities, associated with the post-Bretton Woods developments, corrode the rule of law and thereby the basis of democracy, see Sayer, 2016, pp. 267-84; Stiglitz, 2013, pp. 234-58. For a more general discussion on how the neoliberal world had, in effect, moved to a stage of "post-democracy" already by the early 2000s, thus paving the way for further authoritarianization of politics in the 2010s, see Crouch, 2004. For an early analysis of the relationship between globalization, hegemony, empire, and "neoliberal disorder" see Kiely, 2005.

including the BRICS nations and others, such as Turkey (Gray and Gills, 2016).

This is a time of high and increasing structural tension between the persistence of the territorially bounded and sovereign nation-state system, versus the realities of a highly transnationalized global economic system (Gills, 2000; Gills, 2011). Arguably, a Polanyian "double movement" is still in motion, but of its "left" and "right" ideological manifestations, the latter appears dominant, at least for the time being. The whole idea of a world order, however, is once again contested. The historical outcome of this global contestation, both ideologically and practically, will turn upon how states and social forces around the world will act and respond in the coming period of global history. This outcome is historically indeterminate, as reality involves complex multi-path developmental processes that can be interwoven, or contradictory in numerous ways.

Finally, in our view it is mistaken to prematurely conclude that because historical developments are not smooth and linear, and because many developments at present seem dangerously regressive or chaotic, that there is no rational (and progressive) tangential direction to world history. We claim, from a dialectical perspective, that the rational tendency is manifested in potential toward a system that is capable of increased reflexive self-regulation, in terms of wider wholes and (contested) common good, rather than limitation to actions and responses from particular (powerful) actors' perspectives.

This rational tendency may manifest itself, for example, as democratic global Keynesianism, enabling (even radical) processes of decommodification, and new syntheses in the market/social nexus. Such a historical tendency in response to the present "disorder" would constitute an emerging alternative "democratic world order". Its emergence and consolidation are historically contingent upon new forms of cosmopolitan transformative praxis (Hosseini, Gills and Goodman, 2016). Such a process is also dependent upon the rationality of participating individual actors (cf. Bhaskar, 1993, p. 91). Thus we can anticipate the construction of new common institutions (of international cooperation and global governance) to evolve, in either evolutionary or dialectical fashion, replacing certain aspects of the authority of territorial sovereign states with more adequate (social, Keynesian, democratic) regional and global arrangements. They can be anticipated in terms of overcoming definite lacks, absences, problems, and contradictions of the world economy step-by-step – or more drastically, through many institutional transformations at once, perhaps following a future major global crisis or some form of catastrophe.

As Yeats evoked us to reflect, even as "things fall apart", "surely some revelation is at hand".

References

Alker, Hayward (1996) *Rediscoveries and Reformulations. Humanistic Methodologies for International Studies*, Cambridge University Press: Cambridge.

Alker, Hayward, Amin, Tahir, Biersteker, Thomas and Inoguchi, Takashi (1996) "Concluding Reflections on the Dialectics of World Order", a paper prepared for the ISA-JAIR Joint Convention, 20-22 September 1996, the Makuhari Prince Hotel, Japan; available at
http://dornsife.usc.edu/assets/sites/556/docs/concluding_reflections.PDF

Amadae, Sonja (2015) *Prisoners of Reason. Game Theory and Neoliberal Political Economy*, Cambridge University Press: Cambridge.

Axelrod, Robert (1980) *The Evolution of Cooperation*, Basic Books: New York.

Bhaskar, Roy (1993) *Dialectic. The Pulse of Freedom*, Verso: London.

Braithwaite, John and Drahos, Peter (2000) *Global Business Regulation*, Cambridge University Press: Cambridge.

Brincat, Shannon (2014) "Special Issue: Dialectics and World Politics", *Globalizations* Vol 11, No. 5, October 2014. Routledge, Taylor and Francis.

Brincat, Shannon (Ed) (2016) "Special Issue: From International Relations to World Civilizations. The Contributions of Robert W. Cox", *Globalizations* Vol 13 No. 5, October 2016, Routledge, Taylor and Francis.

Bull, Hedley (1977) *The Anarchical Society. A Study of Order in World Politics*, MacMillan: Houndmills, Basingstoke.

Cox, Robert (1987) *Production, Power and World Order: Social Forces in the Making of History*, Columbia University Press: New York.

Cox, Robert (1996) *Approaches to World Order*, Cambridge University Press: Cambridge.

Crouch, Colin (2004) *Post-Democracy*, Polity: Cambridge.

Fischer, Joschka (2017) "Turning towards Authoritarianism: Is Trump Taking the US down Turkey's Path?", Project Syndicate, posted on Euronews.com 27/02/2017, available at http://www.euronews.com/2017/02/27/view-turning-towards-authoritarianism-is-trump-taking-the-us-down-turkeys-path

Frank, Andre Gunder (2014) *Reorienting the 19th Century: Global Economy in the Continuing Asian Age*, Edited with an Introduction by Robert A. Denemark, Afterword by Barry K. Gills, Paradigm Publishers, Boulder and London.

Gills, Barry K. (Ed) (1994) "The Forum: Hegemony and Social Change", *Mershon International Studies Review*, vol. 38. 361-376 (with contributions by: Christopher Chasse-Dunn, Peter Taylor, Giovanni Arrighi, Robert Cox, Henk Overbeek, Barry Gills, Andre Gunder Frank, George Modelski, and David Wilkinson)

Gills, Barry K. (Ed) (2000) *Globalization and the Politics of Resistance*, Palgrave: Houndsmill, Basingstoke.

Gills, Barry K. (2011) *Globalization in Crisis*, Routledge: London and New York.

Gilpin, Robert (1981) *War and Change in World Politics*. Cambridge: Cambridge University Press.

Gilpin, Robert (1987) *The Political Economy of International Relations*. Princeton, NJ: Princeton University Press.

Glasser, Susan (2017) "The Alpha males are back", *Politico Magazine*, 27 February, 2017.

Gray, Kevin and Barry K. Gills (2016) "South-South cooperation and the rise of the Global South", *Third World Quarterly*, Vol 37 No. 4, pp. 557-576; in Special Issue: "Rising Powers and South-South Cooperation", Kevin Gray and Barry K. Gills (Eds)

Grunberg, Isabelle (1990) "Exploring the 'Myth' of Hegemonic Stability", *International Organization*, Vol. 44(4), pp. 431-477.

Haas, Peter (1989) "Do Regimes Matter? Epistemic Communities and Mediterranean Pollution Control", *International Organization*, 43(3), pp. 377-403.

Haas, Peter (1992) "Introduction: Epistemic Communities and International Policy Coordination," *International Organization*, 46(1), pp. 1-35.

Harvey, David (2005) *A Brief History of Neoliberalism*, Oxford University Press: Oxford.

Hosseini, S.A. Hamed, Barry K. Gills and James Goodman (2016) "Towards Transversal Cosmopolitanism: Understanding Alternative Praxes in the Global Field of Transformative Movements", *Globalizations*, Published online 16 August 2016. pp 1-18. http://dx.doi.org/10.1080/14747731.2016.1217619

Ikenberry, John (1992) "A World Economy Restored: Expert Consensus and the Anglo-American Postwar Settlement", *International Organization*, 46(1), pp. 289-321.

Keohane, Robert (1980) "The Theory of Hegemonic Stability and Changes in International Economic Regimes, 1967-77". In O.Holsti, R.Siverson and A.George (eds.): *Change in the International System*. Boulder, CO: Westview Press, pp. 131-62.

Keohane, Robert (2005) *After Hegemony. Cooperation and Discord in the World Political Economy*. Princeton Classic Edition, with a new preface. Princeton, NJ: Princeton University Press.

Kiely, Ray (2005) *Empire in the age of globalisation: US hegemony and neoliberal disorder*, London: Pluto Press.

Kindleberger, Charles (1973) *The World in Depression 1929-1939*. London: Allen Lane Penguin Press.

Kindleberger, Charles (1981) "Dominance and Leadership in the International Economy: Exploitation, Public Goods and Free Riders". *International Studies Quarterly*, 25(2), pp.242-54.

Kishner, Jonathan (2014) "International Relations Then and Now: Why the Great Recession Was Not the Great Depression", *History Of Economic Ideas*, 22(3), pp. 47-69.

Krasner, Stephen (1976) "State Power and the Structure of International Trade", *World Politics*, 28(3), pp. 317-47.

Layne, Christopher (2012): "This Time It's Real: The End of Unipolarity and the Pax Americana", *International Studies Quarterly* 56(1), pp.203–213.

Leonard, Mark (2017) "Will the Liberal Order Survive? If So, Which Version?", Project Syndicate, posted on Euronews.com 28/02/2017, available at http://www.euronews.com/2017/02/28/view-will-the-liberal-order-survive-if-so-which-version

Mackintosh, Stuart P.M. (2016) *The Redesign of the Global Financial Architecture: The Return of State Authority*, Routledge: London and New York.

Mandel, Benjamin R. (2012) "Why Is the U.S. Share of World Merchandise Exports Shrinking?", *Current Issues*, Federal Reserve Bank of New York, 18(1), available www.newyorkfed.org/research/current_issues

Moser, John E. (2015) *The Global Great Depression and the Coming of World War II*, Routledge: London & New York.

Navidi, Sandra (2017) "American Democracy: Will Trump blow everything up?" Project Syndicate 2017, posted on Euronews 28-02-2017.

Patomäki, Heikki (2008) *The Political Economy of Global Security. War, Future Crises and Changes in Global Governance*, Routledge: London and New York.

Patomäki, Heikki (2010) "What Next? An Explanation of the 2008-9 Slump and Two Scenarios of the Shape of Things to Come", *Globalizations*, 7(1), pp. 67-84.

Patomäki, Heikki (2014) "On the Dialectics of Global Governance in the 21st Century: A Polanyian Double Movement?", *Globalizations*, 11(5), pp.751–768.

Politico Magazine (2017) 1 March 2017. (Summary and report on President Trump's speech before the US Congress on 28 February, 2017)

Rodrik, Dani (2001) "The Global Governance of Trade as if Development Really Mattered", Revised July 2001, John F. Kennedy School of Government: Cambridge, MA, available at http://www.giszpenc.com/globalciv/rodrik1.pdf
Sayer, Andrew (2016) *Why We Can't Afford the Rich*, Policy Press: Bristol.

Springer, Simon, Birch, Kean and MacLeavy, Julie. (ed.) (2016) *The Handbook of Neoliberalism*, London & New York: Routledge.

Steger, Manfred (2009) *Globalisms. The Great Ideological Struggle of the Twenty-First Century*. Third edition. Rowman & Littlefield: Lanham, MD.

Stiglitz, Joseph (2003) *The Roaring Nineties: A New History of the World's Most Prosperous Decade*, W.W.Norton: New York.

Stiglitz, Joseph (2013) *The Price of Inequality*, Penguin Books: London.

Strange, Susan (1987) "The Persistent Myth of Lost Hegemony", *International Organization,* Vol. 41, No. 4 (Autumn) pp. 551-574.

Triffin, Robert (1961) *Gold and the Dollar Crisis*, New Haven, CT: Yale University Press.

Triffin, Robert (1968) *Our International Monetary System: Yesterday, Today, and Tomorrow*, New York: Random House.

Unger, Roberto Mangabeira (2007) *Free Trade Reimagined. The World Division of Labor and the Method of Economics*, Princeton University Press: Princeton.

Wohlforth, William C. (2012) "How Not to Evaluate Theories", *International Studies Quarterly* (56):1, pp. 219–222.

Young, Oran (1989) "The Politics of International Regime Formation: Managing Natural Resources and the Environment", *International Organization*, 43(3), pp. 349-375.

Young, Oran (1991) "Political Leadership and Regime Formation: On the Development of Institutions in International Society", *International Organization*, 45(3), pp. 281-308.

Pussynomics: regression to mean

Susan Feiner [University of Southern Maine, USA]

> "He's a poor person's idea of a rich person. They see him.
> They think, 'If I were rich, I'd have a fabulous tie like that.
> Why are my ties not made of 400 acres of polyester?' All
> that stuff he shows you in his house – the gold faucets – if
> you won the lottery, that's what you'd buy" (Leibowitz, 2016).

The world knows this American president for crude sexist/sexual
declarations, compulsive pathological lying, and friendships with racists,
homophobes and anti-semites. So what? Plenty of liars, bigots and skirt
chasers have called the White House home. Still he's terrifying, conjuring
dread as surely as the Bates Motel in Hitchcock's *Psycho*. Donald Trump –
salesman, TV huckster and sexual predator – triggers primitive, infantile
fears. From his freebie media campaign to his policies and executive orders
he fuels a fear so intense that it works through denial. The hellfire and
brimstone, glitzy gaudy glamor, tough love concoction that is Donald Trump,
masks fears – harbored by many, not just those for whom the economy is
not working – that our beloved caretakers, upon whom we depend for our
daily survival, will not deliver. What explains the appeal of a man who
believes that, "if this country gets any kinder or gentler, it's literally going to
cease to exist" (Trump, 1990).

Right wing populism as fundamentalist religion

> "The point is that you can't be too greedy" (Trump, 1987,
> p. 47).

Between 1987 and 1995 The American Academy of Sciences sponsored the
interdisciplinary "Fundamentalism Project". Studying fundamentalist religions

all over the world, scholars "concluded that, regardless of the religion, fundamentalism has several commonalities". These are:

- Men are to lead and women and children follow. Wives are to be subservient to their husbands. Often, this subservience applies to sisters toward their brothers. A woman's role in life is to be a homemaker (Mike Pence).
- The rules of their religion are complex and rigid and must be followed. Therefore, to avoid any confusion, children of fundamentalists must be sequestered in an environment of like-minded adherents to the corresponding fundamentalist religion. Especially so in their schooling (Besty DeVos).
- There is no pluralism. Their rules apply to everyone everywhere (Jeff Sessions).
- There is a distinct group of insiders and all others are outsiders. Insiders are nurtured and cared for. Outsiders are cast off and fought (Steve Bannon).
- They pine for an older age and a past when their religion was pure, as largely they no longer see it as such. Often, this time never truly existed, but they have a nostalgic view of a Utopian past and they long to acquire it (Make America Great Again).

Fundamentalist religion, the program of Trump, and the regressive economics he promotes are barely distinguishable.

Two trends over the past 30 to 40 years puzzled many social scientists. Wilkinson and Pickett (2010, 36-37) discuss the contradiction posed by surveys that found rising levels of self-esteem across the US population simultaneous with other studies that found heightened experiences of anxiety and depression. Why/how could people with strong self-esteem be increasingly troubled by anxiety and depression? On the face of it these trends are contradictory. But distinguishing between kinds of self-esteem resolves this conundrum. Digging into the data unearthed what is now deemed "unhealthy self-esteem", a pumping up of one's self image as a mode of protection from the "social evaluative threats" generated by rising levels of social inequality. People with healthy self-esteem exhibit "happiness, confidence, (are) able to accept criticism, an ability to make friends, and so on". In contrast, those with unhealthy self-esteem "showed tendencies to violence, to racism, were insensitive to others and were bad at personal relationships". Unhealthy self-esteem – sometimes labeled narcissicim, chuffing one's self up as a defensive strategy to counter a sense of weakness – explains how rising self-esteem can coexist with rising levels of anxiety and depression.

Donald Trump's narcissism triggers his admirer's unhealthy self-esteem. It's not simply his narcissism that drives his acting out (middle of the night tweets about SNL, Meryl Streep or Snoop Daddy). In addition, his narcissism generates an energy loop... his behavior cons many to into seeing themselves in him. This sets up a chain reaction of back and forth reflections from Trump to supporters to Trump. Narcissism and fundamentalist religions feed each other too. As Wilkerson and Pickett demonstrate, the dramatic increases in inequality fuel the many social dysfunctions that are associated with unhealthy high self-esteem. Skinheads, white nationalists and the multitudes of hate groups aligned with Trump are not only the product of long simmering resentments, these movements are also the result of the explosive income inequality that marks the US political economy.

Consider too the ways that dualistic thinking, anti-pluralism, and cognitive rigidity fuel both right wing populism and religious fundamentalism. Dualistic thinkers are naïve. The "proper" authorities know everything, "knowledge is received truth. It is facts, correct theories, and right answers" (Kloss, 1994). Except when facts and theories challenge deeply held certainties... for those occasions there are "alternative facts" and the "lying media".

For college professors, dualistic thinkers are among the most difficult students. Not because they misbehave (quite often they are passive and obedient), but because they are so unwilling to consider multiple, alternative interpretations or modes of analysis. Virtually all scholars of student achievement recognize that intellectual growth requires letting go of the black/white, right/wrong, true/false view of knowledge. But hanging onto dualism is made easier by conformity to religious fundamentalism, since the Church (the one true, right Church) constantly reinforces this mode of thinking. Change and growth are limited by dualism.

Trump's rightwing economic populism unites fundamentalism, narcissism and dualism to create a powerful pull to a dismal past. In the longed for bygone age fathers did know best and education comprised transmission of undisputed facts. Because the one right way of knowing was so obviously correct, violence toward unbelievers – outsiders by definition – was sanctioned by the spurious, imagined "purity". We've known for a long time that economic precarity and soaring inequality generate atavism. "Necessitous men are not free men. People who are hungry and out of a job are the stuff of which dictatorships are made" (Roosevelt, 1944).

Tower trash

> "Owning such beautiful buildings... The Empire State Building, 40 Wall Street, there are a couple of them that are just really incredible buildings. Forty Wall Street is probably the most beautiful tower in New York" (Trump, accessed March 18, 2017).

Neoliberalism worships avarice. Anything that impedes profit maximization is bad, everything that facilitates financial gain is good. Damn the human costs of austerity and deregulation. As Galbraith puts it, "Men, it is assumed, act in economic matters solely in response to pecuniary compensation or, as the only alternative, to force" (1967 [2007], 163). That's what makes grabbing pussy the purrfect analogy for Donald Trump's *Mad Max* economy of rape, pillage and plunder. Run an oil pipeline thru sacred Native lands? Do it. Sell National Parks to the highest bidder? Why not? Wreck public schools? Go for it. Zero out federal support for the arts? Happily. End food subsidies for the elderly and school aged kids? But of course. Actions that initiate flows of dollars to Trump's family and friends cause good things to happen.

It's not difficult to see that monetary incentives are not far removed from corporal punishment. "Compulsion and pecuniary compensation exist in varying degrees of association with each other" (Galbriath, 1967 [2007], 167). This atavistic view of work is motivated by fear of punishment via material deprivation. Intrinsic motivation is an oxymoron. Work, connive, collude... get wealth... buy fancy, glitzy, sparking stuff... flaunt success in the competitive struggle. Joel Grey knew what drove high ranking Nazis, "Money makes the world go round" (*Caberet,* 1972). It's no different for Trump.

The cruelty that is the flip side of money worship was captured brilliantly by Jimmy Breslin when he wrote about the full page ad placed by Trump in every NYC paper following the sexual violene in Central Park.

> "Mayor Koch has stated that hate and rancor should be removed from our hearts. I do not think so. I want to hate these muggers and murderers. They should be forced to suffer and, when they kill, they should be executed for their crimes... Yes, Mayor Koch, I want to hate these murderers and I always will. I am not looking to psychoanalyze them or understand them, I am looking to punish them... I no longer want to understand their anger. I want them to understand our anger. I want them to be afraid (Breslin, 1989).

Losers can't (and no one should let them) avoid their punishment. And punishment should always be as extreme as possible. For the millions swept up by the prison/industrial complex, punishment is literal. For the millions more working at or near the minimum wage, punishment is deprivation. For the tens of millions affected by Trump's budget, punishment is unflinching austerity. The flip side of money worship is deliberately imposed suffering. Sadism as national policy.

Forget art for art's sake or learning for learning's sake. Everything is reduced to a financial calculation. If it doesn't directly inflate the bottom line, cut it. With religious fundamentalism this bankrupt view of human motivation buttresses economic populism, "hailing" subjects, seducing the insecure to celebrate Bentham's *"felicific calculus of pain and pleasure"*, even as that calculus imposes pain on its ardent supporters. National policy of sado-masochism.

Susan Feiner

Are we family?

> "Happy families are all alike, every unhappy family is unhappy in its own way" (Tolstoy, 1877 [2004], p. 1).

A president, even one as unpresidential as Donald Trump, is the nation's metaphorical father. Trump aligns perfectly with Lakoff's (1996) "strict father" model of polity as family. The trademark "You're Fired!" reeks of tough love. Daddy Trump teaches children – everyone less rich than him – self-reliance and self-discipline through punishment. In Lakoff's view, strict father families and nurturant parent families see society through opposing world views.

	Strict Father Families	Nurturant Parent Families
Morality	Evil is all around us, constantly tempting us. Thus, the basis of morality is strong moral character, which requires self-reliance and self-discipline. The primary vices are those that dissolve self-discipline, such as laziness, gluttony, and indulgent sexuality.	The basis of morality is in understanding, respecting, and helping other people, and in seeking the happiness of one's self and of others. The primary vices are selfishness and anti-social behavior.
Child Development	Children develop self-discipline, self-reliance, and other virtues primarily through rewards and punishment, a system of "tough love". Since parents know the difference between right and wrong and children still do not, obedience to the parents is very important. Moral development basically lasts only as long as childhood; it's important to get it right the first time, because there is no "second chance".	Children develop morality primarily through interacting with and observing good people, especially good parents. Punishment is necessary in some cases, but also has the potential to backfire, causing children to adopt more violent or more anti-social ways. Though children should, in general, obey their parents, they will develop best if allowed to question their parents' decisions, to hear justifications for their parents' rules, and so on. Moral development is a lifelong process, and almost no one is so perfect as not to need improvement.
Justice	The world may be a difficult place to live, but it is basically just; people usually get what they deserve. The difficulties in one's life serve as a test to sort the deserving from the undeserving.	The world is not without justice, but it is far from the ideal of justice. Many people, for example, do not seem properly rewarded for their hard work and dedication. We must work hard to improve everyone's condition.

One of Trump Jr's classmates at The University of Pennsylvania offered this vignette of his father.

> "There were quite a few students standing around watching, trying to catch a glimpse of the famed real estate magnate," according to Melker. "Don Jr opened the door, wearing a Yankee jersey. Without saying a word, his father slapped him across the face, knocking him to the floor in front of all of his classmates. He simply said 'put on a suit and meet me outside,' and closed the door" (Melker 2017).

A unique unhappiness if ever there was one.

Picture instead a different mode of family interaction. Nurturant parent families "revolve around every family member caring for and being cared for by every other family member, with open communication between all parties, and with each family member pursuing their own vision of happiness" (Lakoff, 1996). Families living with economic security are much more likely to develop nurturant styles of being.

Trumponomics is focused on undoing economic security and amplifying pressures to restore strict father families. Wiping out the EPA, public schools, Obamacare, Social Security, Medicare, Medicaid, libraries and all manner of other civil institutions, undercuts the stability and security of all but the richest families. Families regress. However unhappy they may have been, they will surely become less happy, each in their unique way.

The atavistic pull at the center of Trump's attraction is revealed by a gendered reading of the images and metaphors which animate it. The following passages, from Lakoff's *Moral Politics* illustrate the intimate connection between visions of family and economic policy. Lakoff riffs on conservative columnist William Raspberry's take on Washington DC's budget crisis:

> "The government of the District of Columbia is reeling from a newly discovered budget shortfall of at least $722 million and there is growing talk of a congressional takeover of the city" (Lakoff, 1996, pp. 5-6).

After an example of spending he considers questionable, Raspberry says,

> "What is about to do us in... is the poor but compassionate mother with a credit card. To put it another way, a huge amount of the city's stupendous debt is the result of the local government's effort to do good things it can't afford."

He then gives a list of examples of good things the city government wants to do and which he thinks it can't afford, and (Raspberry) finishes the column as follows:

> "But a good chunk of the underlying problem is the compassionate mom's attitude that says: 'If it's good for the kid to have, then I ought to buy it—and worry later about where the money will come from.' Well, Mom not only has reached her credit limit: she's in so much trouble that scrimping and saving won't solve the problem. She'll need a bailout from Congress. But then, she has to learn to say no—not just to junk food but to quality cuts of meat she can't afford."

A radically different reading is possible.

> "One could have observed that Washington, D.C., must have city services beyond its population to serve the large number of relatively well-off civil service workers, lobbyists, and others who live in the wealthy suburbs but work in town. One could also have mentioned that it is the *responsibility* of Congress to see that the city is maintained properly and that it lives by a humane standard, indeed that it should set a standard for the country. One could then apply the metaphor of the government as parent to Congress, seeing Congress as a deadbeat dad, refusing to pay for the support of his children, the citizens of Washington, D.C. One could then have drawn the moral that deadbeat dad Congress must meet his responsibilities and pay, no matter how tough it is for him."

Conclusion

Economies and families are inextricably tied in our everyday lives and in our deepest unconscious. Primitive impulses toward exclusion, shame, and painful discipline are unleashed as families crack under the economic pressure of stagnant wages, declining benefits, deteriorating public services, and rising inequality. Pander to the rich. Destroy the social fabric. Adults, suffering the pain of harsh austerities long for the comfort of their imagined, culturally scripted old fashioned families. Such a misdirected wish. Strict-father families and the ethos of punishment are not the stuff of fulfilling household economies. Nurturant household economies require policies that solicit care from all according to their abilities and deliver care to all according to their needs.

Works cited

Breslin, Jimmy (1989) *Newsday.* http://www.newsday.com/opinion/jimmy-breslin-s-columns-on-donald-trump-1.13288319 (accessed 3/22/2017)

Kloss, Robert (1994) *College Teaching*, Vol. 42, No. 4 (Fall) pp. 151-158. Heldref Publications (http://www.jstor.org/stable/27558677).

Lakoff, George (1996) *Moral Politics*. University of Chicago Press. Chicago IL.

Leibowitz, Fran (2016) *Vanity Fair.* http://www.vanityfair.com/news/2016/10/fran-lebowitz-trump-clinton-election (accessed 3/22/17)

Melker (2017) Facebook, quoted in

http://www.deathandtaxesmag.com/308883/donald-trump-jr-diaper-don-college-piss-drunk/ (accessed 2/28/17)

Roosevelt, Franklin D. (1944) *State of the Union Address.* (Several sources cite old English property law, Vernon v. Bethell (1762) 28 ER 838 as the origin of the phrase "Necessitous men are not free men").

Trump, Donald J. http://www.pbs.org/wnet/newyork/series/interview/trump.html, (accessed March 18, 2017)

Trump, Donald J. (1990) *Playboy.* https://www.playboy.com/articles/playboy-interview-donald-trump-1990 (accessed March 18, 2017)

Wilkerson, Richard and Kate Pickett (2007) *Spirit Level: why greater equality is better for everyone.* Bloomsbury Press. London and NY.

Trump's contradictions and the future of the Left

Boris Kagarlitsky [IGSO[1] and MSSES[2], Russia]

The first 100 days of Trump's presidency did not resemble the honeymoon normally enjoyed by newly elected leaders of the United States. The severity and aggressiveness of the debate was unprecedented. Liberals threw at Trump all of their hatred, while the conservative public – all of its delight. Opinions in Russia are split roughly along the same lines as they are in America.

The situation on the Left is much more complex. While some repeat, like well-trained parrots, the talking points of liberal propaganda about Trump's agenda being racist and homophobic, passionately quoting the CNN and the *New York Times*, the others, exhibit at least some schadenfreude about the disintegration of Democratic Party, and the collapse of free trade agreements. However, even in the last case, the discussion, with a few exceptions, does not go beyond the question of whether we like or do not like the 45th president of the US and his decisions.

Assessments of Trump's personality, and even actions, are the last thing we need if we are to understand the perspectives of his term as a president of the US. We would be much better served by an analysis of the processes unfolding before us. Meanwhile, the decisions the new president has made so far are clear evidence of the contradictory character of his policies. Trump and his entourage, perhaps, have not realized the extent of the problem yet, but the future course of events will force them to do so.

---

[1] Institute for Globalization Studies and Social Movements.
[2] Moscow School of Social and Economic Sciences.

Trumponomics: Causes And Consequences

The wavering of Senator Bernie Sanders, who expresses approval of the decisions of the White House one day, while unleashing a fierce criticism the very next, is revealing in its own way.

In fact, a number of actions and statements by Donald Trump put him on par with the anti-globalists who protested in Seattle in 1999. But his other decisions and statements unequivocally portray the president as not just a conservative, but as an ardent supporter of the free market and liberal economic doctrines.

On the one hand, Trump cancels Trans-Pacific Partnership agreement and insists on revising NAFTA, the embodiment of neoliberal principles. He berates NATO, talks about Canada-style public health insurance, calls for lower drug prices and even pushes through the congress six weeks parental leave for women, something never achieved by any Democratic administration with the reputation of being pro-feminist. The president meets with trade unionists at the White House and discusses joint efforts to create jobs. But on the same day, Trump cancels restrictions and regulations governing the activities of the major Wall Street banks, while negotiations on the price control of medicines turn into promises to lower taxes for manufacturers.

The nomination of Betsy DeVos as a head of the Department of Education was a complete scandal. And not only because of her conservative views, but also because the lady who was put in charge of the public schools, was in a sharp conflict with the professional community – how does this fit in with the promise to return power to the people?

It is most likely, though, that from Trump's point of view, there is no contradiction. Yes, Betsy DeVos and teachers experience mutual hatred, but on the other hand, she is in agreement with the most ignorant part of parents, who are confident that the less children learn in school, the better it is for them.

President, like most of his voters, does not believe in global warming, but he believes in free markets and low taxes. At the same time, he believes that the US domestic market should be protected from unfair foreign competition. Simply speaking: liberalism for "our own" protectionism from the "strangers".

This is exactly how American capitalism was developing in the first third of the 20th century.

Alas, the times have changed. Transnational capital, formed by the end of the twentieth century, has changed the rules of the game not only globally, but also in the domestic market. These new rules brought the world to the current systemic crisis. The collapse of the neo-liberal world order is a spontaneous and natural process, generated by its own self-destructive logic, and not by the ideological views of anti-globalists or Trump. Ironically, globalization by weakening and destroying domestic markets, the public sector and the welfare state undermined global demand. Weaker states in the long run mean that we are going to experience not more economic growth and faster expansion of international trade, but on the contrary we are ending up with global stagnation. This process of decay began long before the arrival of the current President in the White House. The victory of Trump is itself a consequence of the crisis, which has already fully unfolded and penetrated into all pores of the society. To the dismay of liberal intellectuals in London, Moscow and New York, this decay is irreversible. Either you change the system or thongs will only get worse, whether you like it or not. In 2016, politics finally synchronized with the economics.

The principal difference between the 45th US president and his liberal opponents is not that he does not believe in globalization, but that he is aware of its collapse, and therefore does not attempt to save the crumbling system, but seeks to build a new policy which would take the new reality into consideration. The question is: which direction this policy will take.

If the collapse of the old system is, to some extent, a natural process, at least at the economic level, the formation of a new social order does not happen automatically. As a consequence of his intent to reconsider the rules of the game, Trump is faced with the need to introduce his own positive program. And here he inevitably faces the objective contradiction between the interests of different social and economic groups which see the necessity of change.

Trumponomics: Causes And Consequences

Consistent implementation of protectionist policies intended to restore the internal market will not be effective without measures aimed at regulation and reconstruction of the US economy. One may call for re-industrialization of the United States on the basis of market principles, but the nature of these principles objectively prevents them from resolving this problem. If the situation were different, not only would the problem have been already solved to a certain extent, but also Trump would probably not have had a chance to occupy the Oval Office at the White House.

Attempts to balance the budget by increasing import duties, while reducing taxes to encourage production without reducing profits of financial corporations and raise wages of workers without affecting the interests of entrepreneurs, sooner or later will lead the US president's policies to a logical impasse. It will be impossible to come out of it without making a political choice in favor of one party or another. Contradictions are only worsening as the government is forced to make decisions on matters of foreign policy, provoking disagreements and crises within the administration.

In fact, the contradictions of Trump's policy reflect the contradictions within the broad cross-class coalition that brought him to the White House. No matter what the liberal pundits say, these were the votes of workers who brought him the victory. Not the so-called "white men", but the working class, who openly and, largely, in solidarity, made a stand against the Washington establishment. To a large extent his election campaign reproduced the ideas and slogans of the Left. The Republican candidate was supported by farmers, clerks and provincial intelligentsia. This really was an uprising of the forgotten and resentful provincial America against the spoiled people in California and the cosmopolitan officials from Washington, who comfortably exploit cheap labor of illegal migrants, against the liberal elite, who turned their back on their own country long time ago.

It's not surprising that we're seeing a rise of the working class. But a substantial part of the bourgeoisie is also unhappy with the current situation. Donald Trump is not a worker or a farmer. He and his entourage are very typical representatives of a medium size American enterprise which is tied to the domestic market and is in conflict with transnational corporations.

All groups that have supported him were equally offended and humiliated by the policies pursued by the metropolitan liberals and were interested in reconsideration of these policies. They all need protectionism. But at this point their unity ends. The interests of classes and groups, who led Trump to the White House, do not coincide in the positive part of the program.

Trump's attacks on political correctness are by no means a manifestation of his personal feelings, his lack of restraint and rudeness; it's a deliberate strategy to consolidate the social groups that have suffered under the dictatorship of political correctness. No matter how different they are, all of them have been hit financially, losing incomes, jobs and revenues.

Trump's propaganda is effective, not because, as intellectuals believe, it resonates with the feelings and prejudices of the people, but because it reflects their real interests, even if expressed in a distorted form. Even Trump's statements that seem ridiculous and anecdotal, such as the promise to build a wall to fence off Mexico, are not totally without meaning. Building the wall would create hundreds of thousands of jobs, not only in the US but also on the opposite side of the border. In fact, it's a Keynesian project, even if fairly absurd from the standpoint of ordinary logic.

Of course, there is nothing progressive about Trump's ideology, but this is not about ideology, which is not so much a factor of social mobilization, as a tool for manipulation. The defeat of financial capital, no matter who brings it about, would open a new era in the development of Western society, inevitably strengthening the working class, and reviving its organizations. The change is under way, not only because of the political and social logic, but also due to the fact that all possibilities of maintaining the current neo-liberal model of capitalism have been exhausted. If the left is unwilling or unable to fight, it will be the right-wing populists like Donald Trump in the US or Marine Le Pen in France who strike the fatal blow against it. Some people will be outraged at the "prejudice" and "irresponsibility" of the working class, but the real moral responsibility would still lie with the leftist intellectuals, who, in times of crisis, will have demonstrated their class position by advocating and defending the interests of financial capital.

Trumponomics: Causes And Consequences

Trump formed a broad coalition for change, something leftists used to talk about for decades but never achieved in practice (and did not even try seriously to achieve). This is what populism is about and this is what made Trump's victory possible in the first place.

The ability to unite a broad cross-class coalition around a single leader or a party has always been the main source of strength for the populist movements. However, the objective contradictions of class interests have invariably been their stumbling block. The long-term success, and often the physical survival of populist leaders have always depended on whether they were able to, by changing the configuration and maneuvering, prevent the collapse of the block they lead. Would the leader be able to reshape it on the go, making a choice in favor of the correct forces at the right moment? Sooner or later the necessity will arise not only to side with one part of his supporters against the other, but also to sacrifice many of his political friends, and sometimes even the interests of his own class.

Donald Trump will inevitably face such choices. Not just a place of 45th president in US history, but also his personal fate, which has potential to be more than dramatic, depends on when, how and for whose benefit he will make these choices. The political and institutional crisis of American society has gone too far. The country is split, and the old order, for the restoration of which the Liberals are clamoring, is not only impossible to restore, but receives blow after blow every day. And the organizers of the liberal opposition campaign are themselves smashing the very public institutions, which they previously have relied upon for their power.

In order to get rid of Trump, they need a coup. Whether this scenario will be tried in the hard (force) or soft (impeachment) variant, it would be a major blow to the institutions of American democracy. And it is exactly the anti-Tump campaign of the Liberals which is creating preconditions for massive populist mobilization of the low class forces that were for decades alienated from politics and rediscovered their strength through voting Trump into the White House.

It can be assumed with good reason that the historic mission of Trump is the destruction of the existing liberal order. The positive work will be performed by other politicians and social movements. But these movements and leaders will only emerging in the struggle that is unfolding today. And how that happens, depends on the fate of Trump and the reforms initiated by him. In that sense the really important struggle is not about supporting Trump or trying to bring him down but about influencing the course of change initiated by the new administration and fighting for progressive reforms whether they are supported by the White House or opposed by it. A new progressive agenda will be formed by grass-root struggles reflecting the practical needs and interests of working people. And this agenda has nothing to do with the ideology of politically correct liberalism.

Institutional crisis, undermining the existing two-party system in the United States and the dominance of the Washington establishment, creates prospects for the left to participate in serious politics. The sudden success of Bernie Sanders in the primaries in 2016 demonstrated the possible scale of the opportunities. But the Left will only be able to use these opportunities on one condition – if it does not allow the Liberal circles to transform them into political extras fighting to protect the dying order. Otherwise, they will go to the bottom together.

This struggle is not only about the future of America, it dramatically affects the rest of the world, creating new dangers, but also impressive new opportunities for social change in many countries. The more the United States becomes involved in solving its own domestic crisis, the more freedom to act will have anti-establishment political forces elsewhere. But which forces will gain from these new conditions? If the international left wants to win the day, it has to reshape itself dramatically, disconnecting itself from the culture of liberal political correctness and returning to the old principles of class struggle based on real practical interests of the masses.

This is the only way to make the Left great again.

Trumponomics, firm governance and US prosperity

Robert R. Locke [University of Hawaii, USA]

Resume

This article focuses on Trumponomics from the perspective of firm governance. It argues that Trump is not interested in economics because the discipline does not offer a useful guide to his kind of management. On the other hand, it questions, using German stakeholder management as a comparative case, whether Trump's views of management, imbibed from his environment, can effectively restore prosperity to white middle class Americans living in rust belt communities. The argument is historical, the conclusion contemporary.

Trumponomics and economics

George Stigler observed that Donald Trump knows no economics, (which is a slight exaggeration, since the President claims a degree in economics, but true conditionally nonetheless, because he is not an economist by long-time practice and so does not have an economist's perspective). Few, however, would suggest that Trump does not understand at least a particular kind of management. MSNBC invited him to address students at his alma mater, the Wharton School, on January 2, 2008, to present management ideas expressed in a book written with Bill Zanker, entitled *Think Big and Kick Ass in Business and in Life*. Brian Halligan, founder of Hub Spot marketing, who attended the session and took notes, summarized with comment ten management lessons that Trump outlined:

> "1. Work Hard – This is a platitude uttered by every speaker at every event like this, but the Don gives this more than the usual lip service. He basically said that everyone he knew that made a lot of money and was

ultra successful worked seven days a week...; they should be prepared for 80-hour weeks for a long time.

2. 'Love' What You Do – He discouraged the audience from joining or switching to a 'hot industry' (i.e. hedge funds) or from going into consulting in favor of getting involved with an industry you love..., even if that industry is not *currently* doing well as a whole. His message was that you will perform so well in your imperfect industry that you will ...end up being a star in the top 1%.... He thought the pay in the top 1% of a crappy industry (in a job you love) would top the 50th percentile in a hot industry (in a job you loathe).

3. 'Know' What You Do – Whatever industry you are in and whatever role you play in that industry, work hard to become a world class expert in it. For example, if you are a marcom manager in a security software company, he suggested that you ought not just focus on getting good at seo [search engine optimization] and email marketing campaigns horizontally, but that you ought to become an expert in that security industry   yourself, so that you can communicate with all levels of people about the technology *simply*, so that you can have detailed conversations with analysts, so that you can write credible blog articles, so that you can explain the future competitive dynamics to potential investors, etc.

4. Luck – According to Don, 'The harder I work, the luckier I get.'

5. Education – A huge advantage that is expensive in the short run, but cheap in the long run.

6. Management – Donald fought the platitude pattern and said 'You want to be smarter than your people'. He thought the notion that you should hire people smarter than you was a poor one.

7. Persistence – He credited his success and the demise of many of his competitors to being patient and persistent over long periods of time to wait out market fluctuations.

8. Negotiation – Always do it face-to-face..., so you can read the other person's body language.

9. Middle men – Donald is not a fan of middle men who do not add value and who extract outsized returns. ... There are so many industries that have middle men filled with old boys clubs that take money out of your pocket. If you want a good example, try leasing some office space or dealing with a technology 'analyst'.

10. Marriage – Marry someone who understands #1 above and make sure to get a prenuptial agreement...."

Classical economics, spawned in an age when the UK was still largely proto-industrial and a forest of small and middle-sized firms, invented the invisible hand to assure consumers that open competition in free markets would serve the public good. Since poor management automatically fails in the firms that go under, the invisible hand regulating free markets guarantees the development of good management. The dictum of the invisible hand of market discipline became the folklore of US political wisdom and the guiding principle of economics. Markets, not management, were the focus of classical economic's investigation.

In the 20th century, the "visible hand" of firm governance, in Alfred D. Chandler, Jr's apt phrase, replaced the invisible hand of market discipline (Chandler, 1977). This led to a separation of ownership from the management, what I called "managerialism" and defined in 2009 as

> "What occurs when a special group, called management, ensconces itself systemically in an organization and deprives owners and employees of their decision-making power (including the distribution of emoluments) – and justifies that takeover on the grounds of the managing group's education and exclusive possession of the codified bodies of knowledge and know-how necessary to the efficient running of the organization" (Locke, 2009, 28).

Chandler and Redlich in 1961 described the managerial hierarchies that emerged in huge multifunctional firms:

> "The centralized coordination, evaluation, and planning for the diverse activities of a large number of sub-units which often carried out several different functions of production, distribution, and transportation within a single, purely private enterprise, were something new in economic history. Such needs brought the managerial enterprise into being. The new enterprise could not run efficiently without formal

internal organizations. They required the generation of internal operating, financial and cost data. Only through a flow of internal impersonal statistics could control of these large enterprises be maintained" (Chandler and Redlich, 1961, 5).

The new managerial hierarchy diversified. Engineers on the shop floors and in the manufacturing divisions of M-form corporations made artifacts. Top management, in which controllers trained in accounting, increasingly replaced the engineers and thought about money, that is, about constantly improving return-on-investment. The controller (today the Chief Financial Officer) became the board of director's indispensable man. He was generally a vice president in the company, with direct access to the chief executive. His function made him a fount of information for policy decisions of a financial, technical, and/or commercial nature. He also had an instrumental role in policy implementation once decisions were taken.

These developments and their consequences drew public attention. In 1932 Adolf Berle and Gardiner Means, in *The Modern Corporation and Private Property*, described the role of management as a functional caste in executive circles; Simone Weil about the same time (1933) recognized that the separation of ownership from control had created a new "oppressive" class, as opposed to the older idea, derived from Marx, of the bourgeoisie as an "exploitive" class (Grey, 1996, 597); James Burnham's *The Managerial Revolution* appeared in 1937. By World War II the management caste became, to use Heinz Hartmann's words, "a fourth production factor... a strategic variable for the development of the firm" (Hartmann, 1963, 113). The emphasis at the top was on financial outcomes.

Concurrently a new management science emerged. A lot has been written about this subject. Suffice it to say that up to the 1930s the study of management focused on firm practice, but the operational difficulties encountered in the war brought scientific methods into the management equation (Locke, 1989, 1-29, Khurana, 2007, 233-290, Locke and Spender, 2011, 10-15). The reference is to science, not to scientists, for it was not just a question of intelligent men and women helping out, but rather of their deploying science's methods to solve unprecedented strategic planning, logistics, and operation problems. Operations research (OR) projects drew on statistical and mathematically informed techniques, such as queuing and transportation theories that were particularly suited to maximizing efficiency in large-scale military operations.

During the Cold War the use of science in government-affiliated OR agencies expanded. In 1946 the US Army Air Force funded a new think tank, the Rand Corporation, to help solve operations problems. In 1947, George B. Dantzig and his Rand associates developed the simplex linear programming algorithms for decision-making. The procedure utilized modern mathematics (vector algebra, matrix theory, symbolic logic) and statistical techniques in an effort to take the guesswork out of decision-making.

Since mathematics and scientific methods prevailed in them, departments of industrial administration, especially in engineering institutions, pioneered the work in higher education. The Case Institute of Technology in Cleveland started the first operations research unit at the urging of industry (with financial support from the Chesapeake and Ohio Railroad Co. and the US Air Force). The institute organized a national conference in November 1951 on OR in business and industry attended by 150 people from all over the country (Page, 1952).

If neoclassical economists still ignored the subject of management, OR's science impressed them, because they had a problem in their own discipline. Since its birth in the late 19th century, it aspired, as it still does today, to become a prescriptive science; consider León Walras' attempt to make it a "mathematical science". (*Elements of Pure Economics*, 1874) In 1944 John von Neumann and Oskar Morgenstern in the foreword to *Theory of Games and Economic Behavior* observed that after decades of effort they had failed. They wrote:

> "The concepts of economics are fuzzy, but even in those parts of economics where the descriptive problem has been handled more satisfactorily, mathematical tools have seldom been used appropriately. Mathematical economics has not achieved very much" (Neumann and Morgenstern, 1944, Introduction).

Economists post World War II came to believe that the new OR scientific toolkit would make the discipline a prescriptive science. Immediately post war, after working at Rand, Kenneth Arrow used it in his work on Rational Choice Theory. His book *Social Choice and Individual Value* (1951) was the "first real classic" on what "is now taken as a given in economics and has spread out into many neighboring disciplines" (Bellah, Introduction 2000, 7). The neoclassical economists Joseph Dorfman, Paul Samuelson, and Robert Solow applied linear programming to their subject (Dorfman, Samuelson, and Solow, 1958). In 1954, Kenneth Arrow and Gerard Debreu announced that they had achieved a mathematical solution of general equilibrium, "the theoretical core of neo-classical economics," which Edward Fullbrook states "has become the central showpiece of academic economics ever since" (Fullbrook, 2003, 5; Arrow and Debreu, 1954).

Managerialism also affected the economists' views about the nature of the firm. Susan Holmberg and Mark Schmitt call this theoretical development the Milton Friedman Doctrine:

> "[Friedman] wrote in 1970 that 'a corporate executive is an employee of the owners of the business [i.e., the shareholders]; he has direct responsibility to them as his employers. That responsibility is to conduct the business in accordance with their desires, which generally will be to make as much money as possible, without breaking the law or cheating people.' ... Michael C. Jensen and William H. Meckling codified Friedman's argument with their seminal 1976 article, 'Theory of the Firm'. The purpose of corporate governance, they argued, is about finding ways to align the incentives of shareholders (whom they referred to as 'principals') and executives ('agents' of the shareholder owners). This theory enraptured economics departments and business and law schools for decades and profoundly shaped how corporate officers, shareholders, taxpayers, policy-makers, and even most Americans think about the roles and responsibilities of corporations" (Holmberg and Schmitt, 2016, 1-2).

Because of the value their performance added to the firms they managed, CEOs' high salaries were worth it.

If neoclassical economics borrowed so heavily from OR methodologies, why would managers not find economics useful? The answer is that the traffic between OR and economics was a one way street; economics borrowed OR science methodologies, but despite taking on its scientific toolkit, the discipline did not subsequently succeed prescriptively, as I noted in chapter two ("The New Paradigm Revisited") of my book *Management and Higher Education Since 1940* (Locke, 1989), and as repeatedly attested to in the blog and articles of the *Real-World Economics Review*.

Nor for similar reasons could managers benefit from the Milton Freedman Doctrine. Holmberg and Schmitt noted that the doctrine's prescriptive value was questioned "at the 2013 annual meeting of the Allied Social Science Associations [when] the French financial economist Jean-Charles Rochet in the keynote address... skewered the very foundation of pay for performance. Cornell Law School professor Lynn Stout calls 'shareholder value a myth' – the idea that corporations exist for shareholders and no one else. Rochet told the conference: 'Everyone knows that corporations are not just cash machines for their shareholders, but that they also provide goods and services for their consumers, as well as jobs and incomes for their employees. Everyone, that is, except most economists, [for whom] shareholder primacy has never been challenged in a serious way'" (Holmberg and Schmitt, 11).

Holmberg and Schmitt continued, citing and quoting Lucian Bebchuk and Jesse Fried's earlier book, *Pay Without Performance* (2004), "...that executive pay could not even be said to be based on stockholder-owners subjective appreciation of executive performance. They (Bebchuk and Fried) 'wrote that skyrocketing executive pay is the blatant result of CEOs' power over decisions within US firms, including compensation'" (quoted in Holmberg and Schmitt, 12). It reflected director, not stockholder, primacy. (On the subject also see Bainbridge, 2006)

Accordingly, why should Trump or any active manager pay attention to the Milton Friedman Doctrine if economists have failed to bring economic thought into line with developments in firm governance. As Gunnar Eliasson concluded:

> "The management teacher as well as the economic theorist needs a realistic model of the firm, [but] no good model of the firm has been created. The moral is... that we have excellent firms, not thanks to but despite management teaching" (Eliasson, 1998, 9).

Trumponomics and social prosperity

The management principles Trump evokes in *Think Big and Kick Ass* are those for self-enrichment reminiscent of robber barons during the Gilded Age. In his election campaign Trump promised to use his knowhow to restore prosperity to the dispossessed white middle class in rust belt communities. Will his management principles, if they served him and other billionaires well, do the same for the white middle class communities? This is a question economists seldom ask since they exclude management systems and methods from their analytical purview. It is also a question that Trump has not asked, inasmuch as he attributes the impoverishment of industrial America's white middle class to NAFTA and other trade agreements, misguided environment policies that destroy jobs, e.g., in coal-mining regions, and tax provisions that encourage corporations to move manufacturing off shore. If economists and Donald Trump ignore the management question, historians have not, and for good reason.

History involves specificities that differ in time and place. The specific time referred to here in US history is when in the 1980s and 1990s the old staple mass production industries (automobiles, steel, rubber, consumer electronics, and their suppliers) succumbed to Japanese competition. Trump is a great believer in what the Germans call the Führerprinzip (leadership principle), which he thinks is the key to success. A good leader is needed to harness the will and energy of the people in the enterprise and the nation, for "without leadership," he says, "organizations slowly stagnate and lose their way... Leaders influence behavior, change the course of events and overcome resistance and therefore leadership is regarded as crucial in implementing decisions successfully."

But in the timeframe under consideration, American director primacy forms of management did not protect American mass production industry and the blue collar populations it succored nearly as well as the stakeholder forms of management that had developed in Germany (and other northern European countries) after the war as alternate forms of firm governance (Albert, 1993).

That the German story is radically different from the American can be demonstrated through comparative analyses of the top twenty firms in each country, ranked by revenues (2012):

USA

1.	Exxon	11.	AT&T
2.	Wal-Mart	12.	Valero Energy
3.	Chevron	13.	Bank of America Corp
4.	Conoco-Philips	14.	McKesson
5.	General Motors	15.	Verizon Communications
6.	General Electric	16.	JP Morgan Chase & Co
7.	Berkshire-Hathaway	17.	Apple
8.	Fannie Mae	18.	CUS Caremark
9.	Ford	19.	IBM
10.	Hewlett-Packard	20.	Citi Group

(Source: Stahl, 2013, 59)

Germany

1.	Volkswagen	11.	Aldi Group
2.	E.ON	12.	BP Europa SE
3.	Daimler	13.	Robert Bosch
4.	Siemens	14.	RWE
5.	BASF	15.	Rewe Group
6.	BMW	16.	Edeka Group

7.	Metro	17. Audi
8.	Schwarz	18. Thyssen Krupp
9.	Deutsche Telekom	19. Deutsche Bahn
10.	Deutsche Post	20. Bayer

(Source: *Ibid.*, 61)

Some firms on each list are classifiable under the same rubric, e.g., retail giants (in the US, Wal-Mart and McKesson; in Germany, the Aldi and Edeka Groups). Others are famous oil and energy firms, mostly on the US list. But there are two big differences between the lists that are of interest here.

Financialization

One is that among the top twenty US firms there are many drivers of financialization (Berkshire-Hathaway, Fannie Mae, Bank of America, JP Morgan Chase Co, Citi-Group, and GE Financial), or US firms that are the creation of financialization (Hewlett-Packard: IPO 1957; Apple: IPO 1980). On the German list, there are none, i.e., not one is a financial institution, not one is a stock market IPO creation.

The financialization referred to is not limited to the concentration on financial outcomes that had become the preoccupation of top management in large firms, although that is part of it. Rather it is the change during the last three decades of the 20th century from viewing a business as a vehicle for earning "returns on investment... based on the value created by productive enterprise" to viewing a business "as assets to be bought and sold for maximizing profits through financial strategies" (Ball & Appelbaum, 2). This is the world that Donald Trump knows and in which he operates.

Dünhaupt describes five ways in which financialization changed executive behavior: 1. It shifted the basis of enterprise finance from banks to capital markets; 2. It reinvigorated the "rentier" class that had been on the decline by creating institutional investors (e.g., pension funds) that base investment decisions solely on stock prices and short-term return on investment; 3. It linked financial trading to new financial institutions (e.g., investment banks, hedge funds, and private equity firms) and new financial instruments (e.g., derivatives, stock options, and credit swaps); 4. It stressed profit-making through financial activities instead of through real productive activity; 5. Under the guise of increasing shareholder value in a firm, it subordinated the interests of stockholders in nonfinancial firms to those of directors (and, implicitly, those of Wall Street analysts, investment bankers, and large investors) (Dünhaupt, 2011, 10).

Financialization of US capitalism expanded the emphasis on maximizing financial gain that top management emphasized in large firms in broader institutional ways – through the spawning of venture capitalist firms, angel investor networks, and IPOs, through the promotion of private equity buyouts, amalgamations, and other schemes of privatization that whet the appetites of the investor class and fill the wallets of their agents with lucrative commissions for dealmakers in hedge funds, private equity firms, and investment banks.

The growth of finance inevitably transformed US management education. Carnegie Institute of Technology's Graduate School of Industrial Administration (to become the Tepper School of Business in 2003) set up a Financial Analyst Security Trading Center (FAST) in 1989, one of the first US educational institutions to replicate successfully the live international data feeds and sophisticated software of Wall Street trading firms. (Bach, 1958) The business school at Carnegie Mellon introduced an MBA in computational finance, an MS in quantitative economics and an MS in computation finance in which the students studied equities, bond portfolio management, and the stochastic models upon which derivative trading, i.e., the Black-Scholes formula, is based. Although early off the mark, there was nothing exceptional in the last decade of the 20th century about the program in mathematical finance at Carnegie-Mellon; all the top business schools developed them.

MBAs increasingly found jobs in the banks, hedge funds, and investment houses of the expanding financialization sector. Khurana's study of Harvard Business School MBAs cites a survey of first jobs for graduating Harvard Business School students: Between 1965 and 1985 students' entry into financial services and consulting "rose from 23 percent to 52 percent" of graduates (Khurana, 2007, 328-29). The same shift happened in "other elite schools, such as Wharton and the business schools at Stanford and the University of Chicago." By 2005 "among the 180 principals and managing directors in the 20 largest investment firms, 73…[held] an MBA from one of the six elite schools (Harvard 51, Chicago 7, Columbia 6, Stanford 5, Dartmouth's Tuck 3, and Northwestern 1" (349).

British and American financialization affected the business of German private commercial banks in their own country; the Anglo-Saxon firms so dominated internationally that by 2004 German financial institutions only transacted 38.3% of the German merger and acquisition business, 21.8 percent of the German equity market business, and 16.3% of the debt market business (*The Economist* 1.11. 2004, 82).

German private commercial banks, fighting back, began trading in securities and engaging in business consultancy. They also, following the UK and US banks, marketed new products and services, including selling loan packages, credit cards, and insurance, and organizing electronic banking through automated machines and on-line services.

But educational and banking traditions hindered Germany from developing institutional arrangements that followed those pushing US and UK financial development. One difference was educational. In the US, the UK, and France members of an ambitious elite, like Trump, study in top-ranked schools; that is, **where** people study is more important to their careers than the subject studied. In Germany **what** people studied was more important than **where**. The absence of national elite schools made recruitment of financially savvy high flyers more difficult, especially when there were few MBA study programs in German institutions of higher education.

When big German commercial banks in the 1990s decided to adopt the US-UK investment banking model, therefore, they had trouble recruiting in Germany. The banks decided to acquire the required expertise through acquisition. Deutsche Bank bought Morgan Grenfell, the British merchant bank, in 1989 and Bankers Trust, the US specialist in hedge funds, in 1999, and moved its investment banking headquarters to London. Dresdner Bank acquired UK-based Kleinwort Benson in 1995 and US-based Wasserstein Parella in 2000, attempting to expand into the global big leagues of underwriting, sales and trading, and merger advice. In other words, running the risk of generalization, it could be said without exaggeration that US and UK financialization, because first off the block and more highly developed globally, co-opted German.

Manufacturing

The second big difference gleaned from a comparison of the top twenty German and US firms pertains to manufacturing. Few of the manufacturing firms on the US list were famous before World War II (Ford, GM, GE), but such firms dominate the list of the German top twenty, many of them prominent even before World War I (Deutsche Post, Robert Bosch, Daimler, BASF, Thyssen Krupp, Bayer, and Deutsche Bahn). The US list would have been different had it been drawn up before the Japanese challenge to mass production US manufacturing had taken effect. In 1996, I described the rapid disappearance of the American staple industries in the early 1980s that the Japanese challenge caused in automobiles and in the related industries of steel, glass, and tires:

> "The total number of workers in the automobile industry declined from 802,800 in December 1978 to 478,000 in January 1983. By 1980 Japan had become the world's major automobile producing nation. American automakers' world market share declined from 27.9 percent in 1970 to 19 percent in 1982. The story in steel was even worse. In 1982 eighteen major steel companies recorded a combined loss in that year of $3.2 billion. Half of the routine steelmakers' jobs vanished between 1977 and 1988 (from 489,000 to 260,000.) To these horror stories could be added many others about American failure in mass-production industries – transistor radios, cameras, binoculars, sewing machines, color televisions, VCRs, compact discs, as well as in glass and tire manufacturing..." (Locke, 1996, 160).

Whatever Donald Trump thinks about the prowess of US management, it is clear that US mass production firms suffered an existential crisis after 1980, and a plethora of comparative management books and articles published in the 1980s and 1990s blamed the outcomes on the superiority of Japanese management to American.

H. Thomas Johnson, for one, traced the US failure in an industry they once dominated (automobiles) to the transformation of management through the financilization of top management, expressed in firm control mechanisms, whose philosophy of managerialism had permeated management school research and teaching. He wrote

> "[US] managers believed they could make decisions without knowing the company's products, technologies, or customers. They had only to understand the intricacies of financial reporting ... [B]y the 1970s managers came primarily from the ranks of accountants and controllers, rather than from the ranks of engineers, designers, and marketers. [This new managerial class] moved frequently among companies without regard to the industry or markets they served... A synergistic relationship developed between the management accounting taught in MBA programs and the practices emanating from corporate controllers' offices, imparting to management accounting a life of its own and shaping the way managers ran businesses" (Johnson and Bröms, 2000, 57).

> "At first the abstract information compiled and transmitted by these computer systems merely supplemented the perspectives of managers who were already familiar with concrete details of the operations they managed, no matter how complicated and confused those operations became. Such individuals, prevalent in top management ranks before 1970, had a clear sense of the difference between 'the map' created by abstract computer calculations and 'the territory' that people inhabited in the workplace. Increasingly after 1970, however, managers lacking in shop floor experience or in engineering training, often trained in graduate business schools, came to dominate American and European

manufacturing establishments. In their hands the 'map was the territory.' In other words, they considered reality to be the abstract quantitative models, the management accounting reports, and the computer scheduling algorithms" (Johnson and Bröms, 186-87).

Johnson observed, in his comparative study of US Big Three automakers with Toyota's Georgetown, Kentucky plant, that the American firms operated under different forms of management than their increasingly successful competitor. He called the American mass production system "management by results", which he presented under seven rubrics:

1. the individual is responsible
2. control results
3. follow finance-driven rules
4. manipulate output to control costs
5. increase speed of work
6. specialize and decouple processes
7. the individual is the cause – blame

By comparison the Toyota Kata at Georgetown operated under "management by means", a system wherein:

1. relationships are reality, and management
2. nurtures relationships,
3. masters life-oriented practices,
4. provides output as needed on time,
5. changes how work is done,
6. enhances continuous flow, and
7. when troubleshooting, considers mutual interaction as the cause of a problem – not individuals (Johnson and Bröms, 2000, 186-87).

Toyota's management at Georgetown reflects Japanese classroom education K-9 of intragroup cooperation that stresses "the process through which results are obtained, not the results themselves" (Locke, 1996, 141); US automobile production management mirrors educational traditions that evaluate an individual's performance (Cummings, 1980, 117).

Robert R. Locke

The US system of management by results is not only different from management by means but inimical to its adoption. Management by results served the needs of top managers and firm outsiders (stockholders, capital markets, and institutional investors) who based decision-making on financial results, but it frustrated management by means, which required attention to work process and people. In the competition between the two, management by means was more efficient.

Johnson's studies have been taken up and explored by other production engineers. Mike Rother and his team spent five years investigating the Toyota Kata (2004-2009), a system of "unseen management routines and thinking" through which the investigator has to find his way "along unpredictable paths through a systematic process of discovery and adjustments". This became particularly challenging to this group of management consultants when they tried to teach management by means in Western firms whose executives have a command and control mindset. Rother ran into the difficulty especially when teaching Western managers about empowerments. "[A command and control approach] is insufficient for tapping the brainpower inside an organization in a purposeful way. If people in organizations are expected to make decisions and navigate rapidly at their level, rather than waiting to be told what to do, they need to be taught effective skills for how to do it" (Rother, 2014, 4).

To appreciate management by means requires the historian's investigative methods, not just those of a mathematically shaped scientific paradigm codified and taught in departments of economics and business schools.

American manufacturing, therefore, has not ignored the Japanese challenge, but the impulse came primarily from manufactures themselves, production engineers, and from regionally or nationally organized associations like the Deming societies, the Association of Manufacturing Excellence organized in 1985, and the current Kata movement in industrial management, which economists ignore.

US business schools in their MBA education neglected the Japanese challenge. Only 1-2% of them had truly been affected, as of early 1991, by the Total Quality Management revolution that sought to install and make permanent a management climate in which the organization continuously improves its ability to deliver high-quality products and services to customers. Instead, beginning in the 1980s, financial strategists in academia and practice increasingly worked with corporate lawyers, stockholders, and financial promoters in various kinds of deal making.

Some converted quite successful public firms through leveraged buyout schemes into private equity companies. Only firms with significant untapped borrowing capacity, undervalued assets, and high cash flows – "common characteristics of many, if not most, of America's largest and more prosperous corporations" (Shad, 1984, 6) – could get involved because buyouts were financed from money borrowed on a target company's own credit line, and the huge debt incurred was paid back from a target company's own cash flow (Kosman, 2010, 151-52).

These deals made money for institutional investment funds that lent the money (e.g., public employees' pension plans), the deal makers, the target company shareholders (who received 50 percent to 100 percent premiums over the current market price of their stock), and managers, who were given golden handshakes. But the buyouts did not do much for stakeholders in the target firms.

Other deal makers targeted firms in economic trouble, especially older firms with high legacy costs (e.g., retirees defined-benefit pensions), in which management sought to shed the fixed costs in a variety of legal ways provided for in takeovers, mergers, and chapter eleven bankruptcies.

The management caste's desire to break pension and benefit agreements motivated it the most. There were 112,000 defined-benefit private pension plans, entered into during the pre-1980s, in the US in 1983, each guaranteeing fixed levels of income to retirees. Many were not fully funded, that is, management, pressed by stockholder desires for good quarterly income statements and dividends to keep the stock price high, had made funding the employee pension plan a low priority.

Tough-minded managers preferred to eliminate pension and benefit plans altogether and to move employees into undefined contribution schemes that did not guarantee fixed incomes for retirees, or, failing that, to establish individual pension savings accounts that greatly reduced company contributions and obligations.

The ruthless, relentless, and radical transformation of private pension plans that the financial management caste carried out during the chaos and restructuring of failed US mass production firms, impoverished white middle class Americans in the country's industrial heartland.

> "From Reagan through [George W.] Bush," Jack Rasmus reported in 2004, "business schools and financial crisis corporations have been terminating and undermining group pension plans by shutting down plants and moving companies, underfunding the plans, diverting funds to other corporate use when they can get away with it, and then, when the plan is in jeopardy, with the assistance of government and the courts, funneling whatever remains into 401-K type personal savings plans. From the passage of the Employee Retirement Income Security Act (ERISA) in 1974 until 2003, more than 160,000 Defined Benefits plans have gone under in the US" (Rasmus, 2004, 3).

During the same time the number of personal retirement accounts mushroomed. Very few households had such accounts in 1982, but by 1995 23 percent of households had a 401-K or an equivalent individual retirement account. That percentage reached 67 in 2004.

Management justifies its behavior on practical grounds: it is looking after shareholder interests. Those who terminated legacy costs even became management heroes, like Richard S. Miller, CEO of Bethlehem Steel, who jettisoned the company's $3.7 billion unfunded pension obligation to its retirees. This obligation removed venture capitalist Wilbur Ross bought the firm, combined it with four other derelict steel firms, and then sold the amalgamated firm, which had cost him $400 million, for $4.5 billion (Walsh, 2005).

Trumponomics: Causes And Consequences

The language that managers and business school academics use in articles about restructuring, mergers, acquisitions, leveraged buyouts and the like rarely, if ever, touches on how employees are affected. Mostly discussions focus on stockholder benefits, profits, and stock market valuation, before and after a deal, and on firm survival rates.

These are the concerns of people in the proprietary firm; and it is they who determine judgments about agency conflict. Since an entity conception of the firm is not in their consciousness, they as management scientists care little about what happens to the firm's employees or retirees. Moreover, they do not look for entity solutions to these problems because employees are not integral to management structures. It is the management caste's show, with the unions kept on the outside.

> "What bothered Mr. Conway, the union leader [at the demise of Bethlehem Steel]," New York Times reporter M. W. Walsh wrote, "was not so much Mr. Ross's inability to wring more money out of the pension system or his remarkable profit on the deal. What troubled him, he said, was that the country seemed unable to take any lessons away from the demise of the steel companies and how it affected so many working people. 'It just staggers us that America's not caught on to what's happening to it,' he said" (Walsh, 2).

American managerialism, therefore, failed the white middle class manufacturing communities twice: once, when it did not save the US mass production firms in which they worked from the Japanese managerial challenge, the second time, when in the shakedown of these industries in the 1980s and after, it made employees pay the price of this failure.

On the other hand, the finance instrumentalities financial deal makers invented promoted the ever yawning income gap between the bottom 90 percentile of income earners and the top one percent. Dünhaupt in fact claims that the increased inequality in incomes can be attributed almost exclusively to one of them: stock options, i.e., that the introduction of stock options into American CEO pay is solely responsible for increasing their share of total incomes from two percent in 2000 to eight percent in 2007 (p. 19).

Why did German manufacturers not fail too? It could not be said that Asian manufacturers did not threaten them. They did, Germans were aware of it, and they, with those allied with them in government and education, carried on a twenty-year campaign to save their manufacturing firms – with success as the 2012 list of German top 20 firms reveals.

One advantage the Germans had over the US when confronting the Japanese challenge was their relative failure in financialization. Whereas it consumed US educational and business energies, its relative absence in Germany meant that it could and did not there.

Moreover, German business economics (BWL, Betriebswirtschaftslehre), when the crisis began, had a special hybrid degree in business economics (Wirtschafts-Ingenieur) – that Willy Prion, a business economist (no engineering degrees) organized in the technical university of Charlottenburg (Berlin) in 1923 and from where it spread to other venues – which kept professors in BWL and their students, unlike in US business schools, from turning their backs on industrial reform. By the late 1960s 11.11% (2,614) of students in German business economics (19,294) were in economics-engineering programs.

 A third advantage German reformers enjoyed was the legacy of shareholder management that grew up postwar at the same time director primacy took control over American firm governance.

In 1994 I visited Germany to investigate the German response to the Japanese challenge to their manufacuring. I learned how the difference in management and management education just mentioned helps explain German success and the US failure. Before leaving for Europe, I asked Robert W. Hall, founding member of the Association of Manufacturing Excellence, about Germans to contact. In his response, he described Horst Wildemann as the "repository of nearly all the coming of manufacturing excellence practice to Germany, a part of it almost from the beginning" (Letter, June 25, 1994).

Trumponomics: Causes And Consequences

In 1994, Wildemann was professor of business economics, with emphasis on logistics, in the Munich Technical University, teaching courses primarily to engineering students on work-process innovation. He headed a substantial group of over 100 research-consultants (30% with degrees in business economics, *Diplom-Kaufleute*, 50% with *Wirtschafts-Ingenieur* degrees, 20% with engineering degrees, *Diplom-Ingenieur*), which included 35 graduate assistants. Their work was heavily oriented to mathematical modeling and computer simulations.

By 1994 the team had already introduced Japanese inspired production processes in 200 European (mostly German) firms, including Daimler-Benz, Grundig, Philips, and Volkswagen, over an eleven-year period. At Volkswagen his group had just (1994) spent three years teaching small-group quality control management techniques in five-day courses to over 2,500 managers. Thirty to fifty percent of German industry had already by that year successfully implemented Total Quality Management, including Just in Time, *Kaizen*, and/or other Japanese work-process techniques. German business economics through its *Wirtschafts-Ingenieur* engineering education tradition made a significant contribution to their work.

Wildemann also reported that in the four years at Volkwagen his group worked closely with works councils and IG Metall shop stewards. The group taught the new techniques to the shop stewards at the same time that they taught them to management. He reported that the works councillors fully appreciated the need to improve work processes but also understood the impact that the changes would have on jobs numbers in the workplace and on the need to reduce work time and pay. The union (IG Metall) not only promoted the implementation of Just-In-Time and other work processes but often led management in their implementation.

The success of the reform did not require German working communities to make heavy financial sacrifices in order to keep their firms. German supervisory boards in large German joint stock corporations have been generous to their managing directors, but never as generous as boards in America's system of director primacy, under which CEOs set their own salaries. With the inclusion of stock options in executive pay packages, adopted in 1997, German executive income in stock market-listed public corporations started to track the skyrocketing incomes of America's CEOs. CEO-to-worker pay ratio in Germany reached a ratio of 1:147 in 2012 compared to US CEO-to-worker pay ratios that year of 1:354, the highest income disparity in the developed world.

Conclusion

Donald Trump is famous for having a sense of his own infallibility. This character trait suits the American director primacy mode of management. Trump and his team of billionaires might jawbone US companies into keeping production facilities in the country, but it is highly doubtful that they will restore the private pension plans and other benefits managers jettisoned over the past quarter century that underpinned white middle class rank and file prosperity. As comparative discussions of the German case illuminate, this would require a shareholder form of firm governance where, as in Germany, employee-elected members of works councils and supervisory boards share in management, for in today's amoral business world employees can protect their interests only if given a voice in the running of firms.

Nor is it possible that the Republican-controlled Congress will do anything to promote government-sponsored entitlement for working people in order to redress the losses in the private sector. This is an important point, because, as Stephen Paul Miller notes,

> "We have not passed beyond the New Deal's assumption, since we have institutionalized much that saves us. Medicare, Medicaid, disability and unemployment insurance, progressive income taxes, and food stamps prevent[ed] a full scale depression after the 2008 economic collapse by keeping consumer demand and the economy afloat" (Miller, 2016, 15).

As Congressional Republicans set their sights on the elimination of the programs, the prospect that a new Trump administration will restore prosperity in white middle class rust belt communities, through governmental any more than through private means, is dim.

With regard to how economists as well as Trump can benefit from this presentation: Until they include systems of firm governance in their calculations, they will never appreciate European economic achievements that the German example in the paper illustrates.

References

Albert, M. (1993). *Capitalism Against Capitalism*. London: FWEW.

Arrow, K. and Debreu, G. (1954). "Existence of a Competitive Equilibrium for a Competitive Economy." *Econometrica*, 22(3), 265–90.

Bach, G. L. (1958). "Some Observations on the Business School of Tomorrow." *Management Science*, 4(4) (July), 351–64.

Bainbridge, S. (2006). "Director Primacy and Shareholder Disempowerment," *Harvard Law Review*, Vol. 119, UCLA School of Law – Econ Research Paper No. 05-25 – available at SSRN
https://papers.ssrn.com/sol3/papers.cfm?abstract_id=808584

Ball, R. and E. Appelbaum, (2013). "The Impact of Financialization on Management and Employment Outcomes." *Upjohn Institute Working Paper* 13-191. Kalamazoo, Mi: W. E. Upjohn Institute for Employment Research.

Bellah, R. N. (2000). "The True Scholar." *Academe, 86.* (January and February), 1-10.

Chandler, A. D., Jr. (1977). *The Visible Hand: The Managerial Revolution in American Business* (Cambridge, Mass.: Harvard University Press).

Chandler, A. D., Jr. and F. Redlich (1961). "Recent Developments in American Business Administration and Their Conceptualization." *Business History Review* (Summer), 1-27.

Cummings, W. K. (1980). *Education and Equality in Japan*. Princeton UP.

Dorfman, J., P. Samuelson, and S. Solow (1958*). Linear Programming and Economic Analysis*. New York: McGraw Hill.

Dünhaupt, P. (2011). The Impact of Financialization on Income Distribution in the USA and Germany. Retrieve on line.

Eliasson, G. (1998). "The nature of economic change and management in the knowledge-based information economy. KTH Stockholm. Department of Industrial Economics and Management.

Epstein, G. (ed) (2005). *Financialization and the World Economy*. Cheltenham: Edward Elgar.

Fullbrook, E. (ed) (2003). *The Crisis in Economics: The Post-Autistic Economics Movement – The first 600 days*. London and New York: Routledge.

Grey, C. (1996). "Towards a Critique of Managerialism: The Contribution of Simone Weil." Journal of Management Studies. 33:5 (September), 591-611.

Hartmann, H (1963). *Amerkanische Firmen in Deutschland: Beobachtungen über Kontakte und Kontraste zwischen Industriegeschellschaften*. Westdeutscher Verlag.

Holmberg, S. and M. Schmitt (2016). *The Milton Friedman Doctrine Is Wrong. Here's How to Rethink the Corporation*. Available at the Roosevelt Institute.

Khurana, R. (2007). From Higher Aims to Hired Hands: The Social Transformation of American Business Schools and the Unfulfilled Promise of Management as a Profession. Princeton UP.

Kosman, J. (2010*). The Buyout of America: How Private Equity Will Cause the Next Great Credit Crisis*. New York: Portfolio.

Locke, R. R. (1989). *Management and Higher Education Since 1940*. Cambridge: CUP.

Locke, R. R. (1996).The Collapse of the American Management Mystique. Oxford UP.

Locke, R. R. (2009). "Managerialism and the Demise of the Big Three." *Real-World Economics Review*. 51 (December 1), 28-47.

Locke, R. R. and J. C. Spender (2011). *Confronting Managerialism: How the Business School Elite and Their Schools Threw Our Lives Out of Balance*. London, JAI Press.

Miller, S. P. (2016). *The New Deal as a Triumph of Social Work*. Palgrave-Pivot.

Page, T. (1952). "The Founding Meeting of the Operations Research Society." *Journal of the Operations Research Society*. 1 (1), 1-26.

Rasmus, J. (2004). *Pension Plans in the Corporate Cross-Hairs*. Kylos Productions. Retrieved from http://www.Kylosproductions.com/articles/pensions.html 1-5.

Rother, M. (2010). *Toyota Kata: Managing People for Improvement, Adaptiveness and Superior Results*. New York: McGraw Hill.

Rother, M. (2014). *About the Toyota Kata Research*. Ann Arbor: University of Michigan.

Shad, J. S. R. (1984). "The Leveraging of America." *Security Exchange Commission News*. Washington DC, June 7, 1-7.

Stahl, C. (2013). "Corporate Social Responsibility in US and German Firms." Master's Thesis. Graduate School of Business, University of Grenoble.

Walsh, M. W. (2005). "Whoops! There goes another pension plan." *New York Times* (October 15)

Donald Trump, American political economy and the *"terrible simplificateurs"*

Kurt Jacobsen and Alba Alexander [University of Chicago; University of Illinois at Chicago, USA]

> "People accustomed to knowing they know everything worth knowing resent having to turn away from the mirror" (Lewis Lapham).

Art historian Jacob Burckhardt in 1889 bewailed what afterward became a cherished conservative term of abuse, *"terrible simplificateurs"*.[1] This memorable epithet, smacking of supreme erudite scorn, demands a closer look in President Donald Trump's USA for all the barbed ironies it actually contains. Burckhardt ably fulfilled the checklist for card-carrying conservatives enamored with an organic status quo, ancient institutions, and lower orders who were revolting solely in their tastes.[2] What he foretold was an age overrun by ambitious apparatchiks who "descend upon our old Europe and make short work with voting rights, sovereignty of the people, material well-being, industry, etc. and will stand upon small ceremony".[3] Burckhardt, make no mistake, prized elite ceremony above all the crude annoyances of democracy. These new barbaric experts would accelerate accumulation of wealth to fantasized levels but in doing so would ruin, as he saw it, harmony among the classes. Next would gallop in wily demagogues to sort it all out. "For this will be the inevitable end of the state based on rule

---

[1] For an example of the conservative application at derisive work see Leslie Mellichamp, "George Orwell: Terrible Simplificateur." Modern Age Spring/Summer 1984.

[2] Historical conservatives were attentive to "an irrational realm in the life of the state which cannot be managed by administration," and whose skill in managing cannot be taught *a priori*." Karl Mannheim, Ideology and Utopia (New York: Harcourt Brace & Co, 1954), pp. 106. "It expressed the ideology of the dominant nobility in England and in Germany..." (p. 107).

[3] The Letters of Jacob Burckhardt (Indianapolis: Liberty Fund, 2001).

of law," Burckhardt anticipated, "once it has succumbed to mere numbers and the consequences".

Little wonder that this hoary old term revived with the mind-boggling election of Donald Trump. No one likes "mere numbers" more than he, evidently because they are so easy to play around with. In today's usage "terrible simplifiers" is synonymous not only with authoritarian twits braying to the masses but also with utopian social engineers who decide for everyone else what is good for them. The engineers' remedies (*pace* Veblen) are imposed one-size-fits-all formulas; hence, free market utopians, flat tax advocates and states' rights proponents, however much they fancy themselves fastidious Burkean conservatives, are ideal candidates for the "terrible simplifiers" label too. Their ardent mission is to harness the state to serve the neoliberal market, Mirowski finds, and their revered freedoms do not include the freedom to criticize the purity of the marketplace.[4] Neoliberals employ politics, in other words, to abolish politics and so relegate power to private actors who, being on intimate terms with the market, really do know best. If neoliberalism isn't utopian social engineering, then what is? Here we glimpse the compulsive schematizing state juggernaut that James C. Scott dourly analyzed, and which is repudiated as much by the anarchist left as by the anarchist right.[5]

President Trump, soon the subject of numerous off-the-couch psychoanalyses, is indeed a *terrible simplificateur*, but this brief essay is a "look in the mirror" exercise regarding many aghast critics who conveniently overlook the wreckage that their own terrible simplifications, appareled in high verbiage and numerical mysticism, have inflicted on the American economy for decades. Trump would not be in the worrying position he is in without immense inadvertent aid from simplifiers of different stripes and partisan leanings. Alan Greenspan, for one, and Lawrence Summers, for two, could not grasp that their economic paradigmatic blinders were

---

[4] The "*neoliberal moment must seek to consolidate power by operating from within the state.*" Philip Mirowski, Never Let a Serious Crisis Go To Waste (London: Verso, 2014), pp. 443, 437

[5] On "Olympian ruthlessness toward victims of their interventions," see James C. Scott, "High Modernist Social Engineering: The Case of the Tennessee Valley Authority," in Lloyd Rudolph and Kurt Jacobsen, eds. *Experiencing The State* (New York: Oxford University Press, 2006)

inadequate to the task before them during the 2007-2008 crash, and amends have yet to be made.[6] So how far can the "terrible simplifier" trope take us in anticipating what the Great Orange One is likely to inflict upon and, or instigate in, what Page and Jacobs conclude is, after all, a "conservative egalitarian" citizenry?

Contrary to favorite media images of a tight-fisted, parochial, and selfish citizenry, Page and Jacobs' survey research finds that "most Americans are philosophically conservative and operationally liberal".[7] Many Americans, moreover, became acutely aware after the recent crash, as Rexford Tugwell discerned during the 1930s version, that "rugged individualism really meant regimentation of the many for the benefit of the few".[8] Americans cannot always find precisely the right words to describe their leanings - although interestingly the word "socialism" reappeared without much incident during the Bernie Sanders campaign. Yet Americans (72%) know and care that inequalities are widening, but, since Congress doesn't seem to heed them anymore, don't know how to fix it. Even majorities of Republicans (56-58%) agree that income inequality levels are "too large" and are willing to make "personal sacrifices to deal with it".[9] Americans may like the sound of conservative values but pragmatism "overcomes philosophical rectitude" so that they "look to government to ensure genuine economic opportunity" in education, housing, health and other arenas.[10] This is the real nation, not the Tea Party prism of it, that Trump and a Congress likewise elected by a minority (through astute gerrymandering and voter suppression) have taken the reins of. Still, the bailout of the thrift industry (157 billion) in the 1980s could have educated every college student with room, board and tuition,

---

[6] Yanis Varoufakis, *The Global Minotaur: America, Europe and the Future of the Global Economy* (2015), p. 3.

[7] Benjamin Page and Lawrence Jacobs, *Class War?: What Americans Really Think about Economic Inequality* (Chicago: University of Chicago Press, 2009), p. xi. An estimable forerunner to this research is Joel Rogers and Thomas Ferguson, Right Turn: The Decline of the Democrats and the Future of American Politics (New York: Hill and Wang, 1986), which demolished the pro-Reagan popularity narrative with poll data regarding public responses to his policies, not his personality.

[8] Cited in Nancy Isenberg, *White Trash* (New York: Viking, 2016), p. 221

[9] Page and Jacobs, *Class War?*, pp. xi, 41, 44.

[10] ibid. p. 97. From 1979 to 2000 the top 1% enjoyed a 184% income rise, the top 20% got a 70% boost and the middle fifth only 12% (p. 7).

Slater reminds.[11] "Americans are very generous when it comes to giving money to the rich." Is this likely to remain the case in the forthcoming Trump years?

The economically astute political science contributors to *The New Politics of Hard Times* embarked on an early appraisal of "a deep economic crisis and its relatively slender effects to date on political realignment and ideational orientation."[12] As of 2013 they were still a bit perplexed that the crash "produced few signs of fundamental political realignment, policy experimentation (apart from Central banks), or mobilizations by new political actors in any of the most seriously affected economies."[13] (The Sanders campaign, Jeremy Corbyn's ascent to UK Labour Party leader, and Brexit were yet to stir.) The volume coeditors, like much of the mass media, jumped anyway to what they curiously depict as a "backlash against increased government spending and rising levels of debt" – as if this "backlash" were not an anticipated element of the bank rescue scheme and essential to inflicting austerity policies afterward. What is oddly labeled "policy experimentation" by central banks was a crimped Keynesianism customized so that federal money funneled to the richest strata and only through their digestive systems in dribs and drabs to the rest of a stricken population. Why, contributors ask, were there no "redefinitions of interest in conditions of crisis"? Well, here was one key moment when the state redefined itself publicly as savior of the wealthy (in order of course to stabilize the system to serve those at the bottom).

Indeed the venerable Ralph Miliband-Nicos Poulanztas "theories of the state" debate abruptly was decided in Gordian knot fashion in Miliband's favor. How can sophisticated analysts prattle about "relative autonomy" structural power, institutional constraints and myriad nuances of capitalist rule when a committee of the not quite whole and entire bourgeoisie is glowering at us across the cabinet table? The executive branch brazenly is

---

[11] Philip Slater, *A Dream Deferred* (Boston: Beacon Press, 1991) pp. 169, 170.
[12] Miles Kahler and David Lake, "Introduction: Anatomy of Crisis: The Great Recession and Political Change," in Miles Kahler and David A. Lake, Eds. *Politics in The New Hard Times* (Ithaca: Cornell University Press, 2013), p. 24.
[13] ibid, p.2. It is strange to argue that TARP was "unthinkable by a Republican administration," except for a crisis, when rolling it out as needed during a crisis was the whole point. (p.10).

populated by members of a class – not least since Bill Clinton appointed Robert Rubin Treasury Secretary – that textbooks say it governs at arm's length. These strategic placements, which in a peculiarly heartening way show that economic elites do not trust the state to act in their interests, ensured that it was Wall Street that got bailed out and not the American people, as should have been the case if the state displayed a legitimating degree of distance from wielders of private power. Donald Trump is a sigh of exasperation, a part of the price that a subsequent decline in legitimacy of the state has cost us.

Right wing coalitions, such as the one Trump erratically presides over, "will satisfy their constituents through asset bubbles and financial deregulation", as Kahler and Lake predict, and Trump, like any Republican, is busy pretending he is doing it for the sake of average Americans, which no one outside his base believes.[14] Although Trump is discovering that his chronic absolutist manner cannot make bureaucracies buckle to his whims, he was never going to threaten major players. "An absolute monarchy", as Ambrose Bierce illuminatingly explained, "is one in which the sovereign does as he pleases so long as he pleases the assassins".[15] In all his accommodations Trump, if one sees him as an ordinary if big-time and thin-skinned huckster, is easy to predict. Many pundits say he baffles them but only because the blustery businessman ditches slick policy theatrics to tell lies he believes in to loyal followers, and makes the further mistake of appointing some of them to high posts. Trump packages himself not so much as a traitor to his class as a bad boy within it. Unlike FDR, he does not welcome the wrath of economic royalists since he remains one of them, one who intends to turn the spigot of federal funds and tax breaks wide open for the rich. What then are the consequences for new and stable coalitions for and against Trump?

An uninhibited businessman's self-serving demeanor ought to, and apparently already does, serve to motivate counter-mobilization. Trump has stepped into a crisis of neoliberalism he is equipped only to exacerbate. The voices warning about fascistic tendencies are probably but not entirely off track inasmuch as intensifying divisiveness is the way Trump instinctively

---

[14] Kahler and Lake, "Introduction," *The New Politics of Hard Times*, p. 11.
[15] Ambrose Bierce, *The Devil's Dictionary* (New York: Neale Publishing Company, 1911), p. 3.

promotes his agenda. Can his mishandlings, blunders and bluster generate a movement that can check him before he sics the not so secret police on all opponents? The prospects for a new New Deal/Great Society style coalition promoting "collective goods and social protection" are slim but should not be discounted, Peter Evans reckons:

> "Leaner, meaner is still more likely, but the possibility that state apparatuses might forge new alliances with civic actors in the early decades of the new millennium is no less implausible than the alliances that were actually forged between labor organizations and the state during the early decades of the twentieth century."[16]

Real estate magnates will thrive as infrastructure spending pours in for however long it lasts, as Galbraith notes,[17] bankers routinely get pampered, the corporate sector wins tax cuts and regulatory "relief," the military is pacified as always with more cash, the medical system – with untenable Obamacare on the ropes – absorbs every spare penny and then some from anyone unlucky enough to need it, so-called entitlements are cut or given short shrift by the most entitled people on the planet, and the police continue to enjoy carte blanche. Anthony Russo of Pentagon Papers fame, by the way, said he knew why they tortured people in Vietnam -because they tortured people in the US, that is, former wardens and cops ran the interrogation programs.[18] William Leuchtenberg, William Appelman Williams, Franz Schurmann and many other scholars noticed that the Democratic Party's progressive vision of regulated capitalist order was no less a natural fit with neo-imperialism than anything Republicans had to offer. Trump at least will behave sanely with Russia, while Hilary Clinton diehards do their best to hang the preposterous collaborator label on him.

Nothing Trump burbles is credible because every phrase is geared to his fleeting notion of what pleases his core crowd. Once they are cheered up,

---

[16] Peter Evans, "The Eclipse of the State?: Reflections on Stateness in the Era of Globalization." *World Politics* 50, 1 (October 1997), pp. 86, 87.
[17] James K. Galbraith, "Can Trump Overcome Secular Stagnation?" This volume.
[18] Jerry Kuzmarov, *Modernizing Repression: Police Training and Nation Building in the American Century* (Amherst: University of Massachusetts Press, 2012), p. 6.

Trump reverts to the shadowy business practices he relished all his life alongside schemers every bit as dubious as he is. No recent public figure, except maybe Halliburton's own Dick Cheney, embodies all the reasons why Plato and the Renaissance Church regarded merchants as unfit as governors: "the astuteness of merchants, fostered by their lust for gain, has discovered so many tricks and dodges that it is hardly possible to see the plain facts, much less to pronounce judgment on them."[19] Trump epitomizes the glib amoral executive who tells any tall tale that serves low purposes. Who hasn't at some time suffered a boss or a provost like him? One swoons, though, at the thought of a fiery Obama fighting just as combatively from the bully pulpit for single payer or military cutbacks to pay for domestic needs as Trump does for his agenda against the media. As the Trump era starts, which indeed feels like an arrival of a demented Roman emperor, it is worth asking in the spirit of Monty Python's "What do we owe to the Romans?" what does Trump owe to Obama and to both Clintons? Trump owes the Obama administration and Bill Clinton's administration the licenses to kill afforded by drone warfare and JSOC, bank and brokerage firm bailouts, steep welfare cuts, habitual deference to market rhetoric, unchecked and unmonitored military expenditure, failures to roll back mass surveillance and police state authority, and promotion of the low bar temporary contract or part-time "gig" jobs which comprised over 90% of Obama's boasted job creation.[20] Nothing in Hilary's own creed of terrible simplifications militated against any of the foregoing list.

Hilary Clinton blithely aided and abetted Trump every step of the way by running on a platform way to the right of Eisenhower's, force-feeding neoliberal nostrums to thinning crowds, and alienating Sanders supporters who discovered that the Democratic party establishment is as deft at dirty tricks as Republicans are (against unwanted insurgents but not Republicans they desperately desired to entice), and scolded Americans that they would never ever afford Canadian-style National health care, wherein her donor

---

[19] The Secretary of the Society of Jesuits to the Council of Trent, 1554, quoted in Chris Bobonich, "Why Should Philosophers Rule?: Plato's *Republic* and Aristotle's *Protrepicus.*" *Social Philosophy & Policy* 24, 2 (2007), p. 158.
[20] "Nearly 95% of New Jobs During Obama Era were Contract, or Part Time." Investing.com, 21 December 2016. Accessed at https://www.investing.com/news/economy-news/nearly-95-of-all-job-growth-during-obama-era-part-time,-contract-work-449057

network, not her statesmanship, was plainly showing. The Washington Consensus, with Clinton buttressing it, so far has proven to be politically impervious, which antagonizes highly mobilizable swathes of the populace. Trump alertly appeases some of them temporarily by balking at mega-trade deals, which antagonizes a quite different band of terrible simplifiers, but he does so more as a matter of hidebound bargaining tactics than principle. Yet no one is better suited in this century than Trump to galvanize a broad and potent counter movement of Polanyiesque proportions.[21]

Trump's tax plan, a Reagan repeat, is geared to raise taxes on working and lower class families, with single parents hit hardest and the lowest tax rate raised for all who barely make enough to pay it.[22] His infrastructure plan is at root a corporate welfare giveaway and a stealth privatization scheme, as Krugman notes.[23] Regarding Trump's proposed repatriation holiday for overseas corporate cash troves, Craig Whitney notes, Goldman Sachs estimates that three quarters is "going go into buybacks that will pump up the equities bubble (that Trump criticized before he was elected) into the biggest colossus of all time. Is that the change that Trump backers were hoping for?"[24] Eyebrows raised at the filling of the White House with minions from Goldman Sachs, an organization that feasts on suckers, which Trump reviled during the campaign. Chief advisor Steve Bannon, Steve Mnuchin (fourth Goldman Sachs Treasury secretary in a row), Gary Cohn and Anthony Scaramucchi snapped into high places, direct from a reptilian outfit that wriggled its way "out from under the mortgage crash by dumping its disastrous mortgage investments on its own clients as it simultaneously bet against them."[25]

---

[21] For a good inventory right out of the gate of the makings of such a many-stranded movement see Peter Dreier, "Preparing for President Trump," Moyers & Company 22 December 2016. Accessed at http://billmoyers.com/story/list-anti-trump-liberals-progressives/

[22] Lily Batchelder, "Families Facing Tax Increases Under Trump's Tax Plan," Tax Policy Center, Urban Institute & Brookings Institution 28 October 2016. Accessed at https://ssrn.com/abstract=2842802

[23] Paul Krugman, "Build He Won't." New York Times 21 November 2016.

[24] Craig Whitney, "The Reason the Fed is Raising Rates and Why It Won't Work." Counterpunch 29 December 2016

[25] Matt Taibbi, "The Vampire Squid Occupies Trump's White House." Rolling Stone 16 December 2016.

One million fewer Americans now work at jobs of any kind than before the Great Recession while the conventional 9 to 5 job with benefits and security increasingly is an endangered species.[26] A billionaire CEO in charge of the Department of Labor is epically ill-suited to reverse course. None of these are things you talk your way out of, and only 27% of the nation's eligible voters went for Trump in the first place. "If only rhetoric remains the rich are in trouble, James Scott observes, "because an inequality in resources can only be justified in terms of their social function".[27] We suspect we soon will see what it takes to ignite a conservative egalitarian nation.

Elsewhere in his *oeuvre* Burckhardt pertinently compared the modern dealmaker's mentality to that of ancient Greek figures who viewed themselves as integral parts of the polis, and he waxes Arendtian about it. Today's "educated men are firmly resolved to make a bargain, with whatever power, for their existence at any given time," he lamented.[28] "There is an enormous veneration of life and property." But in this myopic orientation there is a "mass abdication, and not just on the part of the rulers" from the common good, for there are "numerous bargaining positions and concessions against the worst – and all with great touchiness in matters of recognition and so-called honor." Sounds like someone we know. Keynes scribbled in a rueful and infamous line that for a little longer fair must be deemed foul and foul be deemed fair. Isn't the time up on that one?

---

[26] Lawrence Katz and Alan Kreuger, "The Rise and Nature of Alternative Work Arrangements in the United States, 1995-2015." 29 March 2016. Accessed at https://krueger.princeton.edu/sites/default/files/akrueger/files/katz_krueger_cws_-_march_29_20165.pdf

[27] James C Scott, *Weapons of the Weak* (New Haven: Yale University Press, 1985), p. 308.

[28] Jacob Burckhardt, *Judgments on History and Historians* (Indianapolis: Liberty Fund, 1929), p. 7.

Mexico, the weak link in Trump's campaign promises
Alicia Puyana [FLACSO]

Introduction

Since the Brexit referendum in the UK, whose result surprised us all, a large question looms in the minds of analysts, rulers and politicians: why did voters turn against projects that were, since World War II, the basis of international relations and of the post-World War II social pact?

Events such as Brexit, Trump's election, Le Pen's breakthrough in France and the establishment of right-wing governments in Poland and Hungary (in open defiance to the democratic principles of the European Union), though they are different in many respects, do have common features:

- the crises of the main political parties, abandoned by their constituencies,
- the rejection of political, intellectual and business establishments and the hegemonic economic doctrines of the last three decades (whether referred to as "globalization" or "economic neoliberalism"), and
- a reaction against refugees who are blamed for poverty, violence and the loss of identity.

These ideologies constitute the political phase of the economic crisis that erupted in 2008, the aftermath of which we are still experiencing: low growth, low productive investments, stagnation of productivity and real wages, concomitant with the decline in payments to labor in the functional distribution of income, not to mention the intensification of inequality in developed countries, or the Latin Americanization of the developed world (Palma, 2011). The current swing to the political right echoes the crisis of neoclassical macroeconomics, its general equilibrium models, and the methods of its teaching, which push economists and students away from real-life problems (Fullbrook, 2014; Puyana, 2015). Paradoxically, in recent years, in Latin America, the most unequal region in the world, inequality declined somewhat, although in Mexico it remains above the levels of 1980.

While the 2008 crisis called into question the fundamentals of economic theory over which the model of global growth had been sustained for the last three and a half decades, today we witness the crisis of liberal democracy and neo-liberal economics (Bauman, 2016), of the Social Democracy doctrine, the New Labor and waning The Third Way, as well as the fading out of the unrestricted support of globalization (Rodrik, 2017). Some foresee it as the end of the *Pax Americana*, or US hegemony established since the end of the Second World War and the world order that emerged thereafter (Roubini, 2017). For Trump, the costs of maintaining US imperialism are unacceptable; qualifying NATO as obsolete and its members as free riders and suggesting nuclear proliferation of Japan and Korea while keeping the USA "at the top of the pack" (Trump 2017) would be a sensible strategy, as it would reduce for the US the cost of defending these countries. In reality he is not an isolationist. He aims at controlling word order in his own terms: reinforcing the military power elements of the international security policy and weakening the elements of world peace, that inspired the II WW peace agreements and described in F.D. Roosevelt 1944 State of the Union Speech (Roosevelt, 1944), for whom security was not only preventing foreign aggressions but also avoiding any threats to economic, social and moral security, because a basic element of world peace is "a decent standard of living for all individual men and women and children in all Nations" (Roosevelt, 1944). Furthermore, for Roosevelt, peace depended on "...freedom from fear which is eternally linked with freedom from want" (Roosevelt, op cit.).

Exacerbated globalization has made clear the contradiction between democracy, which proclaims equality among all human beings and a capitalism that sanctions inequality, that inequality in wealth which supposedly guarantees investment and an economic growth and would end poverty. If property is the basis of freedom, the concentration of wealth impedes equality in freedom and in its exercise. One characteristic of neoclassical economics' models and the policies it backs is its lack of support and even disapproval of democracy (Radford, 2016). The same author adds that the principle of efficient allocation under conditions of scarcity leads to rejecting every attempt of redistribution of income and wealth downwards. This rejection is consistent with Lucas (2004) for whom: "Of the tendencies that are harmful to sound economics, the most seductive, and in my opinion, the most poisonous, is to focus on questions of distribution". All this led to the metamorphosis of economics, from a social science to a completely sanitized discipline that subordinates the state and society to the dictates of the market. In this way it came

> "to reject all heresies, in any organized form, that is to say, anything that seems to threaten the sanctity of property, profits, appropriate tariff policy, or the balanced budget, or implied sympathy for unions, public property, or the poor" (Galbraith, 1974, p. 239).

Thus, adds the author,

> "... converting economic theory into a non-political discipline – neoclassical theory destroyed, by the same process, its relation to the real world" (Galbraith, 1974, p. 240).

This distancing from the real world deprived economists and politicians from an understanding of the world and the will of the electorate.

Neoliberal economics and the Third Way political programmes, with its supply side model and its trickle down myths, intensified the innate tendency of capitalism toward concentration of wealth and, by eliminating the mechanisms of distribution and countervailing measures, widened the universe of losers, mainly workers, and reduced that of winners, and rewarded the latter with ever growing profits. This approach was part of the synthesis of Regan-Thatcher market liberalism and social individualism with social democracy distributive policies. The market was to be the means of tackling inequality and avoiding social disintegration. The motto of European Social Democratic parties and left of the centre parties elsewhere was, "equal opportunities for all", while pushing market oriented reforms in education and health. The crisis of 2008 evidenced the extent to which labor had been degraded, wages stalled and social mobility slowed, while services deteriorated and household debt prevented the deterioration of wages hurting even more. Fiscal discipline, or fiscal consolidation, evolved into a permanent austerity, enhancing the effects of the economic contraction, exacerbating inequality and deepening social discontent.

From the growing debate over the kind of government that Trump will lead, it seems that a nightmarish *Plot Against America* might be close to becoming a reality. For some, this is all about the rise to the White House of a determined leader, willing to affect all institutions, to "deconstruct the administrative state" (Bannon, 2017). For others, Trump is a right-wing populist actor in form and language, devoid of ideology. There seems to be no doubt of his authoritarian character and his determination to shake the system, creating conflicts with world leaders, both close and distant allies, and with the judiciary power, the media, members of his party, with women, ethnic minorities, and the intelligence authorities. He also fuels conflicts in the legislative branch between the two parties, given the Republican's willingness to accept all presidential initiatives and to excuse all his outbursts and the conflicts of interest that he defiantly ignores; there is no will to engage in bipartisan politics. So far it appears that he intends to make his proposals a reality, without abandoning his peculiar way of communicating with short, direct sentences that leave a wide margin for interpretation. In his rhetoric truth is not a requirement. How far he will go is not clear. Nor is it clear whether the checks and balances of the system will be able to set brakes on him or on specific policies. The failure to have the health care reform approved could signal that President Trump has to negotiate. It is scary that the most vocal opposition came from the far right of the Republican Party.

In an anachronistic view of reality, Trump's inaugural speech sketched an American society that, besieged and weakened by the harassment of internal and external enemies, has lost its dreams, military hegemony and middle class wealth. The schools deprive American children and youth of knowledge, while the infrastructure collapses and the factories are abandoned to rust. Migration, made up of criminals and terrorists, bleeds the nation and globalization destroys the social fabric by ruining the productive sector through the export of jobs. Since *protection leads to great prosperity,* the recipe to "make America Great Again" boils down to: *buying made in America, by American workers*. Such is the government formula for economic nationalism based on *alternative realism*, in which there is no room to talk about the crisis of 2008, nor about the ravages of financial deregulation and huge mergers, all of which lead to the dominance of large corporations and financial capital in the global economy and the consequent intensification of inequality.

Today, the US economy is growing at a faster rate than similarly developed ones. The number of people receiving unemployment insurance, 1.2 million in 2015, is 70% lower than in 1996, and lower than any time since 2008-2009. With only 4.5% "unemployment" as officially defined, it is close to full employment, judging also by the fact that wages have increased and are finally close to those in 2007. This reality calls into question what it means "to bring jobs back home". More employment? Or higher productivity, with superior technology and robotization? Certainly, the first Labor Secretary candidate is neither a champion of the workers nor the defender of labor income, minimum wages or labor unions. Trump is staffing his economic cabinet with officials from Wall Street corporations and has gone in the direction of undoing previous reforms to the financial system, approved after the crisis of 2008. This indeed is not an agenda that favors workers and the middle classes.

Mexico: the greatest enemy for the United States

Regardless of whether or not Trump can realize his *economic nationalism* agenda, it is clear that he intends to carry out the vision outlined in his inaugural speech: "Decisions in trade, immigration taxes, and foreign affairs will be taken only for the benefit of American workers and American families" (Trump, inaugural speech). The three areas selected by Trump comprise several topics that generate internal and external conflicts.

Trade. Trump proposes reducing the trade deficit, punishing exchange manipulation and retaliating against what he regards as unfair trade practices. The main points of the new government agenda were outlined in a draft of the "annual trade policy agenda" of the United States Trade

Representative (Council of Foreign Relations, 2017). To protect national interests, Trump promised to bilaterally renegotiate multilateral or bilateral trade agreements, especially NAFTA, for him "the worst agreement ever signed". He has signaled the end to the strategy of promoting economic integration as the way to prevent the resurgence of nationalist sentiments and violent conflicts of interest. That was the idea behind the construction of the European Union and of the mega trade projects: the TPP and the TTIP, which were instruments for consolidating USA geopolitical supremacy and restoring the political balance disrupted by the emergence of China as a main political and economic player. Furthermore, Trumps intends to circumvent the WTO, considered by him a medieval institution in which the tyranny of the majority made it impossible to impose a USA hegemony (Lamy, 2003). In effect, it seems Trump's government may not be entirely against free trade, that it is looking to redefine trade rules so as to "defend national sovereignty over trade rules and to strictly enforce USA trade laws" (Council of Foreign Relations, 2017)

Taxes are part of the new trade policy. He has proposed a border adjustment tax, to compensate for the value added tax some countries implement. The VAT tax has been mistakenly described as an unfair tax on imports. Secondly, Trump has proposed a revision of corporate tax, to roll back the Dodd Frank Act and to amend the Volcker Rule. These measures would favor big capital and endanger economic stability as they recreate the conditions which lead to the 2008 crisis.

Migration is at the same time an economic issue due to its impact on US wages and, more importantly, a matter of national security, due to Trump's belief that those who emigrate to the United States are terrorists, violent people, rapists or drug dealers. All this reverberates in the urgency to build the wall on the southern border and in the controversial executive order forbidding the migration from seven Muslim countries. Such criminalization of immigrants echoes the stance towards Afro-American and Latino communities.

In **international relations**, or national security, there are potential conflicts with China, an emerging power with the ability to challenge US supremacy in the Pacific. There are also conflicts regarding the Middle East, North Korea and Iran, but these are not mentioned by Trump as frequently as drug trafficking and the flow of immigrants from Mexico whom he describes as "gang members, drug lords and criminals" (Trump, 2017). President Trump's national security team confirms the militaristic stance in his campaign, as do also the large increases for the military in the projected budget. In a telephone conversation with Mexico's President Peña, Trump offered to dispatch US soldiers to contain Mexican "Bad hombres". The offer was made out of President Trump's perception that Mexican civil and military authorities are unable or unwilling to do their job, suggesting Mexican state is a failed state. Mexico is thus identified as a unique threat to the security of the United States with regard to most of the issues Trump has emphasized in his speeches and summarized in Table 1.

NAFTA, a trade deal not good for the USA. Really?

According to Trump, NAFTA is the most damaging trade agreement to US interests ever signed. It is a result of astute Mexican negotiators gaining commitments contrary to American's national interest. He repeatedly highlights Mexico as the exclusive culprit (with no mention of Canada) of having deceived the US during the negotiations. Nothing could be farther from the truth. This untruthful picture of the agreement calls for an objective description of the negotiating process and an illustration of the trajectory of the Mexican economy since NAFTA, to demonstrate that Trump's criticisms are ill intended and a pretext for imposing a new round of negotiations under conditions of extreme power.

> Truth is far removed from the claim that US negotiators accepted under NAFTA concessions detrimental to US national interests. The negotiations for NAFTA between Mexico and the US were between two deeply asymmetrical countries:
>
> a) they had radically different levels of economic development and influence in the regional markets;
> b) there were large differences in the two country's economic models and their gaps with the implicit model of the agreement;

Table 1 Major threats to United States national security, wellbeing and prosperity, according to President Trump

	NAFTA		Central America	Eurpean Union	North Korea	ISLAMIC STATE			CHINA	JAPAN	NATO	Germany
	Mexico	Canada				IRAN	SYRIA	IRAQ				
FOREIGN AFFAIRS												
SECURITY	X				X	X	X	X	X	X	X	
TERRORISM	X					X	X	X				
MIGRATION	X		X			X	X	X	X			
HOME SECURITY												
DRUGS	X											
VIOLENCE	X	X			X	X	X	X				
EMPLOYMENT	X	X		X					X			
CURRENCY MANIPULATION									X	X		X
VALUE ADDED TAX	X	X	X	X					X	X		X
TRADE DEFICIT	X	X							X	X		X

Source: Own elaboration

c) they assigned different subjective utility to the non-agreement alternative; and

d) there were major differences in their institution building processes and traditions.

By way of Alessina's (2006) war of attrition, the debt crisis (1982), was an opportunity to enforce very radical macroeconomic reforms, liberalizing the Mexican economy, privatizing public sector enterprises, even if these were not at the roots of the crisis. President Salinas (1988-1994) and the political and technocratic elite in power, considered the signing of a free trade agreement with the US as the instrument that would make irreversible the reforms and the modernization of both the Mexican economy and Mexican society. These reforms would increase stability and investor confidence, reassuring the inflows of capital needed to maintain economic growth (Ros, 1994).[1] Therefore, for the Mexican government any other alternative to NAFTA had little value, and US negotiators understood this fact very clearly. Consequently, Mexico needed to offer larger concessions as a result of the lower subjective utility assigned to the Mexican "no agreement" alternative (Wonnacott, 1994). Mexico, the smaller economy and the weaker state, took the initiative to begin negotiations; it was the seeker, looking for a safe haven for its exports, and who was willing to negotiate reciprocity by opening its economy even further, after implementing a far-reaching unilateral liberalization to joining GATT (Drache, 2001).

What were the objectives and interests of the USA behind NAFTA? The largest country (in 1994 the US economy was 17 times larger than the Mexican economy) considered that there were no important changes in prices, nor gains from specialization due to marginal changes in tariffs, because practically all Mexican exports entered the USA almost free, with a 4% average tariff. USA exports to Mexico faced several times higher border and non-border trade barriers. So, the US was interested in extracting from Mexico, on top a drastic cut of all tariff and non-tariff trade barriers, all the

---

[1] Baghawti expressed an abrasive opinion about the reasons and the urgency of the Mexican negotiators to reach the agreement: Mexican architects of NAFTA have a point of view that encouraged them to look at problems from the prism north of Rio Bravo. They were impressed by the US and wanted to emulate it. They said, "The US has done well. If we join with North America, all our problems will be over" (Author's translation), Bhagwati, Jagdish N., *El Financiero*, 22 de noviembre de 1999, p. 24.

concessions Mexico was willing to give. And Mexico was prepared to pay all the costs just to reach the agreement (Heillener, 1991). These included trade and non-trade and even non-economic incentives that could legitimize the United States signing the free trade agreement with Mexico and it was agreed, as early as 1990, that

"Mexico would not be treated as a developing country in the negotiations, meaning that it would not receive preferential treatment in matters such as transition periods for the elimination of tariffs" (Maxwell, 2000).

Mexico granted the USA larger tariff preferences than the ones it received, and in the first year of NAFTA, 50% of the tariff advantages in the US market were lost due to trade agreements the USA signed with countries with an export offer similar to Mexico's. Since the Mexican economy was more protected and regulated, Mexico had to make larger adjustments in the form of "side payments" as entry fees in the "new issues", which were eventually included in the agreement, namely trade in services, regulations and protection of intellectual property rights and in foreign investment, considered the jewel of the crown won by the United States (Drache, 2001). NAFTA was also a pioneer in the Investor-state dispute settlement, later incorporated into the Uruguay Round within GATT, which allows private companies to sue states for policies purportedly damaging to their interests. Furthermore, Mexico wholly and hastily liberalized agriculture and accepted that the US maintained its Farm Bill stimulus, which would later create a dumping effect, or losses to Mexican farmers of up to $13 billion dollars in constant 2005 prices (Wide, 2009), and it is calculated that no less than 5 million rural laborers abandoned this sector, while the imported content (completely from US origin) of the apparent consumption of Mexican staples (maize, beans, barley, rice, soy, among others) grew up to 50%, sometimes even close to 80%, which constitute a serious corrosion of food security. Moreover, Mexico absorbed all the costs of the institutional changes demanded by NAFTA and adopted the North American ones. Therefore, NAFTA did not entail any cost to the United States (Clinton, 1997). In this context, the increase in Mexican exports under NAFTA is more of a consequence of, on the one hand, the revaluation of the dollar rather than the tariff reductions in favor of Mexico and, on the other, the increasing imported content of Mexican manufactured exports (USITC, 2003).

Alicia Puyana

The Mexican economy under NAFTA

Certainly, global economic liberalization went too far, especially regarding financial deregulation, large corporate mergers that nullify the market as well as the ever-growing transfer of national decision-making centers to supranational non-elected entities, of the policies that affected society, creating a sense of denationalization in everybody's daily life. All of this runs parallel to the increase in income gaps between and within countries, which accelerates mass migration and creates global humanitarian problems.

As noted, the primary objective in negotiating NAFTA was to prevent radical changes in the liberal model implemented since the mid-1980s, which amounts to not allowing society to modify economic policy through the electoral process. However, liberalization and the structural reforms eliminated or reduced state interventions on commodity, labor, and financial markets, but did not act to reduce the large concentration of capital or take measures to control its effects. From then until now, the trend of the Mexican economy has been the least favorable since the end of the 1940s, with the smallest GDP growth rates (close to 1.2% per year), with low labor and total factorial productivity, wage repression, declining tradable sectors in GDP and employment and the explosion of informal labor, which is today about 60% of the total labor force employed. If inflation has been controlled, it has been through internal devaluation and permanent fiscal austerity, amidst very low direct taxation (effective tax revenues represent 14% of GDP, excluding oil income). All this has led the economy to a low-growth equilibrium with low-income, limited aggregate demand and limited investments. This trajectory has implied a redistribution from labor towards capital, in which Mexican labor appears as the greater loser when compared to American labor (Figure 1).This change in the functional distribution of income occurred in most countries of the world, but only a few present a scale of change similar to Mexico's. Between 1980 and 2014, the share of wages fell by 11.5 percentage points, a decrease 2.3 and 3.8 times higher than the one in the United States and Canada, respectively, and the highest among OECD countries (OECD. 2016).

Figure 1 Functional distribution of income in the United States, Canada and Mexico,
1970-2014

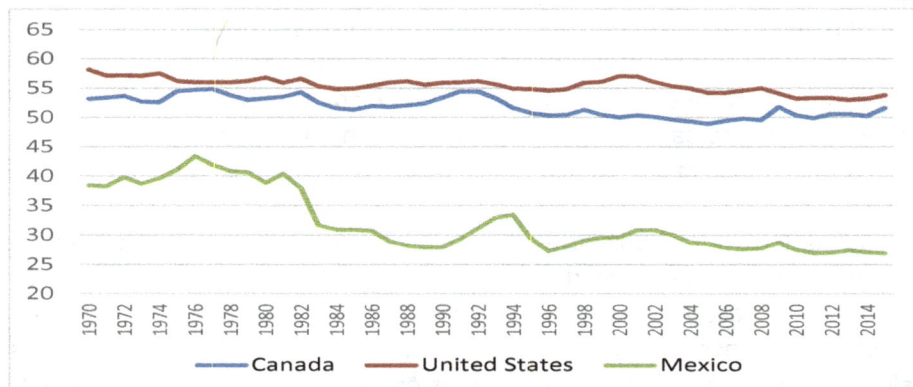

Source: Own calculations based on OECD.Stat2016, accessed 10 February 2017 at:
https://stats.oecd.org

Mexican GDP expanded 3.7 times more than national wages, compared to 1.9 in the US.[2] This confirms that in both cases capital accumulated the profits and labor lost them, and which happened in Mexico to a greater extent. Before the reforms, between 1970 and 1980 and the supply model, the trend between the two countries was in the opposite direction. Mexican labor lost 0.5 points of income while that of the US lost three times more. The situation after the reforms in the Mexican manufacturing sector has been the same but magnified: labor productivity grew twice as much as real wages per worker. From this angle, the impoverishment of Mexican workers is greater than that of the Americans, thus, contrary to Mexico being responsible for the "... looting of other countries that make our products, steal our companies and our jobs" (Trump, 2017). The high presence of investments implies that Mexican workers handed over income in favor of external foreign capital, basically from American origin, the largest foreign investor in the country. This transfer of labor income to capital is a result of having converted the wage bill into the main element of international

---

[2] Mexico was, amongst the 36 countries listed in the OCDE data base, the country with the biggest labour losses in primary distribution of income, after Ireland and Portugal and closely followed by the United Kingdom which occupied fourth place.

competitiveness, therefore a production cost to be reduced. Average real wages for 2015 represent 75% of those for 1980 and real minimum wages, only 35%. This fall in labor income has meant that average real wages in Mexican manufactures are lower than those in China and is ironically presented as an achievement in productive efficiency unleashed by liberalization and NAFTA, as explained by former Mexican Secretary of Economy and main NAFTA negotiator, Jaime Serra (Serra, 2014).

Who depends on whom?

Another fictitious argument is that disadvantageous trade with Mexico, China and other countries made the US economy dependent on such partners.

The US economy is considerably less open than that of Mexico, Canada and China, and practically all OECD countries. The external index of an economy (the total trade of a country as percent of its GDP) shows the degree of openness of an economy to global competition, that is, how much of its product is imported and exported. The United States appears as a relatively self-contained economy with relatively limited penetration of its domestic market by imports and comparatively limited exports. Mexico and Canada are the most open and China is relatively closed, as shown in Table 2. With an external coefficient of 72.8% of GDP (37.5% imports and 35.4% of exports), the Mexican economy is 2.6 times more open to competition in domestic and external markets, than the American one. Even Canada appears less open than Mexico. So it is hard to understand how the US could be dependent on Mexico or China. Whereas Mexico depends much more on trade, for the US the domestic demand is more significant.

Table 2 Canada, Mexico and the USA: External Coefficient of their economies, 1990-2015, as % of GDP

	Canada		China		Mexico		United States	
	1990	2015	1990	2015	1990	2015	1990	2015
Imports	24.9	33.8	10.7	18.6	19.7	37.5	10.5	15.4
Exports	25.1	31.5	14.0	22.1	18.6	35.4	9.2	12.6
Total	50.0	65.4	24.7	40.7	38.3	72.8	19.8	28.0
Trade Balance	0.2	-2.3	3.4	3.5	-1.1	-2.1	-1.3	-2.9
Average	1.1		1.7		-0.5		-1.6	

Source: Own calculations based on World Bank; WDI, 2016

In the context of the aforementioned trade openness, we define dependence as the weight of reciprocal trade in the GDP of each participating country. As shown in Figure 2, about 3.5% of the GDP in the US is linked to trade with

China and about 3% to trade with Canada and Mexico (Panel B). The dependence from the opposite side (Panel A) is surprising, if not alarming. 46.4% of Mexican GDP depends on trade with the US, a dependency 15.7 times more than the one US has from Mexico. In contrast, China's dependence with respect to US trade is almost three times lower than that of Mexico, while the Canadian is 10 points below. With these parameters in mind it is hard to accept the claim that the US depends on Mexico. On the contrary, what stands out is the asymmetrical dependence of Mexico on USA economy

Figure 2 Dependency of the economies of Mexico, Canada, China and the United States, as % of GDP, 1996-2015

Panel A: From USA regarding Mexico, China and Canada

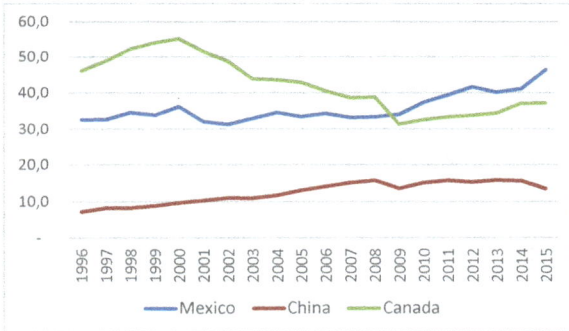

Panel B: From Mexico, Canada and China regarding USA

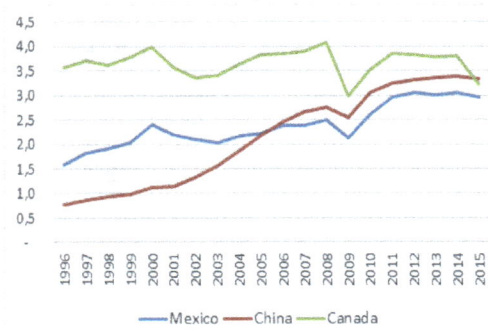

Source: Own calculations based on World Bank, WDI 2016

Second, the diversification of markets of origin and destination of exchange moderates US commercial dependence. Only three countries account each for more than 10% of total imports (China 21%, Canada 13% and Mexico 12%) and exports (Canada 18%, Mexico 15% and China 7.3%). Contrasting these proportions with Mexico's, the United States is the primary destination of 85% of its external sales and the origin of 40% of imports. Note also the imbalance in trade with China, which accounts for 21% of USA imports and only 7.3% of US exports. This asymmetry is most noticeable considering that the Chinese economy is 7.4 times larger than the Mexican and could capture a larger proportion of US exports. In 2016, the trade deficit of the US with China was 18 times greater than the Mexican one, reaching up to 319.3 billion dollars. In this context, the Mexican trade surplus with the United States grew from between 18 to 58 billion dollars between 1996 and 2016, a trend explained by the automotive sector, which accounted for 79.3% of the imbalance, followed by electronics. Mexican total sales of automobiles and auto parts account for 26% of total US automotive imports, but only 2.3% of its total imports.

Table 3 Percentage share of Mexico and China in United States trade, 2000-2016

	US Imports		US Exports	
	From Mexico	**From China**	**To Mexico**	**To China**
2000	11.17	8.22	14.32	12.08
2004	10.61	13.38	13.59	4.22
2008	10.27	16.06	11.75	5.42
2010	12.02	19.08	12.79	7.19
2011	11.91	18.09	13.40	7.02
2012	12.20	18.71	13.99	7.15
2013	12.37	19.42	14.32	7.71
2014	12.53	19.88	14.83	7.63
2015	13.12	21.50	15.71	7.72
2016	13.50	21.12	15.96	7.85
China/Mexico		1.6		0.5

Like no other sector, automobile manufacturing reflects the problems of global value chains: approximately 40% of the exported value are inputs, components and parts, imported from the US companies. An additional 20% is imported from Japanese, Korean and European USA subsidiaries.

Mexican manufacturing exports are intensive in imported value added, which varies in the different branches, Table 4.

Table 4 What is exported? Import content in Mexican and Chinese exports

SECTORS	MEXICO		CHINA		Difference (MX-CH)	
	1995	2011	1995	2011	1995	2011
1 Agriculture, Forestry, Fisheries	8.51	14.54	5.81	7.50	2.70	7.04
2 Mining and extraction	4.50	5.72	9.33	14.87	-4.83	-9.15
3 Foods, beverages and tobacco	14.34	18.50	8.38	11.27	5.96	7.23
4 Textiles and products	21.02	25.85	17.84	14.68	3.18	11.16
5 Leather	16.33	21.02	18.92	14.73	-2.59	6.29
6 Wood and products	12.47	14.96	16.14	16.86	-3.67	-1.89
7 Paper, pulp and printing	18.69	21.16	14.44	18.77	4.25	2.39
8 Coke, refined oil products, nuclear fuel	6.34	8.03	20.68	43.55	-14.34	-35.52
9 Chemicals and products	12.93	16.25	15.35	24.36	-2.42	-8.11
10 Plastics and rubber	24.76	32.29	18.05	23.38	6.71	8.91
11 Other non metallic minerals	10.44	12.56	10.87	16.92	-0.43	-4.36
12 Basic metals	23.37	27.38	15.52	27.32	7.85	0.06
13 Machinery	30.68	34.52	14.85	23.46	15.83	11.05
14 Electric and optical equipment	54.40	61.31	22.25	30.37	32.15	30.94
15 Transportation equipment	34.84	36.79	16.32	22.92	18.52	13.86
16 Manufacturing and recycling	28.93	33.34	15.47	14.77	13.46	18.56

Source: Own elaboration based on World Input Output Database (WIOD) matrices.

Exports with highest imported content are precisely those activities with greater technological content and greater presence of foreign investors. Those are precisely the activities in which the Mexican trade surplus with the US is higher: electrical, electronic and optical equipment, transportation, machinery. In contrast, Chinese external sales contain less imported content, except for some commodity-intensive products.

The highly imported content of Mexican manufacturing exports implies an intensified propensity to import and with more sever external restrictions intensified: for each point of increase in GDP, the imports increased by almost 5%. The final effect is a weakening of the link between growth in manufacturing exports, sectoral and total GDP, and employment (Puyana, 2015) a trajectory evident from Figure 3.

Figure 3 Share of manufactures in total GDP and exports, 1960-2014

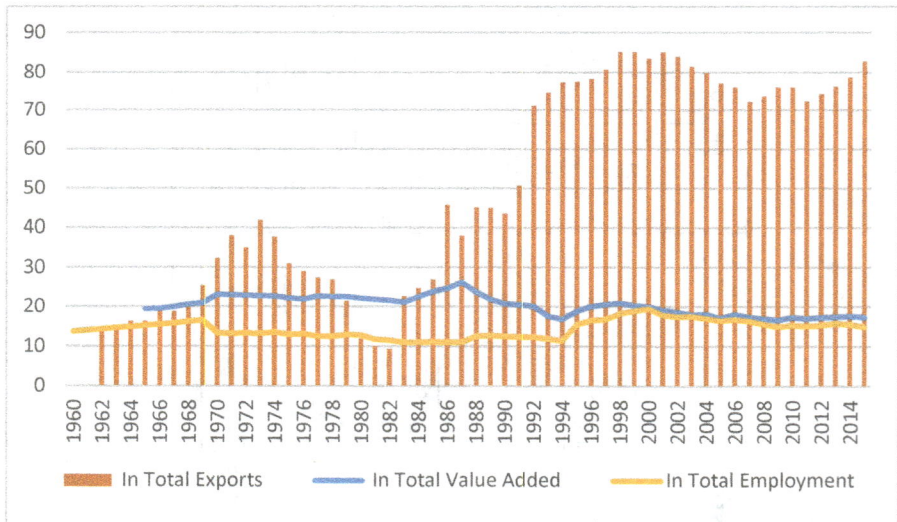

Source: World Bank, WDI, 2016, accessed February 18 2017The decline in GDP manufacturing is associated with a smaller but significant decrease in employment starting in the year 2000. This is the reason why sector productivity has not grown as would be expected by the progress of the sectors' openness, similar to that of total GDP (Romero, 2014). The deindustrialization of the Mexican economy is real, despite its volume of exports.

The trade of manufactured goods between Mexico and the US is vertical intra-industry exchange, in the sense that the two countries exchange goods classified in the same tariff category, which are differentiated by quality and intensity of factors: Mexico exports to the US goods with lower economies of scale and low technological content for lower income markets, and imports the same goods but of more technological sophistication and with higher prices. The effects would be similar to those of inter-industry, Heckscher-Ohlin- type trade (Puyana, 2003). With these considerations, taxes on companies that produce in Mexico and export to the US, either in the form of a Border Adjustment Tax or import taxes, would raise prices in a differentiated manner, punishing mostly consumers in the lower income group. Mexican manufacturing production is found in the most labor-intensive fragments of the production process of the global value chains and represents a tiny share of the value of each product. Therefore, its return to the US will not represent a huge increase in jobs creation but could imply some inflation, especially when considering it parallel to a large plan of public investment.

What to do?

Two facts looks certain: first, Trump and his team will follow through on campaign promises; second, the US presidency is advocating economic nationalism aiming to protect USA production and employment through the relocation of global value chains.[3] This change of focus has left a void for the Mexican leadership, be it in the public or the business sector. The American president pretends to legitimize chauvinist nationalism, presenting it as economic protectionism in defense of employment and reasserting that previous governments forgot to defend the national interest. As if the USA were a developing, commodity-dependent country, Trump says that the US suffers from the effects of an "impoverishing trade" which de-industrialized, turning the country to a low-value manufactures assembling economy. De-industrialization is not a phenomena resulting from trade, but from a higher degree of development, higher per capita income and the consequent change in the structure of demand. Trump's ideological positions which

---

[3] "National Trade Policy Agenda for 2017", presented to Congress in March 2017.

guide the formulation of the trade strategy (USTR, 2017) emerge from the false premise,

> "... that if other Nations are encouraged to raise their standards of living, our own American standard of living must of necessity be depressed" (Roosevelt, op cit.).

So Mexican society received with astonishment both the change of the USA economic policy and the repeated aggressions of Trump the candidate and the president, and refuses to accept them. Notwithstanding the grievances, President Peña invited Trump and gave him the president's platform. Today, a month after his inauguration, the public rejection of the threats of the USA president and the lukewarm Mexican official answers, resonates stronger by the day. The vast majority of Mexicans reject the idea that defense of national dignity and national sovereignty should be interpreted as support for the government or the major political parties or those responsible for the deterioration of the living conditions of the population. The demand for clearer and more energetic attitudes and responses is growing and pushing the government to reject any kind of threats and intimidations and to suggest it would suspend cooperation in migration, drug trafficking and terrorism even to abandon the NAFTA negotiations table if the USA insists in imposing taxes on Mexican exports and on USA investments in Mexico.

Since the US presidential primaries, Mexico has been living in an environment of uncertainty, declining growth and sharp devaluation of the Peso. Different proposals have emerged to resist the crises, which show the deep division in Mexican society. There is unanimity on two issues: first, not to pay for the wall, which is an act of antagonism and xenophobia irreconcilable with the deepening economic integration and ongoing collaboration on security and drug trafficking issues; second, to defend the rights of deported Mexicans, offer them services and assistance of all types, once they arrive in the country, and oppose any measure to tax or to freeze Mexican workers' remittances. So much for the consensus.

Table 5 Views of Mexican society in the face of changes in US policy towards Mexico and NAFTA

Sector Reaction or proposal	Renegotiate and Defend free trade			No to a NAFTA renegotiation		To Transform Current Economic Model					TOTAL
	To Negotiate NAFTA	Defending free trade	Rejecting border tax	Not renegotiate NAFTA without mutual benefits	Abandon NAFTA and opt WTO	Diversify markets	Strenghten internal market	Decrease taxes	Protect Agriculture	Industrial policy, infrastru.	
Gobierno	11	9	9	6	3	9	1	1	2	1	52
Actores politicos	8	10	1	4	10	9	2	2	1	1	48
Empresarios	17	5	1	3	4	17	4	3	8	5	67
Sindicatos, movimientos sociales y ONGs	1	0	0	2	5	0	1	0	3	1	13
Academia	6	3	2	2	3	14	9	1	4	4	48
TOTAL	43	27	13	17	25	49	17	7	18	12	228
Actor responses, absolute values		83		42			73			30	228
Actor responses, porcentual shares		36,4		18,42			32,02			13,2	100

Source: Author's elaboration.

Dissent revolves around whether or not to renegotiate NAFTA or whether to take Trump's policies towards Mexico as the opportunity to revise the development model. In any case, the desirability of diversifying external markets is emphasized as well as reintegrating productive chains and strengthening the internal market, which are at odds with NAFTA. Past economic trends, employment wages, inequality and poverty reinforce the need for changes in economic policies, with or without NAFTA. Table 5, summarizes and groups the views of diverging representative sectors of the society.[4]

While 19% of persons prefer to renegotiate NAFTA, many government and business actors (27 or the 11%) opt to "modernize"[5] NAFTA, and to preserve the free trade ideology that sustains the supply side economic model. They also reject import and export taxes, domestic and foreign. All-in-all pro free trade position comprises 36.4% of answers. This position stems from the premise that Mexico is an important part of the NAFTA region, a fully integrated production area that exports to the world. In that context, any protectionist measure would weaken the region's competitiveness in the world. Therefore, they propose to seize the opportunity to deepen liberalization and expand NAFTA to areas not initially included, such as communications, the energy sector, as well as to extend agreements to the electronic sector, intellectual property, including anti-corruption rules. To strengthen its preferences, the government integrated a group of experts to define the negotiating strategy and lead the negotiations, with the same economists who negotiated the NAFTA in the first place. The group has already stated the main tenets. First, to educate society in the benefits of NAFTA, which has already realized to a greater extent than expected its foremost initial goal: to expand exports. Second, to reiterate that the greatest beneficiaries of the agreement are the consumers, without mentioning how these are first and foremost also producers and workers. Third, to extend NAFTA including themes agreed for the TPP and also discussed in the

---

[4] These are the opinions expressed in articles from the most widely circulated daily and weekly newspapers and in specialized journals, between September 15, 2016 and March 15, 2017. They include 175 notes and articles of some 228 people coming from government, political leaders, representatives of unions, NGOs, academics and entrepreneurs.
[5] Modernize is the euphemism for renegotiate, since so many people rejects the idea of negotiations.

TTIP, eliminating all restriction to trade and to capital. It is still in doubt whether these proposals to "modernize" NAFTA would not intensify the wage repression experienced by the Mexican labor sector since the reforms and NAFTA, and as some critics of TTP and TTIP suggest (Bivens, 2015; Felbermayr, et al., 2013).

The business sector, with its 67 responses appears divided. While some 10% of them propose to negotiate NAFTA, around 16% takes a moderate stance, either rejecting the negotiations in the face of uncertainty and fear that the results will be negative or seeking to expand markets, strengthen the domestic market and to redefine sectoral policies, industrial, agricultural, energy and technology policies.

A diverse group (academia, politicians, and unionists) advocates renegotiating the agreement on condition that it is beneficial to the country and under certain circumstances, namely not building the wall, not imposing border adjustment taxes or any other taxes. To reach positive agreement for Mexico, or if the US decides to abandon NAFTA, the preferred alternative is to go the WTO. Finally, there is a relevant group of political, intellectual and academia actors, proposing not to negotiate, abandon NAFTA and go to the WTO.

A consensus emerges, with 45% support for the need to reform the current economic model, with or without a renegotiation of NAFTA, with industrial policies that reintegrate productive chains, generate added value and national employment, as well as provide protection to agriculture, all with a view to strengthening the market. Finally, the diversification of the destination of export markets gains strength. Some of these proposals would clash with government preferences, but echo Trump's policy. Almost all of these priorities contradict the liberal NAFTA economic policy model.

It is our opinion that Mexico must seize the current opportunity, redefine the policies outlined in NAFTA, and undo the mistakes made in the initial NAFTA negotiations and the structural reforms of the mid-1980s. The answer to this external shock, induced by the stubborn will to change the norms that had governed bilateral relations for the last 24 years, could be the opportunity for a serious reform to the model of national development. There will be losers and winners, it is true. Depending on the players who would lead the changes it would be expected that the balance will not be adverse to labour as it was for the last 30 years.

With oil running out and the US restricting investments and imports of goods made in Mexico, and repressing remittances, the country would not have the resources to invest, accumulate capital and expand production. As in world crises and wars, it is necessary to change course, reindustrialize Mexico and strengthen agriculture.

Following are some premises for change, emerging from our own recollection and reading public opinion in Table 5:

i)   To figure first the direction of the country and its economy and, in this context, establish the space of relations with the US and the rest of the world;

ii) The trajectory of the national economy must rest on sustained and sustainable growth, the generation of more and better jobs to reverse the decline of labor in the functional distribution of income, and reduce inequality;

iii) Protect agriculture, to ensure food security, as the US, EU, Japan and China already do, reversing the imported content of consumption of maize, beans, rice, soybeans and other primary food products;

iv) An agricultural policy with increases in yields and productivity, not oriented exclusively to exports, but to ensure food security and supply inputs to manufactures;

v)   To launch an active industrial policy that incorporates labor and added value, promotes research and, in reaction to the border tax and the import tax, a tariff policy that eliminates negative effective protection and protects national value added;

vi) To structure an energy policy for development, in which the oil that still remains and is to be found becomes a development factor and integrating clean and alternative energies;

vii) To reject elements accepted in the TPP, either as a negotiating strategy with the US or as a policy to expand Mexico's export markets, in the economic restructuring process. That would only aggravate the structural problems generated by the way NAFTA was negotiated. They will deepen the now questioned denationalization of the economy;

viii) In this context, the academy, unfastened from political and economic power centers, must study and explain reality and propose objective interpretations and lines of action.

References

Bannon, E. (2017) Interview at the Conservative Political Action Conference, ACPC, February 23, at http://cpac.conservative.org/speakers/stephen-bannon/

Bivens, Josh (2015) "The Trans-Pacific Partnership Is Unlikely to be a Good Deal for American Workers", EPI Briefing Paper No. 397, Economic Policy Institute, Washington, DC.

Clinton, W.J. (1997). "To the Congress of the United States: Study on the Operation and Effect of the North American Free Trade Agreement". Weekly Compilation of Presidential Documents.
https://www.archives.gov/federal-register/publications/presidential-compilation.html

Felbermayr, Gabriel, Heid Lehwald Sybille Ed. (2013). "Transatlantic Trade and Investment Partnership (TTIP) – Who benefits from a free trade deal?", *Global Economic Dynamic*, Bertelsmann Stiftung.

Fullbrook, Edward, (2014) "New Paradigm Economics versus Old Paradigm Economics", in *real-world economics review*, no. 66,
www.paecon.net/PAEReview/issue66/Fullbrook66.pdf

Heillener, G. (1991) "Consideraciones sobre un área de libre Comercio entre Estados Unidos y México", in G. Vega (coord.), *México ante el libre Comercio con América del Norte*, El Colegio de México y la Universidad Tecnológica de México, Mexico City, 1991.

Lamy, Pascal. (2003) "Commissioner LAMY's closing remarks at 5th WTO Ministerial Conference 0115/ 2016" http://eu-un.europa.eu/commissioner-lamy%C2%92s-closing-remarks-at-5th-wto-ministerial-conference-cancun/

Mayer, F. W. (1998) Interpreting NAFTA: The Science and Art of Political Analysis. New York: Columbia University Press

Puyana, A. (2015) "A never ending recession? The vicissitudes of economics and economic policies from a Latin American perspective", *real-world economics review*, issue no. 72, at:
http://www.paecon.net/PAEReview/issue72/Puyana72.pdf

Radford, P. (2016) "Why Trump?", World Economics Association Newsletter, Volume 6, No. 2, April 2016, at: https://www.worldeconomicsassociation.org/files/Issue6-2.pdf

Roosevelt, F. D. (1944) *State of the Union Message to Congress,* acceded 02/02/2017 at http://www.presidency.ucsb.edu/ws/?pid=16518

Ross, J. (1994) *"Mexico and the North American Free Trade Agreement* in Bulmer-Thomas V. et al eds. *Mexico and the North American Free Trade Agreement. Who Will Benefit?*, Institute of Latin American Studies, University of London, Macmillan, London, 1994

Roubini, N. "'America First' and Global Conflict Next", Project, Syndicate, JAN 2, 2017, at: https://www.project-syndicate.org/commentary/trump-isolationism-undermines-peace-worldwide-by-nouriel-roubini-2017-01

Serra Puche, J. (2014) "TLCAN 20 años", Conference at El Colegio de Mexico, Feb, 2014 http://tlcan20.consejomexicano.org/wp-content/uploads/2014/02/NAFTA-20-a%C3%B1os.pdf
Obama, B. (2015) Declaración de Presidente Obama a raíz de la aprobación del TPP, accedido febrero 10, 2017, en https://obamawhitehouse.archives.gov/the-press-office/2015/10/05/statement-president-trans-pacific-partnership

Lucas, R. (2004) "The Industrial Revolution: Past and Future," (2003 Annual Report of the Federal Reserve Bank of Minneapolis), p. 5.

Trump, D. (2017) "America First': Full Transcript and Video of Donald Trump's Inaugural Address", accessed 14 Feb 2017 in *Wall Street Journal.*

USITC (2003) "The Impact of Trade Agreements: Effect of the Tokyo Rounds, U.S.-Israel FTA, U.S.-Canada FTA, NAFTA, and the Uruguay Round on the U.S. Economy", at: https://www.usitc.gov/publications/332/pub3621.pdf

USTR (2017) The President's 2017 Trade Policy Agenda, at:
https://ustr.gov/sites/default/files/files/reports/2017/AnnualReport/AnnualReport2017.pdf.

Wide, T. (2009) "Agricultural Dumping Under NAFTA: Estimating the Costs of U.S. Agricultural Policies to Mexican Producers", GDE INSTITUTE WORKING PAPER NO. 09-08

"Unemployment": misinformation in public discourse and its contribution to Trump's populist appeal

Edward Fullbrook [University of the West of England, UK]

Piketty et al.

It seems generally agreed that populism tends to rise up after a prolonged period in which governing elites have blocked from public discussion the declining economic welfare of a significant proportion of the population. These declines take two forms, usually simultaneously and interdependently:

1. A decline of income and wealth in absolute terms and/or relative to the elites and their agents.
2. A decline in key characteristics of employment through time (quality, security, real and relative wage levels) creating persistent high level of unemployment.

Though the latter is interdependent with the former, the real level of unemployment can be hidden. Elected elites and their patrons have a strategic interest in holding back public awareness and discussion of both declines for fear of losing elections and for fear that the upward redistributions of income and wealth will be stopped or even reversed.

Until three years ago the ruling elites in the United States were extremely successful at keeping the severe upward income and wealth redistribution that had been "progressing" since the early 1970s out of public view. GINI coefficients and graphs showing from 1970 onwards median income levels and relative shares of the bottom 90% and bottom 50% were never part of public discussion and but rarely of economics. Instead income discussion focused tightly on GDP and GDP per capita, which with rare exceptions increased year by year.

True, from the early 2000s the *Real-World Economics Review* featured numerous papers calling attention to the long-term upward redistributions taking place in the United States,[1] and in other venues Saez and Piketty did the same. But it was not until the publication of Piketty's empirical blockbuster that a substantial hole was opened in the public wall of silence regarding the 40-year relative income and wealth decline of a large proportion of the American population in particular.[2] This cultural breakthrough has made it marginally acceptable for the declining fortunes of the majority of citizens to be mentioned in corporate media and even in some neoclassical journals. Without Piketty's book the rise of Trumpism would have been for our era's overriding neoliberal narrative even more of an unexpected and inexplicable historical phenomenon.

"Unemployment"

The systematic distortion and non-reporting by both journalists and economists of changes in income and wealth levels is not the only way in

---

[1] James K. Galbraith, "The American Economic Problem", *post-autistic economics review*, issue no. 25, 18 May 2004, pp. 23-26,
http://www.paecon.net/PAEReview/wholeissues/issue25.pdf
John Schmitt and Ben Zipperer, "Is the U.S. a Good Model for Reducing Social Exclusion in Europe?", *post-autistic economics review*, issue no. 40, 1 December 2006, article 1, pp. 2-17,
http://www.paecon.net/PAEReview/issue40/SchmittZipper40.pdf
Dean Baker, "Increasing Inequality in the United States", *post-autistic economics review*, issue no. 40, 1 December 2006, article 2, pp. 18-22,
http://www.paecon.net/PAEReview/issue40/Baker40.pdf
Thomas I. Palley, "America's Exhausted Paradigm", *real-world economics review*, issue no. 50, 8 September 2009, pp. 52-74,
http://www.paecon.net/PAEReview/issue50/Palley50.pdf
John Schmitt, "Inequality as Policy: The United States Since 1979", *real-world economics review*, issue no. 51, 1 December 2009, pp. 2-9,
http://www.paecon.net/PAEReview/issue51/Schmitt51.pdf
Edward Fullbrook, "The Political Economy of Bubbles", *real-world economics review*, issue no. 59, 12 March 2012, pp. 138-154,
http://www.paecon.net/PAEReview/issue59/Fullbrook59.pdf
Emmanuel Saez, "Striking it richer: the evolution of top incomes in the United States", *real-world economics review*, issue no. 65, 27 September 2013, pp. 120-129,
http://www.paecon.net/PAEReview/issue65/Saez65.pdf
[2] Thomas Piketty, *Capital in the Twenty-First Century*, Harvard University Press, 2017.

which the reporting and discussion of the economy has been fundamentally distorted so as to keep hidden the decline in the economic welfare of a large proportion of America's population. "Unemployment" is a poignant everyday word, but the media and the economics profession have come to give a meaning to "unemployment" radically different from the meaning that people following the news and voting give it. For them, to be "unemployed" means to want but to be without full-time work.

Led by the Bureau of Labor Statistics (BLS), the economics profession has defined sub-categories of "unemployment" in the real-life meaning of the word and then cunningly reintroduced the same symbol to designate one of those sub-categories – the one which is usually the smallest – of "unemployment" in the real-life sense. Let us look at how this is done.

The BLS's website https://www.bls.gov/cps/ says:

> "There is only one official definition of unemployment – people who are jobless, actively seeking work [in the last 4 weeks], and available to take a job, ..."

There are three idiosyncrasies in this definition.

One idiosyncrasy is immediately apparent. The definition says in effect that if an unemployed person becomes too discouraged to look regularly for a job, then they are no longer "unemployed". It is only those who retain some immediate optimism regarding overcoming their employment situation that will be counted as "unemployed". In other words, under the BLS definition the people who are most psychologically affected by their unemployment are disqualified from being counted as "unemployed". The medical equivalent would be to say that someone who is chronically ill and who has been discouraged from finding a cure for their illness is no longer "ill".

The other two idiosyncrasies of the BLS's use of the symbol "unemployment" are, at least partially, hidden by the meanings it assigns to words in its definition.

It defines "jobless" to mean without any kind of a job whatsoever:

"People are considered employed if they did any work at all
for pay or profit during the survey reference week. This
includes all part-time and temporary work, ..."

So, for example, if an unemployed machinist or supervisor finds eight hours
of work in a week as a dishwasher they are by the BLS definition *not*
"unemployed". But in the real lives of the machinist and the supervisor and in
the minds of their family and friends and the social milieu in which they live,
they are unemployed.

The meaning which the BLS assigns to "actively seeking work" is no less
unworldly. This phrase is interpreted so as to exclude many unemployed
people who *are* looking for work. It makes a distinction between what it
terms "active methods of job search" and "passive methods of job search".
Examples of "active methods" include: contacting "an employer directly or
having a job interview", and "[S]ubmitting resumes or filling out applications".
"Examples of passive methods" include looking for "job openings that are
posted in newspapers or on the Internet". This means that if in the last four
weeks a real-life unemployed person searches every week or even every
day the advertisements for job openings in newspapers and on the Internet
and in the windows and on the walls of employment agencies and finds no
jobs advertised for which they might reasonably apply or inquire about, then
all that effort does not qualify that unemployed person as "looking for work"
and therefore in the official statistics they are *not counted* as "unemployed".
And of course the more serious the unemployment situation in an economy
or sector thereof, the more likely it is that there are no jobs for which an
unemployed person might reasonably contact an employer or fill out forms.

"Labor underutilization"

To avoid referring to the unemployed in general and calling attention to their
numbers and their plight, the Bureau of Labor Statistics has invented the
term "labor underutilization". It gathers and publishes statistics for 6
categories of "underutilization" expressed as percent and calls them: U-1, U-
2, U-3, U-4, U-5 and U-6, the first five being "underutilization" subcategories
of U-6. U-3, which is labelled the "official unemployment rate", is based on

what, as above, the BLS calls "unemployed". U-5 includes U-3's "unemployed" plus what it calls all "persons marginally attached to the labor force" which it defines as the unemployed "who currently are neither working nor looking for work (remember what this "looking for work" means) but indicate that they want and are available for a job and have looked for work sometime in the past 12 months."[3] U-6, in addition to "persons marginally attached", includes "people employed part time for economic reasons", meaning those who cannot find full time employment, like the machinist who washed dishes last Friday night. According to the BLS figures, in January 2017 the number of unemployed people who fall into its U-6 category comprised 9.4% of the civilian labour force, nearly twice its U-3 rate. But U-6 still covers only a subcategory of the real-life unemployed. In does not include people who are unemployed and who "want and are available for a job" but have not "looked for work" in the past 12 months. These workers might be called *very* discouraged, but the fact that they are very discouraged *does not make them any less unemployed.*

Total unemployment

Although the Bureau of Labor Statistics does not compute "U-7" or "U-8" rates, it does count and publish the number of people wanting work but who have not "looked for work" in the past 12 months.

In their 2017 paper, Flavia Dantas and L. Randall Wray note, and their Figure 4 below shows, that when this category of the unemployed is also counted it "boosts the unemployment rate to 12 percent".[4] This means, as Jan Kregel says in his introduction to their paper, that when it comes to reaching full employment "we are still roughly 20 million jobs short of the mark".

---

[3] U-4 is based on U-3's "unemployed" plus "a subset of the marginally attached".
[4] Flavia Dantas and Wray, L. Randall, "Full Employment: Are We There Yet?", Levy Economics Institute, Public Policy Brief No. 142, 2017.

Figure 4 Unemployment Rates, 1994–2016

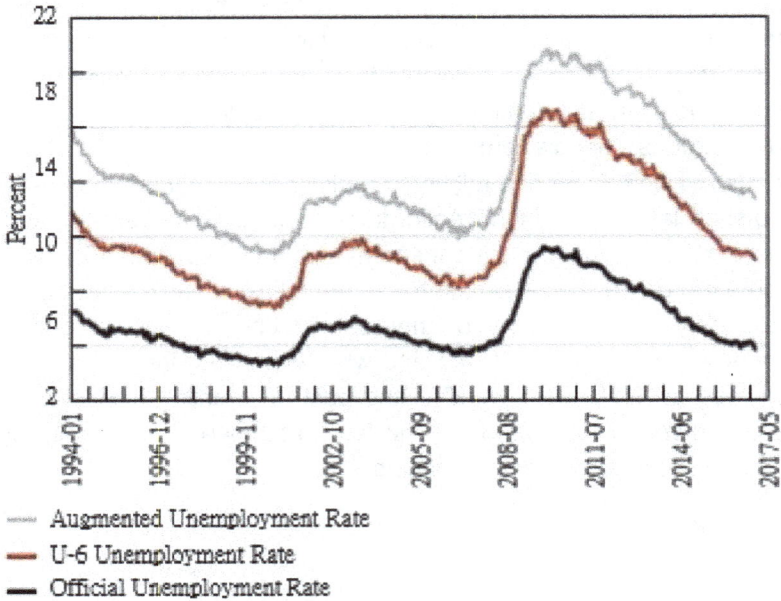

- - - - Augmented Unemployment Rate
—— U-6 Unemployment Rate
—— Official Unemployment Rate

Sources: BLS; author' calculations

But even 12 percent may be a serious understatement of the real-life unemployment rate in the United States at the time of Trump's election, given that the very discouraged unemployed tend to have no contact, direct or indirect, with the BLS's system of counting. Because no official statistics are collected for this category of unemployment, we are here very much in the realm of the statistically semi-unknown. Nonetheless there exist various estimates of what the total unemployment rate might be, one of which, from Shadow Government Statistics is shown in the following graph.

Unemployment Rate - Official (U-3 & U-6) vs ShadowStats Alternate
Monthly SA. Through Jan. 2017 (ShadowStats, BLS)

— Official (U3) — Broadest (U6) — ShadowStats

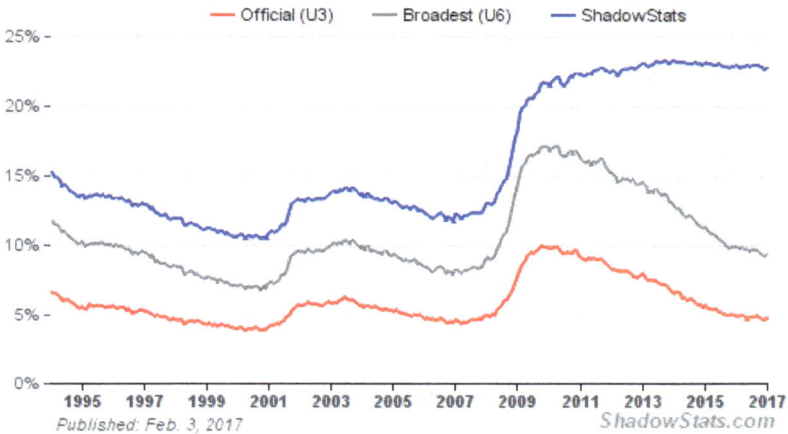

Published: Feb. 3, 2017   ShadowStats.com

Conclusion

Just as failing to acknowledge the upward redistribution of income and wealth does not make its consequences go away, so also defining the majority of the unemployed out of official existence does not eliminate them from real-life existence. But it does humiliate and alienate them by making them feel that their unemployment is a personal failure rather than a failure of the system, of the economy, to provide enough jobs for the number of people wanting and needing them. And when high unemployment persists over a period of years and the flow of public misinformation about it also persists, the probability becomes high that the long-term unemployed and their social milieu will cease to believe the misinformation *and* cease to support the political system that generates it.

Statistics, like everything else, can be used or misused, kept clean or subverted. When public attention is focused on GDP and income per capita and never on relative shares and median income and when, unknown to the many, "unemployment" in public discourse is defined to exclude most unemployment, then statistics instead of serving as means of enlightenment, serve as means of screening ourselves off from reality. In the end, however, reality breaks through. And that is where we are today and why you are reading about Trumponomics.

Trumponomics: everything to fear including fear itself?[*]

Jamie Morgan [Leeds Beckett University, UK]

> "The cause of America is in great measure the cause of all mankind. Many circumstances hath, and will arise, which are not local, but universal, and through which the principles of all Lovers of Mankind are affected, and in the Event of which, their Affections are interested" (Thomas Paine, *Common Sense*).

Introduction: making sense of Donald Trump

Before one can make sense of Trumponomics one must first make sense of Donald Trump. Yet, how to make sense of Donald Trump?[1] Trump is a brand. He is not a career politician. He is not an economist, though he holds a degree in economics earned in the 1960s. In the following paper I set out some well-worn points that help to provide context for Trump in office. These are worth synthesizing because they provide background to the shape and scope of Trumponomics. Despite commentary to the contrary, from a political economy perspective Trump and Trumponomics likely represent business as usual, albeit in angrier intensified and contradictory form. This in turn affects whether Trumponomics will constitute a *structural* transformation in the American economy.

---

[*] Thanks to Brendan Sheehan.
[1] For biography of Trump and his family see, for example, the documentaries Radice (2017); Kirk (2017), and the texts D'Antonio (2017); Blair (2015); O'Brien (2016); Kranish and Fisher (2017).

Jamie Morgan

The capital-mobilising deal maker

As a brand, Trump is also a particular kind of contemporary businessman. He positions himself as a maker of "deals" rather than a maker of things, though his wealth is rooted in construction and property. He is an owner of portfolio assets, who uses these to leverage new ventures where he is able to conjure personal gain from situations where material benefits to the many may be lacking. His skill set is one of concentration and extraction of returns, and the externalisation of costs and losses. Based on that skill set profits can artfully appear and equally disappear (with tax consequences) in ways that have little to do with the simplistic concepts of theory of the firm. The solution to any problem is an additional incorporation, a

transfer of assets, a lawsuit that deters others, a no fault out-of-court settlement that protects oneself, a debt restructure or perhaps a timely Chapter 11 bankruptcy declaration. Being proficient along these lines can make one a billionaire, particularly if one starts with a core of inherited wealth for collateral and has access to a network.[2]

Ultimately, the returns are achieved by surrounding oneself with people able to understand and exploit rules and seize an opportunity.[3] The *ex post* justification for this is that no one prevented it and "wouldn't you do it too?". This is important, because Donald Trump is the first US President to have no experience of political or military office. But he does have experience. His experience is of how to shape and exploit law and convention to achieve goals available only to a narrow interest group. Knowing how to do this does not mean he either knows how to prevent others or is in fact intent on preventing others from doing what he has made a career of. To prevent others would be to deny his own status as entrepreneur and so deny the US the value of such entrepreneurship. Moreover, his business skill set does not simply translate, mirror or reverse. It is not a simple case of poacher turned gamekeeper. For example, being "smart" enough to employ lawyers who

---

[2] Trump's narrative is that he began with a loan from his father. It has also been pointed out Trump could have been as wealthy simply through passive investment. This is arguable and would depend on exactly what Trump is worth, which is difficult to ascertain.
[3] Beginning notoriously with Roy Cohn.

can spot a loophole does not enable one to construct law without loopholes (if it did then the *general* problem would have been solved long ago).[4] In any case, concentration and extraction of returns is quite a different frame of reference than the construction of an overall economy. Developing Trump's skill set created a social subject, some might say anti-social subject. Political economy, meanwhile, is concerned with how we choose to live. But Trump already has a default position. He is by socialisation a particular personification of powerful special interests (capital mobilizing dealmakers). His own sense of uniqueness and superiority should not obscure this nor should it obscure the underlying logic it rests on, which is what is good for this interest group is good for the US economy. This is a deep ambiguity in Trump's appeal once one moves beyond the showmanship.

A US president is the focal-point-as-leader of a system of law. That is, a democratic system of checks and balances and the very point of that system is to constrain powerful special interests; those who exploit, those who behave badly. This includes through impeachment, the president.[5] To function effectively, rather than to be functionally dysfunctional and so also be disintegrating or degenerating, the system requires a president to at least act as though constraint of special interests mattered. Style matters here as much as substance because long-term legitimacy and authority requires convention to have positive meaning. The increasing recognition over the last two decades that the system was not functioning effectively partially explains the appeal of Trump, just as it helped to explain the appeal of Obama. In particular, it was a neat piece of misdirection by the Trump team to construct a campaign that apportioned to one part of a complex the blame for the parlous state of American politics. That is, a Washington-centred political elite. This enabled Trump to appear as a solution of kinds. "Drain the swamp" has disguised the very obvious fact that Trump only has his own

---

[4] One can close loopholes and create law that closes down opportunities existent under former law, but it is the interest in and attitude to exploitation that remains, unless relevant kinds of organization or practice are prohibited. Trump has shown no interest in eradicating the category of "entrepreneur" of which he is a member.

[5] This has already become a source of debate concerning the President's financial affairs and other matters. Article 1, section 9, clause 8 of the constitution only prohibits emolument from a foreign state without permission of Congress. It has been convention to place assets in a blind trust in order to avoid conflicts of interest and Trump has resisted this. Some of his advisors and appointees also carry potential business conflicts of interest.

socialisation to fall back on in making decisions and that of those who can capture his attention. Many of these are also powerful social subjects with narrow interests – articulating hyper-versions of current pathologies. For example, in addition to the Breitbart connection, Trump has increasingly drawn on fellows from The Heritage Foundation (Kopan, 2016). The Foundation has published extensive documents setting out their preferred agenda for the new administration (e.g. Winfree, 2016).[6]

To some degree commentary that emphasises Trump is not "really" a Republican misses the point. He is not a Washington nurtured political animal schooled in Republican tradition of public discourse; but the underlying message that he "knows how things work", has some credence precisely because he is an inside "outsider", both by long-term relations of patronage (he has a history as a campaign contributor) and by broader socialisation. He may have no experience of political office but he has experience with politicians based on the needs of his skill set. What he knows is how things can be broken and who one can hire to get things done in a broken system. This is a pathological form of knowing how things work that indicates also a systemic pathology. Insight and practice (such that they are) along these lines does not translate into ready solutions. It cannot solve partisan antagonism in a system that requires bi-partisanship nor does it lend itself to any clear idea of what good politics or a healthy economy is. That is unless one simply assumes that current politics is an impediment to a vibrant effective economy and all that is needed is for politics to get out of the way. *Political economy* is a reminder that politics never just gets out of

---

[6] Trump's economic advisers include Stephen Moore, Larry Kudlow and Sam Clovis. Moore is a fellow of the Heritage Foundation, and Moore and Kudlow are both adherents of Laffer curve economics. Clovis is a tea party activist. https://ballotpedia.org/Sam_Clovis Carl Icahn has also emerged as a possible economic advisor (billionaire investor) and Peter Navarro is Trump's appointment as head of a national trade council (Navarro is a critic of China's economic and military development). George Monbiot makes the point that many right wing think tanks and ostensibly grassroots campaigning groups are essentially heavily funded corporate lobbying vehicles. A range of staff working for Trump derive from such organizations, including ones funded by the Koch brothers. One should note though that it is a feature of Trump's political career so far that he deviates from core Republican tenets including some advocated by the Heritage Foundation, and there is no necessary unity within his cabinet; for example, ex-general Mattis, is more sceptical of Russia and has taken a more pro-NATO position than Trump (Mattis too has appeared at Heritage Foundation events).

the way. It is a construct. In any case, there is also a basic tension here since Trump has also espoused interventionist policies. Still, the neo-conservative personnel who surround Trump only serve to highlight that his election will ultimately involve intra-elite and intra-class conflict rather than their supersession.[7]

In terms of the economy, long term experience that includes creative use of accounting that tests the law (without necessarily breaking it) and a litigious tendency in order to concentrate and protect wealth does not prepare one to ask basic important questions, such as: what is a sustainable business, how does one distribute wealth fairly, what is the basis of a provisioning economy? As such, and to reiterate, there is no reason to assume that President Trump has an actual interest in preventing what he has profited from or any idea how this can be done, quite the reverse, these will form part of how he views a functioning economy. Prevention-as-transformation requires a fundamental systemic critique (rather than inchoate channelling of many discontents), and a capacity to transcend rather than affirm narrow interests and their socialising (anti-socialising) effects. Moreover, an interest in prevention would require him to embody the role of President in terms of its formal idealisation. That is, a sense of civic duty, the greater good, the welfare of the many (all too easily expressed as the West Wing fallacy). It would require him to have a clear and profound commitment to taking responsibility and acting "responsibly". Yet both of these are ideologically informed and involve reflexive ethical conduct and neither is clearly associated with Trump as a social subject so far. A Trumpian butterfly seems an unlikely metamorphosis. Bullying the badly behaved may get some things done but it is also bad behaviour that ultimately undermines the system through which anything is achieved.

Trump as populist

Though it is questionable that Trump can or will transcend his socialisation his entire campaign hinged on positioning himself as though he *does* transcend it. He is a child of privilege and a publicity seeking television

---

[7] There is also the more controversial issue of the "Alt-Right" and immigration policy has already started to intensify concerns regarding this.

celebrity so this has been a glaring contradiction that has hidden in plain sight. Trump has been positioned as a person able to not only speak for but also empathise with and hence understand the "ordinary Joe". He is by common reference a populist.[8] By definition a populist appeals to the many. However, the context that makes populism significant as a political force is that the many who are appealed to can be swayed, galvanised or co-opted because of their contrastive experience of the world around them, and because they currently are not or feel that they are not represented and recognized. Their concerns as they see them are not given due weight.[9] Trump did not invent income stagnation, deindustrialisation, job insecurity, debt vulnerability, or extreme income inequality. What Trump has done is offer some a future they want to believe in. In a democratic system a populist many need not be the majority, they need only be a significant number able to affect outcomes.[10]

A populist requires a strategy to appeal to the many. Strategy manufactures a link between the past and the future. It warps and repackages nostalgia in the now. Populism is typically associated with the reduction of complex matters to simple causes and consequences for the specific purpose of garnering support. The reduction need not be coherent or consistent it need only be effective. It may well be effective *because* it lacks actual content and *because* it resists or refuses to respond to calls to be substantive, or to justify itself in terms of evidence and realisable projects. It may, therefore, be effective *in its* incoherency and inconsistency rather than merely despite it. Incoherency becomes by a trick of the psyche the grounds for willing

---

[8] For two recent explorations of the concept and proliferation of populism see Judis (2016) and Müller (2016)

[9] There are two different issues here. A system may be problematic in general, and it may also have distributional effects, which are particularly harsh for some. See Morgan, 2017. Populism is focused around parallel issues that involve but are not restricted to distributional effects for some (where moral panic and other manipulations also apply).

[10] Trump lost the popular vote by 2.9 million but won the electoral college vote (confirmed January 6th 2017) by 304 to 227 for Clinton. However, even as a populist '"movement" of protest there is something underwhelming about the actual shift in voting. If one considers the proportions that allowed states to be captured by Trump then the total shift was not only small, it was far less than the average swing away from the incumbent party candidate after a two-term presidency. Since 1952, this has been about 5%. In Trump's case it was closer to 2%. However, 26 of the 30 lowest income states voted Trump.

suspension of disbelief. It enables optimism and hope. The believer may, therefore, respond by a reciprocating resistance to scrutiny of the terms of the reduction. This too helps to make sense of Donald Trump. His socialisation hides in plain sight because his manner and his track record are not secret. However, in plain sight these become something to either set aside (we need a change so why not him?) or laud because he 'tells it like it is' (albeit in a quasi-stream of consciousness form of garbled speech).

There is currently a great deal of reference to a "post-truth" political environment. However, it would be a hysterical response to hysteria to reduce public discourse to simply "post-truth". The desire to know, to reason, to be truth-seeking have not disappeared.[11] At the same time, as Philip Roth once wrote, we live in the real and not in the true. Acting as though truth-seeking did not matter, as though truth-claims were no more than posturing rather than necessary standards for public discourse, is a recognized and significant aspect of reality. It is an anti-Habermasian tendency that has sociological consequences and these extend to Trump. "Telling it like it is" does not require consistency in a post-truth political environment. It can be bombastic and blustering. It only requires a collusive process between participants: the Trump team and a populist-sensitive subset of the electorate.

In a post-truth environment of information silos, confirmation bias, fake news, and positive feedback loops of affirmation, ficts can counter facts, belief can override truth, and fantasy can be more attractive than realism. Against this background, all that is then required for a political movement to take hold is relentless messaging, momentum and an opportunity for capture of existing political mechanisms.[12] Incoherency can be a campaigning strength and communicative capture can exploit weakness. These can shape the nature of optimism and hope. Uncertainty and insecurity can be worked upon to create *angry* and *fearful* hope in an electorate to which the populist is *the* solution. Optimism becomes punitive. This punitive optimism

---

[11] For example, the website of the Factcheck project at University of Pennsylvania scrutinises claims made in US politics and provided a host of material on both Trump and Clinton http://www.factcheck.org See also the EU's East StratCom Task Force, which exposes Russian disinformation campaigns.

[12] And, of course, in the American system, money.

speaks to a more general problem of social justice but does so without ever considering the broader grounds through which social justice is founded, which is a deliberative, inclusive, and fundamentally representative and participatory system. Just as Trump occupies ground that obscures political economy (in deeply political ways), he offers a fundamentalist-as-righteous "movement". The world is represented as Manichean, a place of extremes (the good and the evil, the terrible and the great) in a way that can actively resist reason and shout down evidence to the contrary. Such contemporary populism, of course, has a longer lineage. It speaks to long recognized problems: the demagogue of fifth century Athens, Weber's secularised charismatic authority and so forth. Trump's potential seems rather different than the 'specifically modern form of despotism' Charles Taylor called attention to nearly thirty years ago; a technocratic "mild and paternalistic" democratic authoritarianism licensed by a neglectful inauthentic individualism.[13] So, if we are to make sense of Trump he is, as a political archetype, a populist, but a contemporary populist as a product of the times.[14]

However, Trump's populism has first and foremost been about getting elected. Despite multiple reports of offence caused to a whole array of persons based on denigrating or stereotyping difference (disability, religion, nationality, race, sexuality, gender) he also attempted to be all things to all people, albeit on his own disciplinary terms of punitive optimism. This extended all the way to his appeal to African and Latino Americans: *I am your best hope even if you hate me*. The tension here immediately started to manifest once he became President-elect. Hillary Clinton was now a worthy opponent he had no inclination to see prosecuted, and President Obama was a figure with some wisdom to impart based on his experience as a politician. From a purely instrumental or functionalist point of view the shift needs to be more than rhetoric. The terms of political activity are different

---

[13] See Taylor, 2003.

[14] In terms of antecedents Andrew Jackson is sometimes mentioned as the first to run a populist anti-establishment presidential campaign in the US. Manipulative media distortion is of course also not new. Jefferson and Hamilton employed different newspapers to traduce the policies and supporters of the other. Herbert Hoover was not a populist but he did campaign as a competent man of business. He of course then made the catastrophic mistakes of endorsing the Smoot-Hawley Tariff Act and trying to balance the budget in the wake of 1929.

once elected. Once elected, one can no longer be a strategic, non-substantive populist. One may be an events-led popularity-seeking president, always responding to headlines and seeking to maximise approval; but this is different.

Transitional Trump

Trump's simple mantras and limited expression of policy prior to election provide the grounds for his presidency. A president can be more or less bi-partisan and more or less consensus seeking. A populist agenda may help to shape policy, but policy must still be made. At this point reality starts to bite. The President is not the only source of policy. There is a separation of powers and demarcation of powers. A president has recourse to security directives (these have been variously titled since Truman), memoranda and executive order. The scope of these is limited. Executive orders instruct branches of government to act and are used to bypass Congressional approval. However, they are (notionally) vetted by the Department of Justice and at the extreme they can be overturned by Congress. If the President exercises his veto the Supreme Court can declare an order unconstitutional. Orders and memoranda can still lead to challenges in the courts. A president cannot invoke and impose without consequences. To be effective a president needs to work with the House of Representatives and Senate. One cannot govern by memoranda and order and the US remains a bicameral system where federal law typically requires majorities; both the House and Senate matter. In any case, once office is taken what has been posed, proposed, promised, mooted or suggested cannot remain ambiguous, inconsistent or uncosted as an appeal to a minority-many. It cannot remain profoundly contradictory in also offering something-as-everything to all the electorate (most of whom wanted something else, principally not Donald Trump). Policy must be actually constructed and it must then flow through a system of checks and balances.

Of course, there is nothing new about policy specification as a general issue because there is always a transition from manifesto to governing. Still, there is something qualitatively different about Trump as a political event of significance. Trump's election was shocking to liberal sensibilities and was a curiously foreseeable surprise (the very subject for which the term dread was coined). It also involved an unsettling convergence. Unusually for a candidate, during the campaign Trump was never pinned down and pressed to respond on detailed policy. Trump was elected by a minority-many with expectations of major change and no clear sense of how this will be achieved based on a populist post-truth environment that encouraged and worked with incoherency and inconsistency. Trump is also a social subject with a particular skill set to draw on from within a narrow socialisation and set of experiences. He is constituted from within a sub-set of elites who in turn constitute a further tiny minority of powerful social subjects. *None* of these subjects have a confluence of real economic interests (in the sense of greater income equality and job security) with the populist component of the electorate that gave them victory. *And* Trump's confrontational campaigning style led to highly personal exchanges with many prominent Republicans in Congress, including those who stood in his way as presidential candidates or refused to endorse him as candidate.

Insult and humiliation are not easily forgotten. A Trump presidency thus seems poorly situated to serve as a solution to a dysfunctionally functional system. Furthermore, Trump's inaugural address seemed to set sharp limits to how he sees concession. It was a speech directed at those who elected him rather than to the electorate, and it continued his oppositional tone with a "Washington elite" (both parties), whose cooperation he requires.[15] It was the speech of a man used to people bending to his will, with the implication they will be broken if they do not. Yet a president is not a CEO. He does not employ Congress, and if the people employ Congress, a majority of the people did not vote for him and feel *strongly* he does not speak for them. In 2017 Republicans have a majority of 241 to 194 in the House, but just 52 to 46 (with two independents) in the Senate.[16] It is not a foregone conclusion that Trump can carry either the House or Senate simply because they are Republican.

---

[15] It is odd to think that were Trump's worldview and bearing different he might be lauded as principled yet naïve.

[16] However, Democrats will be defending 23 Senate seats in 2018 and 10 of those are in states won by Trump.

At the same time, the term "Trumpquake" is glib in so far as it seems likely that much of what Trump does will involve combinations of old patterns and policies. A Trump presidency seems set to be an angrier version of business as usual, at least in the sense of continued inequality and job insecurity, despite the headline foci of Trumponomics. He is not conditioned to transcend his own socialisation and he is an opportunity for capture for others within elites.

Personality and the political

One should not neglect the possible significance of Trump's personality. A self-aggrandizing iconoclast is his own contradiction, if not enigma. Many accounts of Trump have now been produced and among his less attractive traits these have positioned him as a hyper-competitive, short-attention span, impulsive, erratic, self-serving narcissistic egotist.[17] Some hope that there is (must be) more to him than this. His more ardent supporters say he is misunderstood and misrepresented. However, these personality traits may matter and this has at least two significant dynamics.

First, we previously suggested that Trump's background as a maker of "deals" does not translate to matters of the economy writ-large, since the skill set involved concentration and extraction of returns, and the externalisation of costs and losses. However, one might argue that Trump is more suited to the foreign policy focus of the role of president: perhaps international trade and international politics and security require an oppositional dealmaker; perhaps such a person is able to put "America first" and so "make America Great again".[18] This line of reasoning assumes that

---

[17] Mudslinging and role playing seem to have become intrinsic parts of Trump's public life so it is difficult to say with certainty how much of what is conveyed and inferred represents a *real* personality. This in itself may be problematic and one can only go on how he appears. See the various biographies from footnote 1 and perhaps watch a few episodes of *The Apprentice*.

[18] Trump's use of "America first" is justified by his defenders as reclaiming the phrase. However, it remains troubling to many that its historical referent is isolationism (see Rothman, 2016). There is also always a danger with analogical reasoning since it assumes sufficient similarity for analogy to lend credence to argument. Sometimes it achieves the opposite. Consider, for example, the powerful hold the basic equation between a household and the state has in terms of attitudes to debt. However, a state is not like a household for the purposes of debt, because its

the international is a zero-sum set of situations where strength-in-conflict allows capture of larger proportions of existing benefits. Such reasoning lacks a sense that current benefits are co-constructed and that future benefits can be greater based on trust and cooperation. If there are currently problems with these then the long-term solution is to build them up not destroy them. A spreadsheet approach to international issues can tell one little about how this is achieved and there is a basic tension between different public projections of Trump; between competent businessman as a maker of deals and the "alpha male" who dominates situations. In terms of the latter, the capacity to do genuine harm to relations is also augmented when one factors in the personality traits attributed to Trump. The consequences here can be extreme and immediate. Impulsiveness is a dangerous X-factor in foreign policy.

Second, it may well be that after a brief flurry of intense activity in the first days of office, because of personality traits Trump is inclined to delegate a great deal of the day-to-day activity of president. He may become a highly visible figure constantly communicating but doing very little. He has already set a pattern of inviting CEOs to the White House for televised meetings. These are very obviously part of Trump's attempt to project an image of activity that places him at the centre of attention. This is despite that the public nature of such events makes them peripheral to his own professed deal-making practices (though they may be part of a strategy to apply pressure). There is no reason to suggest CEOs will continue to accept these invitations if things start to go wrong for Trump (and this had already started to happen over immigration policy at the time of writing). He may retreat to squabble and move markets via Twitter.[19] As an increasingly remote figure his chief concern may be to take credit for any perceived successes of his presidency whilst passing blame for failure to others. Again, he is an

---

finances are differently constructed. The analogy has hampered fiscal policy and given credence to austerity. It may be the case that Trump's appeal trades on the analogy that a country can be run like a business and so to make a country wealthy and secure put a businessman (woman) in charge.

[19] As of January 2017, Trump's @realDonaldTrump Twitter feed has more than 19 million followers and had sent more than 34,000 Tweets; the White House Twitter accounts @potus and @WhiteHouse had a combined 13 million at the end of the Obama administration. Trump has criticised Toyota, Amazon, Lockheed Martin, General Motors and many others, in some cases having immediate material effects on share prices.

opportunity for capture by others within elites. This is already reflected by some of his confirmed and potential advisors and staff:[20]

ADVISORS

Counsellor to the President
Kellyanne Conway, 50 $ NE
Background: founder of the Polling Company,
election campaign manager from August 2016

Chief of Staff
Reince Priebus, 44
Background: Chairman of the Republican National Committee

Chief Strategist
Steve Bannon, 63 $ NE
Background: founding member and later executive chair of Breitbart News, former Goldman Sachs, investor in television assets and film producer,

Senior Advisor
Jared Kushner, 36 $ NE
Background: real estate investor, media owner, husband of Ivanka Trump, son of Charles Kushner (source of conflict with Chris Christie)

National Security Advisor ☠
Michael Flynn, 58 NE
Background: retired army general

Senior Advisor
Stephen Miller, 32 NE
Background: senior economic advisor from August 2016, speech writer

Press Secretary
Sean Spicer,
Background: former communications director of the Republican National Committee

---

[20] The skull and cross bones refers to persons withdrawn, not confirmed or who have resigned since the time of writing. This raises a further important issue. There is no necessary unanimity of purpose surrounding Trump, and competition for his attention can encourage "court politics". Others may be equally vulnerable as power and influence shift. Note also, not all the 23 cabinet posts are represented here and not all had been confirmed at the time of writing. Hundreds of others still await confirmation for other posts. The CIA director is also omitted.

THE CABINET

Legend:
$ multi-millionaire
$$ billionaire
NE never held elected office

Attorney General
Jeff Sessions, 69 $
Background: Senator, dogged by judicial racism controversy, devout Methodist

Secretary of State
Ron Tillerson, 64 $ NE
Background: CEO Exxon Oil 2006-2016; long standing relations with Rosneft and Putin

Secretary of Homeland Security
John Kelly, 66 NE
Background: retired general

Secretary of Health
Tom Price, 62 $
Background: Congress, surgeon, critic of Obamacare

Secretary of Housing
Ben Carson, 65 $ NE
Background: neurosurgeon, author, Christian conservative

The Vice-President
Mike Pence, 57
Background: lawyer, Congress, Governor, Tea Party supporting Christian conservative

Secretary of the Treasury
Steven Mnuchin, 53 $ NE
Background: hedge fund manager, former Goldman Sachs banker, critic of Dodd-Frank finance legislation

Secretary of Defense
James Mattis, 66 NE
Background: retired marine general

Environmental Protection Agency (EPA)
Scott Pruitt, 48
Background: Oklahoma attorney general, long term critic of EPA

Secretary of Transport
Elaine Chao, 63 $
Background: Secretary of Labor in Bush administration, married to Mitch McConnell Senate majority leader

Secretary of Commerce
Wilbur Ross, 79 $$
Background: leveraged buyout and distressed debt specialist, former privatization advisor to Giuliani

Secretary of Labour
Andrew Puzder, 66 $ NE
Background: CEO CKE restaurants, now owned by Apollo private equity, chains pursued for wage violations and has opposed increasing federal minimum wage

Small Business Administration
Linda McMahon, 68 $$ NE
Background: developed World Wrestling Entertainment

Secretary of Energy
Rick Perry, 66 $
Background: longstanding Texas Governor, presidential candidate 2011, proposed eliminating Department of Energy

Secretary of Education
Betsy DeVos, 58 $$ NE
Background: Conservative Christian activist/philanthropist Amway heiress

So, there are many factors to consider when making sense of Trump. However, at this stage making sense of what a Trump presidency may become is not easy. This is not just because there is a limit to what can be set out in a short paper. It remains truistic that politics is typically overtaken by events. Moreover, economists *as economists* struggle at a basic level to provide adequate accounts of economic reality and to extend these into the future. It is also relatively easy in the first few days of office for a president to give the appearance that a great deal is being achieved. However, activity is not achievement. Memoranda and some executive orders do no more than set something in motion. Motion may come to nothing or become something different. Some presidential interventions signal withdrawals, but not all such withdrawals can leave a vacuum. Trump's first week in power is instructive here. The flurry of orders addressed many of his core campaign pledges: the wall, environmental caution affecting economic activity, immigration and extreme vetting etc. The results may be shocking and in some cases immediately damaging or harmful. But it is not yet certain that any or all will survive scrutiny by Congress or challenge in the courts. A great deal of what Trump does will also depend on the day-to-day activity of Congress and of the executive agencies. A great deal hinges on how the American people respond to their president. And a great deal hinges on what other governments do.

All the above provides context for Trumponomics. It is also worth recalling that the US economy is not monolithic and it is not a command economy. It decomposes into regions and sectors and little of it is directly controlled by federal fiat. Trump may be able to shape institutions and apply pressure, but this is not straightforward.

Trumponomics: scope and strategy

Trump's inaugural address reaffirmed an economic nationalist agenda:

> "From this moment on, it's going to be America First. Every decision on trade, on taxes, on immigration, on foreign affairs, will be made to benefit American workers and American families. We must protect our borders from the ravages of other countries making our products, stealing our companies, and destroying our jobs. We will follow two

simple rules: buy American and hire American" (Trump, 2017).

During campaigning the Trump team made reference to a range of proposals bearing on the economy, some of which are now the subject of executive order and *only some* of which now appear on the White House site, under the headings "Bringing back jobs and economic growth", "Trade deals working for all Americans", and "An America First energy plan". These are worth listing, since they indicate the range of stated intent, though the list will quickly become out-of-date:[21]

1. Generate annual economic growth of 4%;
2. Eliminate/reduce/renegotiate the national debt and balance the federal budget;
3. Create 25 million new jobs over 10 years;
4. Award $137 billion in tax credits to business over 10 years to encourage $1 trillion in infrastructure investment (with growth assumed to generate revenues to recoup the cost of the credit); link to buy American
5. Reduce tax rates and simplify the tax code for workers (brackets at 12%, 25% and 33%) and for businesses (reducing corporation tax from 35% to 15%); encourage multinational enterprises (MNEs) to repatriate capital held offshore;
6. Withdraw from the Trans-Pacific Partnership (TPP) and renegotiate NAFTA; "crack down on those nations that violate trade agreements and harm American workers" or "engage in unfair trade practices"; apply up to a 45% tariff on Chinese imports and a 35%/20% tariff on Mexican imports; allow the $ to depreciate to improve exports;
7. Encourage MNEs to repatriate production and jobs; target (for example as tariffs in 6) MNEs that move production abroad to deter such activity;
8. Halt recruitment by federal departments, reduce funding to federal departments; apply a "moratorium on new federal regulations"; identify "job-killing regulations that should be repealed" (such as Dodd-Frank on finance and extending to 9 below);

---

[21] The list is synthesised from initial executive orders, campaign commentary, Trump's September 2016 plan and then from the White House site. All quotation marks refer to "issues" sections from the White House site.

9. Reorient American environmental and energy policy; commit to "clean coal technology"; embrace the "shale oil and gas revolution"; "eliminate harmful and unnecessary policies such as the Climate Action Plan and the Waters of the US rule"; but: "accept responsible stewardship of the environment" and "refocus" the Environmental Protection Agency (EPA) on its "essential mission of protecting our air and water";

10. Increase military spending to develop a comprehensive ballistic missile defence system, develop new cyber-warfare capabilities, expand the number of marine battalions from 24 to 36 and active army troops from 475,000 to 540,000; negotiate buy American arms contracts

11. Build a wall along the Mexican border creating greater security and control at the border and generating construction employment;

Not all the above have economics as their only context but all have spending consequences that affect the economy and so are part of the wider context of Trumponomics. The most appropriate way to analyse this list is to consider that a menu is not a meal, it is not even a recipe. The list contains some aspects that address some important issues. For example, those most ideologically opposed to Trump are still likely to recognize that infrastructure investment can be needed and economically beneficial in basic ways. In so far as modern capitalism in the form of neoliberal globalization is responsible for significant harms then opponents may also agree that the TPP and other international treaties need to be reconsidered. However, it is what is done and how that matters. This is not just about details, it is also about scope, conditioning perspectives and strategy. So, what may happen involves more than Trump, it involves how others respond.

A useful place to start is to ask whether Trumponomics will constitute a *structural* transformation in the American economy. The broad justification and appeal of Trump has been that he will improve American infrastructure, expand domestic energy (fossil fuel) production, and set in motion a wave of investment in industry and manufacturing. This in turn will generate employment and wage effects leading to greater employment security, wealth and economic growth. Some of this depends on how corporations respond to Trump. What might large MNEs do? However, in general it seems unlikely that they will hinge major investment decisions on a president who may last one term and may, within that term, become a lame duck president despite majorities in Congress. Many may adopt a wait and see approach. In the meantime, they may accept the boon of lower corporation tax, repatriate some capital back to the US to show they are sensitive to the concerns stoked by Trump, and they may bring forward or repackage some forms of investment already planned and temporarily transfer some production using existing plant (pushing rather than expanding capacity). This may give a temporary semblance of "more American". In some sectors this may be augmented for some period by consumption effects related to lowering income taxes. This in turn may result in better economic statistics. There is already a Trump-based asset bubble driving equities (a Trubble), though like all bubbles it is unstable and hinges on speculation regarding corporate futures. These are narratives which may come to nothing but allow traders to profit now.

Furthermore, economic variables have multiple influences and no necessary direction of movement. It seems unlikely that large retailers such as Walmart can or will suddenly start to source American (though they may run campaigns emphasising they are doing more of this). It seems unlikely that manufacturers such as Apple or GM will shift all production within US borders. If manufacturers did "in-shore" and retailers did source American then the likely effect would be higher costs (bearing in mind the point of comparison is prior to any protectionist tariffs) passed on in higher prices. Combine this with broader tariffs on Chinese goods to address claims of "unfair trade practices" and Mexican goods to pay for the wall, then inflation could quickly start to erode any income gains provided in the short term by lower income taxes. This could easily be exacerbated by increasing interest rates at the Federal Reserve, in turn raising the costs of borrowing and likely causing the Dollar to appreciate, affecting terms of trade, in turn affecting corporations that are being expected to inshore.

So, amongst other things, initial consumption effects expressed in economic growth could easily be undermined by a complex of consequences. The US is a consumption dependent economy and to match this to manufacturing and industry requires more than fiat. Structural transformation in a disaggregated economy of powerful corporations requires the short term to become the long term in terms of investment commitments and policy. There is thus a basic coordination problem because of how the American economy has already evolved (many corporations will resist, delay or seek to capture or subvert what is intended – just as Trump himself would do; ironically Trump is a potential quasi-regulatory problem for them even though a core commitment is reduced regulation). Trumponomics does not seem set up to address this. It has transformative aspirations but the personnel at its heart are corporate architects and dealmakers. This is not a situation where one can just nudge self-interest in the way game theorists sometimes suggest, nor can one consistently bully powerful interests. If Twitter can move share prices then the eventual effect is persistent uncertainty, which undermines investment of any kind. What seems set to follow is a masked situation of publically dealing with dealmakers *by* dealmakers as though underlying logics were not applying and as though some of the actors within government do not also stand to gain from those very logics. In this context, structural transformation seems deeply problematic and the American worker seems peripheral at best, though some may gain in some ways.

Unemployment in the US is relatively low (less than 5% but with less than a 70% participation rate). Any increase in employment created by initial policies seems likely to draw in non-participants and raise wage rates. This may be beneficial in some ways but may also be short lived and inflationary. If interest rates rise the process will also expose the debt-servicing vulnerability of many workers. Moreover, general wage effects cannot be assumed to be automatic. Trump's Secretary of Commerce, his original pick for Secretary of Labour, and a Republican dominated Congress are opposed by long-term interest and ideology to increasing minimum wages and reducing through law income inequality and job insecurity. This would be more regulation (as protections and empowerments). Trumponomics seems unlikely to empower unions and collective bargaining or to create *institutions* that place the onus on corporations to increase wage levels. It seems set to rely on economic growth as the source of distributed wealth. But the US has had a great deal of economic growth since 1980 and very little if any improvement in wages and incomes (which is one reason why Trump's populism took hold). Ultimately, Trumponomics seems likely to be dependent on trickle down logics and on assumptions that labour markets will simply result in higher wages. Yet if corporations see the consequences of Trumponomics as short lived and uncertain they have no vested interest in transforming wage policy and every interest in sticking to old practices of minimising wage costs and eroding terms and conditions against the background of dubious ideational justifications that emphasise shareholder value and marginal productivity. This is how profit has been made in many sectors for thirty years. Employment relations are not what they were in old industries and new jobs cannot change this alone. Those relations may have globalization as context but they are also localised because they are basic to corporate practice in many sectors. One cannot just assume that withdrawing from globalization (if this is even possible) will change the nature of capitalism at home. Changing capitalism means transforming the political economy and this requires deep institutional reform, not mere elimination or streamlining of regulation. This can simply intensify some current tendencies.

Consider the issue of infrastructure. Tax credits as a means to incentivise private business to invest in infrastructure are essentially an income transfer from the state to businesses that then subsidises the building and hence the ownership of that asset. If it is existing public infrastructure that is being remodelled this is privatisation, but if not or if it is new it can be in any case a variant of corporate welfare. This is basically inconsistent with neo-conservative rhetoric though not reality. It also immediately creates a lobbying interest in influencing how contracts are granted. Deal making can quickly start to look like "the swamp". Moreover, private business will only invest in infrastructure from which it expects to make significant long-term profits. Efficiency is not an unambiguous concept. To most businesses it does not matter how the profits are made, so this can include lobbying for guaranteed high prices paid by users for years to come (tolls, taxes, strike prices etc.). Who will decide whose interests matter most, particularly when this has become *the only* way a given infrastructure project will get done (and there is pressure because of promises made to deliver projects)? Which projects won't get done because they are not deemed profitable priorities by the private sector (either in general or in a particular place of need)? At the very least this framework seems unlikely to address the rural urban infrastructure divide or the problem of tacitly segregated urban decay.[22] Despite the rhetoric, the social value of infrastructure is seemingly

---

[22] To be clear, Trumponomics is not a case of publically funded and owned Keynesian infrastructure expansion. It does not follow the case made that monetary policy has created exceptional circumstances for cheap borrowing by the state for

marginalized by the private sector emphasis expressed via a Trump worldview. There is no normative social direction to any resultant multiplier. The ideas of public goods and merit goods are also deformed.

Infrastructure is not just about profits to business and jobs for people. It is basic to social design that affects how people live. It affects what people do and the consequences of what they do. An infrastructure program may, of course, raise wages in related construction sectors and generate employment demand. For example, through Trump's insistence on the use of American steel. As Dean Baker has pointed out, this may directly improve incomes for disadvantaged groups and may also encourage into work some of working age who have currently fallen out of the labour force (and so are not represented in unemployment statistics); *if* projects are quickly progressed. However, this does not mean all projects are progressive and construction is constructive. The ultimate context here is environmental.

Trump's "America First energy plan" focuses primarily on increasing fossil fuel energy use. The plan's reference to "responsible stewardship" is empty, yet meaningfully so, if one refuses to engage with the problem of climate change.[23] The energy plan refers to the Climate Action Plan as "harmful" and "unnecessary". Trump's focus is on fossil fuel resources as business and employment opportunities rather than as ecological and moral dilemmas. The energy plan states "Lifting these restrictions [regulations] will greatly help American workers, increasing wages by more than $70 billion over the next 7 years." Putting aside the problem of deriving this number, it is the phrase 'lifting restrictions' that is significant. This prioritises the economy over the environment whilst also positioning the two as antithetical – ecologically preferable translates to economically detrimental. In this zero-sum world why not opt for all out exploitation of resources? Clearly initial memoranda paving the way for the Dakota and Keystone pipelines illustrate

---

expansionary fiscal policy. America has a swathe of poorly maintained roads, bridges, railway links, schools etc. as well as a recognized need to update air traffic control, whether these are economically viable private sector initiatives is questionable.

[23] Pruitt, for example, is a longstanding climate change sceptic and was the subject of a *New York Times* investigation in 2014 that claims he and other attorney generals colluded with energy corporations to weaken federal clean-air rules.

this. In combination they require more than 3,300 miles of pipeline and supply a potential 1.3 million barrels of oil a day.

The ultimate issue is not whether jobs are created but rather the baseline assumption that these are the kinds of jobs that *should* be created in a kind of economy that *should* be propagated. This is indicative of Trump's approach to the environment and economy. Rather than transform the economy and its relation to the environment he has chosen to develop along lines that are against the collective interest, including those who may find temporary employment building pipelines. Carbon dioxide emissions can stay in the atmosphere for more than a hundred years so what Trump does now creates a carbon legacy for the rest of the century, and this may be far more enduring than anything else he does (though appointments to the Supreme Court may come a close second). Of course, the impact assumes the pipelines are not blocked in court. Here, one should also note that the UNEP Emissions Gap Report in 2016 finds that the Nationally Determined Contributions (NDCs) under the Paris Agreement are already insufficient to prevent warming of more than 2 degrees. Many are concerned that Trump will withdraw from the Paris Agreement. If he does so it will be mainly for symbolic reasons, since his administration can simply fail to set or pursue stringent NDCs (the system is voluntary and bottom up).

Of course, the US is also home to major investment in new technologies as part of a "fourth industrial revolution". There is little sense of this in Trumponomics. For example, Trumponomics involves no actual strategy to address or realistically assess the impact of the digital economy, robotics etc. on employment. However, putting this aside there is also major investment in alternative energy, transport, farming, and living in the US. These are now embedded. What is clear is that they are not at the core of Trumponomics (meetings with Musk and others not withstanding). Trumponomics is a lost opportunity regarding how the future could be shaped. One can also consider trade policy along these lines. Globalization has been deeply problematic. It is worth recalling that it is not just American workers in some sectors and places that have experienced adverse consequences. Deindustrialization in some parts of America has matching problems of industrialisation in others. This includes Mexico and China. Branco Milanovic's recent work on the "elephant curve" does not ameliorate this. The core issue concerns what kind of economy benefits *all* rather than pursuing a logic where different countries engage in a tussle for industry as is.

Trumponomics treats trade like some Wild West frontierland dispute. Everyone is staking a claim in a world that seems in one sense lawless and in another rule bound. However, it is only lawless if different actors choose to act as though it were. Protectionism fosters trade wars and these are deeply harmful. Others will follow the logic of action you apply. This is antithetical to subsequent bilateral trade treaty "negotiation".[24] There is also a deep contradiction in using protectionist threats to attempt to compel corporations to inshore in order to then create an exporting economy. To assume that the US can act with impunity because others will not dare to reciprocate requires fallacious reasoning. Once one puts aside the empty neoclassical calculative agent one must recognize that just like Trump, other policymakers in other countries have rationales based on constituencies and expectations. If the US can be "irrational" in the strict economic sense, so can they (we simply call this reality). Moreover, the US is not all-powerful and its capacity to inflict damage is highly variable. For example, exports are now only around 20% of China's GDP (in so far as one can rely on the figures), of which around 18% is to the US. So, less than 5% of China's GDP is at direct risk from any actions in the US (though clearly there is more complexity to this).[25] China can also bring the current rules to bear and Trumponomics on trade seems likely to violate World Trade Organization standards. The underlying issue is the way current rules and practices are to the collective detriment of *citizens of the world*. This implies that globalization could be different not that trade is evil. Trumponomics does nothing to contest the current problems of globalization it simply takes them as a given and then seeks isolated advantage for one country in an *interdependent* system. This is perverse,

---

[24] There are also checks and balances here, the president must give Congress 90 days' notice before opening negotiations, 30 days' notice of trading objectives and 90 days' notice before any agreement is signed. This enables scrutiny.
[25] For example, one issue is whether conflict might trigger vulnerable instabilities in the Chinese economy. According to the Bank of England, China's debt currently stands at around 260% of national income and a significant portion of this is provided by unregulated lenders implying lax lending practices and chains of debt linked to non-performing loans.

since the interdependencies will still hold and form the basis of likely damage to all parties.

Again, Trumponomics seems a lost opportunity, just as it fails to consider institutional and organization transformations within the US that could address some of the deep causes of problems, it fails to consider how globalization could be addressed collectively to transform the system that produce adverse consequences everywhere. Problems of races to the bottom, dignity at work, fair wages, "global wealth chains", corporate responsibility, tax avoidance and evasion, environmental harms, and social justice are as applicable internationally as they are domestically.[26] Trumponomics, occupies the territory of transformative change without actual change. Despite the rhetoric it is fight trade not fair trade. One basic reason for this is ideological. Though Trump is not a traditional Republican he shares the basic premise that regulation means more state and more state is interference in the natural order of things. As such, removing regulation will encourage more business activity and this in turn will be economically beneficial. His very first meeting with CEO's emphasised this position. This assumes business can be relied upon to act responsibly and that there is a convergence between business interests and society's interests – so most regulation is simply unnecessary and disempowering, rather than a source of positive empowerment, protections and support that can also mediate interests creating checks and balances. Whatever else Trump may say, this is basically market fundamentalist neoliberalism. However, it is neoliberalism in conflict, since Trumponomics seems set to be disruptive to free movement of capital and labour. Moreover, deregulation is ideology rather than reality since corporations also value regulation (and seek to shape and exploit it). Yet the commitment is important since it also speaks directly to the policy tendencies that resulted in the problems that Trump was then able to position himself as a solution to. The idea that repealing Dodd-Frank or Sarbanes-Oxley will somehow reinvigorate the US economy is deeply flawed.[27] The basic commitments of Trumponomics, such

---

[26] See Seabrooke and Wigan (2017); Morgan (2015, 2016)

[27] As David Dayen has noted potential conflicts in the finance sector are broader. Fannie Mae and Freddie Mac were put in conservatorship in 2008. Various groups have lobbied to have the two recapitalized and these include hedge funds who have invested significant sums in ostensibly worthless assets and who stand to gain from reprivatisation.

that they are, are refuted by the very history that lies behind his presidency and the tenability of the commitment is, arguably, refuted by his own track record in business.

However, the ultimate contradiction still to be played out is between Trumponomics and the most basic of Republican tenets. The aggregate of policies seem set to reduce tax revenues and increase federal spending, despite any freezes on hiring for federal agencies and the likelihood of reduction in scale of many agencies. It seems unlikely that a Republican dominated Congress will support budgets that seem set to increase federal debt. The less popular Trump becomes, the easier it will be for Congress to oppose him. The form this takes will simply mean less of Trumponomics will concern direct fiscal expansion and so more will involve transfer of powers and assets to corporations. This too involves a contradiction, since the potential for some corporations (and financial actors) to benefit from Trumponomics does not mean he will be viewed any differently as a problem of political risk for corporations. So, one can bring the analysis back to where we began from with the problem of strategy and action that will shape how Trumponomics develops.

Conclusion

The problem of low or no growth – of secular stagnation – is widespread. Trumponomics seems set to do no more than create conflict within the system that is experiencing that stagnation. As such, Trumponomics seems unlikely to deliver 4% economic growth, or at least there is nothing transformative about Trumponomics that could justify this claim. This lack of transformation is one way to think about how Trumponomics might be defined, a constituted presence and absence:

1. Trumponomics relies on aggressive, interest pursuing and conflictual action within the current political economy, domestic and global. It seems set to involve hyper-versions of current pathologies and intensifications (albeit in tension) of current tendencies.
2. Trumponomics seeks to remove impediments without due consideration to reconstruction or transformation of the institutional and organizational

basis of the political economy. It involves interest led regulatory removal (combined with streamlined and targeted inducements) that seeks to free capital to work and trades on the assumption this will benefit workers and society in the US, whilst potentially obstructing free movement of capital and labour beyond the US.

It should be emphasised that the above is no more than a framework for context derived, to mix metaphors, from a menu and no more substantive than that menu. Trumponomics will also have reality. It will be contestable and the consequences remain to be seen. However, if we employ popular terms of the day Trumponomics may involve a melange of autocracy, plutocracy and kleptocracy in ways that will not emancipate the "precariat".

For his critics, the best-case scenario restricts Trump to a one-term aberration, one whose failures and contradictions serve as a death knell to neoliberalism.[28] However, there is no necessary reason why a Trump backlash will result in a more reasoned politics and progressive approach to economics. He may be the first in a line of populists, each creating a gravitational pull on the centre ground of politics and preventing any reasonable stability. Also, though his actions so far do not invite confidence, Trump's tenure as president may not manifest as worse case scenarios. Checks and balances still apply and fear-filled rhetoric apart, he inherits an economy that is more stable than the one Obama began with in 2009. What he eventually does remains open. However, it seems unlikely history will judge Trump kindly. Even if Trump manages to deliver some of what he promises the scholastic fallacy will still be invoked by analysts (the danger of seeing subtlety and sophistication where none exists).

References

Blair, G. (2015) *Three Generations of Builders and a Presidential Candidate* London: Simon & Schuster

Chait, J. (2017) *Audacity: How Barrack Obama defied his critics and created a legacy that will prevail* Custom House

---

[28] Chait (2017), for example, argues the future belongs to Obama's legacy rather than to populists.

Trumponomics: Causes And Consequences

D'Antonio, M. (2017) *The Truth About Trump* New York: St Martin's Press

Judis, J. (2016) *The populist explosion: How the great recession transformed American and European politics* New York: Columbia Global reports

Kirk, M. Director (2017) *Frontline: President Trump.* PBS

Kopan, T. (2016) "Meet Donald Trump's think tank" December 7th CNN available at: http://edition.cnn.com/2016/12/06/politics/donald-trump-heritage-foundation-transition/

Kranish M. and Fisher M. (2017) *Trump Revealed* London: Simon & Schuster

Morgan, J. (2015) "Piketty's calibration economics: Inequality and the dissolution of solutions?" *Globalizations* 12(5): 803-823 http://dx.doi.org/10.1080/14747731.2015.1072950

Morgan, J. (2016) "Corporation tax as a problem of MNC organizational circuits: The case for unitary taxation" *British Journal of Politics and International Relations* 18(2): 463-481 http://journals.sagepub.com/doi/pdf/10.1177/1369148115623213

Morgan, J. (2017) "Brexit: Be Careful what you wish for?" *Globalizations* 14(1): 118-126 http://dx.doi.org/10.1080/14747731.2016.1228785
Müller J. W. (2016) *What is populism?* University of Pennsylvania Press

O'Brien, (2016) T. *TrumpNation: The Art of being the Donald* New York: Grand Central Publishing, reissued

Radice, M. Director (2017) *Meet The Trumps: From Immigrant to President* Channel 4, UK

Rothman, L. (2016) "The long history behind Donald Trump's America First foreign policy", *Time Magazine* March 28th

Seabrooke, L. and Wigan, D. (2017) "The governance of global wealth chains", *Review of Political Economy* 24(1): 1-29 http://www.tandfonline.com/doi/pdf/10.1080/09692290.2016.1268189?needAccess=true

Taylor, C. (2003) *The Ethics of Authenticity* Cambridge: Harvard University Press

Trump, D. (2017) "The Inaugural Address, Friday January 20, 2017, Washington DC" The White House, Speeches. Available at: https://www.whitehouse.gov/inaugural-address

Winfree, P. (2016) *Blueprint for Reform: A comprehensive policy agenda for a new administration in 2017* Washington DC: Heritage Foundation

Can Trump overcome secular stagnation?

James K. Galbraith[1] [LBJ School of Public Affairs, University of Texas, USA]

Could the economic program of President Donald Trump, if enacted, overcome secular stagnation? This essay addresses part of that question, focusing on the effects of a changing macroeconomic policy mix and thrust in the present US national and global context. A separate essay will address considerations on the supply side.

The phrase "secular stagnation" is usually attributed to the early post-war Harvard economist Alvin Hansen, one of the first American disciples of John Maynard Keynes, who used it to argue that the American economy would return to the Great Depression once the Second World War ended. *Today,* secular stagnation is defined by Lawrence Summers, who defines it as the condition of a "low real neutral rate of interest", or in Fed-speak a "low R* world". A neutral rate of interest ("R*") is said to be the one that neither increases nor restrains the economic growth rate. If such a rate exists and if it is close to zero, then monetary policy cannot spur growth, and a big-deficit fiscal policy is required.

For this reason, it is argued, the great recession-cure of "Quantitative Easing", so highly touted a few years back, proved to be mostly a dud. But fiscal policy would have better luck, whether through increased public spending or tax cuts, although only so long as the fiscal push is not offset by higher interest rates. If interest rates rise, in a "low R* world" then the fiscal expansion will fail. This tension between fiscal and monetary forces is of

[1] James K. Galbraith holds the Lloyd M. Bentsen Jr. Chair in Government/Business Relations at the LBJ School of Public Affairs, The University of Texas at Austin. His 2014 book, *The End of Normal: The Great Crisis and the Future of Growth*, addresses these issues. His most recent books are *Inequality: What Everyone Needs to Know* and *Welcome to the Poisoned Chalice: The Destruction of Greece and the Future of Europe*. He thanks Lance Taylor, Geoffrey Harcourt, Jason Furman, Grzegorz Kolodko, Mike Lind, Steve Cohen and Robert Skidelsky for comments on drafts.

great importance just now, as Donald Trump assumes the presidency on a program of infrastructure spending and tax cuts, while interest rates are starting to rise.

So, what do economists who argue along the lines described by Summers – a group that includes Paul Krugman, Ben Bernanke and other substantial figures – say that they think governs the interest rate? One might say: it's obvious, Janet Yellen and Stanley Fischer decide the interest rate. But this is not what our leading economists appear to believe. Instead, they appear to believe – or anyway, they argue – that a panoply of natural and social forces lie behind the interest rate. And therefore, if interest rates rise to block the Trump expansion, it will be because those stars are aligned against him.

We have seen this movie before, in the early 1980s, when interest rates rose dramatically in advance of the Reagan tax cuts. Those high interest rates – reaching twenty percent briefly, and sustained at high levels for two years, generated a deep recession. They destroyed much of heavy industry in the Mid-west and of the trade union movement, previously the backbone of the Democratic Party. They were, in their way, the forebear of the economic conditions that have brought Donald Trump to power now.

In this paper I will first explore the intricate doctrines of the interest rate which are still circulating among high-profile economists, and which have the effect of obscuring a basic reality. The reality is that in the modern world of integrated global finance, the central bank of the largest economy determines the core financial conditions for the United States and also for the world at large. Whether a change in those conditions will serve, or undermine, the Trump program is the question.

To straighten the matter out, it is necessarily to plumb a number of rabbit-holes in the deep history of economic thought. Investigating, one finds especially the ghosts of two academic scribblers: Knut Wicksell of the late 19th century and Dennis Robertson of the early 20th century. Wicksell, a Swede, advanced the doctrine of a "natural rate of interest", while Robertson, of Cambridge University, is associated with a "loanable-funds" theory of the actual interest rate. Both doctrines appear prominently in recent attempts by leading economists to explain themselves on the question of the interest rate.

According to the loanable funds theory, the actual interest rate is set in something called the "capital market", by a balancing between household savings and business investment. A recent report from the Council of Economic Advisers states this bluntly: "The interest rate settles at the level that equates the supply of saving with the demand for investment." This is pure Robertson, which is perhaps not surprising, given that the CEA Report is by (at least in part) my 1975 King's College (Cambridge) contemporary Maurice Obstfeld, the international economist at the Obama White House.

So what determines the supply of savings and investment demand? Evidently, "loanable funds" is today a global theory. In a recent Federal Reserve paper cited by Summers as "thoughtful," John C. Williams of the Federal Reserve Bank of San Francisco gives the "underlying determinants" as "the global supply and demand for funds, including shifting demographics, slower trend productivity and economic growth, emerging markets seeking large reserves of safe assets, and a more general global savings glut." In other words it's a grab bag, based loosely on reports from the Council of Economic Advisers, the International Monetary Fund and leading lights of MIT and elsewhere. One can search the pudding for a theme, in vain. Except possibly in the perception that if interest rates are governed by obscure global forces, they cannot also be anything so banal as the decision of a committee sitting at the Board of Governors of the Federal Reserve System, on Constitution Avenue in Washington, DC.

To compound the confusion, leading mainstream economists are often unclear as to what it is, exactly, that the supply of savings and investment demand are supposed to determine. For Obstfeld, to judge by the quote above, supply and demand apparently determine the actual rate of interest. Specifically, this would be the rate of interest paid by private banks for funds, as they draw on Chinese savings and compete with the Russians or the Indians for a safe reserve asset. In this model of the world, it would appear, the central bank of the United States plays no role at all.

But for Summers, supply-and-demand govern the *neutral* rate – not the rate of interest actually paid by banks for funds, but a notional benchmark rate, a characteristic of the world economy, a standard against which actual rates are measured to judge whether they are likely to be contractionary or expansionary in effect. The neutral rate is not something that you can actually observe. Against the neutral rate, the central bank sets a *policy rate*. Again, if the policy rate is below the neutral rate, then policy is expansionary; otherwise it's contractionary.

The natural rate – yet another notional benchmark rate – is something else. Simple and clear by comparison, it stipulates a larger equilibrium of financial *and physical* forces, driven by the prevailing "marginal product of the capital stock". As with the neutral-rate theory, an actual rate below the natural one is a disequilibrium, which will (it is said) stimulate investment, by making new capital more profitable than its physical productivity would justify. The CEA report, co-authored by Obstfeld, links the natural rate directly to the concept of productivity, and explains why (in this theory) the actual rate should be influenced by the natural rate over the long run:

> "A high return on investment should trigger a reallocation of resources from consumption toward capital accumulation, driving down the marginal product of capital and the real interest rate over time. Similarly, a low return on investment should induce consumers to increase current consumption and reduce capital investment, eventually driving up the real interest rate. Such economic forces should limit extremely high or extremely low real interest rates and work to push the rate back to intermediate levels" (p. 1).

In other words, the world is constructed in an orderly way, such that the state of economic development progresses on a path determined by the role of capital in the country. If the country is capital-rich, the rate of interest will fall, and if it is capital-poor, the rate of interest will rise. This view of things, firmly rooted in the eighteenth and nineteenth centuries, tells one a great deal about the idle mentality of the economists at the Obama White House, just at the moment when dark forces were building in the depressed heartland, preparing to sweep the vestiges of liberal America into the dustbin of history.

James K. Galbraith

Reference to the marginal product of capital raises another ugly little issue from the history of economic thought: namely, the specter of capital theory and the Cambridge-Cambridge capital controversies. This topic, now obscure, was very hot back at Cambridge in 1975 – although it seems that Obstfeld missed it, or he could never have signed off on a paragraph like the one quoted. As far back as 1966, the MIT neoclassical Paul Samuelson had already conceded that the underlying theory was, in point of mathematics, wrong. A larger "amount" of capital (whatever that means) or an increase in capital accumulation over time does *not* necessarily lead to a lower "marginal product" or to a lower "natural" rate of interest. Nor would a reduction in later capital investment lead to a rise in the natural rate, even in the long run. *In short, there is no such thing as a "natural rate of interest".*

If there is no *natural* rate, and if Summers were right that the *neutral* rate is governed by world financial forces, then (as he argues) the force of monetary policy is governed by the relationship of the actual rate and the neutral rate. In that argument, the actual rate is set by Yellen and Fischer after all. It is the cost of funds to banks, established by the Federal Open Market Committee of the Federal Reserve System, at their meetings every six weeks, and known to the world as the rate on "federal funds". In this concept, the apposition is not between deep technological factors and financial market factors, but rather between financial market factors on one side and the will of the policy-makers on the other.

But this is also nonsense. The apposition requires that saving, and the supply of funds, be governed by the decisions of households, and that it be wholly separate from the decisions of government. But what is the Federal Reserve if not a central bank? And what does a central bank do, if it does not supply funds? If the Federal Reserve is not in position to supply funds, if it is not a participant in the "loanable funds" market in which the "neutral rate" is determined, then what the devil are open-market operations, and what is Quantitative Easing, the principal tool of monetary policy for the past decade?

Of course the Federal Reserve supplies funds. "QE" is nothing more than large-scale purchases by the Federal Reserve of long-term securities for cash. On the short end of those same markets, funds are something which the Federal Reserve can create at will. It has done so, in recent years, to the tune of trillions, in order to put and keep the short-term policy rate where it is. Therefore, separating the policy rate from a supposed neutral interest rate determined by the supply of household saving and the demand for loanable funds makes no sense.

What then? It is difficult to say, exactly, whether the prevalent confusions are the result of sloppy thinking, an incoherent textbook pedagogy, or a deliberate desire to cover for the Federal Reserve and to obstruct potential criticism of the independent central bank. As a next step, let us ask: is there a better theory of interest rates out there, somewhere in the great work of the economists?

In the CEA paper, as in most of this so-called literature, the 20th century British economist John Maynard Keynes is not cited. Yet it is a fact that Keynes did write an influential book with the word "Interest" in the title. It was called *The General Theory of Employment Interest and Money,* published in 1936. In which Keynes states, of the classical theory of interest – that theory of loanable funds overlying a natural rate – that his own analysis "will have made it plain that this account of the matter must be erroneous" (p. 177). Perhaps it is worthwhile to seek Keynes's counsel at this point?

Keynes's theory of interest does not rest on the capital stock. And in Keynes as in the real world, there is no "capital market" that equates household saving with business investment.

Instead, Keynes's theory of interest is about the *market for money* – a market that definitely does exist in the real world. He wrote: "The rate of interest is not the 'price' which brings into equilibrium the demand for resources to invest with the readiness to abstain from consumption. It is the 'price' which equilibrates the desire to hold wealth in the form of cash with the available quantity of cash" (p. 167). In other words, interest rates are a portfolio issue. They are determined in the money markets, by how – *in what form* – people with wealth choose, at any given time, to hold that wealth. You pay interest, in order to get people to hold their wealth in less-liquid forms, such as bonds – and this is what provides firms with a secure source of financing, which then permits them to invest.

James K. Galbraith

Keynes's theory of interest is the pure common sense of how financial markets work. So why is it treated, by our leading liberal economists, as though it didn't exist? Why all this confusing folderol about natural and neutral rates? The apparent answer is damning. In the theories our economists like, a technical theory of interest creates a technical theory of income distribution, since interest rates govern the incomes of creditors against debtors, of the rich against the poor, of profits against wages. Thomas Piketty's recent book is a nice instance of this point, with its argument that the great inequalities of capitalism are due to interest rates higher than the rate of economic growth. If interest somehow reflects the physical productivity of the capital stock, then the consequences may be unfortunate – but they are inevitable and not something of which it is proper to complain.

Keynes's theory offers no such bloodless rationale for profits, maldistribution and gross inequalities. If you accept Keynes, as for Marx before him, distribution is political. For that reason above all, Keynes and his ideas on this theme had to be forgotten. (Otherwise, among other things, the Democratic Party's current alliances with Wall Street would be seen too clearly for what they are.) And the upshot is that Trump, as his Federal Reserve – especially if augmented by numerous hard line appointments – drives interest rates up, will be able to hide behind a bipartisan phalanx of academic obfuscation.

Keynes's theory isn't the last word. In the period of the gold standard and just afterward, there was a certain definiteness to the "available quantity of cash". Cash was what the government could print up and make available to banks on short notice. But financial markets have changed since the 1930s.

Today, we live in a world of what is called "fiat money", backed by nothing except the legal-tender declaration and the taxing power of the state. Moreover, most money is created outside the state itself; it is bank money, created through explicitly- or implicitly-insured electronic bank balances. These can be increased by private bankers at will. And so in our time government can create (or guarantee) liquidity as much as it likes, and governments with control of their monetary systems do exactly that, since they don't want the banks to run dry. And so there is (or can be) as much liquidity around as anyone – anyone with funds to trade, that is – would like to have.

This is the world in which we have all lived since the demise of the Bretton Woods monetary system in 1971, which broke the last link of the dollar to gold. In this world, the base rate of interest is the policy rate, nothing more or less. It is what it seems: the decision of the central bank. And so, we're back to ordinary common sense: the Federal Reserve does control the money-market dollar interest rate, as surely as OPEC used to control the price of oil. Today, the price of cash, which is the rate of interest in the overnight money markets, is an administered cost of funds. It's called the Federal Funds rate or, in England, Bank Rate. This is the price the central bank sets for a bank wishing to obtain cash on short notice; the US Federal Open Market Committee sets it, normally, at meetings once every six weeks.

This interest rate can be set at any level, and the level at which it is set, at any given time, is the object of competing political and economic pressures. For a long time, thanks to the crisis, it was set at or nearly at zero, giving banks access to funds, to meet their reserve requirements, at close to no cost. To determine the rates that banks charge customers, of course, other factors come in: a markup covering bankers' cost, the alleged risk of the loan, and what the market will bear. But that is another matter; monetary policy in the first instance focuses on the short-term cost of funds to banks.

Long-term rates are, of course, what matters to business borrowers and homeowners, among many others. But once one has a clear understanding of the administered character of short-term rates, then the trajectory of *long-term* interest rates also becomes much easier to understand. As even the CEA paper admits, long rates are a function (in large part) of the expected sequence of short rates. Short rates are policy rates. And so as the prevalence of low short rates became the norm, through persistence of policy over time, low-risk long rates followed them down. Simple as that. This is a process which has been going on since the early 1980s, and although I and other dissidents have been following it for decades, according to a new paper by Jason Furman, chair of the CEA under Obama, the economic mainstream seems only just to have noticed.

In this light the entire problem of "secular stagnation" can be radically simplified. There is no natural rate, and no neutral rate independent of policy. The fear of risk has risen. The desire to borrow, for all purposes including to invest – except perhaps in cheap imported electronics – has declined. That is all that is necessary. The supposed physical productivity of capital and the supposed global supply of savings have nothing to do with it. Low realized rates of growth, of productivity, and high liquidity are effects, not causes, of a general climate of fear and reluctance to borrow and invest. So too is a high markup on a slim volume of new loans. So too is the proliferation of intermediaries who obscure who exactly is bearing the risk. Against these forces, the inability of a low cost of funds to produce robust economic growth is no surprise; in the absence of borrowers, low short policy rates are weak tea.

In this simplified world, even with no "neutral rate" to act as a fulcrum, it is still very easy to see why raising rates is dangerous. Rising interest rates are not a sign of a stronger economy. They are not a market response to stronger investment demand or a shortage of funds. They are an action of the central bank. But the Federal Reserve acts immediately on the short-term rate, not the long-term rate.

Normally, long-term rates lie above short-term rates, thanks to liquidity preference. But as short rates rise, this relationship, which is called the yield curve, flattens out. Soon enough it will invert, as short rates rise above sluggish long-term rates. In financial markets, this provokes a rush to cash. Often an inverted yield curve provokes a financial crash, and from that, follows a recession.

So now the economy is Trump's problem, and what does he propose? On the fiscal side, there will be tax cuts, especially for business, and (we are told) vast new public-private spending, especially for infrastructure. In other words, if the fiscal program is for real it will resemble the American Recovery and Reconstruction Act, Obama's early stimulus program. Tax cuts and public spending work; if there is a large fiscal stimulus then the economic growth rate will rise. But Trump promises to reinforce the "inflation hawks" – the high-interest-rate caucus – at the Federal Reserve. Taken together, so far as the broad outlines are concerned, and so far as we know now, Trump proposes to repeat the Reagan formula. And the question becomes, what will happen if he does?

As with Reagan, higher interest rates – especially if they come before the fiscal effects kick in, will play havoc with credit-dependent sectors of the economy. Here at home, the pinch may fall largely on corporate borrowing and on automobile and student loans. The net depends on scale and timing: under Reagan the recession came first, because the monetary shock was very strong and it hit before the tax cuts and military spending boom took effect. This pattern could be repeated, even though the level of nominal interest rates need not approach the extremes of the early 1980s. But an equally or more important effect could come from the consequences of this policy mix for a price that Trump and his team do not directly control: the exchange rate of the US dollar.

Expected higher interest rates have already raised the value of the dollar. Higher interest rates will drive it up even more. As in the early Reagan years, this will hurt exports and import-competing traded goods, offsetting the benefits of fiscal expansion for manufacturing. Only the most severe and sustained protection, which Trump in his inaugural did promise, can mute or reverse this effect. But such protection would bring inflation, product shortages, unemployment in the distribution and retail sectors, a massive decline in real consumption – since new production facilities would have to be established on a vast scale to replace the disappeared plants of the older manufacturing sector, and this takes time. Much more likely, there will be a wide expectation that the policy cannot last, and so there will be little gain, under the policy we're going to get, in manufacturing jobs. Symbolic gestures apart, industrialists are not going to invest in factories to make shirts and shoes, when they know very well that a future government can reopen trade and bankrupt them all, in a matter of days.

So where will the money go? Where will private investors, seeking low taxes on quick profits, want to invest? The answer seems clear enough: real estate. Infrastructure spending, after all, is not only or even necessarily in support of production. Most of it, whether in roads, bridges, water systems or airports, supports household consumption and offices and – therefore – land values. A high dollar attracts foreign capital. A low corporate profits tax rate diverts loose funds from other countries. Real estate – practically alone – can turn these factors into capital gains in a fairly short time. Trump of course knows this; he's a real estate man.

It is darkly amusing that the entire US economy may be run in such a way that so well serves the personal interests of the President, of his children, his son-in-law and his friends. Those who voted for him to make America great again – by restoring manufacturing jobs – will be disappointed. And those who may lose many other benefits they now receive, including health insurance and perhaps parts of Social Security, Medicare, Medicaid and other programs, will be unhappy. Trump and his team may not care very much, for as a good businessman, he and his team will know when to cash out. But to the extent that they wish to survive politically, they must be relying on the obvious fact that the Democratic Party has had no strategy for the Mid-west since the 1960s, that it has become a bicoastal party of professionals, with no plan to earn back the votes that carried Wisconsin, Michigan, Pennsylvania and Ohio for Obama in 2008 and 2012. That's probably a safe bet for at least the next four years.

References

Council of Economic Advisers, "Long Term Interest Rates: A Survey," Executive Office of the President: July 2015. At https://obamawhitehouse.archives.gov/administration/eop/cea

Furman, Jason, "The New View of Fiscal Policy and Its Applications, Conference: Global Implications of Europe's Redesign, New York, October 5, 2016.

Galbraith, James K. *Created Unequal*. New York: Free Press, 1998.

Galbraith, James K.,*The End of Normal: The Great Crisis and the Future of Growth*, New York: Free Press, 2014.

Keynes, John Maynard, *The General Theory of Employment Interest and Money*, New York: Harcourt Brace, 1936.

Levhari, David and Paul A. Samuelson, "The Nonswitching Theorem is False", *The Quarterly Journal of Economics* (1966) 80 (4): 518-519 doi:10.2307/1882912

Summers, Lawrence, "The Age of Secular Stagnation: What it is and what to do aboutit", *Foreign Affairs*, February 2016.

Taylor, Lance, "The 'Natural' Interest Rate and Secular Stagnation: Loanable Funds Macro Models Don't Fit Today's Institutions or Data", manuscript for *Challenge*, October 2016

Varoufakis, Yanis, *The Global Minotaur,* Economic Controversies, 2011.

Williams, John C. "Monetary Policy in a Low R-Star World" *FRBSF Economic Letter*, August 15, 2016, http://www.frbsf.org/economic-research/publications/economic-letter/2016/august/monetary-policy-and-low-r-star-natural-rate-of-interest/

Trump through a Polanyi lens: considering community well-being

Anne Mayhew [University of Tennessee, Knoxville, USA]

Introduction

At least in outline, the economic policies that new presidents of the U.S. will attempt to put in place are generally known when they take office. Economic advisors who have given speeches, written papers, testified before Congress are usually known. However, we know little about what Trump actually intends or what he can accomplish. Rather than trying to write about what I have absolutely no confidence in predicting, I am, in this paper, going to suggest some parallels between Trumps' incoherent, and yet apparently popular campaign proposals, and some themes from an earlier period of populist anger in the U.S., the period that began in roughly 1870 and culminated in the presidential election of 1896. In drawing these parallels I will accept that in calling the Tea Partiers and Trump voters populists, observes are correct in thinking that there is an anger abroad in the U.S. that bears resemblance to the anger of that earlier period.

My conclusions will be three: In both periods of populist anger the causes of that anger are hard to explain using standard measures of economic well-being. People had many reasons for voting for Trump, but even given that, it is hard to make sense of the economic causes of his victory, just as it was hard to account for the electoral success of the earlier populists. Secondly, even though Trump and his administrative colleagues may not truly care about that anger now that they are in office, it is important that those in opposition understand what people want and why they are angry. It is not sufficient to write Trump off as a cowbird, a bird whose characteristics I will explain shortly. And, finally, there is a growing literature that suggests that we need to devise not only new policies but quite possible a new way for economists to think about national economic policy.

285

Trumponomics: Causes And Consequences

Two populisms

In the last three decades of the 19th century American farmers joined the Grange, Farmers' Alliances, and in the 1890s in the Peoples (or Populist) Party. They enjoyed considerable success in electing third party candidates at the state level.[1] In recent work such as John Judis' *The Populist Explosion,* as well as older standard works such as John D. Hicks' *The Populist Revolt,* and Norman Pollack's *The Populist Mind,* the discontent that led to what we might today describe as an effective Tea Party uprising, is said to have been falling agricultural prices and the economic power of the newly important railroads and their attendant political power. This is not surprising for that is pretty much what the farmers themselves said.

The story is, however, more complicated. Statistics compiled by Douglass North in 1966 reveal that the last three decades of the 19th century was a period when agricultural terms of trade improved and when railroad rates were falling. Markets for Midwestern crops were expanding rapidly. Further and more recent support for the proposition that life on American farms, at least in the Midwest where the protest was strongest, was improving comes from Robert J. Gordon's very recent book, *The Rise and Fall of American Growth: The U.S. Standard of Living since the Civil War.* In short, statistical evidence does not really support the complaints of the farmers but we do know that they were very clearly unhappy.

There has also been an easy explanation for the recent anger of Tea Partiers and Trump supporters that does not quite stand up to closer examination. It was easy during the long primary season and even in the first days after his November victory to believe that Trump's successes were coming from the votes of those who had not enjoyed the benefits of the post-2009 economic recovery. Much of the rhetoric of Trump's campaign and much of the early coverage suggested that his unexpected support in areas that had previously been safely Democratic resulted from a continued loss of jobs, whether because of globalization or automation or both.

---

[1] This section is based on Mayhew, 1972 and the sources cited there. See also Turner (1980).

A corollary of this analysis of Trump's win was the conclusion that many of those who voted for Trump voted against their own economic interests. It has all along been difficult to believe that Trump could or would extend and strengthen a government-provided safety net would seem crucial to protect those caught in the undoubtedly real structural change that has produced the depopulating towns and empty and crumbling factories that served as backdrops for the election. Analysts have puzzled over why voters assumed to be concerned about a loss of jobs were willing to accept the vague and sometimes contradictory prescription that Trump offered as a remedy and why they voted for a man and a party that promise to take apart the existing safety net.

There was a parallel in the late 19th century. After the Populists allied with the Democratic Party in 1896, there were also suggestions that the farmers had been "duped" into an alliance that even though it did ultimately lead to Democratic progressivism removed the farmers and their concerns from center stage. William Jennings Bryan, with his oratorical skills and a popular call for "free silver" was, according to the muckraker Henry Demarest Lloyd, a cowbird. For those readers not up on their ornithology, I should explain that cowbirds lay their eggs in the nests built by other species of bird and leave the parenting duty to the builder of the nest. At least some of the eggs do not hatch and cowbirds are often described as crowding out those with more legitimate rights to the nest and the parenting that goes with being there. For the Tea Partiers and other angry voters of 2016, we could say that Donald Trump is the cowbird with the mélange of interests that he now represents is in the process of shoving the hopes and plans of "the people" out of the nest.

Different interpretations

There is some justification for calling Bryan a cowbird and even more for calling Trump out on this score. If, however, the important thing is to understand the anger of voters, that is not sufficient. It is important to look behind the slogans of "free silver" and "bring jobs back" and explore more fully why voters and protestors were angry and why they allowed the cowbirds entry into their political nests at all. I begin this process by noting that as part of the political process, vote seekers must articulate the concerns of the people in a way that resonates with the voters and, at the same time, state those concerns in a ways that are addressable by the policy makers on whom they will rely. In the case of Donald Trump, the policy maker may be Trump rather than independent experts but the generalization still holds. Concerns must be articulated in a way that both yields policy and at the same time appear to the electorate to address their problems.

My conclusion (see Mayhew 1972) about the 19th-century populists was that the farmers were actually angry about their sudden immersion in a thoroughly commercial and nation-wide market for agricultural crops that resulted from the new rail network and the availability of ocean-going steam ships. They were angry because prices that emerged from processes that played out in Chicago and New York and London determined their success. To oversimplify just a bit, most U.S. farmers, and particularly those who were populating the Midwest were successful if they grew enough to feed and clothe their families. By the 1870s this was no longer a measure of success. New goods, mail order catalogs, and a rising standard of living, required more and that more depended upon prices over which the farmer had no direct control. In the political language available to these farmers they blamed the railroads and the "trusts" and "monopolists".[2]

When these complaints were heard by politicians, policy makers, and academics, the message was transformed into anger about prices and about "monopolies". This was confusing for economists. The railroads, even as they merged into networks did not conform to the models of monopolies that economists and other academics had to hand. Nor did the "trusts" conform to such models. In fact, most economists at the beginning of the 20th century argued that there was too much competition in the American economy. Combinations were needed to avoid what they labelled "ruinous competition". The near-unanimous congressional support for the Sherman

---

[2] A word about terms. Because of the way in which laws of incorporation then existed in the U.S. setting up a "trust" was the way used by John D. Rockefeller and others to concentrate control over multi-product and geographically dispersed firms such as Standard Oil. Even as laws of incorporation and combination changed, the word "trust" continued in American discourse as a name for a firm deemed to have too much power. In popular language, a "trust" was the same thing as a "monopoly".

Antitrust Act in 1890 did not jibe with expert opinion and clear-cut policies to deal with farm anger were not easy to formulate. Following creation of state regulatory bodies and then in 1887, the creation of the Interstate Commerce Act, railroads were regulated in ways that sometimes did and sometimes did not please protesting farmers, but answers for other industries remained elusive and the issue of what to do about "monopoly" remained a major issue in elections up until WWI changed the national conversation.[3] It also made sense to the experts and the politicians to place an emphasis on money and hence on the gold versus silver issue that had long dogged American political discourse. This was especially so as there were no measures available to deal with "power" as power was being wielded by Rockefeller and his colleagues who ran the railroads.

Since the 2016 election there has been a growing body of evidence that this most recent "populist" revolt has also been muddled in the translation among voters, candidates, and economists and for a similar reason: the measures of economic well-being thought by experts to be at issue may simply not be adequate to address concerns of unhappy voters. Perhaps today we also lack a good measure of what is wrong in those counties that swung hard from traditional Democratic support to vote for Trump. Evidence that these are not counties of high unemployment cast doubt upon the easy conclusion that this was an election about jobs even before the votes were finally counted. That is confusing.

What were voters angry about in 2016?

To try to understand this apparent paradox there has been a rush by journalists and scholars to look more closely at those places that, often to the surprise of political observers, voted for Trump. One such effort that illustrates the paradox well is that which appeared In an article in *MINNPOST,* a regional Minnesota news source, where reporter Jeff Ernst describes how for the first time since 1924, Morrison County, a county located northwest of Minneapolis in central Minnesota, voted for someone

---

[3] I have written about this in Mayhew (1998) and Mayhew (2008).

other than the Democratic nominee for President.[4] This was particularly striking because the candidate for whom the majority of Morrison County residents voted in 1924 was Robert M. La Follette, Sr. who was running as the nominee of the Progressive Party, a third party created by liberal Democrats and Republicans. It is also striking because Trump's margin of victory over Clinton was 53 points. Morrison County has long been a liberal bastion but went strongly for Trump. What happened?

The Republican state representative for Morrison County identified need for jobs as the reason for his own and Trump's win. But, as Ernst reports, the unemployment rate in Morrison County in 2008, when Obama took office, was nearly 14%, while in 2016 it was only 4 percent. After reading Ernst's article, I did a little further digging and while I cannot claim any in-depth knowledge of the area, there is little evidence that a lack of jobs was causing hardship in this one area that swung heavily from left to right in the 2016 election. The evidence is that Trump's emphasis on the need for jobs, "good jobs", resonated even in areas where unemployment had declined and where there are no signs of the poverty that plagues some regions of the U.S.

It would, of course, be easy to attribute unhappiness with economic conditions to underemployment, a concept that got considerable play from Trump. But that also does not appear to explain what happened in Morrison County, Minnesota. The median income is relatively close to the national median, the poverty level much lower, and the highest concentration of poverty is among women over the age of 75, hardly a group affected by currently low wages or shortage of jobs. I could find no evidence in the local newspaper of anxiety about loss of employment. In other words, all standard measures of economic well-being in 2016 indicate that Morrison County, Minnesota is and has been for some time a relatively prosperous county in a prosperous state.

So, what did persuade people in Morrison County, Minnesota to vote for Trump? Fortunately, over the months since the election there have been more and more reports on places like Morrison County, Minnesota. Those

---

[4] I thank Doug Veum who keeps up with his native Minnesota for calling this article to my attention.

reports, in turn, serve as guides to a considerable body of work done before the 2016 election by sociologists, political scientists, journalists, and others on areas of the U.S. where Tea Party anger was strong but jobs not necessarily lacking. "Post-Election Disorientation: Bibliography" compiled by Siobahn McAndrew is a particularly useful guide to some of this literature. I, like many others, have also found the work of Katherine Cramer on rural residents of Wisconsin and that of Arlie Hochschild on southern Louisiana particularly interesting. There is a theme that runs through these studies that goes something like this: The supporters of the Tea Party and of Trump are no dummies and are not being irrational. Cowbirds are not going to fool them. These voters themselves may be comparatively well off, may not have been directly affected by loss of jobs overseas, and in general do not display the other characteristics that might have been expected from a simple story of voters reacting to unemployment or low wages. These people are, however, deeply angry about what they see as a system in which an urban elite governs with both intent and effect to deprive those who live in small towns and on farms of what should rightly be theirs.

But the story is also not simply about growing inequality of income. In southern Louisiana where Hochschild, a sociologist, interviewed people, there was great concern about environmental degradation. This surprised Hochschild for these same people were decidedly against regulation, particularly at the Federal level. What she discovered was that these people had reached a not unreasonable conclusion that regulation was applied to them but not to the big firms. They might be regulated as to fishing rights and use of "their Bayous" but the non-resident owners of big firms that caused heavy pollution were not punished in any ways obviously harmful to them. Hence they opposed regulation and had little faith in government programs that had failed them. They were also persuaded by the prevailing rhetoric that without the ineffectual regulation now in place even in polluted Louisiana there would be more jobs available so that their children would not have to leave a place that was dear to them. The tradeoff that they perceived was not so much environmental regulation versus jobs as it was biased-against-common people-regulation versus little or no regulation and more jobs in addition. In other words they were fully aware that executives of BP and other large and polluting firms were not made poor, but they saw themselves as regulated in petty ways and in an area of the country that could only grow if they accepted environmental degradation. They voted for Tea Party candidates and Trump because that offered the slightly better of two bad choices.

In Wisconsin, Cramer, a political scientist found what she calls a "rural consciousness" that fuels a similar resentment against the elite who live in places like Madison and Milwaukee and beyond. Much has now been written about the importance of the rural/urban divide that characterizes American politics but Cramer and Hochschild add depth to this understanding by emphasizing *place*. As Cramer puts it, "place matters more than just as a proxy... It is a part of at least some voters' fundamental sense of self" (p. 217).

The conclusions of Hochschild and Cramer are borne out by Jonathan Rothwell's analysis of 87,000 interviews with Trump supporters undertaken by Gallup. Rothwell used statistical analysis to reject both income and direct effects of foreign trade as plausible explanations of why Trump voters voted as they did in the primaries. He concluded that Trump supporters came from *places* (emphasis mine) where their neighbors endure or are at risk for other forms of hardship, including poor health and a lack of opportunity for upward mobility (Ehrenfreund and Guo). According to Rothwell, "Trump's supporters are concerned less about themselves than about how the community's children are faring."

Cramer's words can be used to summarize what is probably the best understanding that we currently have of why so many were persuaded to vote for Trump in those counties that swung unexpectedly his way and in some that have long been bastions of Tea Party strength:

> "When we start to ask why people vote against their interests, we need to acknowledge that interests are subjective. In a simplistic view, this means that interests are not necessarily what we as observers would predict based on objective facts, such as a person's income. But in a more useful view, this means that interests are interpretations that people arrive at through thinking about the world as particular types of people—people with identities. The

simplistic view paints voters as ignorant. The latter view acknowledges their humanity" (p. 209).

Hochschild, Cramer, Rothwell, and now many others are reaching the conclusion, which should not surprise us that voters vote not as economistic rational individuals, but as members of society and of a particular community.

Let me be clear and emphasize that it is not simply the case that voters vote for a candidate without full knowledge of the policies that will be implemented and their effect. It is also the case that skilled specialists can manipulate fear, hope, disappointments and so on into passion for simply stated slogans and simplistic promises. But the point that Hochschild, Cramer, and Rothwell are making goes beyond these common observations. It is also the case, they tell us, that voters bring to be ballot box fear and hope for the communities with which they identify.

How to think about the future

What makes this conclusion important is that it is the context in which we need to think about policies that will allow a more robust alliance of urban and rural folk, both elite and not. Much is currently being made of the rural/urban divide that helps to account for Trump's electoral victory, but there is a danger in that. My suspicion is that the emphasis on "place" in the work of both Hochschild and Cramer should not be understood simply as an emphasis on attachment to a geographic location but rather to a community with which one identifies. Communities may be either rural or urban, and both rural and urban communities may be seen as marginalized by their inhabitants. Saying this is not to say anything really new but it does suggest a change of focus for economic policy makers.

Most economic measures of well-being and most policy formulations focus on individuals or, at most, on individual families: the unemployed person versus the employed person, the person below the poverty line versus individuals in the top 1%, the highly educated versus the high-school dropout. These measures are important but community identification is also needed in order to understand both voter anger and the routes to greater well-being. For this purpose it is important to recognize that communities should not be thought of as collections of individuals with the same economic, social, demographic characteristics. There is much social science evidence that thriving communities are also diverse communities. What we need for better policy formulation and for better political campaigns are measures of community well-being. Some of these already make the news. Is water polluted in the community? What is the rate of opioid addiction? Is there a future for the town and its schools or will they too be boarded up in the near future?

Karl Polanyi laid blame for the turmoil and destruction of the 1930s and WWII on an "economistic fallacy", the notion that attitudes, affiliations, social status, friendships, and, yes, voting, are determined by narrowly conceived economic factors. The idea that a self-regulating market of the sort still idealized in textbooks could yield a good human society was based on this fallacy. When protective measures were put in place to shield people and nature and nations from the workings of the self-regulating market the system collapsed. The rush to create working economies led to both the welfare state created in the U.S. of the 1930s and elsewhere in the West and to the fascism of Hitler's Germany. In the U.S. today the road ahead still has those forking paths.

As all readers of these essays almost certainly know, one reason for the welfare-state path taken in the U.S. and in much of Western Europe, was recognition that humans needed income and jobs. The importance of John Maynard Keynes was that he incorporated this understanding into a Marshallian view of the ideal liberal economy. This incorporation was both fed by and in turn fed the development of new and aggregated measures of economic well-being. These measures of labor participation, joblessness, and real wages all remain important, just as the measures of price and output that informed the reformers who responded to the 19th century populists remained and remain important. But seeing humans as members of communities whose place in a larger world has been fundamentally altered by globalization and the internet, makes these measures insufficient. Even if all are employed and with a living wage, there may be anger based on comparison of place. Humans want to live in and be part of thriving communities, whether those communities are geography bound or internet created. As against this view, the 19th-century liberal ideal was that of a world that served individuals whose primary needs and concerns were purely economic. What worries me is that even though an emphasis on jobs and a living wage is certainly an advance on the kind of 19th-century economics that understood full employment to be a naturally occurring condition and wages beyond the reach of policy, it may not be sufficient.

I am not confident in predicting the extent of damage that Trump, working with a Congress that seems wedded to the 19th-century economic ideal, may do. I have more confidence in saying that those of us who hope to minimize that damage need to develop and put to use better measures of economic and social well-being and to put them to use. In addition to measuring environmental degradation and declines in human health and longevity, we need to incorporate measures of community well-being into our policy formulations.

References

Cramer, Katherine J. (2016) *The Politics of Resentment: Rural Consciousness in Wisconsin and the Rise of Scott Walker.* Chicago: The University of Chicago Press.

Ernst, Jeff. (2016) "What Made Morrison County the most pro-Trump place in Minnesota? *MINNPOST,* 12/05/16. Available at https://wwwminnpost.com.

Ehrenfreund, Max and Guo, Jeff. (2016) "A Massive New Study Debunks a Widespread Theory for Donald Trump's Success," *The Washington Post,* August 12, 2016.

Gordon, Robert J. (2016) *The Rise and Fall of American Growth: The U.S. Standard of Living since the Civil War.* Princeton, NJ: Princeton University Press.

Hicks, John D. (1961) *The Populist Revolt.* Lincoln: University of Nebraska Press.

Hochschild, Arlie Russell (2016) Strangers in Their Own Land. New York: The New Press.

Judis, John B. (2016) *The Populist Explosion.* New York: Columbia Global Reports.

McAndrew, Siobhan (2016) "Post-Election Disorientation: Bibliography". Available at https://medium.com/SocSciMcAndrew/post-election-disorientation/bibliography

Mayhew, Anne (1972) "A Reappraisal of the Causes of Farm Protest in the United States, 1870-1900", *The Journal of Economic History,* Vol. 32, No. 2, pp. 404-475.

Mayhew, Anne (1998) "How American Economists Came to Love the Sherman Antitrust Act", in Mary S. Morgan and Malcolm Rutherford (eds.) *From Postwar Pluralism to Postwar Neoclassicism.* Durham and London: Duke University Press.

Douglass C. North (1966) *Growth and Welfare in the American Past.* Englewood Cliffs: Prentice-Hall, Inc.

Pollack, Norman (1967) *The Populist Mind.* New York: The Bobbs-Merrill Company, Inc.

Polanyi, Karl (1944) *The Great Transformation.* Boston: Beacon Press.

Turner, James (1980) "Understanding the Populists", *The Journal of American History,* Vol. 67, No. 2, pp. 354-373.

Trump is Obama's legacy. Will this break up the Democratic Party?

Michael Hudson [University of Missouri at Kansas City, USA]

Nobody yet can tell whether Donald Trump is an agent of change with a specific policy in mind, or merely a catalyst heralding an as yet undetermined turning point. His first month in the White House saw him melting into the Republican mélange of corporate lobbyists. Having promised to create jobs, his "America First" policy looks more like "Wall Street First". His cabinet of billionaires promoting trickle-down corporate tax cuts, deregulation and dismantling Dodd-Frank bank reform repeats the Junk Economics promise that giving more tax breaks to the richest One Percent may lead them to use their windfall to invest in creating more jobs. What they usually do, of course, is simply buy more property and assets already in place.

One of the first reactions to Trump's election victory was for stocks of the most crooked financial institutions to soar, hoping for a deregulatory scythe taken to the public sector. Navient, the Department of Education's knee-breaker on student loan collections, accused by the Consumer Financial Protection Bureau (CFPB) of massive fraud and overcharging, rose from $13 to $18 now that it seemed likely that the incoming Republicans would disable the CFPB and shine a green light for financial fraud.

Foreclosure king Stephen Mnuchin of IndyMac/OneWest (and formerly of Goldman Sachs for 17 years; later a George Soros partner) is now Treasury Secretary – and Trump has pledged to abolish the CFPB, on the specious logic that letting fraudsters manage pension savings and other investments will give consumers and savers "broader choice", e.g., for the financial equivalent of junk food. Secretary of Education Betsy DeVos hopes to privatize public education into for-profit (and de-unionized) charter schools, breaking the teachers' unions. This may position Trump to become the transformational president that neoliberals have been waiting for.

But not the neocons. His election rhetoric promised to reverse traditional U.S. interventionist policy abroad. Making an anti-war left run around the Democrats, he promised to stop backing ISIS/Al Nusra (President Obama's "moderate" terrorists supplied with the arms and money that Hillary looted from Libya), and to reverse the Obama-Clinton administration's New Cold War with Russia. But the neocon coterie at the CIA and State Department are undercutting his proposed rapprochement with Russia by forcing out General Flynn for starters. It seems doubtful that Trump will clean them out.

Trump has called NATO obsolete, but insists that its members up their spending to the stipulated 2% of GDP – producing a windfall worth tens of billions of dollars for U.S. arms exporters. That is to be the price Europe must pay if it wants to endorse Germany's and the Baltics' confrontation with Russia.

Trump is sufficiently intuitive to proclaim the euro a disaster, and he recommends that Greece leave it. He supports the rising nationalist parties in Britain, France, Italy, Greece and the Netherlands, all of which urge withdrawal from the eurozone – and reconciliation with Russia instead of sanctions. In place of the ill-fated TPP and TTIP, Trump advocates country-by-country trade deals favoring the United States. Toward this end, his designated ambassador to the European Union, Ted Malloch, urges the EU's breakup. The EU is refusing to accept him as ambassador.

Will Trump's victory break up the Democratic Party?

At the time this volume is going to press, there is no way of knowing how successful these international reversals will be. What is more clear is what Trump's political impact will have at home. His victory – or more accurately, Hillary's resounding loss and the *way* she lost – has encouraged enormous pressure for a realignment of both parties. Regardless of what President Trump may achieve *vis-à-vis* Europe, his actions as celebrity chaos agent may break up U.S. politics across the political spectrum.

The Democratic Party has lost its ability to pose as the party of labor and the middle class. Firmly controlled by Wall Street and California billionaires, the

Democratic National Committee (DNC) strategy of identity politics encourages any identity *except* that of wage earners. The candidates backed by the Donor Class have been Blue Dogs pledged to promote Wall Street and neocons urging a New Cold War with Russia.

They preferred to lose with Hillary than to win behind Bernie Sanders. So Trump's electoral victory is their legacy as well as Obama's. Instead of Trump's victory dispelling that strategy, the Democrats are doubling down. It is as if identity politics is all they have.

Trying to ride on Barack Obama's coattails didn't work. Promising "hope and change", he won by posing as a transformational president, leading the Democrats to control of the White House, Senate and Congress in 2008. Swept into office by a national reaction against George Bush's Oil War in Iraq and the junk-mortgage crisis that left the economy debt-ridden, they had free rein to pass whatever new laws they chose – even a Public Option in health care if they had wanted, or make Wall Street banks absorb the losses from their bad and often fraudulent loans.

But it turned out that Obama's role was to *prevent* the changes that voters hoped to see, and indeed that the economy needed to recover: financial reform, debt writedowns to bring junk mortgages in line with fair market prices, and throwing crooked bankers in jail. Obama rescued the banks, not the economy, and turned over the Justice Department and regulatory agencies to his Wall Street campaign contributors. He did not even pull back from war in the Near East, but extended it to Libya and Syria, blundering into the Ukrainian coup as well.

Having dashed the hopes of his followers, Obama then praised his chosen successor Hillary Clinton as his "Third Term". Enjoying this kiss of death, Hillary promised to keep up Obama's policies.

The straw that pushed voters over the edge was when she asked voters, "Aren't you better off today than you were eight years ago?" Who were they going to believe: their eyes, or Hillary? National income statistics showed that only the top 5 percent of the population were better off. All the growth in Gross Domestic Product (GDP) during Obama's tenure went to them – the

Donor Class that had gained control of the Democratic Party leadership. Real incomes have fallen for the remaining 95 percent, whose household budgets have been further eroded by soaring charges for health insurance. (The Democratic leadership in Congress fought tooth and nail to block Dennis Kucinich from introducing his Single Payer proposal.)

No wonder most of the geographic United States voted for change – except for where the top 5 percent is concentrated: in New York (Wall Street) and California (Silicon Valley and the military-industrial complex). Making fun of the Obama Administration's slogan of "hope and change", Trump characterized Hillary's policy of continuing the economy's shrinkage for the 95% as "no hope and no change".

Identity politics as anti-labor politics

A new term was introduced to the English language: Identity Politics. Its aim is for voters to think of themselves as separatist minorities – women, LGBTQ, Blacks and Hispanics. The Democrats thought they could beat Trump by organizing Women for Wall Street (and a New Cold War), LGBTQ for Wall Street (and a New Cold War), and Blacks and Hispanics for Wall Street (and a New Cold War). Each identity cohort was headed by a billionaire or hedge fund donor.

The identity that is conspicuously excluded is the working class. Identity politics strips away thinking of one's interest in terms of having to work for a living. It excludes voter protests against having their monthly paycheck stripped to pay more for health insurance, housing and mortgage charges or education, or better working conditions or consumer protection – not to speak of protecting debtors.

Progressive politics used to be about three major categories: workers and unionization, anti-war protests and civil rights marches against racist Jim Crow laws. These were the three objectives of the many nationwide demonstrations. That ended when these movements got co-opted into the Democratic Party. Their reappearance in Bernie Sanders' campaign in fact threatens to tear the Democratic coalition apart. As soon as the primaries were over (duly stacked against Sanders), his followers were made to feel unwelcome. Hillary sought Republican support by denouncing Sanders as being radical and utopian in advocating a public option for health care and in seeking to rein in Wall Street – the Democratic Donor Class. Her aim was to counter Sanders' attempt to convince diverse groups that they had a common denominator in needing jobs with decent pay – and, to achieve that, in opposing Wall Street's replacing the government as central planner – the Democrats depict every identity constituency as being victimized by every other, setting themselves at each other's heels. Clinton strategist John Podesta, for instance, encouraged Blacks to accuse Sanders supporters of distracting attention from racism. Pushing a common economic interest between whites, Blacks, Hispanics and LGBTQ always has been the neoliberals' nightmare. No wonder they tried so hard to stop Bernie Sanders, and are maneuvering to keep his supporters from gaining influence in their party.

When Trump was inaugurated on Friday, January 20, there was no pro-jobs or anti-war demonstration. That presumably would have attracted pro-Trump supporters in an ecumenical show of force. Instead, the Women's March on Saturday led even the pro-Democrat *New York Times* to write a front-page article reporting that white women were complaining that they did not feel welcome in the demonstration. The message to anti-war advocates, students and Bernie supporters was that their economic and anti-war cause was a distraction.

The march was typically Democratic in that its ideology did not threaten the Donor Class. As Yves Smith wrote on *Naked Capitalism*: "the track record of non-issue-oriented marches, no matter how large scale, is poor, and the status of this march as officially sanctioned (blanket media coverage when other marches of hundreds of thousands of people have been minimized, police not tricked out in their usual riot gear) also indicates that the officialdom does not see it as a threat to the *status quo*."[1]

Hillary's loss was not blamed on her neoliberal support for the TPP or her pro-war neocon stance, but on the revelations of the e-mails by her

---

[1] Yves Smith, "Women Skeptical of the Women's March," *Naked Capitalism*, February 10, 2017.

operative Podesta discussing his dirty tricks against Bernie Sanders (claimed to be given to Wikileaks by Russian hackers, not a domestic DNC leaker as Wikileaks claimed) and the FBI investigation of her e-mail abuses at the State Department. Backing her supporters' attempt to brazen it out, the Democratic Party has doubled down on its identity politics, despite the fact that an estimated 52 percent of white women voted for Trump. After all, women do work for wages. And that also is what Blacks and Hispanics want – in addition to banking that serves *their* needs, not those of Wall Street, and health care that serves *their* needs, not those of the health-insurance and pharmaceuticals monopolies.

Bernie did not choose to run on a third-party ticket. Evidently he feared being accused of throwing the election to Trump. The question is now whether he can remake the Democratic Party as a democratic socialist party, or create a new party if the Donor Class retains its neoliberal control. It seems that he will not make a break until he concludes that a Socialist Party can leave the Democrats as far back in the dust as the Republicans left the Whigs after 1854. He may have underestimated his chance in 2016.

Trump's effect on U.S. political party realignment

During Trump's rise to the 2016 Republican nomination it seemed that he was more likely to break up the Republican Party. Its leading candidates and gurus warned that his populist victory in the primaries would tear the party apart. The polls in May and June showed him defeating Hillary Clinton easily (but losing to Bernie Sanders). But Republican leaders worried that he would not support what they believed in: namely, whatever corporate lobbyists put in their hands to enact and privatize.

The May/June polls showed Trump and Clinton were the country's two most unpopular presidential candidates. But whereas the Democrats maneuvered Bernie out of the way, the Republican Clown Car was unable to do the same to Trump. In the end they chose to win behind him, expecting to control him. As for the Democratic National Committee, its Wall Street donors preferred to lose with Hillary than to win with Bernie. They wanted to keep control of their party and continue the bargain they had made with the Republicans:

The latter would move further and further to the right, leaving room for Democratic neoliberals and neocons to follow them closely, yet still pose as the "lesser evil". That "centrism" is the essence of the Clintons' "triangulation" strategy. It actually has been going on for a half-century. "As Tanzanian President Julius Nyerere quipped in the 1960s, when he was accused by the US of running a one-party state, 'The United States is also a one-party state but, with typical American extravagance, they have two of them'."[2]

By late 2016, voters had caught on to this two-step game. But Hillary's team paid pollsters over $1 billion to tell her ("Mirror, mirror on the wall ...") that she was the most popular of all. It was hubris to imagine that she could convince the 95 Percent of the people who were worse off under Obama to love her as much as her East-West Coast donors did. It was politically unrealistic – and a reflection of her cynicism – to imagine that raising enough money to buy television ads would convince working-class Republicans to vote for her, succumbing to a Stockholm Syndrome by thinking of themselves as part of the 5 Percent who had benefited from Obama's pro-Wall Street policies.

Hillary's election strategy was to make a right-wing run around Trump. While characterizing the working class as white racist "deplorables", allegedly intolerant of LBGTQ or assertive women, she resurrected the ghost of Joe McCarthy and accused Trump of being "Putin's poodle" for proposing peace with Russia. Among the most liberal Democrats, Paul Krugman still leads a biweekly charge at *The New York Times* that President Trump is following Moscow's orders. Saturday Night Live, Bill Maher and MSNBC produce weekly skits that Trump and General Flynn are Russian puppets. A large proportion of Democrats have bought into the fairy tale that Trump didn't really win the election, but that Russian hackers manipulated the voting machines. No wonder George Orwell's *1984* soared to the top of America's best-seller lists in February 2017 as Donald Trump was taking his oath of office.

---

[2] Radhika Desai, "Decoding Trump," *Counterpunch*, February 10, 2017.

This propaganda paid off on February 13, when neocon public relations succeeded in forcing the resignation of General Flynn, whom Trump had appointed to clean out the neocons at the NSA and CIA. His foreign policy initiative based on rapprochement with Russia and hopes to create a common front against ISIS/Al Nusra seemed to be collapsing.

Tabula rasa celebrity politics

U.S. presidential elections no longer are much about policy. Like Obama before him, Trump campaigned as a *rasa tabla*, a vehicle for everyone to project their hopes and fancies. What has all but disappeared is the past century's idea of politics as a struggle between labor and capital, democracy vs. oligarchy.

Who would have expected even half a century ago that American politics would become so post-modern that the idea of class conflict has all but disappeared. Classical economic discourse has been drowned out by modern economist's neoliberal junk economics.

There is a covert economic program, to be sure, and it is bipartisan. It is to make elections about just which celebrities will introduce neoliberal economic policies with the most convincing patter talk. That is the essence of *rasa tabla* politics.

Can the Democrats lose again in 2020?

Trump's November victory showed that voters found *him* to be the Lesser Evil, but all that this meant was that all voters really could express was "throw out the bums" and get a new set of lobbyists for the FIRE sector and corporate monopolists. Both candidates represented Goldman Sachs and Wall Street. No wonder voter turnout has continued to plunge.

Although the Democrats' Lesser Evil argument lost to the Republicans in 2016, the neoliberals in control of the DNC found the absence of a progressive economic program less threatening to their interests than the critique of Wall Street and neocon interventionism coming from the Sanders camp. So the Democrats will continue to pose as the Lesser Evil party not really in terms of policy, but simply *ad hominum*. They will merely repeat Hillary's campaign stance: They are *not* Trump. Their parades and street demonstrations since his inauguration have not come out for any economic policy.

On Friday, February 10, the party's Democratic Policy group held a retreat for its members in Baltimore. Third Way "centrists" (Republicans running as Democrats) dominated, with Hillary operatives in charge. The conclusion was that no party policy was needed at all. "President Trump is a better recruitment tool for us than a central campaign issue," said Washington Rep. Denny Heck, who is leading recruitment for the Democratic Congressional Campaign Committee (DCCC).[3]

But what does their party leadership have to offer women, Blacks and Hispanics in the way of employment, more affordable health care, housing or education and better pay? Where are the New Deal pro-labor, pro-regulatory roots of bygone days? The party leadership is unwilling to admit that Trump's message about protecting jobs and opposing the TPP played a role in his election. Hillary was suspected of supporting it as "the gold standard" of trade deals, and Obama had made the Trans-Pacific Partnership the centerpiece of his presidency – the free-trade TPP and TTIP that would have taken economic regulatory policy out of the hands of government and given it to corporations.

Instead of accepting even Sanders' centrist-left stance, the Democrats' strategy was to tar Trump as pro-Russian, insist that his aides had committed impeachable offenses, and mount one parade after another. Rep. Marcia Fudge of Ohio told reporters she was wary of focusing solely on an "economic message" aimed at voters whom Trump won over in 2016, because, in her view, Trump did not win on an economic message. "What Donald Trump did was address them at a very different level – an emotional level, a racial level, a fear level," she said. "If all we talk about is the

---

[3] "Pelosi denies Democrats are divided on strategy for 2018," Yahoo News, February 10, 2018. https://www.yahoo.com/news/pelosi-denies-democrats-are-divided-on-strategy-for-2018-194337876.html

economic message, we're not going to win."[4] This stance led Sanders supporters to walk out of a meeting organized by the "centrist" Third Way think tank on Wednesday, February 8.

By now this is an old story. Fifty years ago, socialists such as Michael Harrington asked why union members and progressives still imagined that they had to work through the Democratic Party. It has taken the rest of the country half a century to see that Democrats are not the party of the working class, unions, middle class, farmers or debtors. They are the party of Wall Street privatizers, bank deregulators, neocons and the military-industrial complex. Obama showed his hand – and that of his party – in his passionate attempt to ram through the corporatist TPP treaty that would have enabled corporations to sue governments for any costs imposed by public consumer protection, environmental protection or other protection of the population against financialized corporate monopolies.

Against this backdrop, Trump's promises and indeed his worldview seem quixotic. The picture of America's future he has painted seems unattainable within the foreseeable future. It is too late to bring manufacturing back to the United States, because corporations already have shifted their supply nodes abroad, and too much U.S. infrastructure has been dismantled.

There can't be a high-speed railroad, because it would take more than four years to get the right-of-way and create a route without crossing gates or sharp curves. In any case, the role of railroads and other transportation has been to increase real estate prices along the routes. But in this case, real estate would be torn down – and having a high-speed rail does not increase land values.

The stock market has soared to new heights, anticipating lower taxes on corporate profits and a deregulation of consumer, labor and environmental protection. Trump may end up as America's Boris Yeltsin, protecting U.S. oligarchs (not that Hillary would have been different, merely cloaked in a more colorful identity rainbow). The U.S. economy is in for Shock Therapy. Voters should look to Greece to get a taste of the future in this scenario.

---

[4] *Ibid.*

Without a coherent response to neoliberalism, Trump's billionaire cabinet may do to the United States what neoliberals in the Clinton administration did to Russia after 1991: tear out all the checks and balances, and turn public wealth over to insiders and oligarchs. So Trump's best chance to be transformative is simply to be America's Yeltsin for his party's oligarchic backers, putting the class war back in business.

What a truly transformative president would do/would have done

No administration can create a sound U.S. recovery without dealing with the problem that caused the 2008 crisis in the first place: over-indebtedness. The only one way to restore growth, raise living standards and make the economy competitive again is a debt writedown. But that is not yet on the political horizon. Obama's doublecross of his voters in 2009 prevented the needed policy from occurring. Having missed this chance in the last financial crisis, a progressive policy must await yet another crisis. But so far, no political party is preparing a program to juxtapose Republican-Democratic austerity and scale-back of Social Security, Medicare and social spending programs in general.

Also no longer on the horizon is a more progressive income tax, or a public option for health care or for banking, or consumer protection against financial fraud, or for a $15-an-hour minimum wage, or for a revived protection of labor's right to unionize, or environmental regulations.

It seems that only a new party can achieve these aims. At the time these essays are going to press, Sanders has committed himself to working within the Democratic Party. But that stance is based on his assumption that somehow he can recruit enough activists to take over the party from Its Donor Class.

I suspect he will fail. In any case, it is easier to begin afresh than to try to re-design a party (or any institution) dominated by resistance to change, and whose idea of economic growth is a trickle-down pastiche of tax cuts and deregulation. Both U.S. parties are committed to this neoliberal program –

and seek to blame foreign enemies for the fact that its effect is to continue squeezing living standards and bloating the financial sector.

If this slow but inexorable crash does lead to a political crisis, it looks like the Republicans may succeed in convening a new Constitutional Convention (many states already have approved this) to lock the United States into a corporatist neoliberal world. Its slogan will be that of Margaret Thatcher: TINA – There Is No Alternative.

And who is to disagree? As Trotsky said, fascism is the result of the failure of the left to provide an alternative.

Causes and consequences of President Donald Trump

Ann Pettifor [PRIME (Policy Research in Economics) UK]

Introduction and context: 2016, the year that shook the foundations of globalisation

2016 was a year of momentous events for the United States. A major insurgency was triggered by resistance to the utopian ambitions of economists, financiers and politicians – namely, to detach markets – in money, trade and labour – from the US's regulatory democracy. Americans reacted to an economic system that appeared to many to be beyond the control of public authorities, and beyond that of democratically elected politicians. Both Democrat and Republican administrations had presided over a steep rise in inequality. At the same time while millions of middle class Americans were impoverished or made insecure by "liberalized" finance, or globalisation, the system fabulously enriched the 1%. Exposed, through no fault of their own, to the 2007-9 financial crisis and its aftermath, many experienced the economic system as threatening to their life chances, their incomes, their futures, and their way of life. Despairing of their democracy, and of politicians and political institutions, Americans turned to a "strong man" – a billionaire who led them to believe that he alone could protect them from the predations of markets in trade and labour.

The rising tide of American nationalism and populism, was manifest in the slogan: "America First". The determination to build walls against migrants and free trade represents a major challenge to the utopian ideal of "globalisation". For some time now advocates of globalisation have complacently believed that the globalised financial system is a given, and unchallengeable. President Bill Clinton embraced globalisation as the overarching solution to the country's problems – the "bridge to the twenty-first century".[1] Tony Blair told the Labour Party Conference in 2005 that there was no need to stop and debate globalisation: "you might as well debate whether autumn should follow summer." Like many others Blair ignored the rising threat to globalisation: nationalism. In a 1940 lecture delivered at Bennington College, Karl Polanyi, the political economist and author of *The Great Transformation* (1944)[2] argued that:

> "The more intense international cooperation was and the more close the interdependence of the various parts of the world grew, the more essential became the only effective organizational unit of an industrial society on the present level of technique: – the nation. Modern nationalism is a protective reaction against the dangers inherent in an interdependent world.
>
> The apparently simple proposition that all factors of production must have free markets implies in practice that the whole of society must be subordinated to the needs of the market system."[3]

On the opening page of his book Polanyi explained that society "inevitably... took measures to protect itself" from job and income losses, and from economic forces that generated anxiety, insecurity, risks and threats. Self-protection would invariably take the form of a counter-movement to *laissez faire*, or self-regulated markets. The movement, Polanyi argued, can be spontaneous, often leaderless and attracts supporters from all classes. Unlike Marx, Polanyi believed that the counter-movement could include the business and finance sectors. These, as Fred Block has argued need protections, or

---

[1] Quoted in George Packer, 31 October, 2016: *Hilary Clinton and the Populist Revolt.* The New Yorker. http://www.newyorker.com/magazine/2016/10/31/hillary-clinton-and-the-populist-revolt

[2] Karl Polanyi, 1944, *The Great Transformation*, Beacon Press, 1957, p. 114.

[3] Karl Polanyi,1940, in the first of Five Lectures at Bennington College on *The Present Age of Transformation: The passing of 19th century civilisation.* Re-published by Policy Research in Macroeconomics (PRIME) in February, 2017. http://www.primeeconomics.org/articles/our-polanyi-week-the-1940-bennington-college-lectures

"limits, especially regulatory initiatives, to avoid destructive social, environmental, and economic consequences."[4]

Back in May 2016, pollster Nate Silver analysed Trump's primary campaigns and noted that the "movement" to elect Donald Trump as President was diverse.

> "As compared with most Americans, Trump's voters are better off. The median household income of a Trump voter so far in the primaries is about $72,000, based on estimates derived from exit polls and Census Bureau data. That's lower than the $91,000 median for Kasich voters. But it's well above the national median household income of about $56,000. It's also higher than the median income for Hillary Clinton and Bernie Sanders supporters, which is around $61,000 for both."

Trump either won, or closely contested all the US's traditional manufacturing states Ohio, Wisconsin, Indiana and even Michigan, where union voters did not support Clinton as they had Obama and where trade was a big issue. Silver writes:

> "The slower a county's job growth has been since 2007, the more it shifted toward Trump. (The same is true looking back to 2000.)
>
> ...The list goes on: More subprime loans? More Trump support. More residents receiving disability payments? More Trump support. Lower earnings among full-time workers? More Trump support. 'Trump Country,' as my colleague Andrew Flowers described it shortly after the election, isn't the part of America where people are in the worst financial

---

[4] Karl Polanyi, as above, Lecture Three of Five Lectures at Bennington College.

shape; it's the part of America where their economic prospects are on the steepest decline."[5]

Two days after the presidential election, Politico noted that "between 2007 and 2014, the median incomes of white males without college degrees fell by 14 percent. Trump carried them by nearly 40 points Tuesday."[6]

The "counter-movement" was not confined to the US. Nationalist, right-wing, anti-globalisation and even fascist movements are active across Europe, as this goes to press.

The slogans used by Trump: "Make America Great Again" and "America First" did not just echo the fascist-leaning Charles Lindbergh's 1930s "America First" campaign in support of Hitler. It was also a theme of the far-right French presidential candidate, Marine Le Pen's: "On est chez nous" in 2017 and of the Italian leader, Silvio Berlusconi's earlier "Forza Italia". The UK's Brexit campaign slogans included: "Take Back Control", "Take Back Our Country" and "Britannia waives the rules". They all represented an attempt by political leaders of insurgencies to use the nation as a "protective reaction" against unfettered globalised markets in capital, trade, and labour.

In this essay we hope to trace the underlying and deep-seated economic causes that led to this rise of nationalisms and protectionism.

From beasts on an 18th-century Pacific island to today's globalised financial markets

Back in the 1770s a story circulated about two families of "beasts" – goats and dogs – placed on a remote Pacific atoll, Juan Ferdinand island, by Spanish and English sailors. In a natural condition of scarcity, the goats and dogs fought viciously over food, but ultimately learned to live in harmony –

---

[5] Nate Silver, 9 January, 2017: *Stop Saying Trump's Win Had Nothing to do with Economics.* Accessed 15th February, 2017. https://fivethirtyeight.com/features/stop-saying-trumps-win-had-nothing-to-do-with-economics/
[6] Carl M. Cannon, 10 November, 2016. Real Clear Politics, *How Trump Won.* http://www.realclearpolitics.com/articles/2016/11/10/how_donald_trump_won_13232 1.html. Accessed 15 February, 2017

without political interference – or so we are led to believe. The author of an influential dissertation on the Poor Laws used this experience as an incentive for the alleviation of poverty. Hunger he argued,

> "will tame the fiercest animals, it will teach decency and civility, obedience and subjection, to the most brutish, the most obstinate, the most perverse."

In this tale, and in the political economy that emerged from it, lay the origins of a theory that underpins classical and neoliberal political economy to this very day. Namely that without government interference, self-regulating markets in money, trade and labour may become vicious and unsettled, but can ultimately be expected to reach a state of equilibrium. The author of the pamphlet was one Rev. Joseph Townsend and the 1786 publication was his *Dissertation on the Poor Laws*.[7] Despite its relative obscurity, the *Dissertation's* contribution to political economy represented a decisive episode in the history of economics, as Philipp H. Lepenies explained in a 2014 paper.[8]

Townsend made the "scientific" case that hunger, or scarcity, represented a "natural law" that governed human appetites and markets for food:

> "There is an appetite, which is and should be urgent, but which, if left to operate without restraint, would multiply the human species before provision could be made for their support. Some check, some balance is therefore absolutely needful, and hunger is the proper balance; hunger, not as directly felt, or feared by the individual for himself, but as foreseen and feared for his immediate offspring. Were it not for this the equilibrium would not be preserved so near as it is at present in the world, between the numbers of people and the quantity of food."

---

[7] Joseph Townsend, 1786. *A Dissertation on the Poor Laws.*
http://socserv2.socsci.mcmaster.ca/econ/ugcm/3ll3/townsend/poorlaw.html
[8] Philipp H. Lepenies, 2014. *Of goats and dogs: Joseph Townsend and the idealisation of markets – a decisive episode in the history of economics.* Cambridge Journal of Economics, 38 (2): 447-457.

In other words, it was not men, but the *natural* fear of hunger that governed markets for scarce food. Polanyi noted that:

> "Hobbes had argued the need for a despot because men were like beasts; Townsend insisted they *were* actually beasts and that, precisely for that reason, only a minimum of government was required."[9]

Lepenies believes that Malthus plagiarised Townsend in his famous *Essay on the Principle of Population* – which is "similar" to Townsend's Dissertation,

> "not only in their argument, ideas and structure but in their use of the device of scientific abstraction and generalisation. It is therefore not Malthus alone who should be revered as the father of modern economic logic and market fundamentalism but also Townsend."[10]

Townsend was also a close friend of Jeremy Bentham who quoted at length the example of goats and dogs in his Pauper Systems Compared of 1797 (Quinn, 2001).[11]

For Townsend, society, as fundamentally biological, was best left as a self-regulating system that when untouched by political intervention, will tend toward equilibrium and order. His crude and brutish conception of self-regulating markets – previously understood as embedded in regulated social and political institutions – was to inform much of classical and neoclassical economics, and has persisted to this day in market fundamentalism.

More recently Townsend's theory was extended from labour and trade markets and applied to markets in money – with devastating economic and political consequences. It was the application of this flawed theory to the monetary system that led, I will argue, to recurring and catastrophic financial market failures, and ultimately to the election of President Donald Trump.

---

[9] Karl Polanyi, 1944. *The Great Transformation*, Beacon Press, 1957, p. 114.
[10] Philipp H. Lepenies, as above.
[11] Cited in Lepenies, as above.

The neoclassical conception of money

Adam Smith first conjured up the idea of money as a "veil" over economic activity when he asserted that money is "a *neutral* medium that facilitated exchange on the 'great wheel of circulation'".[12] Paul Samuelson explained to millions of students of his Economics 101 textbooks that:

> "Even in the most advanced industrial economies, if we strip exchange down to its barest essentials and *peel off the obscuring layer of money*, we find that trade between individuals or nations largely boils down to *barter.*"[13]

While the classical or neoclassical school of economists pay little attention to "neutral" money or to "the obscuring layer of money" in designing models of the economy, they simultaneously conceive of it as akin to a commodity and therefore, as Samuelson explains, as a form of barter. Money, in their view, is representative of a tangible asset or scarce commodity, like gold or silver. As with corn for example, money in this orthodox view, can be set aside or saved, accumulated and then loaned out. Savers lend their surplus to borrowers. Bankers, Krugman and Wells argue in their textbook, Macroeconomics,[14] are mere intermediaries between savers and borrowers.

Because neoclassical and some post-Keynesian economists conceive of money as like gold or silver, having a scarcity value, they theorise as if money is subject to market forces. In other words, as if money's "price" – the rate of interest – is a "natural" price, subject to the law of supply and demand, rather than a socially constructed "price" on every loan determined by risk assessors in banks. Many argue that like commodities, the supply of money or savings can become scarce. In February, 2017, the British government's Chancellor was quoted in the Financial Times as saying (to MPs clamouring for extra funds): "There is no pot of money under my

---

[12] Adam Smith.
[13] Paul Samuelson,
[14] Krugman and Wells, Macroeconomics, 4th Edition.
https://www.amazon.co.uk/Macroeconomics-Paul-Krugman/dp/142928343

desk."[15] *Mrs Thatcher in a speech to the 1983 Tory party conference echoed the neoclassical theory that money exists as a consequence of economic activity when she* said:

> *"The state has no source of money, other than the money people earn themselves.* If the state wishes to spend more it can only do so by borrowing your savings, or by taxing you more. And it's no good thinking that someone else will pay. That someone else is you. There is no such thing as public money. There is only taxpayers' money." (My emphasis.)

This misunderstanding of the nature of money and of a monetary economy is entrenched in classical and neoclassical (neoliberal) economic theory. It helps explain the "blind spot" that economists have for money, banks and debt, and for the finance sector.

The economist Andrea Terzi, explains the difference between a monetary economy and a non-monetary economy:

> "When people save in the form of a real commodity, like corn, the decision to save is a fully personal matter: if you have acquired a given amount of corn, you have the privilege of consuming it, storing it, wasting it, as you please, without this directly affecting other people's consumption of corn. *Only if you decide to lend it will you establish a relationship with others.*
>
> In a monetary economy, saving is not a real quantity that anyone can independently own, like corn or gold or a collection of rare stamps. In a monetary economy, as opposed to a non-monetary economy, saving is an act that [establishes a relationship with others]... in the form of a financial *claim*.
>
> Unlike a commodity such as corn, financial saving always

---

[15] George Parker, Jim Pickard and Gemma Tatlow, in the Financial Times, 21 February, 2017: *Hammond Warns No "Pot of Money" for Extra Budget Funds*. https://www.ft.com/content/6c786540-f844-11e6-bd4e-68d53499ed71

appears as a financial relationship, as it exists only as a claim on others, in the form of banknotes, bank deposits or other financial assets. Personal savings are claims of one economic unit on another, and any change in savings entails a change in the relationship between the 'saver' and other economic units. This does not appear on national accounts, which only expose aggregate values.

If we then look at savings by zooming out of the individual unit and considering the interconnections between units and between sectors, we find that each penny saved must correspond to a debt of equal size. A banknote is a central bank's liability. A bank deposit is a bank's liability. A government security is a government liability. A corporate bond is a private company liability, and so on. This means that when we discuss financial savings we are also discussing debt. Every penny saved is someone else's liability ... every penny saved is somebody's debt.

In a monetary economy, savings do not fund; they need to be funded."[16]

"Nixon Shock" as lightning rod for international financial liberalisation

On the evening of Sunday, 15 August 1971 in a TV announcement, and without consulting allies or the IMF, President Nixon unilaterally dismantled the architecture of the international financial system. At the time, the "Nixon Shock" represented the biggest sovereign default in history, and was a reckless decision the foolhardiness of which President Donald Trump (up until this point) has failed to match. Its effect was to accelerate the process of de-regulation by restoring *private authority* over the finance sector, and to trigger recurring financial crises.

---

[16] Andrea Terzi, 2015, *The Eurozone crisis: debt shortage as the final cause.* Contribution to a panel at INET Annual Conference, Paris, 8-11 April, 2015.

The Bretton Woods system had been carefully constructed by an international gathering of economists, including Britain's JM Keynes and Harry Dexter White of the United States, at a grand New Hampshire hotel in 1944.[17] The international financial architecture constructed at Bretton Woods was a response to the recurring crises of the 1920s and 30s under the deeply flawed gold standard. That in turn was based on a fallacious understanding of the nature of money as a commodity, gold; and not as a socially constructed system of obligations and claims; assets and liabilities; debits and credits, all managed by regulatory democracy.

One of the primary motivations behind the construction of Bretton Woods was Keynes' and White's determination (backed by President Roosevelt) to restore *public authority* over the monetary system and to thereby restore policy autonomy to democratic governments. The latter had been stripped of such autonomy by the mobility of capital, and by the exercise of *private authority* over the creation of credit and the determination of interest rates. Keynes and White understood that fundamental to the restoration of public authority over finance was the introduction of controls over the mobility of capital.

The process of dismantling Bretton Woods began almost as soon as agreement had been reached at the conference hotel. Roosevelt had barred private bankers from attending the 1944 conference, but this did not deter their lobbying. An IMF Working Paper explains that both Keynes and White realized that "capital controls would not be effective unless applied 'at both ends' of the transaction, and their original plans therefore mandated IMF member countries to cooperate in enforcing each other's measures."[18] But as the IMF documents "last minute intervention by powerful New York bankers... succeeded in watering down these proposals, and in the final version of the IMF Articles agreed at Bretton Woods on 22nd July 1944, capital controls were not included as a permanent feature of the international financial landscape."[19]

---

[17] Ed Conway, 2014, *The Summit: The biggest battle of the Second World War – fought behind closed doors.* Little, Brown
[18] IMF Working Paper February, 2016, by Atish R. Ghosh and Mahvash S. Qureshi *Capital Controls What's In a Name? That Which We Call Capital Controls.* https://www.imf.org/external/pubs/ft/wp/2016/wp1625.pdf
[19] As above

In this otherwise excellent paper by the IMF's Ghosh and Qureshi the authors, like many other economic historians, overlook the "Nixon Shock". Yet the collapse of the Bretton Woods system in 1971 represents a decisive episode in the process of financial globalisation begun soon after Bretton Woods, and with it the corresponding weakening of regulatory democracy. As the OECD explains:[20]

> "the easing of capital controls, and the international branching of business firms or establishment of their finance companies, made domestic regulations easier to circumvent by conducting financial transactions outside national boundaries."

Up until the early 1970s, financial systems in most western, democratic economies were governed by the regulation of market forces, enacted within the policy-making boundaries of democratic nation states. These included: interest rate controls; securities market regulations; quantitative investment restrictions on financial institutions; line-of-business regulations and regulations on ownership linkages among financial institutions; restrictions on entry of foreign financial institutions; and controls on international capital movements and foreign exchange transactions.

According to the OECD:[21]

> "Direct controls were used in many countries to allocate finance to preferred industries during the post-war reconstruction period; specialised credit institutions have also been in place to ensure access to credit by smaller enterprises; restrictions on market access and competition were partly motivated by a concern for financial stability; protection of small savers with limited financial knowledge was an important objective of controls on banks; and

---

[20] Edey, Malcolm and K. Hviding (1995), *An Assessment of Financial Reform in OECD Countries*, OECD Economics Department Working Papers, No. 154, OECD Publishing. doi:10.1787/515737261523
https://www.oecd.org/fr/eco/monetaire/35235099.pdf
[21] As above.

controls on banks and financial institutions were frequently
used as instruments of macroeconomic management."

The "interventions of bankers" and the establishment of the Eurodollar
market in the late 1960s, led to the removal of controls over the mobility of
capital.[22] Democratic governments were gradually stripped of the powers of
oversight and of *the management* of the financial equivalent of the Juan
Ferdinand island.

From the perspective of Keynes, the consequences were entirely
predictable: recurring financial crises. These began at the periphery of the
global economy (in indebted third world countries) but gradually moved to
the core of the global economy: the Anglo-American economies. These
recurring crises after the "liberalisation" of the 1970s are best illustrated by
this chart from Reinhart & Rogoff's book: *This Time is Different*.

Capital Mobility and the Incidence of Banking Crisis: All Countries, 1800-2007:

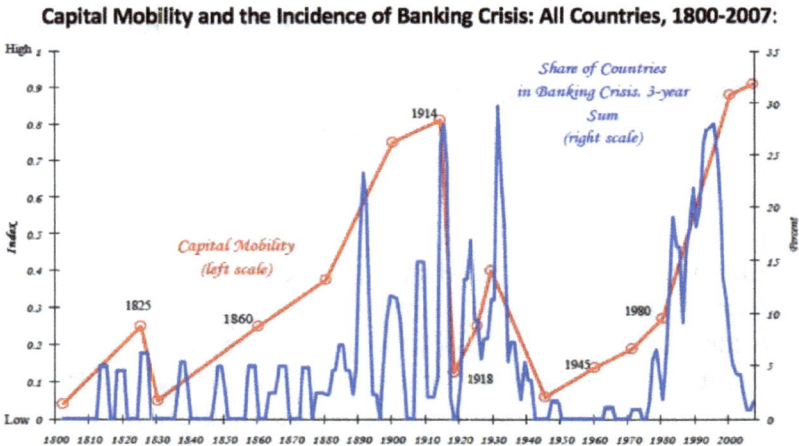

Chart taken from "This Time is Different: A Panoramic View of Eight Centuries of
Financial Crises" by Carmen M. Reinhart, University of Maryland and NBER; and
Kenneth S. Rogoff, Harvard University and NBER.

---

[22] Eric Helleiner, 1995, pg 152 *Great Transformations: A Polanyian Perspective
on the Contemporary Global Financial Order*
file:///Users/annpettifor/Downloads/9379-15190-1-PB.pdf

In Britain one of the most significant de-regulatory measures was introduced in 1971, the same year as the "Nixon Shock", and was dubbed "Competition and Control" (CCC or "the New Approach"). It was "the biggest change in monetary policy since the Second World War" and is often described by economists as "all competition and no control" over credit creation.

Duncan Needham, of the Cambridge University Centre for Financial History, has written at length on the subject, and argues that:[23]

> "CCC swept away the restrictions on... bank lending to the private sector, that had been in place for much of the 1960s. Henceforth, bank lending would be controlled on the basis of cost, that is, through interest rates. Loans would be granted to those companies and individuals that could pay the highest rate rather than those that fulfilled the authorities' qualitative criteria. By allocating bank credit competitively 'on the basis of cost', CCC replaced years of credit rationing 'by control'."

CCC was not a success. While it aimed to control "the money supply", the effect was the opposite. The money supply grew by 72 percent as commercial bankers engaged in a wild lending spree, and two years later inflation peaked at 26.9 percent.

The ending of restrictions on bank lending in the UK was paralleled in the United States by the Supreme Court's Marquette decision, which initiated interest rate deregulation.[24]

"Price" or the rate of interest, was to become to bank borrowers what "hunger" was to the goats and dogs on Townsend's Juan Ferdinand island.

---

[23] Duncan Needham, September, 2012. *Britain's money supply experiment, 1971-73* University of Cambridge, http://www.econsoc.hist.cam.ac.uk/docs/CWPESH%20number%2010%20Sept%202012.pdf

[24] FDIC, Diane Ellis, March, 1998: *The Effect of Consumer Interest Rate Deregulation on Credit Card Volumes, Charge-Offs, and the Personal Bankruptcy Rate.* https://www.fdic.gov/bank/analytical/bank/bt_9805.html

The FDIC charts the immediate impact interest rate deregulation had on bankruptcy filings:

The Long-Term Rise in the Personal Bankruptcy Rate Started Shortly after Interest Rate Deregulation

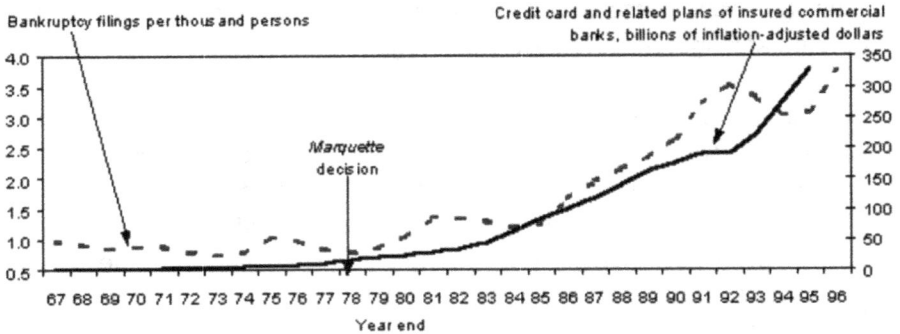

Source: Bank call reports, Administrative Office of the U.S. Courts, and Census Bureau

Back in Britain the inflation caused by financial deregulation of lending in the 1970s, and the impact of high real rates of interest on bankruptcies of firms did not trouble a conservative government Minister, Lord Cockfield who said:

> "Control of the money operates through the simple but brutal means of butchering company profits. Ultimately insolvency and unemployment teach employers and workers alike that they need to behave reasonably and sensibly."[25]

As Needham writes:

> "With nominal interest rates peaking at seventeen percent as the authorities tried to rein in the money supply, and the pound at its highest level since 1975, company profits were indeed butchered."

---

[25] Duncan Needham, 2014, p. 134: *UK Monetary Policy From Devaluation to Thatcher, 1967-82*. Palgrave Macmillan.

Cockfield's words echoed those of the 18th-century father of market fundamentalism, Joseph Townsend. He believed that like bankruptcies in the market for money, hunger in the market for food:

> "will tame the fiercest animals, will teach decency and civility, obedience and subjection, to the most brutish, the most obstinate, the most perverse."

It was these ideas, and their related policies that led to high, real rates of interest after 1971 and to the build-up of the overhang of private debts that ultimately became unpayable, leading to recurring financial crises, and to the catastrophe of 2007-9. Self-regulating financial markets, "untouched" by elected governments have for more than 30 years inflicted loss and suffering on populations around the world. As Karl Polanyi predicted, these societies, in a "counter-movement" to globalisation and recognising the failure of democratic governments to protect societies from the depredations of self-regulating markets, have reacted by electing "strong men" (and women) that do offer protection. Donald Trump posed as a strong protector, and won the support of those Americans "left behind" by globalisation.

Explaining the rise of Donald Trump

Marshall Auerback [Levy Economics Institute of Bard College, NY, USA]

Donald Trump's ascension to the Presidency last November is not as incredible as Establishment pundits profess. Nor is it a surprise that a big portion of Trump voters were working-class Americans displaced from their jobs by globalization, automation, and the shifting balance in manufacturing from the importance of the raw materials that go into products to that of the engineering expertise that designs them. These are the people Trump referred to in his Inaugural Address as "the forgotten men and women of our country".

In fact, during the campaign, Trump became the voice for an increasing number of Americans, who count themselves amongst the biggest losers of globalization and free trade, many of whom are located in key rust belt states (Ohio, Pennsylvania, Wisconsin, and Michigan), which ultimately turned the election in his favor. Commentators may lament the fact that his inauguration address did not have the poetry of previous Presidential addresses, but his references to "a small group in our nation's capital [who have] reaped the rewards of government while the people have born the cost" rang very true to many, even those who did not vote for Trump.

Globalization's winners and losers

For decades, the gap has widened between the winners and losers of globalization and free trade. And each election year, U.S. politicians express concerns for the losers in this increasingly globalized world of free trade and more open borders, then conveniently ignore these same people when they reach power and implement policies from the same Washington Consensus that has dominated the past 40 years. In Trump, the electorate has somebody who is playing a very different game, even if his policies lack the coherence and elegance so beloved in the world of economic policy seminars and think tanks.

Trump broke with traditional economic mantra on both the right and the left. While Hillary Clinton and Republican rivals such as Jeb Bush and Marco Rubio tried to build coalitions based on cultural issues and partisan traditions, Trump and Sanders set their sights squarely on what mattered most to voters: a political economy in which elected officials strongly promoted a broad-based prosperity that included them.

As Robert Johnson, Senior Fellow and Director of the Project on Global Finance at the Roosevelt Institute, wrote,

> "[T]heir efforts to attract a broad spectrum of voters were constrained by a system that makes it extremely difficult to fund a credible political campaign without catering slavishly to the wealthiest sliver of American society. That system invited rebellion, and Trump and Sanders – by self-financing and grassroots fundraising, respectively – were ideally positioned to lead one."

The author further noted that other candidates were also constrained by the prevailing neoliberal orthodoxies, which dominates in both parties, and therefore has precluded any "mainstream" politician

> "from willingly addressing the structural inequities in the American economy head-on. Doing so would require candor about such hard issues as technological disruption and globalization. It would also require confronting the legacy of decades of lobbyist-written free-trade agreements, regulations, bailouts, and tax policies that have been funneling economic gains up the income ladder, while imposing budget austerity in response to the needs of most Americans. The story Trump told of a 'rigged' system

resonated with voters more than anything they had heard from their political leaders in quite some time."[1]

Quality of jobs vs quantity of jobs – a rising source of inequality?

Johnson touches on the heart of the issue: rising inequality, under both conservative Republican administrations, and ostensibly progressive Democratic presidencies. For the past 3 decades, many Americans have been left behind economically and culturally for so long, and were furious about it; additionally, from the 2008 financial crisis onwards, they had accumulated so much contempt for the political elites. For these voters, then, the election ultimately was distilled down to a single question that Ronald Reagan first posed in the 1980 Presidential debates against then incumbent Jimmy Carter: "Are you better off than you were 4 years ago?" Many answered no, despite the fact that the usual economic metrics, such as GDP growth, unemployment, and the overall health of the credit system, would seem to paint an unambiguously positive picture.

These conventional metrics, however, ignored the fact that the QUALITY of the jobs was poor. The newly-created jobs in many respects were sub-optimal and in turn exacerbated the continued growth in inequality. This trend meant that much of the economic improvement was experienced by an increasingly smaller number of people. Professors Emmanuel Saez and Gabriel Zucman have analyzed b decades of US tax data and conclude that:

> "wealth inequality has considerably increased at the top over the last three decades. By our estimates, almost all of this increase is due to the rise of the share of wealth owned by the 0.1% richest families, from 7% in 1978 to 22% in 2012, a level comparable to that of the early twentieth century"[2]

As the authors illustrate, the current evolution of Capitalism is taking the world back to where it was in the early 20th century, before trade unions were

---

[1] https://www.project-syndicate.org/commentary/trump-misrepresentative-democracy-by-rob-johnson-2017-01?referrer=/xCtZP0Jk64ic
[2] http://gabriel-zucman.eu/files/SaezZucman2014.pdf

strong enough to protect workers' rights, before central governments were willing to mediate the class struggle and step in to make sure workers had the means to enjoy the material prosperity that the system generated, before wages growth allowed workers to share in productivity growth and build a modicum of material wealth.

And the unemployment data ignores the quality of the types of jobs being created. Recent research by Professors Lawrence Katz of Harvard and Alan Krueger of Princeton based on non-labor force survey data (private sampling) suggests that "all of the net employment growth in the U.S. economy from 2005 to 2015 appears to have occurred in alternative work arrangements."[3] That is, standard jobs with predictable income, pension benefits and health care coverage, have disappeared and are being replaced by more precarious contract work and other types of alternative working arrangements. Quantifying this trend, the authors conclude the following:

> "The increase in the share of workers in alternative work arrangements from 10.1 percent in 2005 to 15.8 percent in 2015 implies that the number of workers employed in alternative arrangement increased by 9.4 million (66.5 percent), from 14.2 million in February 2005 to 23.6 million in November 2015."[4]

Thus, these figures imply that employment in traditional jobs (standard employment arrangements) slightly declined by 0.4 million (0.3 percent) from 126.2 million in February 2005 to 125.8 million in November 2015. Unfortunately, we cannot determine the extent to which the replacement of traditional jobs with alternative work arrangements occurred before, during or after the Great Recession. But it appears that as of late 2015, the labor market had not yet fully recovered from the huge loss of traditional jobs from the Great Recession.

---

[3] https://krueger.princeton.edu/sites/default/files/akrueger/files/katz_krueger_cws_-_march_29_20165.pdf
[4] Ibid.

Delusions of the "punditocracy" and the response of the disenfranchised

All in all, a toxic brew, which surely helped to pave the way for an iconoclastic non-ideologue like Donald J. Trump, who explicitly addressed those peoples' anxieties during the election campaign a way in which the Democratic nominee, Hillary Clinton, could not (or would not). Trump aligned his campaign with those who were furious with executive pay / corporate looting (about 99% of the country). In spite of being a billionaire himself, he aligned himself with the public who felt let down by the system. Credible or not, it worked. Trump became an imperfect vessel for voter discontent with the status quo (whereas Hillary Clinton was seen as its embodiment).

Trump's description of a rigged system extended to the "punditocracy" in the media, which failed to recognize this underlying anger. Perhaps because it was germinating under the Obama Presidency and that Obama himself remained likeable, and pundits confused the President's personal approval ratings with voter satisfaction, rather than seeing the underlying truth: which is that for many outside the prosperous coastal regions (so-called "flyover country") a number of voters who ultimately voted for Trump had barely recovered from the 2008 recession. By contrast, those largely responsible for the 2008 global financial crisis – the politicians and bankers and businessmen on Wall Street – kept raking in the money and seldom bore the cost of the bailout. The banks were "too big to fail" and the bankers were "too big to jail."

Living in these same coastal areas, a large portion of the media failed to pick up on this ongoing seething anger. The pundits continued to predict confidently a victory by Clinton and did not, (and arguably still do not), appreciate that these "experts" are seen by most people as part of the same corrupt system.

The punditocracy may not control the money, but they control the message that is disseminated. They also control the social capital. They set/define what is acceptable, what is allowable, and what is frowned on. In other words, they define what is valid cultural capital.

Failing to see an electorate frustrated repeatedly with broken promises, the media failed to recognize the desperation of the voters in "flyover country". They decided to reject the knowable (i.e. Hillary Clinton) and went with "the Devil they didn't know". They chose Trump because they felt undervalued, disrespected and increasingly desperate. They felt stuck and were mocked by those very elites which failed to acknowledge their reality.

Trump's election has indeed introduced a degree of unpredictability and volatility into the process of governing that did not exist before. But what is decried by the elites and the media is irrelevant to Trump's supporters. Their support for him constitutes a way of breaking down a system that no longer works for them. If Trump's sledgehammer approach creates "collateral damage", then so be it, a predictable response to those who increasingly see themselves as having nothing to lose.

Free trade and immigration

All of this social and cultural ferment has been occurring against a global backdrop in which the dominant force in the development of the world economy remains hyper-globalization. The single biggest factor which accelerated this process was China's entry into World Trade Organization. In the process, distance simply evaporated as a concept. Businesses moved to China, India, Latin America, and other emerging markets in search of cheaper places and means to produce goods and services for Western economies. As a result, several hundred million people in underdeveloped economies were lifted into urbanization from centuries of debilitating rural poverty.

At the same time, globalization created losers. Revolutionary technological advances enabled an unprecedented outsourcing by American companies seeking to maximize profits by employment of low-cost foreign labor. The scale of the outsourcing was made possible because of advances in technology, global trade treaties and capital-account liberalization. For all of the vaunted gains in profitability, it is unclear that globalization has been the huge win-win, as its apologists argue. Internationally, the richest five percent of people receive one-third of total global income, as much as the poorest 80 percent.[5]

In the U.S., workers have been replaced by low-cost foreign workers. As a result, a huge number of Americans have experienced stagnant wages and incomes for more than a quarter century, with trade agreements exacerbating the problem. And, as economists such as Dani Rodrik and Dean Baker have pointed out,[6] more recent "trade" agreements have had very little to do with the classic benefits associated with liberalized trade, and more to do with entrenching the oligopolistic privileges of the leading dominant corporations. Furthermore, the benefits of real world trade results have not lined up so neatly with trade economists' assumptions.[7]

"Synthetic immigration" and globalization

Trump has taken this one stage further with his hardline stance on immigration. For all the media attention devoted to a wall along the Mexican border, or an outright ban on Muslim immigration, there is method to Trump's madness which goes well beyond racism. By linking immigration and trade, however crudely, Trump has exposed the paradox and inherent contradictions which lurk between the two.

Historically, immigration law in the U.S. and Canada has concerned itself with many considerations, key being the displacement of domestic workers. By contrast, advocates of free trade ignore this consideration, or blithely suggest that the resultant unemployment in a displaced sector (e.g., the automobile industry), is a "negative externality", which is offset by the resultant gains in competitive efficiency, and lower cost goods. Cheap imports, then, outweigh the displacement of workers.

---

[5] http://www.truth-out.org/opinion/item/35300-fools-or-liars-on-the-trans-pacific-partnership
[6] https://www.project-syndicate.org/commentary/tpp-debate-economic-benefits-by-dani-rodrik-2016-02?barrier=accessreg
[7] According to research by Professor Branko Milanovic, a visiting presidential professor at CUNY's Graduate Center and a senior scholar at the Luxembourg Income Study Center.

But we do not extend this logic to immigration, or we would move straight to a policy of open borders. Historically, the answer to the question why we do not have open borders is because it would substantially drive down the wages of American workers. Low costs for traded goods are okay; low-cost labour, not so good, at least that is implicit in the application of current immigration policy.

Businesses have sought to evade this inconvenient immigration restriction via offshoring manufacturing facilities, resulting in the displacement of workers by low cost foreign labor. The economic impact subverts the policy goal behind American immigration policy. In many respects, it mirrors the impact of a hypothetical open-borders policy, in effect creating "synthetic immigration", which reduces employment and lowers wages as investment is increasingly outsourced abroad.

Globalization advocates argue that the resultant profits to U.S. corporations spur re-investment, which in turn creates employment. In reality, the profits that accrue to corporations do not go toward domestic re-investment (and, hence, more jobs), but to increasing investment abroad. That is, of course, when they are not using corporate cash to buy back stock and inflate share prices and CEO executive compensation.

To offset the economic drag that outsourcing and synthetic immigration impose, policymakers have largely abandoned fiscal policy in favour of austerity, whilst the major central bankers (starting with the US Federal Reserve) have been pursuing a reckless and increasingly ineffective program of Quantitative Easing (QE) in unprecedented amounts, both absolutely and relative to GDP. Designed to stimulate consumption and ultimately investment by pumping up housing and stock markets, the promise did not match the reality. We got booming stock markets, but not much else. Inequality continued to grow (arguably exacerbated by QE) and wage growth remained stagnant. Conventional policy measures, such as free trade, did not help.

The paradox of outsourcing

In regards to free trade, tens of thousands of automobile workers in Michigan are displaced because we attach primacy to being able to buy the cheapest cars available. The theory is that the savings will generate sufficient demand elsewhere to offset the impact of displaced workers. The implicit assumption is that this "good" outweighs all other considerations, even though the relative consumption problem that occurs as one person buys the lower-cost good creates a consumption equivalent to Keynes's "paradox of thrift" – insofar as consumers fail to realize that if they all do it, then many more of them ultimately end up unemployed or underemployed.

Consider a thought experiment: imagine a country with one worker and that worker was the sole consumer. The worker would understand that by consuming foreign-made goods produced by the synthetic immigrant, he would soon have no income and, as a consequence, no consumption. In the real world, people want to maximize their welfare and most do so by maximizing current consumption, which is said to be one of the benefits underlying free trade. Maximizing current consumption means purchasing the lowest-priced goods at any particular level of quality.

This behaviour cascades because in the short-run the increased standard of living offered by low-cost goods swamps the longer-term effects of chronic job losses. Thus, the paradox of consumption is the idea that a rational person in a one-person world would never behave in the same way as many rational utility-maximizing individuals behave, even if many understand the possible outcome.

In periods prior to the post-Cold War period of globalization, this was not a problem because displacement by immigrants generally began at the most menial level of the labour force, and policy changes adopted in the aftermath of each successive immigration wave (at least until 1965) generally prevented massive amounts of displacement and consequently, stopped the migration of jobs at the menial labor level.

America first?

The ethics debate regarding immigration is similar to that regarding trade. Should policy be constructed with respect to domestic or global welfare? For the most part, it seems as if domestic concerns dominated immigration policy; whereas trade policy, haunted by misconceptions regarding the Smoot-Hawley Tariff of the 1930s, is generally obsessed with global considerations. Today, false ideas about great prospects for exporting into the enormous Chinese market hinder national policy and enable employee displacement. Because of technological advances, today's trade policies are effectively an immigration policy.

There are differences to be sure, but those differences work to the detriment of American workers. Typically low-cost labour attracted long-lived capital investment. Today, synthetic immigration via global outsourcing leads to capital investment in the immigrant's country (China) resulting in a greater capital stock there and increased competitiveness.

It is, and always has been, the government's duty to provide for and protect its citizens. Immigration policies differ everywhere and change as the government's responsibility to its citizens is enforced. Protection of U.S. workers from synthetic immigrants is long overdue and the cost of government neglect is huge. And yet we never apply the same principles that underlie our immigration policy for trade. At least until now, where it became a major feature of the Trump campaign and continues to be a focal point in the early days of his presidency, which is why, for example, the Carrier "solution" had such symbolic importance for Trump, even as many people on both the left and right of the spectrum dismissed it as "crony capitalism".

As the author Thomas Frank noted in the *The Guardian*:

> "There's a video going around on the internet these days that shows a room full of workers at a Carrier air conditioning plant in Indiana being told by an officer of the

company that the factory is being moved to Monterrey, Mexico, and that they're all going to lose their jobs."[8]

And Trump used this during his campaign and then came back to it after the election when he announced that Carrier had backed down thanks to the political pressure he applied. "Experts" derided this as micro-managing worthy of a planned economy, but it played well in Peoria and Kenosha. Mainstream economists would have had a greater impact on the public debate had they stuck closer to their discipline's teaching, instead of mindlessly siding with globalization's cheerleaders.

As globalization has intensified, companies have increasingly competed with each other. Those with substantial low-cost advantages have generally prevailed, eliminating competitors which sought to preserve well-paying American jobs. Therein lays the paradox of outsourcing. It is the responsibility of government to construct policies that stop, or least restrict, the cascading of outsourcing because of its adverse impact on employment and the negative incentives outsourcing imposes on domestic investment.

We have historically considered these factors in our immigration policy. Why is trade so sacrosanct? Trump is the candidate who has been most persistent, however crudely and coarsely, in asking these questions. Odd as it seems, and as much as he probably didn't even mean to, Trump raised important questions. For an increasing number of Americans, he is providing answers they find far more palatable than the traditional neo-liberal nostrums that have dominated global policy making for the past 30 years and these voters elected him president.

Conclusion

Suffice to say, the lack of detail and policy coherence in the Trump campaign and his subsequent chaotic start in officer suggests that the new President does not have all of the answers to the current economic malaise. But he does understand that his supporters find the status quo

---

[8] https://www.theguardian.com/commentisfree/2016/mar/07/donald-trump-why-americans-support

unacceptable. Whether he will indeed craft a policy response that navigates to everyone's benefit, (not just the elites who have profited from the globalized free trade environment that has created as many losers and as winners) is still unknown. If Trump continues to tweet about every perceived slight, he will confirm the prevailing narrative that he is temperamentally unfit to be President. At the same time, the near hysterical responses to his victory and his first 100 days of governing suggest that our existing political class (including the MSM) have yet to internalize the results of the 2016 election and what does need to change. Indeed, the more abuse that Trump and his "basket of deplorables" suffer, the more determined the latter are to support the President. The wise and the reasonable "experts" take their best shots. They catalogue what he has said; the contradictions, hypocrisies, beliefs unsupported by evidence or science. They go blue in the face winning every argument against "fake news" by any objective measure, but, but Mr Trump won't go away. He has rendered the traditionally powerful powerless. The learneds who are just so smart, the commentators who are just so smug, the know-everythings – he ignores them all. Now the question is: can he deliver?

Class and Trumponomics

David F. Ruccio [University of Notre Dame, USA]

> "The globalists gutted the American working class...The issue now is about Americans looking to not get f—ed over" (Steve Bannon).

Right now, after Donald's Trump surprising electoral victory in late 2016 and in the midst of the chaotic assumption of power in early 2017, everyone is curious about how the U.S. economy will change if and when the new president's economic policies are enacted.

But first things first. We need to have a clear understanding of what the U.S. economy looks like now, during the uneven recovery from the Second Great Depression. In particular, it's important to analyze the class dimensions of that recovery, even before the new administration formulates and enacts its policies.

Why class? One reason to focus on class is because it played such an important role in Trump's victory. Not alone, of course, but class interests, resentments, and desires did – in different ways – affect Trump's ability to challenge and win out over his rivals in both the Republican primaries and the presidential election. The other reason is that Trump made a whole host of class promises during the course of his campaigns – promises both to working-class voters and to members of the tiny group at the top, which led him to victory (at least in the electoral college).

We don't know, of course, if Trump will keep those class promises. A lot depends on the balance of power inside the administration and among it, the Republican Congress, and the Democratic opposition, not to mention the debates and struggles by groups and movements outside the corridors of power. But, even as the new alliance assumes control and new economic goals are formulated, we need to make sense of the class dynamics that at least in part have defined the U.S. economy in recent years, before and during the two terms of the administration of Barack Obama.

Class before Trumponomics

What is most striking about the economic situation over the course of the past eight years is that, while economic policymakers managed to create the conditions for capitalism to recover from its worst set of crises since the First Great Depression, it has otherwise been pretty much business as usual. What I mean by that is the economic recovery has mostly assumed the same shape and general features that characterized the U.S. economy before the crash of 2007-08.[1]

That's not to say nothing has changed (a point to which I return below). But the fact that the benefits of the recovery – in terms of both income (Figure 1) and wealth (Figure 2) – have been captured mostly by those at the top, and left pretty much everyone else behind, is exactly what was happening prior to the crash.

One way to see this in particularly class terms is to examine the relationship between the "two great classes," capital and labor. Underlying the growing gap between the top 1 percent and everyone else, which is now well known (because of the persistent and detailed research of Thomas Piketty, Edward Saez, and their collaborators), is the much-less-remarked-upon divergence in the capital and wage shares of national income.[2] After the recovery began in 2009, the share of income going to corporate profits increased dramatically, from 12 percent to 15 percent (in 2014, falling slightly in 2015 to 13.7 percent). Meanwhile, the share going to workers declined by 4 percent (between 2009 and 2014, increasing slightly in 2015 by about 1.5 percent).

---

[1] As I see it, that's the major reason Hillary Clinton and the Democratic Party lost the elections – not the leaks of the Democratic National Committee emails or FBI Director James Comey's late announcement about Clinton's emails, but their decision to embrace Obama's economic legacy.

[2] I have relied heavily in this paper on the data Piketty, Saez, and Gabriel Zucman (2016) have made publicly available from their NBER working paper. See also their web site: World Wealth & Income Database (http://wid.world/).

Figure 1 Income inequality: top 1 percent and bottom 90 percent average pre-tax incomes, 1949-2014

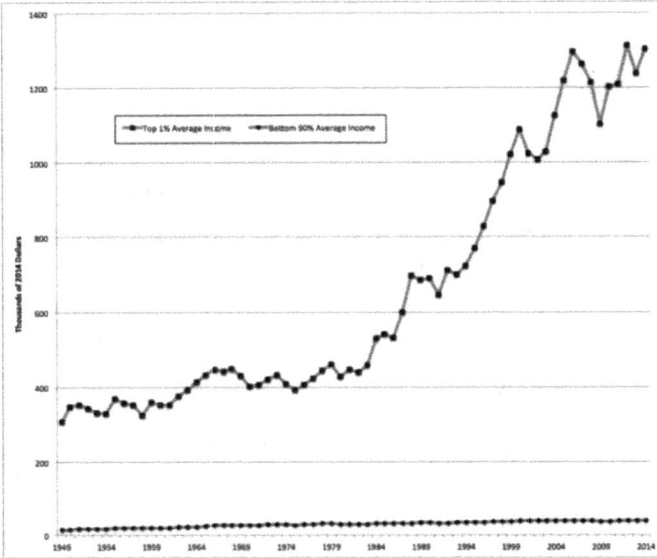

Figure 2 Wealth inequality: top 1 percent and bottom 90 percent average wealth, 1949-2014

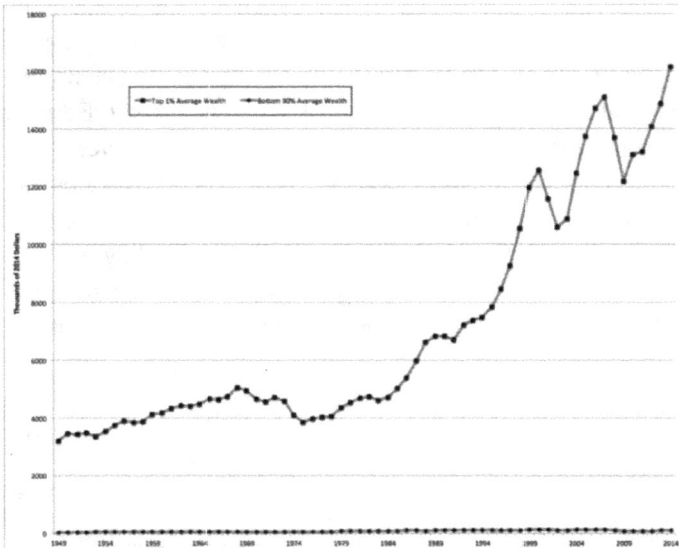

Source for Figures 1 and 2: T. Piketty, E. Saez, and G. Zucman, Distributional National Accounts: Appendix Tables II (http://gabriel-zucman.eu/usdina/).

As readers can see from Figures 3 and 4, those short-term trends represent a continuation of longer-term dynamics. The profit share had reached a low of 7 percent (in 1986) – and therefore has just about doubled (by 2015). The labor share has moved in the opposite direction for an even longer period of time, declining by about 12 percent (from 1980 to 2015).

Figure 3 Profit share of national income (before tax, without IVA and CCAdj), 1949-2015

Source: U.S. Bureau of Economic Analysis, retrieved from FRED (https://fred.stlouisfed.org/).

Figure 4 Wage share of gross domestic income, 1949-2015

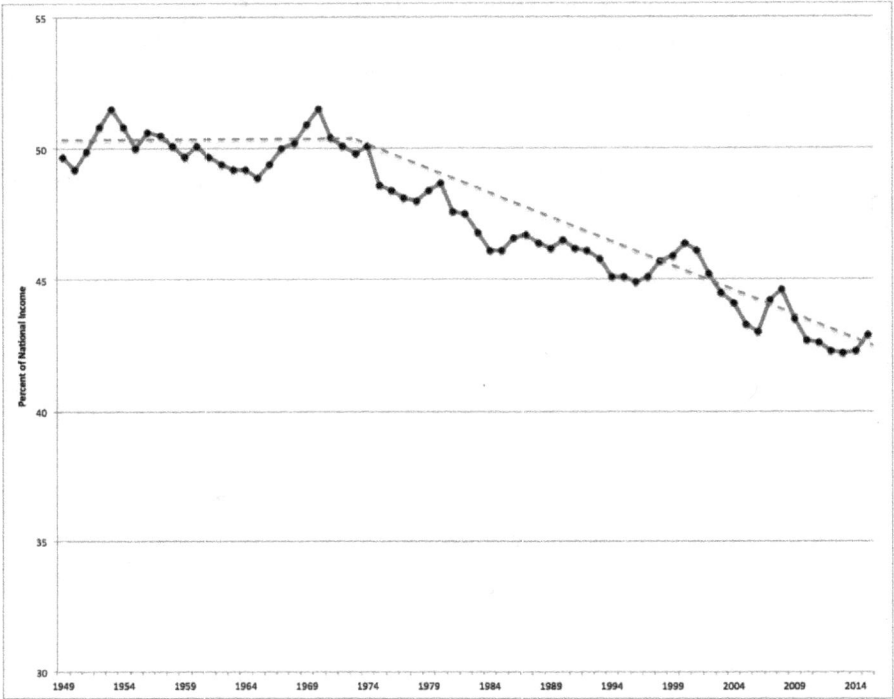

Source: U.S. Bureau of Economic Analysis, retrieved from FRED (https://fred.stlouisfed.org/).

In other words, the so-called recovery, just like the thirty or so years before it, has meant a revival of the share of income going to capital, while the wage share has continued to decline. That, in my view, is the overall class dynamic within the U.S. economy of both the decades leading up to the crash and the years of post-crash recovery prior to the elections of 2016. During both periods, U.S. corporations managed to capture the growing surplus that was being produced by the working-class – both American workers and, importantly, workers around the world.[3]

---

[3] Loukas Karabarbounis and Brent Neiman (2013) have documented the fact that "the global labor share has significantly declined since the early 1980s, with the decline occurring within the large majority of countries and industries."

But that general trend isn't the whole picture. In the next two sections, I analyze some of the salient details with respect to the contrasting fortunes of both capital and labor.

Labor before Trumponomics

Let me start with labor. In the first section above, my analysis actually understates the capital share and overstates the labor share. That's because a large share of the surplus was actually included in wages, and thus attributed to labor, when in fact it properly belongs in the share captured by capital. The idea is that high-level executives and others (e.g., Chief Executive Officers and those working in finance), while much of their income is reported as "wages," are actually receiving a distribution of the surplus from their employers. Therefore, their wages are actually part of the capital share, while the incomes of the rest of workers form the basis of the labor share properly understood.

This is clear from the data illustrated in Figure 5, where I've split the labor share by income fractiles. Based on a rough class analysis of the U.S. labor force, the labor share actually includes the first two components (making up the bottom 90 percent of the labor force), while the other fractiles (those making up the top 10 percent) represent for the most part distributions of the surplus from capital. As is evident from a quick glance at the figure, the share of total wages going to the working-class has been declining for decades (from about 72 percent in 1972 to 60 percent in 2014), while the share representing distributions of the surplus has grown (from 28 percent to 40 percent).

The consequence of making such a distinction is that the fall in the labor share and the rise in the capital share are actually much more dramatic – both in the decades leading up to the crash and during the so-called recovery – than when we look just at conventionally defined workers' wages and corporate profits.[4]

---

[4] It also means that there's no one-to-one correspondence between, on one hand, the profit-wage ratio and, on the other hand, the Marxian notion of the rate of exploitation. For example, because of the modification I discuss in the text, it's quite

Figure 5 Shares of pre-tax labor income, by fractiles, 1962-2014

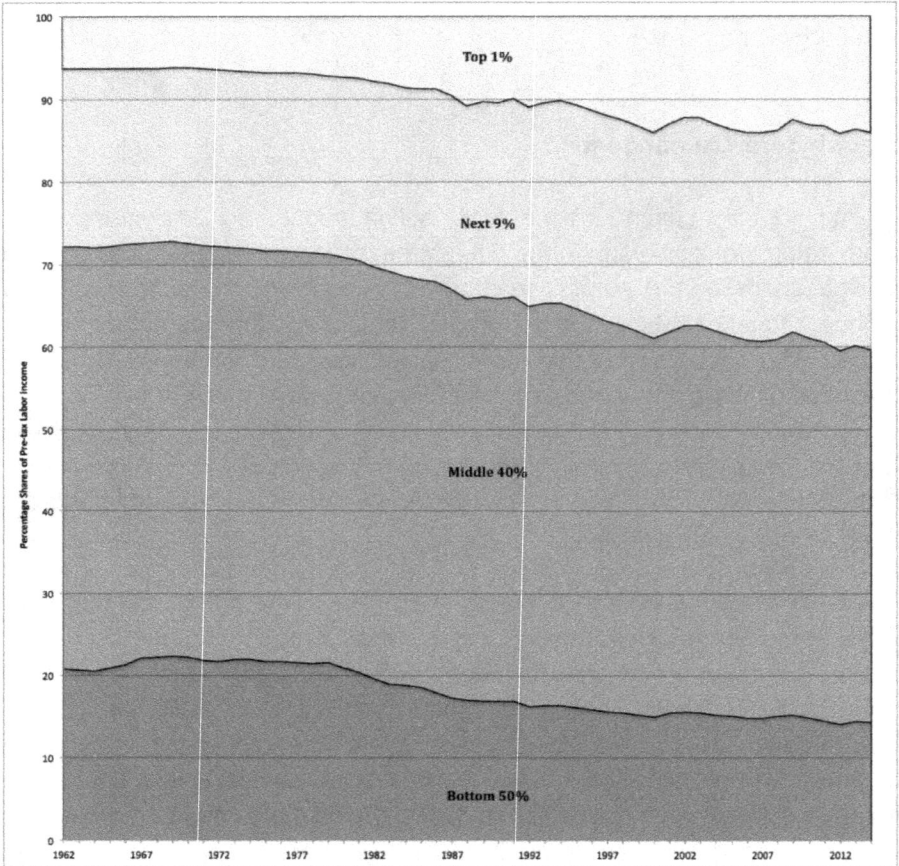

Source: T. Piketty, E. Saez, and G. Zucman, Distributional National Accounts: Appendix Tables II (http://gabriel-zucman.eu/usdina/).

The U.S. working-class has also changed over time, especially in the decades leading up to the crash, as the economy itself was fundamentally transformed by a combination of automation, the offshoring of production, and imports from other countries. In terms of sectors and thus types of jobs,

---

possible for the profit-wage ratio to remain constant (the stylized Kuznets fact for the immediate postwar decades) while the rate of exploitation rises. And if the profit-wage ratio rises (as it has in recent decades), it's even more likely that the rate of exploitation has increased.

the biggest change that can be seen in Figures 6, 7, and 8 was the decline in Manufacturing, which took place mostly between 1980 and 2007 – from 21 percent of total employment to only 10 percent – with a further decrease (to 8 percent) by 2016. The sectors that grew as shares of total employment include Leisure & Hospitality, Education & Health, and Business Services. Mining and Logging, which was never more than a tiny share of total employment, began and remained very small. Similarly, the percentage of jobs in FIRE (Finance, Real Estate, and Insurance) remained constant. And Government jobs, as a share of total employment, actually declined (from 18 to 15 percent). The result is that, over time, American workers have been forced to have the freedom to sell their ability to work less to employers in the production of goods (who have off-shored production and automated many of the manufacturing jobs that remain) and more to those involved in the production of services (who are already engaged in a new round of automation, thus threatening service-sector jobs).

Figure 6 Employment by sector, 1980

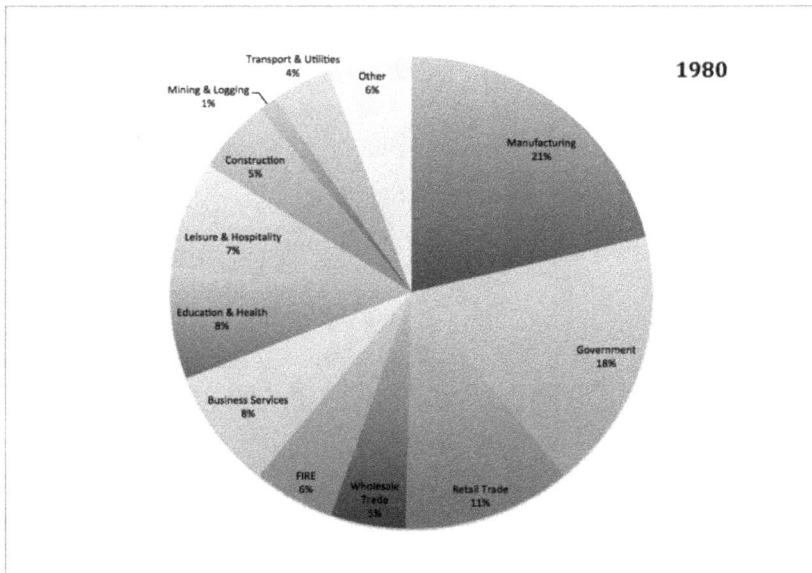

Source for Figures 6, 7 and 8: Author's calculations, based on U.S. Bureau of Labor Statistics, retrieved from FRED (https://fred.stlouisfed.org/).

Figure 7 Employment by sector, 2007

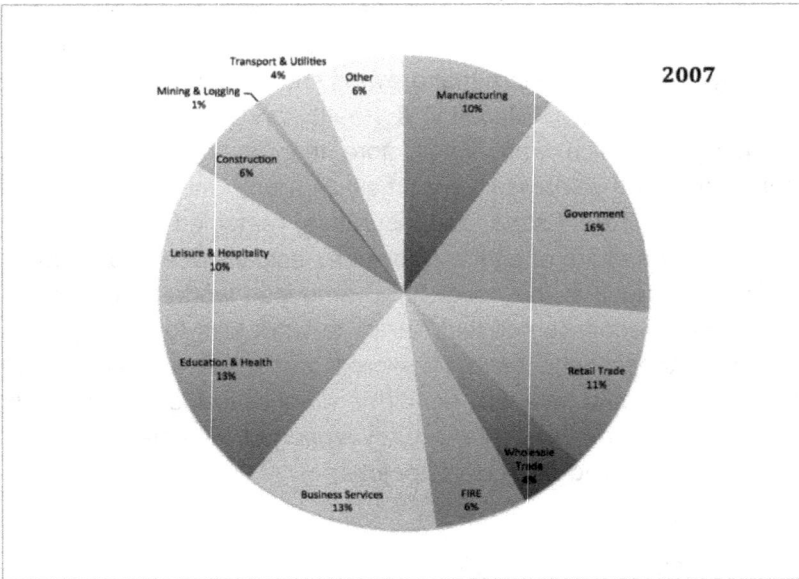

Figure 8 Employment by sector, 2016

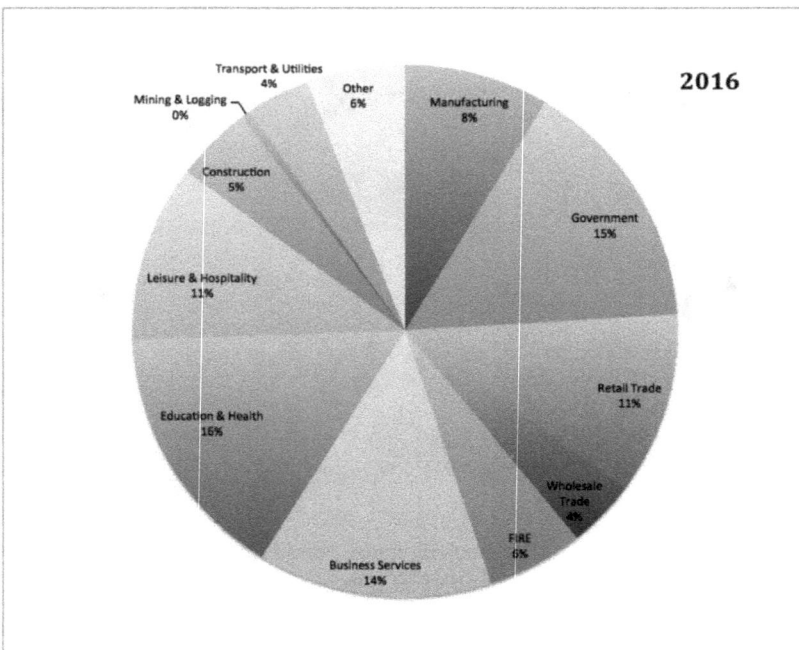

The U.S. working-class has also changed in many other ways over the course of the past few decades.

Figure 9 Union density, 1983-2016

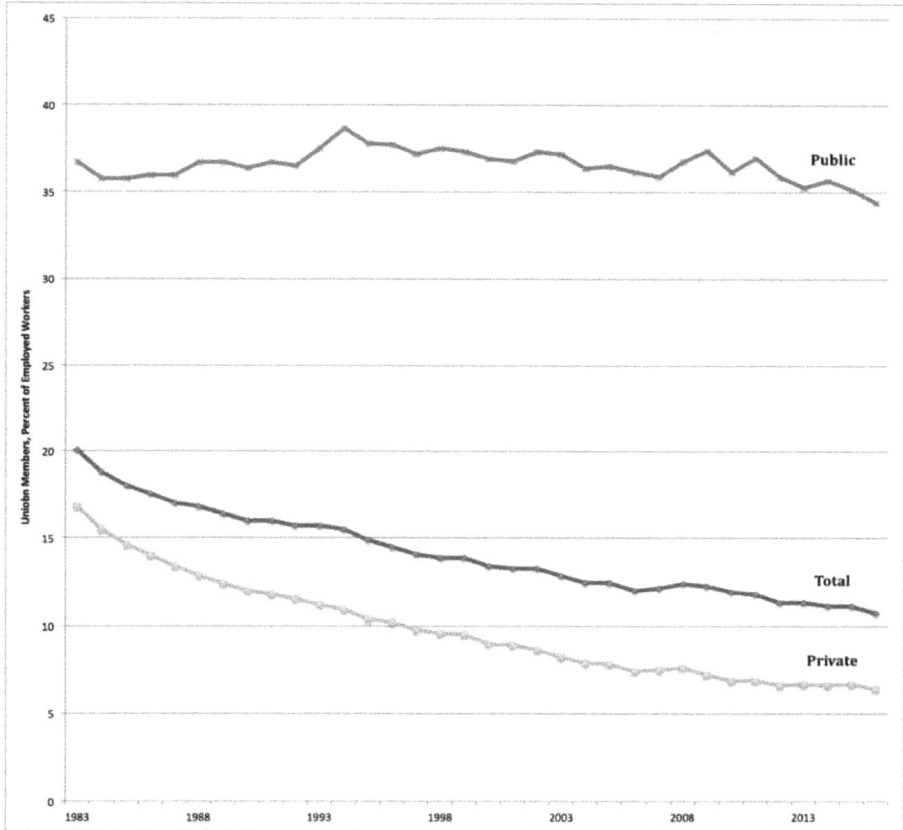

Source: U.S. Bureau of Labor Statistics,
(http://www.bls.gov/webapps/legacy/cpslutab3.htm).

For example, union membership has steadily declined in the United States. In 1983, 20 percent of all workers in the United States belonged to unions, which negotiated wages and benefits on their behalf. By 2016, however, only 10.7 percent of all U.S. workers were union members, the lowest level on record.[5] The decline has almost entirely been driven by a large decrease in private-sector union membership. In 1983, union members accounted for 16.8 percent of private-sector workers, and in 2016 they only accounted for 6.4 percent. Public-sector unions, meanwhile, remain quite prevalent among government workers. In 2016, 34.4 percent of government workers were union members, which is virtually unchanged from 1983.[6]

Not only do U.S. workers enjoy less protection as a result of the decline in labor unions; the wage floor, represented by the minimum wage, has also fallen over time. The real value of the federal minimum wage is now less than it was in 1968 (when it was equal to $9.63 in 2016 dollars) – and it is now much less than what it would be had it grown at the same rate as average wages, the growth in productivity, or, especially, the increase in incomes of the top 1 percent.

Another major change in recent decades has to do with foreign-born workers (both legal and undocumented), which increased dramatically from 1970 through 2010 – from 4.3 to 24.7 million workers and, as a percentage of the U.S. labor force, from 5.2 to 15.8 percent. After the crash, however, the growth in both the number and the percentage slowed considerably.

---

[5] According to the latest OECD data [2016], the United States is an outlier on both trade-union density (10.7 percent versus an average of 16.7 percent) and coverage of collective bargaining agreements (11.9 percent versus an average of 50.4 percent).
[6] Although public-sector workers are more likely than their private-sector counterparts to be union members, there are still more private-sector union members (7.4 million) than public-sector union members (7.1 million). That's because, as shown above, public-sector workers account for only about 15 percent of the U.S. workforce.

Figure 10 Number and percentage of foreign-born workers, 1910-2015

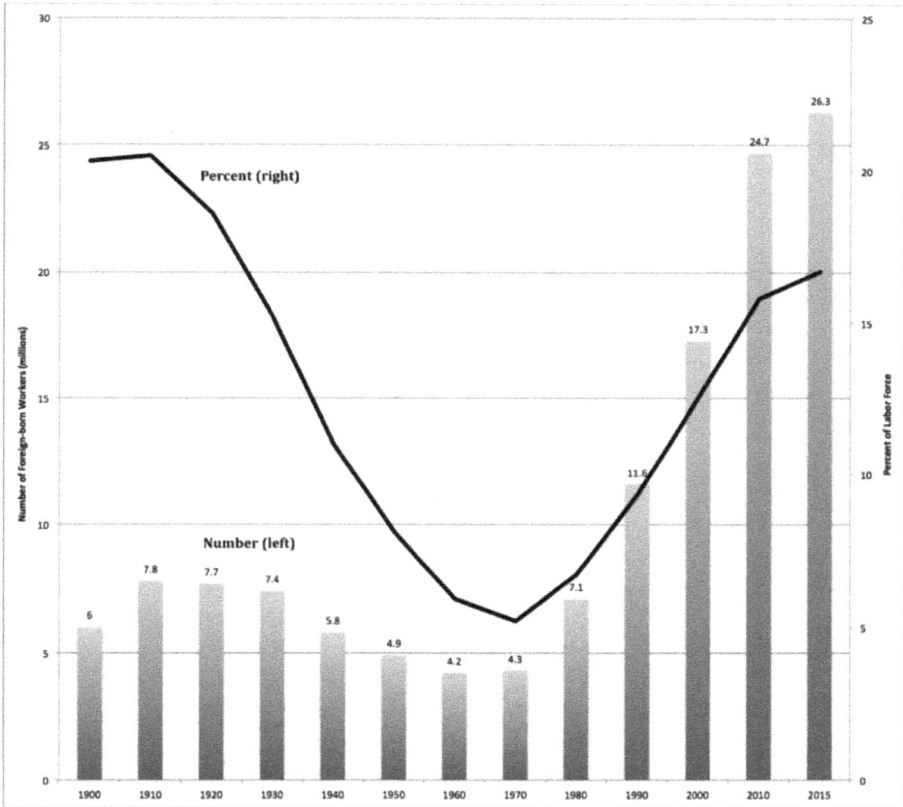

Sources: U.S. Bureau of Labor Statistics and U.S. Census Bureau.

What about other segments of the U.S. working-class? As is clear from Figures 11 and 12, wages for all workers – regardless of race, ethnicity, or gender – have fallen far short of the growth in economy-wide productivity. It's true that most groups (with the exception of Black men) have narrowed the gap with white men since 2000. That's in part because the real earnings of some groups have increased (especially Hispanic men and women) but mostly because the wages of white men have barely changed (increasing by only 2.3 percent). And, as with the earlier period, all wages have registered increases much less than the growth in labor productivity (which has almost doubled since 1979, increasing by 33 percent just since the beginning of the millennium).

Figure 11 Productivity and real weekly earnings for men and women, 1979-2016

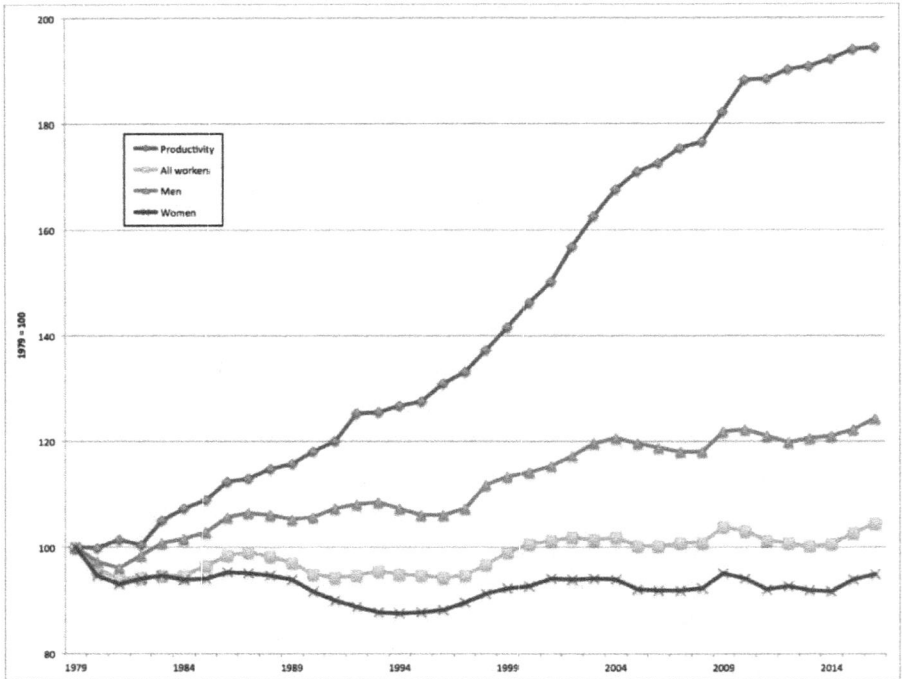

Source: U.S. Bureau of Labor Statistics, retrieved from FRED (https://fred.stlouisfed.org/).

David F. Ruccio

Figure 12 Productivity and real weekly earnings by gender and race/ethnicity, 2000-2016

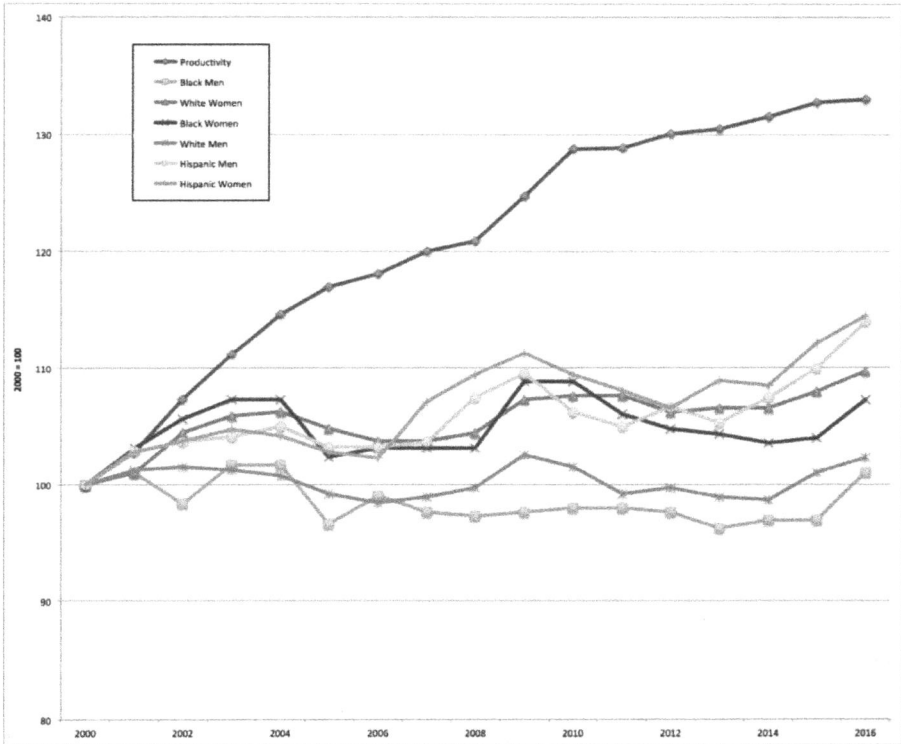

Source: U.S. Bureau of Labor Statistics, retrieved from FRED
(https://fred.stlouisfed.org/).

We also need to consider the other side of that relationship – that increased racial and ethnic disparities reinforce the growing gap between productivity and the wages of all workers. Black and Hispanic workers are paid less than their white counterparts (of both genders), and all workers' wages are as a result less than they otherwise would be. That's because employers are able to pit one group against the others, thus undermining the bargaining position of all workers. As a result, wealthy individuals and large corporations, who capture the resulting surplus, are the only ones who benefit from racial and ethnic wage disparities.

349

Figure 13 Precarity: part-time workers compared to full-time workers, 1968-2016

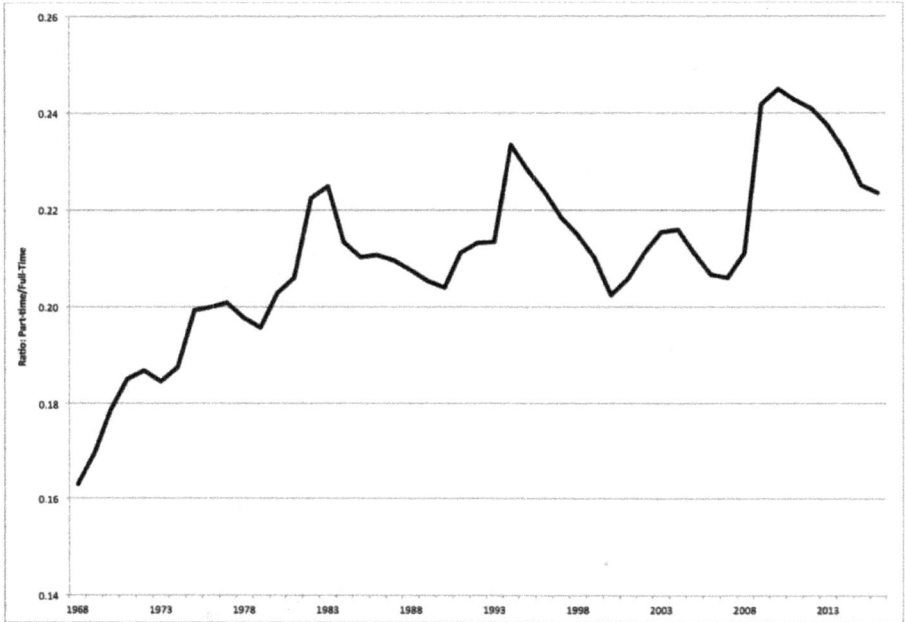

Source: U.S. Bureau of Labor Statistics, retrieved from FRED (https://fred.stlouisfed.org/).

The final major change I want to draw attention to is the increasing precarity of the U.S. working-class. They're increasingly employed in part-time jobs (as can be seen in Figure 13, which tracks the ratio of part-time to full-time workers) and in "alternative" work arrangements. As Lawrence Katz and Alan Krueger (2016) have shown, just in the past decade, the percentage of American workers engaged in alternative work arrangements – defined as temporary help agency workers, on-call workers, contract workers, and independent contractors or freelancers – rose from 10.1 percent (in February 2005) to 15.8 percent (in late 2015). And, it turns out, the so-called gig economy is characterized by the same unequalizing, capital-labor dynamics as the rest of the U.S. economy.

What is clear from this brief survey of the changes in the condition of the U.S. working-class in recent decades is that, while American workers have created enormous additional income and wealth, most of the increase has been captured by their employers and a tiny group at the top – as workers have been forced to compete with one another for new kinds of jobs, with fewer protections, at lower wages, and with less security than they once expected. And the period of recovery from the Second Great Depression has done nothing to change that fundamental dynamic.

Capital before Trumponomics

In this section, I want to focus on a more detailed analysis of the other side of the class relationship – capital.

Figure 14 Gross output of FIRE (finance, insurance, and real estate) as a share of gross output of private industries, 1970-2015

Source: U.S. Bureau of Economic Analysis.

It should come as no surprise that one of the major changes in U.S. capital over the past few decades is the growing importance of financial activities. Since 1980, FIRE (the combination of finance, insurance, and real estate) has almost doubled, expanding from roughly 12 percent of the gross output of private industries to over 20 percent.

Figure 15 Profits of FIRE (finance, insurance, and real estate) as a share of corporate profits, 1970-2015

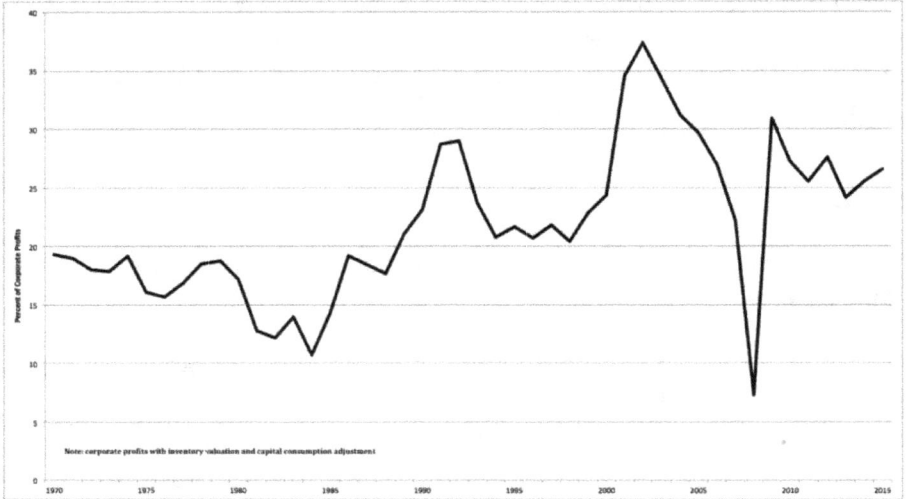

Source: U.S. Bureau of Economic Analysis.

The rise in the share of corporate profits from financial activities was even more spectacular – from 10.8 percent in 1984 to a whopping 37.4 percent in 2002 – and then falling during the crash, but still at a historically high 26.6 percent in 2015.[7]

By any measure, U.S. capital became increasingly oriented toward finance beginning in the early 1980s – as traditional banks (deposit-gathering commercial banks), non-bank financial entities (especially shadow banking, such as investment banks, hedge funds, insurers and other non-bank financial institutions), and even the financial arm of industrial corporations

---

[7] I should point out that it is only by the conventions of national-income accounting (as they are heavily influenced by neoclassical economic theory) that banking and other FIRE services generate "output" (counted via an "imputation for implicitly priced intermediation services"), which in turn is said to give rise to the "profits" received. According to Marxian economic theory, most FIRE activities are considered "unproductive" – and thus do not represent an addition to the social value-product. Therefore, FIRE profits represent a transfer, not a new creation, of value. See Roberts (2014) for an elaboration and discussion of this argument.

David F. Ruccio

(such as the General Motors Acceptance Corporation, now Ally Financial) absorbed and then profited by creating new claims on the surplus.

This process of "financialization" was the flip side of the decreasing labor share in the U.S. economy: On one hand, stagnant wages meant both an increasing surplus, which could be recycled via the financial sector, and a growing market for loans, as workers sought to maintain their customary level of consumption via increasing indebtedness. On the other hand, the production of commodities (both goods and services) became less important than capturing a portion of the surplus from within the United States and from the rest of the global capitalist economy, and utilizing it via issuing loans and selling derivatives to receive even more.

Figure 16 Internationalization: exports and imports as a percentage of GDP, 1970-2016

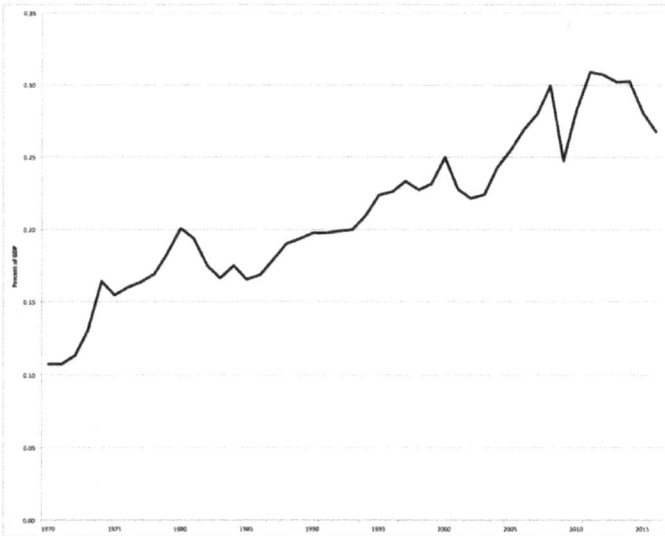

Source: U.S. Bureau of Economic Analysis, retrieved from FRED (https://fred.stlouisfed.org/).

Not only did finance become increasingly internationalized, so did the U.S. economy as a whole. As a result of employers' decisions to outsource the production of commodities that had previously been manufactured in the United States and to find external markets for the sale of other commodities (especially services), and with the assistance of the lowering of tariffs and

353

the signing of new trade agreements, the U.S. economy was increasingly opened up from the early-1970s onward. One indicator of this globalization is the increase in the weight of international trade (the sum of exports and imports) in relation to U.S. GDP – more than tripling from 1970 (9.33 percent) to 2014 (29.1 percent).

Figure 17 Bank concentration: Assets of five largest banks as a share of total commercial banking assets, 1996-2014

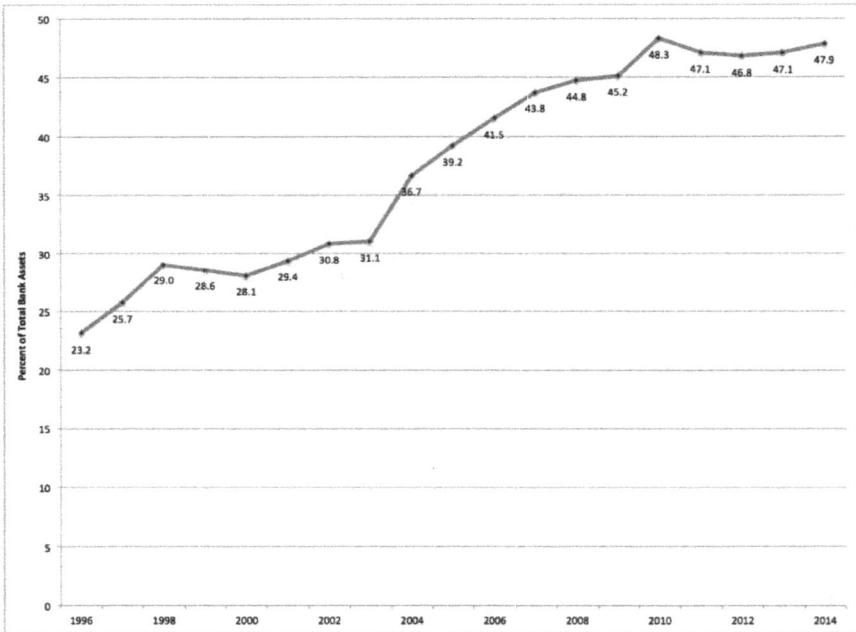

Source: World Bank, retrieved from FRED (https://fred.stlouisfed.org/).

The third major change in U.S. capital in recent decades is a rise in the degree of corporate concentration and centralization – to such an extent even President Obama's Council of Economic Advisers (2016) had taken notice. A wave of mergers and acquisitions has made firms larger and has increased the degree of market concentration within a broad range of industries. In finance, for example, the market share of the five largest banks (measured in terms of their assets as a share of total commercial banking assets) more than doubled between 1996 and 2014 – rising from 23.2 percent to 47.9 percent.

Figure 18 Selected U.S. airline mergers and acquisitions, 1929-2013

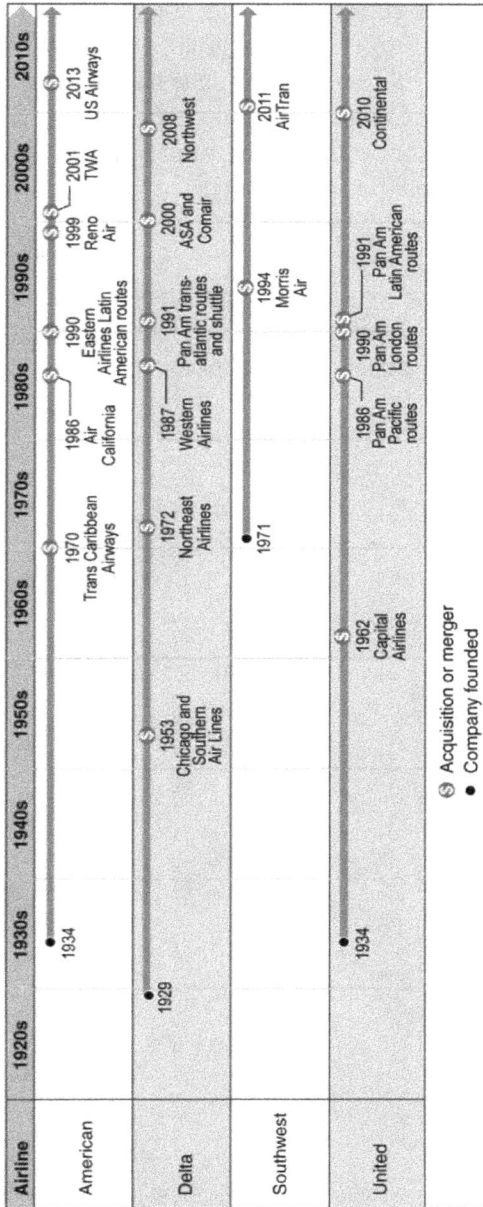

Airline	1920s	1930s	1940s	1950s	1960s	1970s	1980s	1990s	2000s	2010s
American		1934				1970 Trans Caribbean Airways	1986 Air California	1990 Eastern Airlines Latin American routes	1999 Reno Air	2001 TWA	2013 US Airways
Delta	1929			1953 Chicago and Southern Air Lines		1972 Northeast Airlines	1987 Western Airlines	1991 Pan Am trans-atlantic routes and shuttle	2000 ASA and Comair	2008 Northwest
Southwest						1971		1994 Morris Air		2011 AirTran
United		1934			1962 Capital Airlines		1986 Pan Am Pacific routes	1990 Pan Am London routes	1991 Pan Am Latin American routes	2010 Continental

Ⓢ Acquisition or merger
• Company founded

Source: U.S. Government Accountability Office, *Airline Competition* (June 2014).

The U.S. airline industry also experienced considerable merger and acquisition activity, especially following deregulation in 1978. Figure 18 (from a report by the U.S. Government Accountability Office [2014]) provides a timeline of mergers and acquisitions for the four largest surviving domestic airlines – American, Delta, Southwest, and United – based on the number of passengers served. These four airlines accounted for approximately 85 percent of total passenger traffic in the United States in 2013.

More generally, according to David Autor et al. (2017), between 1982 and 2012, six large sectors of the U.S. economy – manufacturing, retail trade, wholesale trade, services, finance, and utilities and transportation – showed a remarkably consistent upward trend in concentration (measured in terms of both sales and employment).

Figure 19 Oligopoly rents: Corporate profits as a share of national income and real interest-rates, 1981-2015

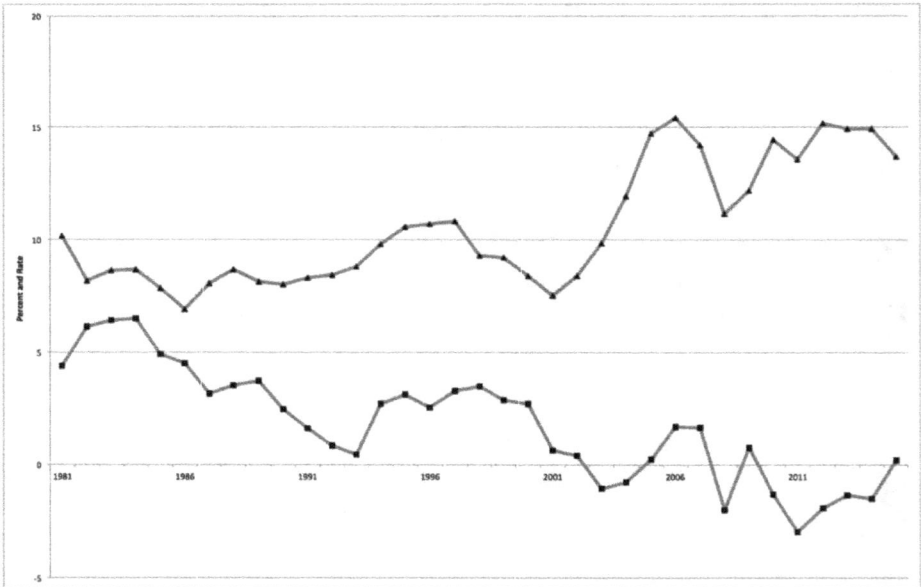

Sources: Author's calculations from U.S. Bureau of Economic Analysis, Federal Reserve, and U.S. Bureau of Labor Statistics, retrieved from FRED (https://fred.stlouisfed.org/).

A final piece of evidence that concentration and centralization have increased within the U.S. economy is (following Jason Furman [2016]) the growing gap between corporate profits and interest-rates. The fact that corporate profits (as a share of national income, the top line in Figure 19) have risen while interest-rates (the nominal constant-maturity one-year rate estimated by the Federal Reserve, less inflation defined by the Consumer Price Index, the bottom line in the figure) indicates that the portion of profits created by oligopoly rents has grown in recent decades.[8]

Figure 20 Manufacturing and FIRE: Value-added by industry as a share of GDP, 1970-2015

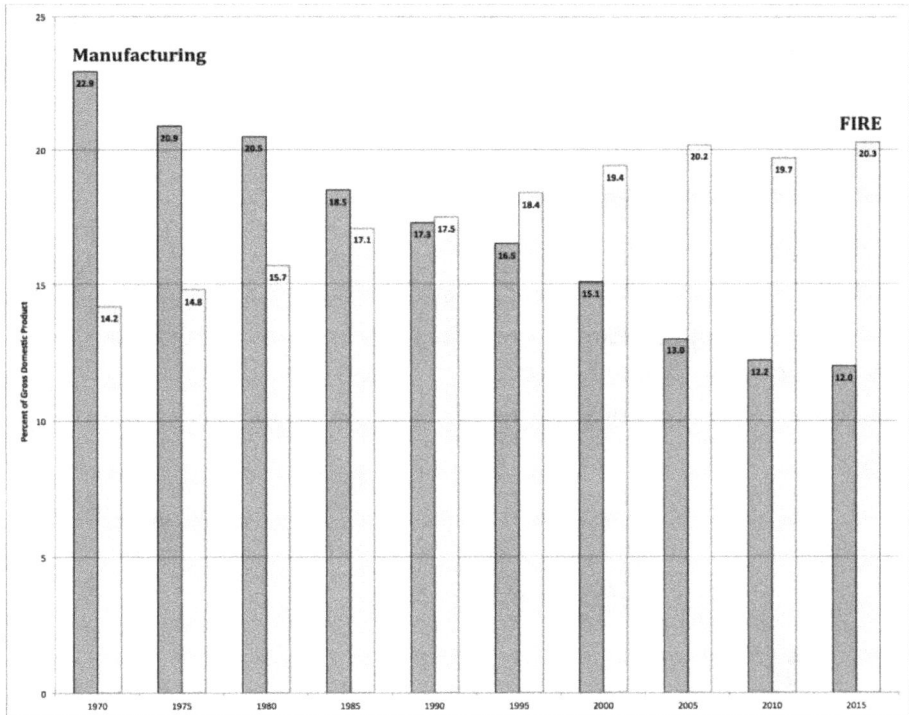

Source: U.S. Bureau of Economic Analysis.

---

[8] Another way to get at these oligopoly rents is to distinguish between the narrowly defined capital share and the so-called profit share. According to Simcha Barkai (2016), the decline in the labor share over the last 30 years was not offset by an increase in the capital share, which actually declined. But it *was* accompanied by an increase in the profit share, due to a rise in mark-ups.

Together, the three main tendencies I have highlighted – financialization, internationalization, and corporate rents – indicate fundamental changes in U.S. capital since the 1980s, which have continued during the current recovery. One of the effects of those changes is a decline in the importance of manufacturing, especially in relation to FIRE, as can be seen in Figure 20. Manufacturing (as measured by value added as a percentage of GDP) has declined from 22.9 percent (in 1970) to 12 percent (in 2015), while FIRE moved in the opposite direction – from 14.2 percent to 20.3 percent. Quantitatively, the two sectors have traded places, which qualitatively signifies a change in how U.S. capital manages to capture the surplus. While it still appropriates surplus from its own workers (although now more in the production and export of services than in manufacturing), it now captures the surplus, from workers inside and outside the United States, via financial activities. On top of that, the largest firms are capturing additional portions of the surplus from other, smaller corporations via oligopoly rents.

What we've witnessed then is a fundamental transformation of U.S. capital and thus the U.S. economy, which begins to explain a whole host of recent trends – from the decrease in rates of economic growth (since capital is engaged less in investment than in other activities, such as stock buybacks, hoarding profits in the form of cash, and mergers and acquisitions) to the rise in the ratio of corporate executive pay to average worker pay (which has ballooned, according to the Economic Policy Institute [Mishel and Schieder 2016] from 29.9 in 1978 to 275.6 in 2015).

In my view, the decisions by and on behalf of U.S. capital, as it changed over the course of recent decades, helped to create the conditions for the crash of 2007-08 and the unevennesses of the subsequent economic recovery – which, in turn, culminated in Trump's victory in November 2016.

It should come as no surprise that the return to economic growth, so celebrated as the basis for the post-crash recovery, has felt so hollow to so many – given that a rising portion of the measured increase in output and productivity is a fantasy created by conventional national-income accounting rules, an illusory consequence of real class-driven shifts in income from wages to profits (based on a return to decades-old trends in the relationship between labor and capital). The frustration that many voters clearly had with the cheery optimism of mainstream economists and politicians (who asserted, in response to Trump's candidacy, that "America is already great") has a solid foundation, even if the causes of that sense of abandonment and neglect (including the recent trends in U.S. capitalism that I focus on in this essay) were mostly papered over or ignored during the primaries and the national presidential campaigns of both major political parties.

Class under Trumponomics

Clearly, the new Trump administration has inherited an economy that is as divided as the electorate. The question is, what will that economy look like if and when Trump's right-wing national-populist promises and post-election proposals are enacted?

As I have shown in the three preceding sections, over the course of recent decades and continuing through the crash and recovery, the class nature of the U.S. economy was transformed in dramatic fashion. Capital was able to pump more surplus out of U.S. workers and, through the combined processes of financialization, globalization, and concentration, to capture more of the surplus from workers both at home and around the world. Labor, too, was radically transformed – and weakened by many forces, including automation, declining unionization, ethnic and racial disparities, immigration, and a declining real minimum wage. Overall, underlying the grotesque levels of inequality that characterize the United States today have been the opposing forces of an increasing capital share and a declining labor share.

That's what the U.S. economy looks like as Trump celebrates his victory and, along with his Cabinet and advisers and Republican majorities in both houses of Congress, develops a set of economic plans to "make America great again".

What will things look like moving forward? There is, of course, a high degree of uncertainty concerning the changes we can expect from the Trump administration's proposals. For a variety of reasons, we don't know what those proposals will be – not only because Trump put forward different versions of his "promises" (and, in some cases, like saving the Carrier plant jobs, he didn't even remember he'd made such a promise on the campaign trail), but also because his Cabinet members, advisers, and the Republican Congress have their own ideas of what they'd like to do. Plus, unexpected developments in the United States and around the world will surely require changes to whatever proposals are formulated or implemented.

All we can do, then, is analyze the potential effects of proposals that have been announced – on the assumption they will be at least general guides to the policies the members of the Trump administration and their allies attempt to enact.

I don't pretend here to be able to analyze the effects of all of the economic proposals associated with Trump, his economic team, and the new Congress, which run from repealing the Affordable Care Act to renegotiating international trade agreements. Instead, I want to focus on three that were prominent during the campaign and, by virtue of their size, have the potential of dramatically altering the current class landscape: tax cuts, reducing regulations on business, and deporting undocumented immigrants.

While the details remain to be worked out, the centerpiece of Trump's economic strategy – as he explained in speeches in Detroit (Charles 2016) and New York (Trump 2016a) – is a plan to cut taxes on both individuals and corporations. While others have focused on whether the plan's numbers are consistent (they aren't, according to Greg Ip (2016) for the *Wall Street Journal*) and its effects on the national debt (the Tax Policy Center [Nunns et al. 2015] argues it could increase the debt by nearly 80 percent of GDP by 2036), I want to concentrate here on the class implications of the tax plan.

It should come as no surprise that, based on the analysis by the Tax Policy Center (Nunns et al. 2015, 9), the highest-income households would receive the largest benefits from the proposed individual income-tax cuts, both in dollars and as a percentage of income.

> The highest-income 1.0 percent would get an average tax cut of over $275,000 (17.5 percent of after-tax income), and the top 0.1 percent would get an average tax cut worth over $1.3 million, nearly 19 percent of after-tax income. By

contrast, the lowest-income households would receive an average tax cut of $128, or 1 percent of after-tax income. Middle-income households would receive an average tax cut of about $2,700, or about 5 percent of after-tax income.

Given the fact that the income of taxpayers at the top comes mostly from distributions of the surplus (in the form of executive salaries, interest, dividends, and so on), the Trump tax plan implies they will be able to keep more of the surplus they have managed to capture and to decide individually what to do with their share of the surplus – to spend it on conspicuous consumption and utilize it to acquire even more private wealth.

Figure 21 Corporate taxes: Federal receipts by source, 1934-2015

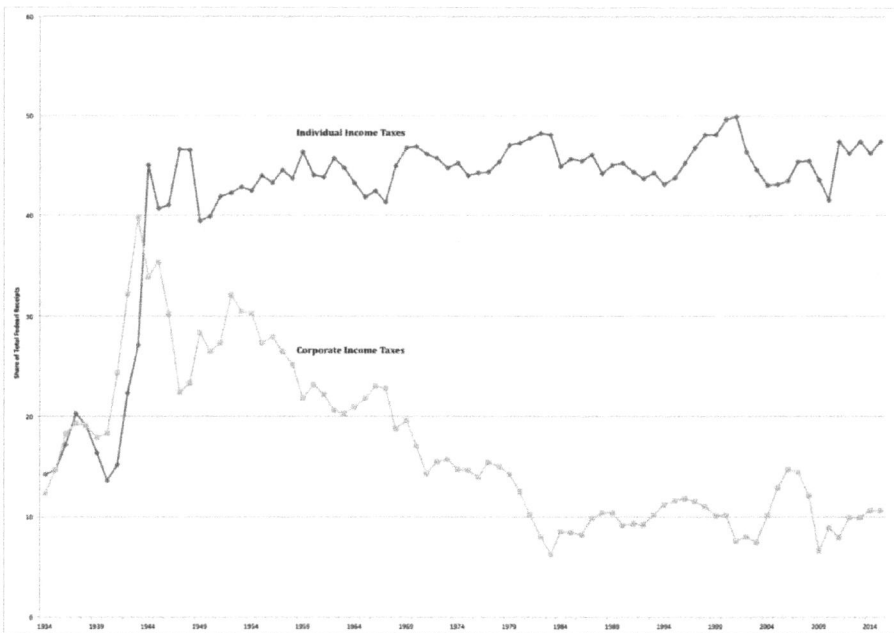

Source: Office of Management and Budget
(https://www.whitehouse.gov/omb/budget/Historicals).

Trump also proposes to cut the top corporate tax rate from 35 percent to 15 percent. But because the effective corporate tax rate (16.1 percent in 2012, according to the U.S. Government Accountability Office, 2016) is much lower than the statutory rate, if corporations were required to pay the proposed lower statutory rate, the status quo would be largely unchanged. In other words, U.S. corporations would pay no more than they currently do in the form of taxes (and possibly less, if the future effective rate falls below the lower statutory rate), and the contribution of corporate income taxes to total federal revenues (only 10.6 percent in 2015) would continue to be low by historical standards (23 percent as recently as 1966).

It is impossible to predict what corporations will do with the share of the surplus that is not subject to federal taxation. However, if the current pattern holds, we can expect a continuation – and perhaps even an acceleration – of mergers and acquisitions, stock buybacks, and job-displacing investment in robotics and other forms of automation that will boost the profits, especially of large corporations.

As I see it, the result of proposed cuts in both individual and corporate taxes is that more of the surplus would be captured and kept in private hands and consequently less will be available – via taxes – for social spending. And the only way to prevent fiscal deficits and the federal debt from increasing (as Republicans have long claimed is one of their goals) will be to decrease spending on federal programs, cuts that will be felt mostly by workers and their families.

Throughout the presidential campaign, Trump also promised "to cut regulations massively" – and according to Stephen Mnuchin (Yu, 2016), Trump's Treasury Secretary designee, revising Dodd-Frank is "the number one priority on the regulatory side". Here there is no clear proposal but it's likely four features of Dodd-Frank will come under scrutiny and perhaps be undone or seriously revised: capital controls (the rule stating that the eight largest banks in the country should maintain an additional layer of capital to protect against losses), "enhanced supervision" (which requires the Federal Reserve evaluate banks with assets of at least $50 billion more closely than those with fewer assets), the so-called Volcker Rule (which prohibits banks from proprietary trading and restricts investment in hedge funds and private equity by commercial banks and their affiliates), and the Consumer Finance

Protection Bureau (which regulates the offering and provision of consumer financial products and services under federal consumer financial laws).

Figure 22 FIRE profits: Profits of finance, insurance, and real estate (with inventory valuation adjustments), 1978-2018

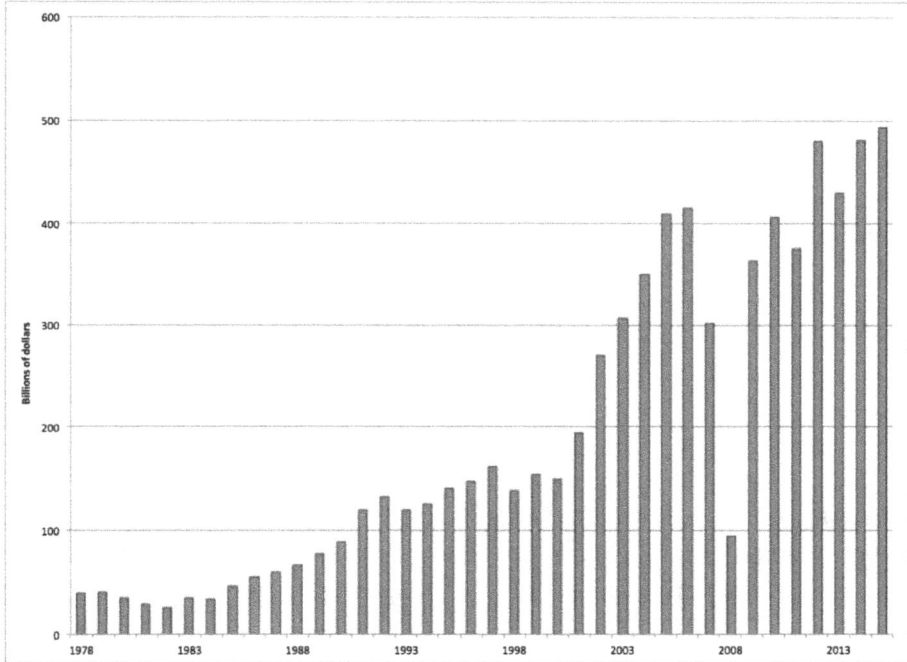

Source: U.S. Bureau of Economic Analysis, retrieved from FRED (https://fred.stlouisfed.org/).

As a result of the stabilizing effects of both the financial bailout and the Dodd-Frank legislation, the amount of the surplus captured by the financial sector has recovered – and is larger now ($493.3 billion) than it was even before the crash ($415.1 in 2006). It's likely, if the Trump administration succeeds in revising or repealing key provisions of the new legislation, financial activities will continue to expand and the share of the surplus they manage to siphon off from other sectors – in the United States and around the world – will also continue to grow.

Finally, Trump promised to "prioritize the jobs, wages and security of the American people" by establishing new immigration controls, with a series of measures outlined in his 10-point plan (2016b). A great deal depends on whether or not the administration is able to fund the activities required by the plan, such as deporting the estimated 11.1 million immigrants living without documents in the United States (which would require large increases in funding from Congress to increase the current workforce of immigration agents and judges to be able to lawfully handle that many deportations – not to mention the logistical challenge of locating so many immigrants, many in the country for years with deep family and community ties). In my view, what is more likely is that there will be a great deal of talk about curbing immigration (with some selective high-profile anti-immigrant actions), which will serve to increase the level of fear within immigrant communities and make existing undocumented workers even less likely to seek assistance from private agencies and public departments.

The obvious beneficiary of such a public campaign against undocumented workers will be their employers – especially in such industries as farming, maintenance, construction, and food (according to the Pew Research Center [Passel and Cohn, 2015]). They will continue to be able to hire undocumented farmhands, maids, groundskeepers, laborers, and cooks at wages that are less than those paid to legal immigrants and native-born workers – in addition to subjecting them to more violations of labor laws (including minimum wages, overtime pay, and so on).[9] And because undocumented workers will be driven even further underground, with fewer viable alternatives, the position of both legal immigrants and low-wage U.S.-born workers who are also employed in those industries will likely be weakened, thus increasing the profits of corporations that hire anyone from the three groups of workers.

---

[9] According to a landmark 2009 survey of thousands of workers, by Annette Bernhardt et al. (2009), 37 percent of unauthorized immigrant workers were the victims of minimum wage-law violations at the hands of their employers (meaning they were not paid the legally required minimum wage). And an astonishing 84 percent of unauthorized immigrant workers who worked full-time were not paid for overtime, that is, they were not paid the legally required time-and-a-half rate for the hours they worked in a week beyond 40 hours.

David F. Ruccio

While we need to be cautious in terms of an analysis of the effects of the Trump administration's promises and proposals, for the reasons I offer above, it is likely we are going to see an accelerated or supercharged version – instead of a softening, much less a reversal – of the class dynamics of the U.S. economy in recent years and decades. There's a good chance corporations that appropriate the surplus from workers, as well as wealthy individuals who manage to capture a portion of that surplus, will be able to get and keep even more of the surplus – and they will continue to be able to make their own private decisions about what to do with it. For its part, the financial sector will likely continue to grow in importance, with even fewer limits or safeguards, thus channeling more of the surplus into the profits of banks and insurance companies and the salaries of their highest-paid employees. And a campaign against undocumented workers will undoubtedly make their situation—and that of other low-wage workers, both immigrant and native-born – much weaker *vis-à-vis* their employers.

Therefore, I expect the class transformations that have come to characterize the U.S. economy, between and within labor and capital, will likely continue in an even more intense fashion under the aegis of the new administration. The only real change I envision, at least at this early date, is Trump's willingness to target specific groups and entities according to a right-wing populist sense of the "national interest", which may serve to deflect attention from the class inequalities and injustices inherent within the existing set of economic institutions.

Alternatively, the pronouncements and policies of the Trump administration may end up mocking the arrogance and ignorance of the existing economic and political elites – and thus, however ironically, highlighting those inequalities and injustices.

Acknowledgments

I want to thank Jack Amariglio for encouraging me to embark on this project, Edward Fulbrook for inviting me to submit this essay, and Dwight Billings and Bruce Roberts for their comments on the initial draft.

References

Autor, D. et al. 2017. "Concentrating on the Fall of the Labor Share." IZA Institute of Labor Economics Discussion Paper 10539, January (https://papers.ssrn.com/sol3/papers2.cfm?abstract_id=2911477, accessed 18 February 2017).

Barkai, S. 2016. "Declining Labor and Capital Shares." Stigler Center for the Study of the Economy and the State New Working Paper Series No. 2, November (https://research.chicagobooth.edu/~/media/5872FBEB104245909B8F0AE8A84486 C9.pdf, accessed: 5 December 2016).

Bernhardt, A. et al. 2009. Broken Laws, *Unprotected Workers: Violations of Employment and Labor Laws in America's Cities*. New York: National Employment Law Project.

Charles, J. B. 2016. "Transcript of Donald Trump's Economic Policy Speech to Detroit Economic Club." The Hill, 8 August (http://thehill.com/blogs/pundits-blog/campaign/290777-transcript-of-donald-trumps-economic-policy-speech-to-detroit, accessed: 29 November 2016).

Council of Economic Advisors. 2016. "Benefits of Competition and Indicators of Market Power." April (https://www.whitehouse.gov/sites/default/files/page/files/20160414_cea_competition _issue_brief.pdf, accessed: 29 November 2016)

Furman, J. 2016. Forms and Sources of Inequality in the United States." Vox, 17 March (http://voxeu.org/article/forms-and-sources-inequality-united-states, accessed: 29 November 2016).

Ip, G. 2016. "Donald Trump's Economic Plan, Up Close, Doesn't Add Up." *Wall Street Journal*, 18 October (http://blogs.wsj.com/economics/2016/10/18/donald-trumps-economic-plan-up-close-doesnt-add-up/, accessed: 29 November 2016).

Karabarbounis, L. and B. Neiman. 2013. "The Global Decline of the Labor Share." NBER Working Paper 19136 (June).

Katz, L. and A. Krueger. 2016. "The Rise and Nature of Alternative Work Arrangements in the United States, 1995-2015." March (https://krueger.princeton.edu/sites/default/files/akrueger/files/katz_krueger_cws_- _march_29_20165.pdf, accessed 28 November 2016)

Mishel, L. and J. Schieder. "Stock Market Headwinds Meant Less Generous Year for Some CEOs" (http://www.epi.org/publication/ceo-and-worker-pay-in-2015/, accessed: 29 November 2016).

Nunns, J. et al. 2015. "An Analysis of Donald Trump's Tax Plan" (http://www.taxpolicycenter.org/publications/analysis-donald-trumps-tax-plan/full, accessed: 29 November 2016)

Organization for Economic Cooperation and Development. 2016. "Coverage rates of collective bargaining agreements and trade union density rates: Percentage." In *Economic Policy Reforms 2016: Going for Growth Interim Report* (http://www.keepeek.com/Digital-Asset-Management/oecd/economics/economic-policy-reforms-2016/coverage-rates-of-collective-bargaining-agreements-and-trade-union-density-rates_growth-2016-graph54-en#page1, accessed: 10 February 2017).

Passel, J. S. and Cohn, D'V. Share of Unauthorized Immigrant Workers in Production, Construction Jobs Fall Since 2007." Pew Research Center Hispanic Trends, 26 March (http://www.pewhispanic.org/2015/03/26/share-of-unauthorized-immigrant-workers-in-production-construction-jobs-falls-since-2007/, accessed: 5 December 2016).

Piketty, T.; E. Saez; and G. Zucman. 2016. "Distributional National Accounts: Methods and Estimates for the United States." NBER Working Paper 22945 (December).

Roberts, B. 2014. "Productive/Unproductive: Conceptual Topology." *Rethinking Marxism* 26 (3): 336-59.

Trump, D. 2016a. "Trump Delivers Speech on Jobs at New York Economic Club." 15 September. (https://www.donaldjtrump.com/press-releases/trump-delivers-speech-on-jobs-at-new-york-economic-club, accessed: 29 November 2016).

Trump, D. 2016b. "Immigration Plan." (https://www.donaldjtrump.com/policies/immigration, accessed: 5 December 2016).

U.S. Government Accountability Office. 2014. "Airline Competition" (http://www.gao.gov/assets/670/664060.pdf, accessed: 29 November 2016).

U.S. Government Accountability Office. 2016. "Corporate Income Tax" (http://www.gao.gov/assets/680/675844.pdf, accessed 29 November 2016).

Yu, R. 2016. "Dodd-Frank, in Place After Finanical [sic] Crisis, Targeted by Trump and Mnuchin." *USA Today*, 1 December (http://www.usatoday.com/story/money/2016/11/30/dodd-frank-place-after-finanical-crisis-targeted-bytrump-and-mnuchin/94684080/, accessed: 5 December 2016).

Trump's growthism: its roots in neoclassical economic theory

Herman Daly [University of Maryland, USA]

I. Introduction

By Trumpism, or "Trumponomics", I mean an unrestrained commitment to growth – deregulated markets with little attention to monopoly or distributive equity, high government spending on military and infrastructure, low taxes on the rich, low interest rates, policies of drill it, pump it, burn it, cut it down, dig it up, pave it over, buy it, consume it, and if it threatens to slow growth, then run over it or bomb it. One hopes it will not be that bad, but if it is not, it will not be due to any restraining influence from neoclassical economics, nor from the Democratic Party.

In fact it is the multiple, long-standing errors of the neoclassical-Keynesian growth synthesis that have encouraged growthmania in general and Trumpism in particular. My purpose in this essay is to identify the main neoclassical errors, and show their connection to the general growthism that Trump has raised to a higher power.

II. Paradigm error

The foundational error occurs in the first chapter of the standard economics textbooks: the diagram representing the economy as a circular flow of exchange value between firms and households. Firms supply goods and services to satisfy the demands of households. Households supply factors of production to satisfy the demands of the firms, who use them to produce the goods and services demanded by the households, etc. This circular merry-go-round has its virtues. It unites in one diagram the microeconomics of markets and price determination by supply and demand in the goods market, and in the factors market, with the macroeconomics of aggregate national product of goods, and aggregate national income to factors of production. The value of national income equals the value of national product thanks to the residual definition of profit as the difference between the value of product and cost of factors. We can also include the financial sub-circuits of Government Expenditure and Taxes, Savings and Investment, and Exports and Imports. But the total flow of exchange value remains circular. That is a lot to bring together in one picture, so it is not hard to see why it has been so influential as a representation of the economic process as a whole, and has served as what Schumpeter called a "preanalytic vision", and philosopher Thomas Kuhn later referred to as a "paradigm". I confess that I used to teach this vision to sophomores, with considerable conviction and satisfaction.

But the vision embodies an astonishing omission, a critical flaw: nothing enters from the outside, nothing exits to the outside. The economy is seen as an isolated system – it has no outside, no environment, much less any dependence on its non-existent environment. It is a perpetual motion machine that, contrary to the entropy law, just recycles matter and energy forever to generate a continuing, nay *growing*, circular flow of exchange value, *somehow* embodied in physical goods and factors, with no need of replenishment from outside. What is absent from this preanalytic vision, namely the metabolic, entropic throughput from the environment as natural resource inputs and waste outputs, cannot be introduced by subsequent analysis. You have to alter the preanalytic vision itself, reform the paradigm, go back to the beginning, to give analysis something to work on. Starting over from the beginning requires some recantation and reworking. Later we will indicate the major consequences of this flawed vision for current theories of macroeconomics and microeconomics, as well as for monetary and international trade theories.

It does not take a genius to re-imagine this preanalytic vision. First draw a larger circle around the original diagram of the economy and label it "ecosphere" or "environment". Then give it an input of solar energy from space, and an output of heat back to space. Give the economic subsystem inputs of useful matter and energy from the ecosphere, and outputs of waste matter and energy back to the ecosphere. Not hard at all. Some of us have been doing this for many years. Most economists resist it.

I remember vividly trying to do it in the World Bank's *1992 World Development Report on Sustainable Development.* An early draft contained a diagram of the economy with no environment. As an internal reviewer I suggested enclosing it in the ecosphere in the manner suggested above. The team of traditional World Bank economists writing the Report could not argue against my suggestion, since it was so obvious and simple, but neither could they face the difficult questions it would require us to address – namely, how big is the economy relative to the containing ecosphere? How big can it be? How big should it be? How much do the resource inputs deplete the ecosphere? How much do the waste outputs pollute the ecosphere? What are the consequences for the environment and economy of the entropic nature of the metabolic throughput from depletion to pollution? What is the optimal scale of the economic subsystem relative to the ecosphere? And most challenging: how do we cure poverty without growth? Explicitly drawing the containing ecosphere with matter/energy throughput flows, an innocent and simple correction, implicitly said that the ecosphere is finite, that the economy depends on it, and that sharing, more than growth, is the ultimate solution for poverty.

Yet the World Bank was very much committed to growth, if not forever, at least for a very long time, and by a very large amount. The Bank economists knew that any recognition of limits to growth would not fly with the higher-ups. Their resolution was simply to abandon any attempt to represent the relation of economy and ecosphere in a diagram. Too much clarity can be inconvenient! Whatever "sustainable development" (the new buzzword) meant, it could not be allowed to compromise growth. Better to keep the old vision of the economy as an isolated system, that presumably grows into the void, than to risk raising questions that would embarrass the World Bank's commitment to growth.

Trumpism in 2017 is even more committed to this growth paradigm than was the World Bank in 1992.

There are many specific neoclassical errors that derive from this faulty preanalytic vision. Let us trace out some of them in the fields of macroeconomics, microeconomics, money, and international trade.

III. Macroeconomic errors

In macroeconomics, National Income counts only "value added", that is to say, value added by labor and capital to a presumably valueless flow of matter ("free gifts of nature") whose existence was not even recognized in the preanalytic vision, but somehow must be smuggled in, if the circular flow of money is to have a real counterpart in terms of physical commodities. Natural resources are just background "stuff", valued at their labor and capital cost of extraction. True, royalties are sometimes paid for resources *in situ* if they are easier to extract relative to marginal mines or wells. But the royalty is simply the savings in labor and capital costs relative to the marginal mine. No independent value is attributed to the resource throughput in our national accounts. Yet that entropic metabolic flow is the source of our life and wealth! As physicist Erwin Schroedinger put it in his classic *"What is Life?"*, we live by "sucking low entropy from the environment". A paradigm that totally abstracts from natural resource flows prevents neoclassical economists from registering the very sap of life and wealth, the most basic of all biophysical facts. As a consequence the category of "externalities", things left out of the theory but too obvious to completely ignore, has expanded enormously. When destruction of the very capacity of the earth to support life has to be classed as an "externality", it is past time to make our theory more inclusive!

Economists mesmerized by the circular flow of value, as measured by GDP, naturally have difficulty imagining how growth in GDP, measured in value units, could affect anything outside the isolated circular flow – including the climate. Trump and his advisors have the same difficulty and think climate change is a hoax.

Whether they consider climate change a hoax or not, neoclassical economists think it cannot be economically important. Consider the following three examples.

1. Reporting on a National Academy of Science study on climate change and greenhouse adaptation, *Science* magazine quotes Yale economist

Trumponomics: Causes And Consequences

William Nordhaus (1991) as saying the following:[1]

"Agriculture, the part of the economy that is sensitive to climate change, accounts for just 3 percent of national output. That means there is no way to get a very large effect on the US economy" (p. 1206).

2. Oxford economist Wilfred Beckerman, in his 1995 book, *Small is Stupid*, also tells us that greenhouse-gas-induced climate change is no worry because it affects only agriculture, and agriculture is only 3 percent of GNP. Beckerman elaborates,[2]

"Even if net output of agriculture fell by 50 percent by the end of the next century this is only a 1.5 percent cut in GNP" (p. 91).

3. In the November/December 1997 issue of *Foreign Affairs*, former president of the American Economic Association (and subsequent 2005 Nobel Laureate in Economics), Thomas C. Schelling, elaborates a bit more:[3]

"In the developed world hardly any component of the national income is affected by climate. Agriculture is practically the only sector of the economy affected by climate and it contributes only a small percentage – 3 percent in the United States – of national income. If agricultural productivity were drastically reduced by climate change, the cost of living would rise by 1 or 2 percent, and at a time when per capita income will likely have doubled" (p. 9).

---

[1] Nordhaus, W., 1991 *Science*, Sept. 1991, 1206.
[2] Beckerman, W., 1997. *Small is Stupid*. Duckworth, London
[3] Schelling, T.C., 1997 "The Cost of Combating Global Warming", *Foreign Affairs*, November/ December, p. 9.

What is wrong with these three statements? First, it is simply not true that agriculture is the only climate-sensitive sector of the economy – just ask the insurance firms (and the citizens of New Orleans after Katrina!). Second, it is not at all clear what makes Schelling think that per capita income is likely to double in spite of a drastic reduction in agriculture. But those are not the errors that most concern me.

The error that concerns me here is to treat the importance of agriculture as if it were measured by its percentage of GDP – its contribution to the presumed macro bottom line. These distinguished economists know all about the law of diminishing marginal utility, consumer surplus, and the fact that exchange value (price) reflects *marginal* use value, not total use value. They know that GDP is measured in units of exchange value. They surely know that other economists have long referred to agriculture as *primary* production and understand the reason for that designation. They also know that the demand for food in the aggregate is famously *inelastic*. Probably they have even explained the famous "diamonds-water paradox" to their Econ 101 students in something like the following words:

> Imagine an economy in which GDP consisted of only two commodities, water and diamonds, with water so abundant that its price was almost zero, while diamonds were scarce and very expensive. GDP might consist, say, of 99% value of diamonds and 1% value of water. Imagine that climate change causes a severe drought. The marginal utility of water and its price become very high, and the terms of trade of diamonds for water moves drastically against diamonds – people would trade all their diamonds for just a glass of life-sustaining water. Now GDP might well be 99% value of water and 1% value of diamonds. You see how important marginal utility is to price and GDP, and what a bad indicator it is of total utility and welfare!

With that familiar pedagogical parable in mind it should be evident that in the event of a climate-induced collapse of agriculture the relative price of food would skyrocket and the percentage of GDP accounted for by agriculture, which is not a constant of nature, could rise from 3 percent to 90 percent. No doubt, adaptation would be possible, since in the past agriculture did account for 90 percent of national product and we (many fewer of us, consuming much less per capita) survived. Clearly, the percentage of the GDP derived from agriculture is a measure of the importance only of marginal (very small) changes in current agricultural output – certainly not Beckerman's (1995) "50 percent fall", or Schelling's (1997) "drastic reduction", or Nordhaus' (1991) unqualified "no way". One way of looking at the error is therefore that it represents an elementary failure to distinguish marginal from infra-marginal utility – to ignore consumer surplus.

A less elementary dimension of the error is neglect of the structural interdependence of GDP. These economists are surely familiar with Leontief's input – output matrix showing the amount of input that each sector of the economy requires from all other sectors in order to produce its output. And each input used by each sector is itself an output of another sector that also required inputs from nearly every other sector – likewise for the inputs to those inputs, and so on. All these technical interdependencies of production are abstracted from in GDP, which leaves out intermediate production, counting only what goes to the final consumer. But the economy functions as an integrated whole, not a loose collection of final consumption goods. What happens to the output of non-agricultural sectors when agricultural inputs to them are drastically reduced? Well, they decline, and their reduced output results in lower inputs to other sectors, etc.

Yet another related dimension of the error is that it treats all parts of GDP as substitutable. If GDP declines by 3 percent due to disruption of agriculture that will presumably be no problem if GDP simultaneously increases by 3 percent due to growth in information services. A dollar's worth of anything is assumed to be indifferently substitutable for a dollar's worth of anything else. Likewise for a hundred billion dollars' worth. Although money is indeed fungible, real GDP is not. We measure GDP in units of "dollar's worth", not "dollars". A dollar is a piece of paper or a book- keeping entry; a dollar's worth of something is a physical quantity. GDP is a price- weighted index of aggregate quantity of final production. The part of that aggregate quantity accounted for by agriculture is something necessary to support not only other sectors, but life itself. The fungibility of dollars does not imply the fungibility of food and, say, information services. Unless we first have enough food, we just will not be interested in information services. If I am hungry, I want a meal, not a recipe, not even a lot of recipes. That is why economists traditionally have called agriculture "primary" and services "tertiary".

True, agriculture accounts for only 3 percent of GDP, but it is precisely the specific 3 percent on which the other 97 percent is based! It is not an indifferently fungible 3 percent. The foundation of a building may be only 3 percent of its height, but that does not mean that we can subtract the foundation if only we add 3 percent to the flagpole on top of the building. Like a building, GDP has a structure – neither is just a pile of fungible stuff.

In addition to technical interdependence, this structure reflects objective valuation by consumers, a kind of "lexicographic ordering" of wants. No amount of information services will substitute for food until basic food needs are met – just as the second letter of words is irrelevant to the alphabetical order of a dictionary unless the first letter is the same.

It is hard to understand how such distinguished economists could ignore these fundamental principles of their own discipline. In all three cases, the mistake was part of a larger defense of economic growth. Maybe the conclusion in favor of growth, the undoubted *summum bonum*, lent credence to the faulty reasoning leading to it. I do not know. But I am sure that the error cannot be attributed to ignorance or stupidity of these three economists – people whom I know and respect. If these economists were ignorant or dumb, their error would be of little interest. *It is precisely because of their legitimately high prestige that one suspects that the error is to be found in the presuppositions of the dominant "Keynesian-neoclassical growth synthesis", to which all three firmly adhere, along with the majority of modern economists.* This is not to say that no economists have ever criticized GDP. Many have. Kenneth Boulding even suggested, tongue only partly in cheek, that it should be re-labeled Gross Domestic *Cost*. But the stonewalling mainstream[4] has simply ignored any argument that casts doubt on

---

[4] For more on "stonewalling", see H. Daly, *From Uneconomic Growth to a Steady-State Economy*, Edward Elgar Publishing Co., Cheltenham, U. K., 2014. pp. 59-62.

growthism. And that is why the repeated error is important and needs repeated correction.[5]

IV. Microeconomic errors

In admirable consistency with omitting natural resources from national income accounting, the neoclassical economists also omit natural resources from their basic microeconomic production function, $Y = f(K, L)$, where Y is product, K is capital and L is labor. The form of the function is nearly always multiplicative, as in the usual Cobb-Douglas. Sometimes to avoid embarrassment at obviously violating the first law of thermodynamics, neoclassical economists will insert an R in the function to represent natural resource inputs to provide the material basis of physical product Y. But since the function is multiplicative the math allows any given Y to be produced, even as R approaches zero, as long as K or L is increased in a compensatory fashion. Thus we can bake a ten pound cake with only a few ounces of ingredients, as long as we use more ovens and cooks – still violating the first law! It is as if a "product" resulted from the multiplication of

---

[5] The earliest of the three quoted statements was made in 1991, and the error was soon pointed out in a letter to *Science* (18 October, 1991, p. 358) where Nordhaus' statement had been published. No reply from Nordhaus. Since the error was subsequently repeated by Beckerman in 1995, and by Schelling in 1997, I thought it worth a further correction and commentary in 2000 ("When Smart People Make Dumb Mistakes", *Ecological Economics*, July, 2000, Vol. 34, No. 1, pp. 1-3). To my knowledge there has been no response, defense, or recantation by any of the three distinguished economists, or by their many disciples. Nobody enjoys having their mistakes pointed out – I certainly do not. It would be churlish to harp on old mistakes if they had been corrected, or if they were not important. But neither is the case. The egregious statement was thrice delivered by prestigious economists, *ex cathedra* from the National Academy of Sciences, Yale University, Oxford University, the American Economic Association, and the Nobel Prize for economics. Trump's growthist advisors and climate deniers can claim encouragement from neoclassical economists. Scientific claims delivered from such high platforms merit (indeed demand) serious consideration, but still are required to withstand and respond to criticism. Conjecture and refutation form the very definition of scientific method, as famously argued by Karl Popper (*Conjectures and Refutations: the growth of scientific knowledge*, Routledge Classics, 1963). But since growthism is more ideology than science, the conjectures (and errors) of growthists are given a free pass. Indeed, mainstream economists, along with Trumpists, consider it bad manners to refute them!

"factors" (as in mathematics), rather than from the physical transformation of natural resources by the agency of labor and capital (as in actual production). Georgescu-Roegen made this criticism years ago in his fund-flow model of production,[6] and has never been answered.

At this point the growthists will appeal to technological progress. But improved technology is a qualitatively new production function, not just substitution of factors in a given production function. In the empty world technological progress has aimed at increasing productivity of the limiting factor (capital or labor), by transforming a greater flow of natural resources which were considered non limiting. In today's full world natural resources are limiting, and raising resource prices by severance taxes, a carbon tax, or cap-auction-trade would help induce new resource-saving technology. But these policies are usually opposed by the growthists, although increasingly advocated by some mainstream economists.

The mistake is to treat *all* factors of production as substitutes. Labor and capital are to a large degree substitutes because they are both agents of transformation of the resource flow from raw material to finished product and waste (waste is also absent from the neoclassical production function). Likewise, one natural resource ingredient can often substitute for another. But natural resource flows are complements to, not substitutes for, the transforming fund agents of labor and capital. Nothing could be clearer than that capital and labor are not at all embodied in the final product, while natural resources are entirely embodied in the product (and waste). Natural resources are the material cause of production, capital and labor are efficient causes. Capital and natural resources are not substitutes; they are complements.

Yet prominent neoclassical economists maintain the opposite. Nordhaus and Tobin[7] are specific on this point:

---

[6] *The Entropy Law and the Economic Process*, Harvard University Press, Cambridge, MA, 1971.
[7] Nordhaus, W. and J. Tobin (1970), *Is growth obsolete?* National Bureau of Economic Research, Colloquium, San Francisco, December 10, 1970.

"The prevailing standard model of growth assumes that there are no limits on the feasibility of expanding the supplies of nonhuman agents of production. It is basically a two factor model in which production depends only on labor and reproducible capital" (1970, p. 14).

How is this neglect of resource flows justified? According to Nordhaus and Tobin,

"the tacit justification has been that reproducible capital is a near perfect substitute for land and other exhaustible resources".[8]

When factors are complements the one in short supply is *limiting*. In the empty world capital was limiting and natural resources abundant. Capital's controlling social power came from the fact that it was the limiting factor. But thanks to growth we now live in a full world in which remaining natural resources have become limiting, while capital is relatively abundant. For example, the fish catch is no longer limited by the number of fishing boats, but by remaining fish and their capacity to reproduce. Cut timber is not limited by the number of chain saws or lumberjacks, but by remaining forests and their growth rates. Pumped crude oil is not limited by number of drilling rigs, but by remaining accessible deposits, and the capacity of the atmosphere to absorb CO_2. Economic logic says invest in the limiting factor and maximize its productivity. The logic stays the same, but the limiting factor has changed. As natural resources became limiting we should have seen an increase in fallowing-type investments in increased regeneration and productivity of natural resources. But instead neoclassicals denied that resources were the limiting factor.

They claimed that there was no limiting factor, because capital and natural resources were really substitutes, in fact nearly perfect substitutes.

In the empty world these economists saw man as dominating nature because manmade capital was limiting. In the full world, rather than

---

[8] Ibid.

accommodating to the new fact that natural capital and resources have become limiting, they abandoned the very idea of limiting factor by declaring that capital and natural resources are substitutes, not complements. Yet they must have previously considered capital and natural resources to be complements or they could not have claimed that capital was the limiting factor. Both cases illustrate the neoclassical animus against the importance of nature, emphasizing the dominance of man. So they continue to advocate investing in manmade capital, the non-limiting factor, in the false belief that it is a substitute for the limiting factor of natural capital. This is wrong for reasons just given; but consider one more. If manmade capital were a substitute for natural capital then natural capital would also be a substitute for manmade capital. Substitution is reversible. But then why would we have gone to the trouble to make and accumulate capital if nature had already endowed us with a good substitute?

In reply to these criticisms growth economists often point to modern agriculture, which they consider the prime historical example of substitution of capital for resources. But modern, mechanized agriculture has simply substituted one set of resource flows for another, and one set of funds (capital) for another. The old resource flows (soil, sunlight, rain, manure) were to a significant degree replaced by new resource flows (chemical fertilizer, fossil fuels, irrigation water), not by "capital"! The old fund factors of labor, draft animals, and hand tools were replaced by new fund factors of tractors, harvesters, and so on. In other words new fund factors substituted for old fund factors, and new resource flows substituted for old resource flows. Modern agriculture involved the substitution of capital for labor (both funds), and the substitution of nonrenewable resources for renewable resources (both flows). In energy terms it was largely the substitution of fossil fuels for solar energy, a move with short-term benefits and long-term costs. But there was no substitution of capital funds for resource flows. The case of mechanization of agriculture does not contradict the complementarity of fund and flow factors in production, nor the new role of natural resources as limiting factor.

A production function is often aptly compared to a recipe. But unlike the neoclassical production function, real recipes in real cookbooks always begin with a list of ingredients. Trump's economic cooks are at least more realistic than neoclassical economists – they know they need limiting natural resources as ingredients, but rather than economize on them, are quite prepared to tear the world apart to get ever more of them. But then, for the neoclassicals, there is no world outside their isolated system, so what happens in the unrecognized biophysical world doesn't count in GDP, and doesn't enter into production functions. It is an "externality".

V. Monetary errors

Neoclassical economics considers money as a veil, or a *numeraire*, a kind of common denominator for expressing prices in comparable units, thereby facilitating trade, and avoiding the inconvenience of barter. It is that, but has become much more with the development of fiat money and fractional reserve banking. The close connection of fractional reserve banking with alchemy was recently emphasized by Mervyn King, former head of the Bank of England, in the very title of his recent book, *The End of Alchemy: Money, Banking, and the Failure of the Global Economy*. He refers to the more thorough development of this connection by Swiss ecological economist H. C. Binswanger in his brilliant study, *Money and Magic*. Given this connection to alchemy, it is more than a coincidence that the earliest and most thorough critique of fractional reserve banking came, not from an alchemist, but from a real chemist, Nobel Laureate Frederick Soddy.[9] Soddy's advocacy of full reserve banking was later picked up by Irving Fisher, and by Frank Knight and others of the early Chicago School. The proposal seemed to die with the Great Depression, because it was correctly perceived to limit growth, the new panacea. Mervyn King stops short of advocating full reserve banking, but clearly is unhappy with the fractional reserve system.

Most Central Banks, however, seem to favor the alchemy of fractional reserves as a key part of their hyper-Keynesianism: the quest to stimulate real growth by increasing monetary growth, first by low, then by zero, and now by negative interest rates. Why hasn't it worked? Because real growth today is constrained by real resource shortages – those same resources that were absent in the pre-analytic vision, and the national accounts, and the

---

[9] See H. Daly, "The Economic Thought of Frederick Soddy", *History of Political Economy*, 1980, 12:4.

production function. In the 1930s traditional Keynesianism's assumption of unemployed resources was reasonable. Now there is still unemployed labor to be sure, but not unemployed natural resources, which have become the limiting factor in today's full world. As growth converts more of nature into economy we see that these newly appropriated natural resources were not unemployed at all, but were providing ecological services that often were more valuable than the extra production resulting from their enclosure into the economy. But this fact is invisible to those whose preanalytic vision denies any importance to natural resource throughput, much less to natural services. In the real world aggregate growth in wealthy countries has become *uneconomic* – a condition unrecognized by economists long fixated on growth as panacea in their circular isolated system.

It is time to reconsider the proposal of full reserve banking. What are its advantages?

1. The private banking system could no longer live the alchemist's dream of creating fiat money out of nothing, pocketing the seigniorage, and lending the created money at interest. These enormous privileges would be transferred to the public treasury. Money would be a public utility – a medium of exchange, a unit of account, a store of value. The idea is to nationalize money, not banks http://steadystate.org/nationalize-money-not-banks/.

2. Every dollar borrowed would be a dollar saved, and unavailable to the saver for the life of the loan. This restores the classical discipline of balancing investing and saving, rather analogous to chemistry's law of conservation of matter- energy. Savers and Investors cannot both claim the same dollar at the same time. Banks would be intermediaries, charging interest to borrowers and paying interest to savers. The interest rate exists as a price equating savings with investment, but not as a price paid to the banks for their unnecessary and expensive "service" of creating money as private interest-bearing debt. That the public utility of money should be the by-product of the private activity of lending and borrowing is no better than when it was the by-product of the private activity of gold mining.

3. With full reserve banking there would be no possibility of bank failure due to a run on the bank by depositors, and therefore no need for deposit insurance and its consequent moral hazard. The entire debt pyramid would no longer collapse with the failure of a few big banks, bringing down the basic system of payments with it. The bargaining power of the banking system to extort large bailouts by taxpayers would be lost.

4. No longer would the money supply expand during a boom and contract during a slump, reinforcing the cyclical tendency of the economy. And the reserve ratio could be raised gradually. Also, under fractional reserves the money supply is always threatening to decline as bank loans are repaid, unless new loans compensate. New loans are made in the expectation of growth, so unless those expectations are met, new loans will cease and the money supply diminish. So fractional reserve banking imparts a growth bias to the economy that is absent with 100% reserves.

5. Money would be issued by the Treasury, and spent into existence for public goods and services. *The amount of money issued should be limited by the amount of money that people are voluntarily willing to hold instead of exchanging it for real wealth.* If the Treasury issues more than that amount people will spend it on real goods, driving up the price level. That is the signal to the treasury to print less money and/or raise taxes. The Treasury's policy target is a constant price index, not the interest rate, which is left to market forces, and would thus never be negative (http://steadystate.org/the-negative-natural-interest-rate-and-uneconomic-growth/). The internal value of the currency is determined by maintaining a constant price index, and thus the dollar ceases to be a "rubber yardstick" of value. The external value of the currency would be determined by freely fluctuating exchange rates.

Trump's growthmania is financed by money creation and cheap credit from the big banks. Banks hate the idea of 100% reserve requirements on demand deposits the way 17th-century counterfeiters hated Sir Isaac Newton, who, in his extra job as Controller of the Mint, had many of them hanged.

VI. Trade errors: globalization versus internationalization

Finally we come to a place where we must give some credit to Trumponomics for having opposed neoclassical economics rather than blindly following it. Whether this was out of conviction, or devious political expediency, or both, is a question I will leave to the reader. Free trade, off-shoring, capital mobility, and uncontrolled immigration added up to the neoclassical cheap labor policy, nominal opposition to which gave Trump his big issue and political victory. Of course it was sold as "pro-growth" rather than "cheap labor". The Democrats, under the influence of neoclassical free traders and global corporations, were blind to the devastation and resentment their cheap labor policy had caused in working class and rural America. Bernie Sanders understood, and almost got the nomination, but Hillary Clinton and the Democratic establishment failed to learn the lesson.

The presidential election revealed a deep-seated discomfort with globalization and its costs, and as Donald Trump sets the agenda for his new administration, some fear he will move the United States towards isolationism and nationalism. There is another alternative open to him that served the country well for over fifty years, neither globalization nor nationalism, but internationalism.

Globalization is frequently conflated with internationalism but is something quite different. Globalization refers to the global integration of many formerly national economies into one global economy. "Integration" derives from "integer", meaning one or whole, and when we integrate, we combine into one the previous parts. Since there can only be one whole, the disintegration of the national economy is necessary to reintegrate its pieces into the new global economy.

As the saying goes, "To make an omelette you have to break some eggs". Under globalization the disintegration of a nation's economic boundaries is achieved through globally integrated capital markets, labor pools and trade agreements.

Internationalism refers to international trade, treaties, protocols, alliances and other structures where nations rely on each other and work together towards common goals. "Inter-national" means between or among nations, and under internationalism the basic unit of policy and decision-making remains the nation. Internationalism was the post-WWII goal of the Bretton Woods institutions; globalism has become the goal with the WTO, TPP and transnational corporations. As nations outgrow their domestic resource base they expand, via globalization, into the global commons, and into the ecological space of other nations.

In internationalization, trade is conducted between nations with their own self-interests in mind. Countries determine what they are best at doing, specialize in those goods or services, and trade with each other on that basis. In the classic example, England trades its wool and textiles for Portugal's wine and vice versa. It would be unproductive for English investors or workers to attempt large scale winemaking in the English climate, and England's resources are better put to use in sheep farming and wool-making. Through trade based on comparative advantage, both England and Portugal benefit.

In a globalized economy with free capital mobility, nations no longer specialize in their own "comparative advantage", but instead global capitalists and corporations follow "absolute advantage" – allocating their resources to maximize global productivity and global profit. They function as components of an integrated global economy. U.S. corporations or investors shift capital to China to produce goods with less expensive Chinese labor for sale back into the U.S. By doing so, the same investment generates more product at lower cost, thereby growing the global economy. However, these global gains can inflict enormous cost at the national level.

While the global economy may grow more with globalization, each nation no longer necessarily benefits. With globalization the nation loses its ability to enforce its own laws and standards. The U.S. has national policies, for example, governing workers' rights and workplace standards – minimum wages, non-discrimination, fair pay, child labor laws, and environmental and safety regulations. These agreements have been reached through generations of national debate, elections, strikes, lockouts, court decisions, and, at times, violent conflict. They affirm national values and strike a balance between how the economic pie is split between "capital" and "labor". These policies become meaningless in a globally integrated economy.

If a U.S. corporation run by U.S. executives closes a plant in Michigan, lays off its workers and opens a new one in Mexico facing much less stringent compliance standards, staffs it with lower salaried Mexican workers who do not require health insurance or unemployment benefits, and then ships products back to sell to U.S. consumers at a much higher profit, the result is not what most Americans think of as "free trade". It is instead freedom from regulation and responsibility done under the cover of globalization.

The restoration of internationalism re-establishes the nation as the locus of policy and reasserts the principle of interdependence – not integration – as the basis for international collaboration. Interdependence is to integration as friendship is to marriage. Strong friendships lead to a long and happy life, but few people attempt or survive a multi-lateral marriage.

Trump has recognized the distributive flaws of globalization, but it remains to be seen if he will limit capital mobility in order to make the world safe for trade based on comparative advantage. Or will he opt to maintain capital mobility and accept the consequence of substituting absolute advantage for comparative advantage in the quest for global growth? Probably, like neoclassical economists, he is not aware that the logic of comparative advantage is based on the assumption of internationally immobile capital, as explicitly stated by David Ricardo in his famous comparative argument. Probably global growthism will win out in the Trump regime, since it is in the interests of the billionaire US elite, from which he has entirely drawn his cabinet of advisors.

VII. Conclusion

Many of the excesses of Trumpism are firmly rooted in the neoclassical growth paradigm that is still taught in the economics departments of all major universities, to the near exclusion of other views. The discipline of neoclassical economics itself requires a good dose of the "creative destruction" that it so often advocates for businesses. A friend told me how, at an individual level, he is helping this creative destruction of mainstream economics. In reply to letters from his alma mater dunning the alumni for contributions, he says, "When your Economics Department stops advocating infinite growth on a finite planet, I will donate. Until then, save the postage."

Trumponomics: causes and prospects

L. Randall Wray [Bard College, NY, USA]

I do not want to dwell excessively on the politics, but it is necessary to examine how we got here before we can begin to discuss the prospects.

Why Trump?

To say that the election of someone like Trump to the American presidency is merely unprecedented for the United States would make too light of our current situation. Trump has the self-control one would normally expect to find in an impulsive and petulant six-year-old. He has truly unparalleled experience as a businessman – and I do not mean that in any positive way. His behavior in polite company has fallen to a standard usually reserved for failed states. He fancies himself a "pussy grabbing" predator and stays up late at night to compulsively tweet personalized nasty comments about women's bodies and the supposed foreign nationality and incompetence of our nation's judges.

Even as he thoroughly trounced every candidate the Republicans could throw in front of him, all of the country's elite remained convinced that there was little chance that he would become president – right up to and through the early evening of election day. The Democrats were so confident of the impossibility of Trump's winning that they insisted on running a weak and unpopular candidate to challenge him. There probably has never been a "democratic" election on this planet in which two more unpopular candidates faced off. Still, most pundits had Hillary winning in nearly an electoral college landslide. Trump would go the way of Hillary's first political infatuation, Barry Goldwater, to an historic defeat.

And, yet, Trump trumped. How could that have happened? Tom Frank provided part of the answer last October: the official pundits "are professionals in the full sense of the word, well educated and well connected, often flaunting insider credentials of one sort or another. They are, of course, a comfortable bunch. And when they look around at the comfortable, well-educated folks who work in government, academia, Wall Street, medicine, and Silicon Valley, they see their peers.

Now, consider the recent history of the Democratic Party. Beginning in the 1970s, it has increasingly become an organ of this same class. Affluent white-collar professionals are today the voting bloc that Democrats represent most faithfully, and they are the people whom Democrats see as the rightful winners in our economic order. Hillary Clinton, with her fantastic résumé and her life of striving and her much-commented-on qualifications, represents the aspirations of this class almost perfectly. An accomplished lawyer, she is also in with the foreign-policy in crowd; she has the respect of leading economists; she is a familiar face to sophisticated financiers. She knows how things work in the capital. To Washington Democrats, and possibly to many Republicans, she is not just a candidate but a colleague, the living embodiment of their professional worldview. In Bernie Sanders and his "political revolution," on the other hand, I believe these same people saw something kind of horrifying: a throwback to the low-rent Democratic politics of many decades ago."[1]

Frank documents the stance that the Washington Post – Washington's official mouthpiece – took from the beginning of the Primaries: "On January 27, with the Iowa caucuses just days away, Dana Milbank nailed it with a headline: NOMINATING SANDERS WOULD BE INSANE." That Sanders over the course of the Primaries would become the most popular politician in

---

[1] Thomas Frank 2016, http://harpers.org/archive/2016/11/swat-team-2/.

America was beside the point.[2] The mainstream media never changed its views – Sanders had to be stopped so that Hillary could fulfill her manifest destiny to follow in her husband's footsteps to the Whitehouse, to secure Washington for the neoliberals. And when it came down to Trump versus Clinton in November, even many prominent Republicans jumped ship to endorse a Democrat who had always been loathed by the party's base. The punditry was united by its common belief that Clinton would – and should – triumph.

In truth, the Democratic primary was a charade. The Democratic National Committee (DNC) had long before decided that Hillary Clinton would be the party's candidate, and did everything it could to ensure that voters' preferences would play no role in the election.[3] When proof of the DNC's Nixon-like dirty tricks campaign surfaced,[4] the official media did its best to divert attention away from Hillary's misdeeds and toward President Putin. Over the course of the Republican Primaries, the DNC's confidence grew as it looked increasingly likely that Trump would be Clinton's challenger as he dispatched with no fanfare all of that party's stars. The DNC considered him to be the weakest candidate. Of course this clown with no experience would be easily bested by Hillary, the most over-qualified candidate ever.

Many of the speeches given at the Democratic Convention could have been delivered by *Dr Strangelove's* Brigadier General Jack D. Ripper – with no

---

[2] Even today, Sanders remains the most popular politician in America as a recent survey shows: "Everyone Loves Bernie Sanders. Except, It Seems, the Democratic Party" by Trevor Timm, *Guardian* UK,18 March 17

[3] I was an early voter in Hillary's own county. I took my ballot to the local postmaster two days before the deadline, signed the ballot and envelop under the postmaster's watchful eye, and had him postmark it in front of me. After the election I received a letter from the DNC informing me that my ballot had been tossed out because it was either late or unsigned. In fact, it was rejected because I did not vote for the DNC's designated winner. I was told by an insider in the Bernie campaign that such fraud was common all over the country but that Bernie had committed to working within the system and thus would not protest the rigged outcome.

[4] For a dirty laundry list of the DNC's acts against the will of the voters see http://www.salon.com/2016/07/29/10_reasons_why_demexit_is_serious_getting_rid_of_debbie_wasserman_schultz_is_not_enough/ and http://observer.com/2016/07/wikileaks-proves-primary-was-rigged-dnc-undermined-democracy/.

change of content or tone.[5] After the Primaries ended, Trump's unwillingness to join the red scare bandwagon against the "Ruskies" provided more fuel to the fire. National Public Radio's supposedly liberal commentators began to habitually place the term "enemy state" in front of "Russia". Soon they added the preface to China, too. The Clintonistas made it clear that only Hillary could stand up to our rediscovered cold war enemies. If anything, Trump was just a Manchurian candidate, following directives from the Reds. Forget about Trump, Hillary was running against Putin.

The DNC wrote off the majority of US states – those in which Trump's "deplorables"[6] made it too difficult to win. With the US's electoral college votes in the bag, Hillary was going to win – in a landslide – by taking the handful of coastal states plus a few big states in the fly-over middle. There was no way the Democrats could lose, as Trump's racist and misogynist tweets and twits handed them female, young, and minority voters to supplement the usual union members and low income folks who would vote their own economic interests.

Right up to the night of the election, the electoral college was Hillary's, although some worried that she might not capture the popular vote – because the Bernie "Bros" stubbornly refused to support her. The DNC tried

---

[5] The Democrat convention featured plenty of Jingoism, assertions that the 21st century will be the "American Century", odes to "American Exceptionalism" and claims that the rest of the world longs for a return of aggressive American "leadership". Speeches by Rear Admiral John Hutson, Leon Panetta, and General John Allen all could have come straight out of the Cold War. Hillary has made her own hawkish position clear; see http://www.theglobalist.com/is-hillary-clinton-a-warmonger/.

[6] As Hillary Clinton put it, "You know, to just be grossly generalistic, you could put half of Trump's supporters into what I call the basket of deplorables... The racist, sexist, homophobic, xenophobic, Islamaphobic – you name it" who support Trump. She estimated their number at 11 million – only about 17.5% of the number who actually voted for Trump (implying either she underestimated the number of deplorables, or "misunderestimated" Trump's support).
http://www.politifact.com/truth-o-meter/article/2016/sep/11/context-hillary-clinton-basket-deplorables/ However, the number who *thought* she was speaking of them is undoubtedly much higher – particularly among white males and young black males (some of who would have recalled that she once tagged young black males as "superpredators"). In any event, this probably played some role in her defeat in the key states of Wisconsin, Michigan, Ohio, Pennsylvania and Florida – all of which had been won by Obama.

to shame the supporters of Bernie and Jill Stein into throwing their principles to the wind; and, indeed, most did – holding their noses and voting for Wall Street's candidate.

However, the election was a shocker. Hillary lost white women and performed worse across the entire spectrum of voters who had elected Obama. She failed to bring in the minority and young voters the New Democrats had been counting on. She even lost across most of the traditional categories of Democratic voters.

Putin won, or at least his surrogate did.

The white-collar professionals that form the New Democrat base that did support Hillary come from the "new" economy – the FIRE (finance, insurance and real estate) sector, Silicon Valley, and social media (broadly defined to include the burgeoning targeted marketing sector – which is really what social media is all about). What they share in common is that they benefit from the neoliberal policies that fuel globalization. This coalition of socially liberal but economically Goldwater conservatives thought that by moving right they could force the Republicans so far right on social issues that changing demographics would ensure Democratic control of government. In a "normal" election, that might have worked. While Gore proved to be too weak of a candidate, Obama succeeded twice with that strategy. In spite of Hillary's unpopularity, she might have been able to beat another "legacy" candidate, like Jeb Bush. But poor Jeb was destroyed in the debates.

When I saw one of Trump's first press conferences, before the Republican debates, I thought he would stomp the likely Democrat, Hillary, and that there was only one candidate who could beat him – Bernie. (I will admit that I waivered in the final days of October, when seemingly plausible projections of the electoral college vote put Hillary in front by a mile.) But, as we know, the primaries were rigged. The Democrats were not going to run him. They would have been "crazy" to run the candidate who could win.

Still, we need to explain how Trump won. It largely comes down to popular disaffection with the mainstream of both parties, each of which quite publicly dismisses the interests of most Americans. Perhaps the "deplorables" did

391

vote their economic interests, realizing that the Democratic party no longer shared them. If you add together Hillary's deplorables plus Romney's 47%, you have a large proportion of the US population, if not the majority, even after striking those that are double-counted. These are the people that neither party wants. Trump welcomed them. Although they have lower voting rates, they make up a sizable block – and many of them were enthusiastic Trump supporters. Trump took the presidency with 19.5% of Americans voting for him; Clinton lost with 19.8%; almost 59% did not vote (of which half were not eligible); and far more of those who were eligible to vote chose to stay home (30% of Americans) compared to the number who voted for the winner or the loser (less than 20%).

Both the Republicans and the Democrats are content with low turnout largely made up of white collar elites enriched by neoliberal policies. Republicans typically play the race and crime card to capture more votes, while Democrats pull in minorities. What separates the two is morals, not economics. The Dems think it is important to emphasize the pain of those left behind, without embracing policies that would actually provide relief. Indeed, they profess to share the pain even as they embrace the policies that cause it: ending entitlements, enacting job-destroying "free trade" agreements, and deregulating the financial system. The Republicans (rightly) blame the government for inflicting the suffering (although they point to the wrong policies as the cause) while promising to get government off our backs.

Both parties assert that the best hope for the underclass is for its denizens to become more like "us" – upper class, highly educated, urban coastal elites. What they did not count on was a Trump.

Careful examination of Trump's voters show that they view themselves as left behind – in regions devastated by job loss, slow growth, low income, high poverty rates, and declining living standards. But their perceptions turn out to be largely false – at least in a relative sense. Pundits point out that they live in regions with above average incomes, and lower than average rates of unemployment and poverty; in comparison with the urban core of cities like Detroit and Chicago, or the ghost towns of the farm-belt, they have it pretty damned good.

Those Trump voters have no reason to complain – they are better off than the average American! Maybe that explains their vote – they are as delusional as Trump, who emphasizes the dire straits in which America finds itself, a stark contrast to the Pollyanna-ish view our nation's elite holds.

But what the pundits do not understand is that voters are not comparing their situation to the devastation found across America. Their reference is both to where they thought America would be in the 21st century, as well as to how it has been pictured in movies and on television since the mid 1980s when John Hughes forever altered expectations of American living standards. Instead of Opie in Mayberry, the Waltons, or the Ingalls family – all with lifestyles that Americans in the 1980s or 90s could view with nostalgia – our movies (*Ferris Bueller, Pretty in Pink*) showed us teens "borrowing" the dad's Ferrari and attending lavish Sixteen parties, while TV featured "Lifestyles of the Rich and Famous". The "middle class" lifestyles increasingly depicted on the screen were enjoyed only by the top single digits of the income distribution.

Furthermore, the reality that Americans faced at the turn of the 21st century fell far short of what we baby-boomers of the 1950s and 60s had been groomed to expect. Where's my flying car? Heck, I'd settle for a decent paved highway to JFK airport that didn't have Hummer-swallowing potholes. And, while not that many Trump voters have traveled to China to see what modern infrastructure looks like, it is obvious that if anyone is going to be commuting to work in swift comfort, Americans will not be at the front of the line.

For an unexpurgated look at the views of the underclass held by our white collar elite, we need look no further than the comments made by their unelected representatives in Washington, the FOMC[7]. As transcripts from the Fed's meetings reveal, FOMC members enjoy poking fun at those left behind by America's neoliberal policies. In 2011, when the unemployment rate was still a shocking 9%, the FOMC focused on drug addiction as the major cause:

---

[7] Federal Open Market Committee – the decision-making body of the Fed.

"I frequently hear of jobs going unfilled because a large number of applicants have difficulty passing basic requirements like drug tests or simply demonstrating the requisite work ethic," said Dennis Lockhart, a former Citibank executive who ran the Atlanta Federal Reserve Bank. "One contact in the staffing industry told us that during their pretesting process, a majority -- actually, 60 percent of applicants -- failed to answer '0' to the question of how many days a week it's acceptable to miss work..." The room of central bankers then broke into laughter. Charles Plosser, the president of the Philadelphia Federal Reserve, cited "work ethic" as a common complaint he heard in his district, both in rural and inner city areas. A contact of his who owned 60 McDonald's restaurants said "...passing drug tests, passing literacy tests, and work ethic are the primary problems he has in hiring people".[8]

In other words, the "deplorable" unemployed -- particularly those in inner cities and rural areas -- have no one to blame but themselves.

If that was the belief back in 2011, it is no wonder that Fed officials believe that today's official unemployment rate -- around 4.7%[9] -- represents "full employment". Even the drug-addled must already have jobs. So the Fed has resumed monetary policy tightening to slow growth. Facing no reelection and with long terms, Fed officials enjoy nearly unbridled freedom to speak their minds in a less constrained manner than that adopted by politicians who have to face voters every few years. They can openly represent today's elite -- the professional class in the FIRE, "knowledge", and "social" media circles who fear full employment and the higher costs they would face hiring informal sector workers as nannies, housekeepers, and groundskeepers. As Plosser's "contact" complained, even at the 9% unemployment rate he was already having trouble hiring the right kind of people to flip burgers and mop

---

[8] https://theintercept.com/2017/01/27/federal-reserve-bankers-mocked-unemployed-americans-behind-closed-doors/

[9] The broader U6 figure was 9.3%, and if we include those who have left the labor force but who would accept a job offer, the number of unemployed is probably above 20 million. See Dantas and Wray 2017, http://www.levyinstitute.org/pubs/ppb_142.pdf.

up his 60 fast food franchises that are euphemistically called "restaurants". (Yes, even the 47% gets to enjoy the occasional sumptuous *restaurant* meal under the golden arches! Albeit, without the Merlot, one supposes.)

It probably should not be surprising that our elite cannot understand that it is the poor prospect for the average American worker that is contributing to the "deplorable" behavior, including drug use and weak "attachment" to the labor force. In truth, the low official unemployment rate is in good measure due to declining labor force participation rates. Until the GFC, the overall labor force participation rate was held up by women, in spite of a long-term declining participation rate by men.[10] It is significant that prime age women now have experienced a reversal – even in the "recovery" from the GFC, their participation remains depressed. The usual explanation for the falling participation rate of men – that it is due to demographic changes (aging of the population) – doesn't hold water. Participation rates of the elderly are *rising* – while rates of prime-age men continue to fall – and even taking account of the demographic changes, we find that most of the decline of male participation is not due to aging – but rather to prime age dropouts.[11] On any given day, just about one out of every six men of prime working age has no paid job of any kind.

True, incarceration and drug use explain some of the dropouts, but poor job and wage prospects are more important. Note that a large majority of prime age male dropouts are single – without the support from a working spouse and with little access to government safety nets. In other words, they have little alternative to working. Finally, they are not gainfully using the time freed up to care for family members, clean house, or pursue more education; in comparison with employed and unemployed men, those out of the labor force simply engage in more leisure activities – about four more hours per day – mostly watching television. While the survey data do not report what they are watching, a good bet is that a lot of their TV time is devoted to programs that help to produce sympathy for Trump's agenda: right wing

---

[10] The overall labor force participation rate reached its peak in 2000 and has been falling ever since; it has now fallen back to its 1977 level. This is not simply due to aging, as it has been falling since 2000 even for prime age and younger workers. See Dantas and Wray 2017.
[11] See Dantas and Wray 2017

"news" programs that stoke fears of immigrants, international trade, and the take-over of the White House by a foreign-born Muslim.

Those that do find jobs are increasingly trapped in contingent, often part-time work at pay that does not offer an American living standard. Trump's voters can beat the averages because the average isn't that great. Too many "average" Americans have little job security, too much debt, mandated health insurance they can't afford (even with Obamacare subsidies), and no savings for rainy days or retirement. They are only a couple of paychecks away from losing their homes to foreclosure fraud, their kids attend schools facing budget problems, and they see no light at the end of the tunnel.

As Rick Wolfe has documented, real median wages have been stagnant since the early 1970s in spite of steadily rising productivity. This opens a tremendous demand gap – wages are not even close to sufficient to buy the output our workers produce. And because we run an overall trade deficit, foreigners aren't buying them, either. Our domestic rich folk do more than their share of the buying, no doubt, but they are rather like Malthus's parsons and landlords. Ricardo correctly concluded that capitalists would do just as well to burn their extra output as to sell it to the nonproductive classes. Wall Street found the solution: fill the gap with loans to the working class so that the capitalists can sell the output and our rentier class can collect interest on the loans. Workers spend more than their incomes to keep the system afloat.

As a result, the dire strait of America's workers was long hidden behind a growing mountain of debt, and by a plethora of amazing gadgets (smartphones and flat screen TVs) kept cheap by outsourcing to foreign labor and purchased on credit. This was revealed in the GFC that began in 2007. Americans all over the US are still losing their homes to Wall Street's banks, hedge funds, and private equity – and remain burdened with mortgage debt even after they've lost the home that they now rent at exorbitant rents paid to the vultures scooping up blocks of foreclosed homes. They are also servicing debt on their autos and their student loans and their medical bills. Is it any wonder that they no longer feel middle-class, even if their incomes are above average? To add insult to injury, the "deplorables" heard Ms Clinton justifying her six-figure pay for cheerleader speeches given to Wall Street on the basis that "that's what they offered me".

Is it really so puzzling that they "voted against their own economic interests" when they chose Trump, who promised to throw a wrecking ball into the machinery that destroyed America's middle class? He would punish firms moving jobs overseas, tear up "free trade" agreements, go after Wall Street, drain the swamp, build a wall to block undocumented immigrants, fund infrastructure and create jobs, and Make America Great Again.

Above all, he would put America's interests first – a return of overt nationalism and rejection of foreign entanglements, in line with popular revolts that spread from the Arab spring to mainland Europe and finally to the UK before coming to rest in the USA. He had the answers to the questions most Americans were asking, while Hillary was busy creating technocratic policies to address questions most Americans had never thought to ask. And while Americans wanted jobs at decent pay, the mainstream media was obsessed with gender testing for bathrooms right up through the final days of the campaign. If there really are any aliens out there receiving American televised news channel signals, they will think that the biggest problem facing earthlings at the end of 2016 was finding a pot to piss in.

To conclude, in spite of the revelations of earlier shockingly misogynous behavior of Trump during the final weeks of the campaign, the loss of voters seems to have been in the "safe" states so that while Trump fell behind in the popular vote, he held on to the electoral college.
And we got Trumped.[12]

---

[12] As I wrote in 2012, "Here in the U.S., Donald Trump is known as a cartoonish buffoon – But he's no laughing matter in Scotland where he buys off the government and destroys a pristine and fragile coastal sand dune to build the world's biggest golf course. This moving documentary follows the efforts of the ordinary folk to preserve a fishing and farming community that, supposedly, stands in the way. You've Been Trumped is essential viewing for developing an understanding of the issues surrounding unchecked development, its impact on environmental sustainability, the unholy alliance of big money and public policy, and the consequence of excessive inequality that has divided our modern world between the 99% 'have-nots' and the one per-centers who've got it all but still want more." Wray 2012:

Economic prospects under Trump

Immediately after the election and long before the inauguration, the official media – as well as left-leaning websites – had a field day trying to best one another by imagining the most outlandish economic policies that Trump might propose, and then predicting the disastrous consequences. On taking office, Trump upped the ante by confirming expectations that neither he nor his staff has the competency required to run the Oval office. He really only attempted to implement one of his promised policies – blocking entry by Muslim terrorists and deporting undocumented residents – but disastrously bungled it by targeting particular nations as well as travelers with proper documents. By the third week in office he had already established a new kind of revolving door policy, as his designees either dropped out, or were forced to resign at an unprecedented pace. The White House was in complete disarray as insiders leaked info designed to demonstrate their boss's incompetence, and his party's leadership openly doubted his ability to serve.

To make matters worse, the Russian bear came back to haunt him.[13]

---

http://www.economonitor.com/lrwray/2012/11/15/youve-been-trumped-essential-viewing-for-the-99/.

[13] The media conveniently forgets that there is ample precedent for negotiations behind the back of a sitting president. The Nixon campaign tried to spoil President Johnson's peace talks with the Vietnamese, and there are reports that the Reagan campaign negotiated for a delay of the release of the hostages in Iran to undermine President Carter. So far, it appears that deals the Trump campaign struck with the Russians do not rise to the level of treason and did not directly endanger American lives. The Russians released information that was damaging to Clinton, but it was information Americans deserved to see. Trump's campaign might have talked with the Russians about lifting sanctions that were imposed by President Obama to punish them for letting Americans know that the Clinton campaign had rigged the primaries. Bad form? Yes. Illegal? Perhaps. Prolonging a war that would kill thousands of additional Americans? Not even close. See *Nixon Tried to Spoil Johnson's Vietnam Peace Talks in '68, Notes Show, New York Times,* https://www.nytimes.com/2017/01/02/us/politics/nixon-tried-to-spoil-johnsons-vietnam-peace-talks-in-68-notes-show.html?utm_source=huffingtonpost.com&utm_medium=referral&utm_campaign=pubexchange&_r=0 and *New Reports Say 1980 Reagan Campaign Tried to Delay Hostage Release, New York Times,* http://www.nytimes.com/1991/04/15/world/new-reports-say-1980-reagan-campaign-tried-to-delay-hostage-release.html

In recent days, the odds have risen that Trump will not make it through his first term in office. There are four ways Trump might leave office early: "(1) death; (2) impeachment by House and conviction by Senate; (3) suspension due to disability under the 25th Amendment; and (4) resignation."[14] Eighteen percent of US presidents died in office, half of them by assassination. Trump is the oldest president we've ever had, but life spans have risen and he has no known serious health problems. But he is wildly unpopular and has made a lot of enemies – including many in the US security establishment (not exactly the kind of enemy one wants). Dean Falvy puts the probability of death at 10%. Three presidents have been impeached (including Clinton), but only one was forced out of office (Nixon). Falvy puts Trump's chances at 25% if the Democrats regain control in the midterm elections. Removing a president from office due to incapacity is quite difficult; Falvy gives that a 10% chance. Trump would appear to be too vain to resign, but one could envision circumstances in which resignation might better preserve the value of the Trump brand than would serving out a miserable term of office. Falvy gives that 10%. Actual bettors are far more optimistic about the prospects of Trump leaving office: "Ladbrokes, the British oddsmaking giant, has Trump's chances of leaving office via resignation or impeachment and removal at just 11-to-10, or just a little worse than even money."[15]

In my view, it is more likely that Trump will finish his term. However, he will not be able to implement his agenda. He might cave to the mainstream Republicans and sign-off on some policy-making around the edges, but he will not successfully shepherd through any of his big ideas. Still, it is worthwhile to analyze what might have been. I will not attempt to fathom what Trump really wants, but rather will quickly assess a few proposals that were prominently featured in his campaign. But first let me add one anecdote.

Last spring I was approached by a well-known individual with Wall Street experience who claimed to be one of Trump's closest advisors. He had

---

[14] https://verdict.justia.com/2017/02/02/youre-fired-four-ways-donald-trumps-presidency-might-not-last-four-years.
[15] http://www.politico.com/story/2017/02/trump-impeachment-bets-234931.

come across some articles on "modern money theory"[16] in the mainstream press and wanted to compare notes. He agreed that sovereign governments face no financial constraints and budget deficits are not a problem; he understood that government spends through "keystroke" credits to bank accounts and cannot run out of keystrokes. He noted that Trump understands debt (during the campaign Trump proclaimed "I'm the king of debt").[17] Instead, he said, America faces three problems that Trump must resolve: unemployment remains too high, American wages are too low, and our infrastructure is a mess. He assured me that no matter what Trump might say during the campaign, these would be the main policy issues after Trump won. We went on to discuss a job guarantee – in which the government provides wages to ensure a job for anyone who wants to work.[18] While he agreed that the federal government can fund such a program, he doubted it would be competent to run one. Hence, he would have the federal government pay contractors to create the jobs. He asked me not to reveal his name as he preferred to work behind the scenes, but assured me he had Trump's ear. After the election he assumed a prominent position in the Trump administration.

What should we make of this? Does he really have Trump's ear? I suppose he does. However, it is becoming increasingly clear that Trump will not be able to manage Congress. It would take a powerful and trusted president to overturn nearly four decades of deficit hysteria, whipped up by both parties. Trump is weak, perhaps mortally wounded, and he never had the trust of his party's leadership. At best, what follows is a list of what might have been, focusing on three main areas Trump has addressed. I will not explore any of the areas that are typically of concern to mainstream Republicans: repealing Obamacare, ridding the nation of "welfare", deregulation, exercising greater control over women's bodies, arming the population with deadly military-style weapons, denial of the science of evolution and climate change, integrating church and state, and stacking the courts with troglodytes. I'll stick to Trump's more unusual proposals.

---

[16] See: https://www.washingtonpost.com/business/modern-monetary-theory-is-an-unconventional-take-on-economic-strategy/2012/02/15/gIQAR8uPMR_story.html?utm_term=.7bae6bdd44df.

[17] http://www.politico.com/story/2016/06/trump-king-of-debt-224642.

[18] http://www.nytimes.com/roomfordebate/2016/07/11/are-we-ready-for-the-next-recession/a-guaranteed-federal-jobs-program-is-needed.

1. Jobs and Infrastructure

Over the past year, much was made of our nation's infrastructure shortfall, with both Trump and Sanders promising major investments, and both of them made this part of their proposal to create jobs. A dozen years after Hurricane Katrina, and after countless other preventable deaths caused by deteriorating infrastructure, Northern California faces the prospect of collapse of its largest dam.

> "The nation's dams, which are 52 years old on average, earned a D grade from the American Society of Civil Engineers. The nation's levees, which were initially used to develop farmland but now often protect communities directly, earned an even worse D-minus. Overall, ASCE estimates that $3.6 trillion in investment is needed by 2020 to revitalize the nation's infrastructure... One of Trump's biggest promises for his first 100 days was to deliver a $1 trillion infrastructure plan to Congress. But Senate Majority Leader Mitch McConnell (R-Ky.) poured cold water over the idea of a large spending package in December, telling reporters he hoped to avoid "a trillion-dollar stimulus."[19]

Note that this $3.6 trillion would just fix what we've got – it would not move us into the 21st century. The problem is that our nation's elite do not rely on America's public infrastructure. They helicopter to and fro in Manhattan – from heliport to heliport far above the filth and decay; they ride in increasingly lavish "upper class" lounges on jets (if they cannot afford their own gold-plated personal airliners) as they circle the globe; they've got immaculate, gated communities with private security; their kids attend elite private schools in idyllic preserves in the Northeast. They don't need "a trillion-dollar stimulus", and they really don't care if China – or even Vietnam

---

[19] http://www.huffingtonpost.com/entry/oroville-dam-infrastructure-spending_us_58a21be4e4b03df370d922c0?iooux06vgnbmg3nmi&&utm_medium=email&utm_campaign=The%20Morning%20Email%20021417&utm_content=The%20Morning%20Email%20021417+CID_d3859488c36e68160b30ceee2c941d99&utm_source=Email%20marketing%20software&utm_term=about%20American%20infrastructure&.

– sets the global standard for public infrastructure. Trump is not going to get a major infrastructure plan through this Congress.

What might have been? While I would prefer a New Deal-style jobs program to repair the old and invest in the new, Trump would most likely have used government contracting plus tax incentives to build infrastructure. This would make the investment much more expensive (and more open to corruption) and less responsive to public needs. It would create some jobs, but construction would be capital intensive and require skilled labor. It would probably come up against capacity constraints – at least in many areas – raising skilled wages and total costs. While some jobs and perhaps higher wages would trickle down, the program would not provide enough jobs where they are most needed, and would not significantly raise wages at the bottom.

By comparison, a New Deal-style program would create jobs for those of lower skill levels; it could be designed to be less capital-intensive; projects could be targeted where infrastructure needs are greatest and where joblessness is highest; and wages could be compressed – as a matter of policy – by raising them at the bottom. The New Deal's WPA[20] played an important role in bringing USA into the 20th century, putting in place the infrastructure needed to "make America great"; a WPA-style jobs and infrastructure program could help to "make America great again" for the 21st. But Trump is not likely to be the President to see that through.

Note that Trump promised to create 25 million new jobs over the next decade, and while that number is in the right ballpark if we are to reach full employment *now (not ten years from now)*, his infrastructure plan would have provided only a small fraction of the jobs needed to reach the goal. Any serious job creation program will have to include an array of jobs across the entire country. Many of these will need to be in provision of public services (elder care and child care, for example) – not only is that a neglected area but it will provide jobs for those who cannot work in construction. The

---

[20] Works Progress Administration, which employed nearly 8.5 million workers during the New Deal mostly for construction of public projects. The US today still enjoys many of those projects. See Taylor 2008, *American Made: The enduring legacy of the WPA: when FDR put the nation to work*, Tantor Media.

infrastructure-oriented focus adopted by both Trump and Sanders will neglect women as well as older workers and those with disabilities. An inclusive nation-wide program that creates useful jobs in every community will be necessary.

2. *The Wall and NAFTA*

One of Trump's favorite policies is to build a "Great Wall" along our southern border. The current estimate is that a system of fences and walls running 1250 miles will take about three years to complete and cost about $22 billion – almost twice the $12 billion figure Trump used in the campaign. (He claims his negotiating expertise will cut that higher figure significantly; history provides reason to expect the actual costs will exceed even the high estimate by a substantial amount: big government projects usually run over budget.)[21] The Wall is too popular among Trump's broad base for Republicans to ignore it. The most likely compromise with Congress will lead to substantially less than Trump's $12 billion figure; the construction will be scaled back, and it will not be finished before the end of Trump's first (and only) term.

Even the smaller project will face labor and equipment shortages, price gouging and localized wage pressures. Relying on regional companies and local labor will create bottlenecks in the construction sector. While the US still has ample unemployment around the country, the unemployed are not where they are needed and they do not have the skills and experience required by firms using sophisticated construction equipment and capital-intensive labor on the border. While we would not want to precisely replicate the 1930s projects, a New Deal-style WPA and CCC approach[22] would use unemployed labor. It would be less likely to cause inflation and would create the kinds of jobs our unemployed need.

---

[21] http://www.huffingtonpost.com/entry/trump-border-wall-cost_us_589cf9d9e4b0ab2d2b13ae7b?ytwsf6htga11exw29&&utm_medium=email&utm_campaign=The%20Morning%20Email%20021017&utm_content=The%20Morning%20Email%20021017+CID_3664cee32f01ecd126a0fd90bff70fea&utm_source=Email%20marketing%20software&utm_term=Reuters&

[22] Civilian Conservation Corps; a New Deal program that employed 3 million young men to work on public lands.

Trumponomics: Causes And Consequences

Trump has promised to send the bill to Mexico for payment. While this is popular with the base, it has created tensions with Mexico and problems for President Nieto – whose popularity is now far below Trump's. Here's a better idea: let Mexico build it and send the bill to the US.

Trump must change course. First he must issue a public apology for his derogatory statements and insulting behavior. Second, he should propose a bilateral commission to study border security to determine how best to reduce the flow of undocumented migrants, human trafficking, and drugs across the border. Presumably, at least some sections of the border will be recommended for barrier construction. The "Wall" must be a joint project, with the US providing the funding and with the construction jointly managed. Mexico needs good paying jobs – the lack of which fuels immigration to the US in search of them. The slack labor markets in Mexico will help to minimize inflationary impacts there, and spending on Mexican labor is not likely to fuel inflation in the US – unlike the case in which skilled American workers are hired to build the wall. Mexico needs dollars to replace the remittances she lost when the US economy slowed and the dollars she will lose if the flow of migrants to America is attenuated.

In addition to funding the construction, Trump would negotiate a plan for cooperative management of the completed wall – each nation benefits from secure borders, and co-management would increase trust. Both Presidents come home as winners. New facilities should be built along the border to quickly and humanely process people who want to cross. Cooperation on the Wall also helps to take the rhetoric about retaliatory trade sanctions down a notch. For the squeamish who insist that a border wall is by its very nature unacceptable, note that we've already got 654 miles of "fortification" along the border, and we are not alone in erecting new walls – Europe is busy building more of them than any other region. While the construction crews are at it, they can repair and build new public infrastructure (roads, public utilities, and waterways) along the border to better link our two nations. Both nations will benefit by improved relations, secure borders, less trafficking in humans, drugs, and guns, and legitimized border crossings. This might make it easier to get rational immigration policy in the US.

And while we are on the topic, renegotiation of NAFTA is long overdue.[23] From inception, this was a neoliberal treaty that operates against the interests of the majority of the population in both countries. It is bad for American labor and bad for Mexican agriculture. It benefits "intellectual property rights", finance, and megacorporations – all of which fuel growing inequality in the US and migration from Mexico. While discussion of NAFTA is always put in the context of the supposed benefits of "free trade", this framing benefits the neoliberal interest and has almost no basis in reality. Trump is right when he says NAFTA is a bad deal for America, but he probably neither understands what the problem is, nor has a snowball's chance in hell of gutting the treaty.

3. End globalization and bring the jobs home

Trump has put forward a number of proposals related to the theme of ending globalization – including renegotiating NAFTA and pulling out of the TPP – many of which were directed at China and other exporters. Like many American politicians, Trump has claimed that China is a "currency manipulator" and promises to pursue an investigation. He's proposed large tariffs to be slapped on imports (variously suggested as 45% on Chinese exports to the US, 20% on all imports, and 35% on Mexican imports)[24], and particularly on American firms that move jobs overseas (proposing a 15% tax on firms that do so). As mentioned, he promised to create 25 million good jobs over the next decade, many of those by bringing the jobs home. One of his first acts was to "save" jobs at Carrier that had been destined to go to Mexico – supposedly proof of his touted negotiation skills – and suggests he will continue to put pressure on individual firms to stay put.

At the same time, Trump has proposed to reduce the tax burdens that presumably discourage job creation and encourage tax avoidance (including corporate inversions). He has variously proposed a flat tax on firms of 15%, and a one-time repatriation of corporate profits at a special 10% rate. Here's a better idea: eliminate the corporate income tax. Economic theory suggests that the tax is largely passed forward to consumers or backward to workers.

---

[23] http://readersupportednews.org/opinion2/277-75/41658-in-fight-with-trump-mexico-has-plenty-of-ways-to-punch-back.

[24] https://www.politiplatform.com/trump.

It induces firms to make many decisions – such as location of headquarters as well as taking on debt – on the basis of tax avoidance rather than sound business principles. To the extent that profits are paid out in the form of dividends, they get taxed as personal income. In theory, we should also tax retained earnings to the extent that these drive up share prices and hence increase personal wealth – otherwise elimination of the corporate income tax might increase the incentive to retain earnings and thereby exclude them from ever getting taxed (except for capital gains, which are taxed at a lower rate than income). In practice, imputing retained profits to individuals so that they can be taxed as income might be too difficult. In this particular case, the good should not be seen as the enemy of perfection: let's just drop the corporate income tax, increasing the incentive to make and report profits, as well as eliminating the disincentive to seek low tax havens.

With regard to the promise to punish "currency manipulators", this is as silly as punishing countries that are "fiscal policy manipulators" (who, for example, keep domestic unemployment high and wages low so that they can export), or punishing "monetary policy manipulators" (who use interest rate policy to pursue perceived self-interest). I am sympathetic to those who call for pushing "fair trade" over "free trade" – we should not accept the exports produced by slave or child labor, or by labor working in dangerous conditions or below subsistence wages. However, the exchange rate is a legitimate policy tool in the same way that interest rate targets or inflation targets or fiscal balance are used to pursue national economic interests. While the US has embraced floating exchange rates as useful in promoting its national interests, many nations (rightly or wrongly) see control over exchange rates as necessary to promote theirs. In truth, China has been letting its exchange rate rise (the recent large capital outflow reversed course) while pursuing a strategy of rapid wage increase in spite of trend inflation.

Trump needs to understand that the US issues the international reserve currency – the dollar. The rest of the world wants and needs dollars and so will operate domestic policy to ensure dollar inflows. No matter how many tariffs Trump imposes and no matter how much he tries to keep jobs in the US, the US current account balance largely will be determined by the rest of the world's desire for dollars. Making them scarce by restraining imports will only increase global efforts to undermine Trump's policy. "Bringing the jobs home" will not be a significant source of job creation anyway – we need to focus on creating new jobs at home, not on enacting penalties or tariffs. The US is too big (and too rich) to engage in beggar-thy-neighbor policy.

And we need to provide decent pay for those new jobs. There might be some role for trade policy to promote "fair trade" in specific instances to protect American wages. Trump is right to reject the claim that "free trade" is always good, and to insist that domestic policy should consider the interests of American workers. That is what democratic representation is all about.

Conclusion

There is growing resistance to neoliberalism, as promulgated by the Clintons, the Bushes, and unfortunately, by Obama. There is growing recognition of neoliberalism's role in creating job losses, reducing national sovereignty, and losing ability to control domestic corporations, corporate agriculture, and big finance. It is convenient for the neoliberals to push "Tina" – the argument that there is no alternative to the neoliberal globalization agenda; that people must serve the economy; that the market is supreme. But we must not be fooled. Neoliberalism is a choice we can reject.

Supporters of Trump and Sanders realized that there's something wrong with this picture. They are not sure what it is. Some grasp at strawmen: immigrants, minorities, women. Some align with despicable characters: white supremacists, anarchists, fascists, homophobes, misogynists, nativists. In any case, they are tired of playing along. The promise that if they'll subject themselves to the global economy, it will eventually pay off, rings hollow. They've held wages in check while labor productivity grew tremendously, but all they got was pain and no gain.

Our comfortable elitists – whether Democrats or Republicans – focus on the despicables, on the deplorables, on the takers. The last 45 years of neoliberalism has been good to the elite, even very, very good. They dismiss the most recent election as an aberration, a mass exercise in delusion. Both parties focus on Trump's peculiarities – this is one of those black swan events that will not be repeated for another hundred thousand years. Trumpism has an expiration date. Neither party need change its strategy.

The Democrats will win the next presidential election, but that does not mean the people that the party supposedly represents will win. The recent election of the new leader of the DNC has determined that the party will stay the course: the Clinton/Obama candidate, Tom Perez, defeated the Sanders candidate, Keith Ellison. There will be no reform; Wall Street remains in the saddle. The DNC (as well as the GOP – "Grand Old Party", the Republicans) hopes that the energies of the disaffected will be exhausted by the 24-7 protests against Trump. But the residual anger could help to push through a better candidate than Hillary.

What we need is a recognition that it does not have to be this way. The economy should serve the people. We do not have to accept "market" outcomes. There is no "invisible hand" guiding us toward equilibrium. All economies are always controlled – the only questions are *by whom* and *for whom*. Our economy has increasingly become controlled by and for the top one percent, or – really – by and for the top one-tenth of one percent. The election of Trump (or of Clinton) could not change that. It is possible that a perfect storm is building – fueled by the election of Trump and also by the bail-out of Wall Street that makes another global financial crisis all but inevitable.[25] If that happens sooner rather than later, there could be an opening for real change.

---

[25] Geithner argues that a crisis is inevitable, although he blames the restrictions placed on policy-makers by Dodd-Frank.
https://www.foreignaffairs.com/articles/united-states/2016-12-12/are-we-safe-yet.

The fall of the US middle class and the hair-raising ascent of Donald Trump

Steven Pressman [Colorado State University, CO, USA]

1. Introduction

According to Thomas Piketty (2014), between 1980 and 2010 the share of total US income going to the top 10% of earners rose from around 30-35%, where it stood for several decades, to nearly 50%. These are very conservative estimates. Piketty's figures come from the distribution of adjusted gross income (AGI), reported by the US Internal Revenue Service. AGI subtracts from income things like investment losses, retirement account contributions and their returns (see Pressman 2015, Chapter 2). With large adjustments, someone can make a lot of money but have little AGI; or, as in the case of Donald Trump, you can report a *negative* AGI of nearly $1 billion. In addition, tax-free income (such as unrealized capital gains and interest on municipal bonds), as well as returns on money hidden in tax havens, are not reported to the IRS and do not appear in AGI. Like the adjustments helping Trump avoid taxes, this income mainly goes to the wealthy and has been growing for several decades (Zucman, 2015).

As the rich received a bigger piece of the pie, everyone else got relatively less. We can see this in the falling share of income going to the middle-three income quintiles (Figure 1).

One standard economic argument for great inequality is that it generates incentives to make money and contributes to economic growth, which increases average living standards. Even if this is true, not everyone benefits from growth. Saez and Piketty (2013) estimate that since the late 1970s nearly 60% of all gains from growth have gone to the top 1%, roughly those making $500,000 or more in 2016.[1] Consequently, a typical US household

---

[1] The thresholds in Saez and Piketty (2013) need to be increased due to inflation and income not included in AGI.

has seen little improvement in their absolute standard of living for several decades. We can see this in figures on real median household income, which increased only slightly over the past quarter century – growing from $54,432 in 1988 to $56,516 in 2015.[2]

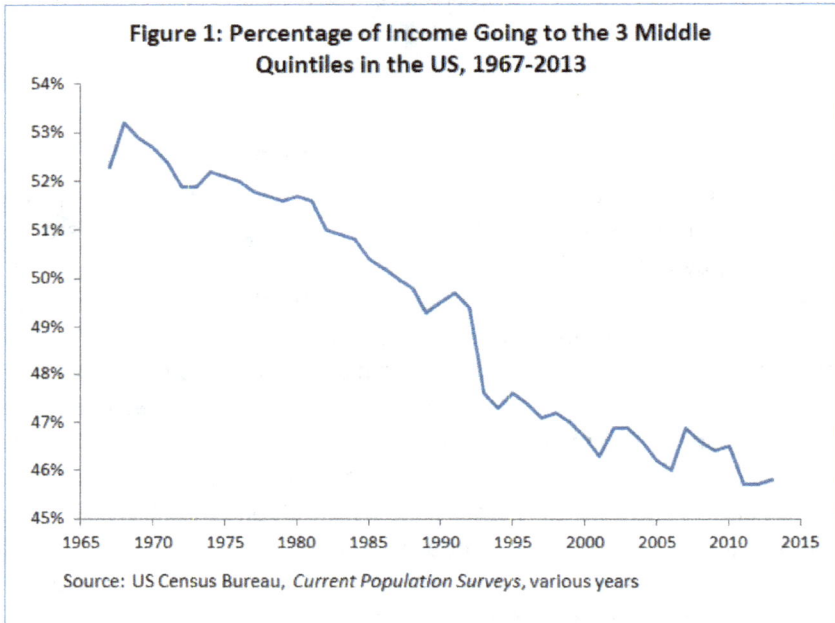

Figure 1: Percentage of Income Going to the 3 Middle Quintiles in the US, 1967-2013

Source: US Census Bureau, *Current Population Surveys,* various years

We focus here on another distributional measure – the size of the middle class. A thriving middle class is important for a number of reasons. First, there are political factors. Rothstein & Uslaner (2005, p. 52) argue that inequality reduces social capital or the trust needed to sustain democracy. Second, Robert Malthus (2008[1803], p. 594) noted: "Our best grounded expectations of an increase in the happiness of the mass of human society are founded in the prospect of an increase in the relative proportions of the middle parts." For Malthus, the additional income that moves one from poverty into the middle class is what makes life worthwhile. Finally, a large middle class improves economic performance. Alfred Marshall (1920, pp. 529-32, 566-9) noted that higher earnings may improve the habits of working

---

[2] Remarkably, the 2014 figure was *below* the 1988 figure.

people, thereby improving productivity and everyone's standard of living. From a Keynesian perspective, a large middle class increases consumption, effective demand and economic growth because middle-class households tend to spend larger fractions of their income than wealthy households.

This paper focuses on one particular political consequence of a shrinking middle class. It contends that this was a key factor in Donald Trump becoming President of the United States. Then it argues that the policies promulgated by Trump will not help the US middle class but will exacerbate recent inequality trends. The paper concludes with some suggestions for reviving the middle class. But first a measurement issue.

2.   Who is middle class and what has happened to the middle class?

Numbers are important for understanding how economies work and developing policies that improve economic performance. Simon Kuznets developed national income accounting to measure economic growth. Irving Fisher developed price indices to compute the rate of inflation. And Mollie Orshansky developed the official US poverty rate. These enabled us to study the factors affecting these variables, and how we might increase growth, control inflation and reduce poverty.

Presently there is no accepted definition of "middle class", and no figures get calculated and reported regularly. This makes it difficult to ascertain if the US middle class has declined, identify factors that expand or shrink the middle class, or develop policies that might bolster the middle class. To measure the size of the middle class this paper follows the Orshansky methodology for measuring poverty.

Orshansky (1965, 1969) began with data on the minimum food requirements for families of different sizes to survive during one year; then she estimated the cost of purchasing this food. Government surveys of household expenditures, undertaken during the 1940s and the 1950s, found that families (on average) spent around one-third of their income on food. So Orshansky multiplied the cost of a minimum food budget for each family size by three in order to arrive at their minimum income needs. These became the official US poverty thresholds. Each year they get increased by the annual rate of inflation.

To measure the size of the middle class we start, like Orshansky, with some data. In 2010 the Pew Research Center asked people how much income was necessary for a four-person family to be middle class in their neighborhood. While answers varied by location and income level (those living in cities and making more money provided larger figures), $70,000 was the median response. Wider Opportunities for Women (WOW) estimated that a household with two working parents and two children needed $68,136 in 2010 to have some economic security. This bought basic necessities and allowed some savings for retirement and emergencies. Finally, median income for a family of four in the US in 2010 was $68,274. If the Pew figure stems from the fact that people like nice round numbers, we can take the median income for a four-person family as the midpoint of the middle-class income range for a family of four.[3] The Pew Research Center (2012) also found that a preponderance of responses fell between two-thirds and twice the median income. Some differences stemmed from different perceptions regarding what was necessary to be middle class and some from regional cost of living differences.

Rather than focusing on income, we focus on *disposable income* to define the "middle class" because this is what people care about and what households use to purchase a middle-class standard of living. Moreover, changes in taxation over time affect a family's standard of living. One frequent criticism of the Orshansky poverty definition is that it failed to account for taxes paid by low-income households (Pressman 2013).

To compute the size of the middle class for any country in any given year, we start with the median income for a family of four. Next we convert this to median disposable income based on income taxes and payroll taxes paid, as well as government benefits received, and compute the percentage of households whose disposable income falls between two-thirds and twice median disposable income. For households of other sizes, we adjust median income for a family of four using the Orshansky adjustments for families of

---

[3] This is a better data source than the similar WOW estimate because it is available annually and over a long time period.

different sizes. Middle-class households are those whose disposable incomes fall between 67% and 200% of the median disposable income for a household of that size.

Table 1 shows middle-class income ranges in 2013 based on market income (rather than disposable income) since this is the typical reference point for most people. These numbers all seem reasonable. The lower figure is more than twice the Orshansky poverty thresholds, meeting the Horrigan and Haugen (1988) criterion for defining the middle class, and the top figure is not so high that we would consider a family wealthy.

One minor flaw in this procedure is that it doesn't account for falling median household income, as occurred during the Great Recession. In such situations, households may still be counted as middle class because of the fall in median income, but they will not feel middle class any longer. To deal with this issue we make one adjustment to our estimates. When real median income falls, we use the *highest previous real median income* and calculate the size of the middle class using that figure.

Table 1: Middle-Class Income Range for 2013	
HOUSEHOLD SIZE	INCOME RANGE (Household Income)
1	$28,569-$85,281
2	$37,140-$110,865
3	$45,710-$136,449
4	$54,281-$162,033
5	$62,852-$187,617
6	$71,422-$213,201
7	$79,993-$238,786
8	$88,564-$264,370
9+	$97,135-$289,954
Source: See Paper	

Figure 2 plots the percentage of middle-class households in the US between 1974 and 2013 using our methodology and the Luxembourg Income Study (LIS),[4] an international database of income and socio-demographic information. LIS data for the US came from annual Census Bureau household surveys.

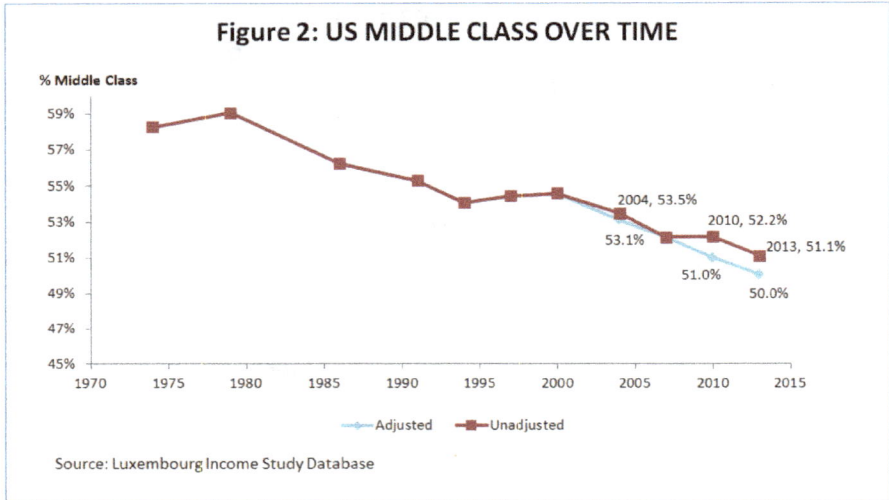

Figure 2: US MIDDLE CLASS OVER TIME

Source: Luxembourg Income Study Database

Undoubtedly the US middle class has shrunk since the 1980s, when it comprised 59% of all households. The only exception was the economic boom of the late 1990s when the size of the US middle class held steady. Figure 2 also shows what happens when our computations do not allow median household income to fall. The main adjustments occur after the Great Recession. In 2010, median household income for a family of four was $4,800 below the inflation-adjusted figure for 2007. Taking this into account reduces the size of the middle class by 1.2 percentage points. In 2013 median household income for a family of four was more than $5,100 below the inflation-adjusted figure for 2007. Using the higher real median income from 2007 reduces the size of the US middle class to just 50% in 2013.

For comparison purposes, Figures 3–5 show changes in the size of the middle class over time in eight other developed nations. Nations are divided

---

[4] For more on LIS, see their homepage at www.lisdatacenter.org.

into three groups – Anglo-Saxon countries, continental Europe and the Nordic nations. These three figures make clear that what happened in the US did not happen elsewhere. In some countries (Canada, Italy and Norway) the size of the middle class has remained relatively stable since the 1980s; in other countries (France) the middle class increased in size. Some countries show a U-shaped curve over time (the UK), while for others it looks more like an inverted U (Canada).

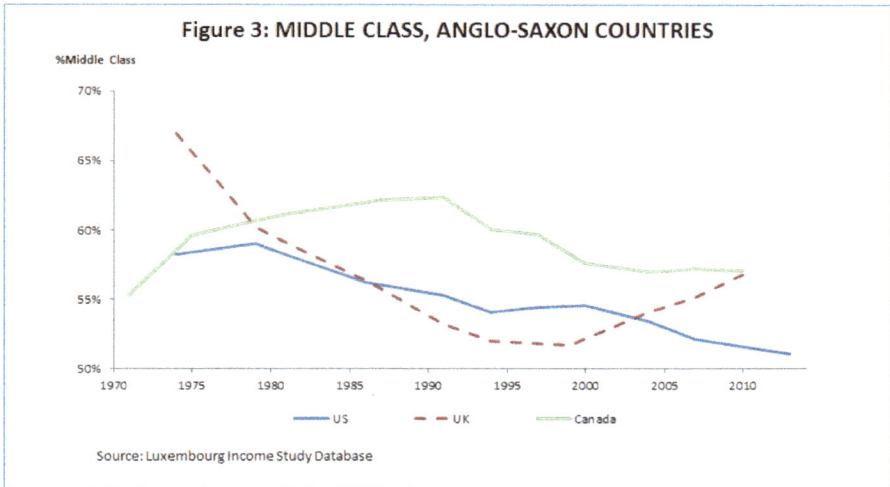

Figure 3: MIDDLE CLASS, ANGLO-SAXON COUNTRIES

Source: Luxembourg Income Study Database

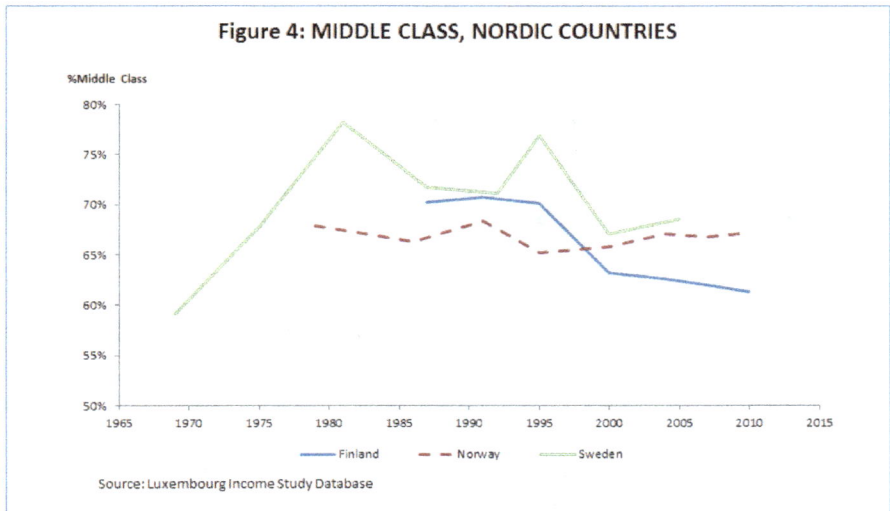

Figure 4: MIDDLE CLASS, NORDIC COUNTRIES

Source: Luxembourg Income Study Database

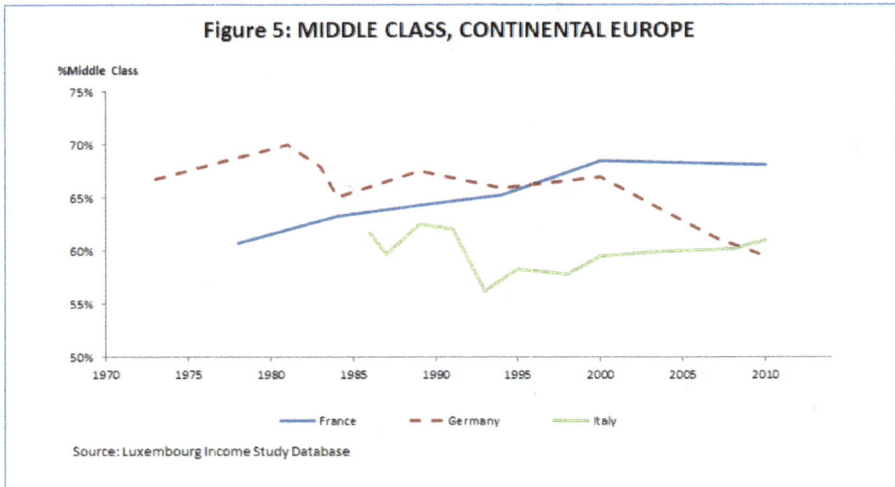

Figure 5: MIDDLE CLASS, CONTINENTAL EUROPE

Finally, like Piketty's computations of top income shares, these figures underestimate the true decline of the US middle class. More people work in a typical household today compared to 1980, and people work more jobs. This increases living costs because households must spend more on clothing, food and transportation. Most important is the additional cost of child care (Giannarelli and Barsimantov 2000). This means that the higher income from sending another family member into the workforce does not result in an equivalent increase in the family living standard. In addition, a weaker social safety net means that in hard economic times most people must resort to borrowing. Households must then repay this debt, with interest, thereby lowering their standard of living. Consumer debt (excluding mortgage debt) has been rising sharply in the US with time. Subtracting just the interest on consumer debt, reduced the size of the US middle class by 3.6 percentage points in 2010 according to Scott and Pressman (2013).

3. The decline of the middle class and the rise of Donald Trump

The American Dream of a middle-class life has been slowly receding. This is evident in Figure 2, and in survey data (Pew Research Center 2012). It is not clear from other government data. At the end of 2016 the US unemployment rate fell below 5%, inflation was under 2%, real wages were rising, and GDP grew at a 2% rate. Such good numbers typically result in victory for the political party currently in power. Not in 2016 – mainly due to distributional factors. Recovery from the Great Recession bypassed many households. Those without a college degree fared worst of all. Feeling the effects of this, and worried about their future, many Americans lashed out the only way possible – at the voting booth.

Donald Trump's political genius was to tap into this rage and fear. Appealing to millions of families who felt left behind in 21st-century America, Trump promised a return to the glory days of the mid-20th century, when the future appeared bright and middle-income households did much better. He denounced Washington, especially the trade and immigration policies that he blamed for destroying the America he wanted to make great again.

Trump's Democratic opponent, Hillary Clinton, failed to address the problems facing average Americans and failed to develop a simple message about restoring middle-class jobs. She rejected future trade deals like the Trans-Pacific Partnership, but said nothing about old trade deals like NAFTA, which was signed by her husband President Bill Clinton. More positively, she talked about raising the minimum wage, providing free education and improving Obamacare (rather than replacing it with something better). But it is not clear how any of this solves the problem of a shrinking middle class. A $15/hour minimum wage does little good if there are few full-time jobs available. Free college education doesn't help people not prepared to go to college. And while Obamacare has provided some security to tens of millions of American families, it hasn't generated jobs or higher incomes; yet it requires everyone to buy health insurance or pay a tax penalty.

Instead of attacking Trumponomics, Clinton went after the low-hanging fruit – Trump's personality and behavior. For those struggling on a daily basis, with little savings for emergencies and worried about the future, this provided little hope. Many people cared more about their own economic prospects than Trump's misogyny or his mocking impersonation of a disabled reporter.

Trump became President because he won several states that typically vote Democratic (Pennsylvania, Michigan and Wisconsin) in Presidential elections plus two key swing states (Florida and Ohio). With one exception, these are all states where real median incomes dropped considerably between 2007 and 2015. While the average state decline was $600, Florida ($-3,524) Michigan ($-2,234), Ohio ($-2,826) and Wisconsin ($-3,192) all experienced sharp drops in median household income. Only in Pennsylvania (+$5,019), a state that Clinton lost by only around half a percentage point, did median household income rise. But Pennsylvania also experienced one of the largest increases in equality over several decades (measured in terms of the share of state income going to the top 10%); only three reliably blue New England states (Connecticut, Massachusetts and Rhode Island) did worse on this metric (Frank, 2014). While other factors affect voting, polling data also indicate that Trump's greatest support came from those groups experiencing the greatest financial problems over the previous decade (Kolko, 2016). Clinton's support came from well-educated voters; she did poorly, and Trump did extremely well, in counties with a small share of college graduates (Silver, 2016). And those with a college educated did best in recovering from the Great Recession.

4. Will Trumponomics help the middle class?

"Make America Great Again" is essentially Trump's promise to revive the US middle class. But sometimes promises are hard to keep. According to Trump, the problem is that immigrants and the US trade deficit took good jobs from hard-working Americans. Going further, his inauguration speech claimed that the wealth of the middle class was ripped away and distributed to the rest of the world. This analysis gets most everything wrong.

Foreign countries did not abscond with US wealth. Housing, the largest source of wealth middle-class wealth (Piketty, 2014), was lost because large US financial institutions traded campaign contributions for deregulation (such as repealing Glass-Steagall). This enabled these institutions to develop an array of toxic securities, leading to the housing bubble, its implosion and the Great Recession.

Likewise, immigration and large US trade deficits are not destroying good jobs with high incomes. Here's one way to clearly see this. Developed nations look rather similar in terms of the size of the middle class based on market income; large differences arise only when we look at disposable income (Pressman, 2010). This indicates that the problem is *not* globalization or foreign competition, since all developed countries experienced greater competition from low-wage nations. Nonetheless, many counties managed to maintain the size of their middle class; a few even saw a growing middle class. The reason for these cross-national differences, it seems, depends on what happens within each nation or on the government policies that transform market income into disposable income.

The problem is that the US government has failed to support working Americans, believing that the free market will solve all economic problems. This belief system has led to lower incomes and less wealth for many households. It has decimated the US middle class. This belief system also underpins Trump's main policy prescriptions – deregulation and large tax cuts for the wealthy, protectionism ("the wall") and repealing Obamacare. None of these policies will actually help Trump supporters or help rebuild the US middle class.

The US has given large tax cuts to the wealthy many times, most notably during the Reagan years and the 2000s with George Bush. In part, the policy was successful; Keynes (1936) was right that tax cuts boost spending and output. But tax cuts provide a smaller bang for the buck than increased government expenditures.

Even with large tax cuts stimulating demand, business investment also depends on what Keynes (1936, p. 161) called "animal spirits". Trump is his own worst enemy here. If a company makes a decision that Trump dislikes or a CEO says something critical of him, Trump can rant on Twitter, leading his supporters to boycott the company. We have already seen such behavior by Trump after Nordstrom dropped his daughter Ivanka's clothing line from their department stores. It is impossible to predict who Trump might lash out against and what economic impact it might have. Facing such uncertainty, firms will be reluctant to invest in the US. And without large business investment, large job gains are unlikely.

Further, large tax cuts for the wealthy provide incentives to cut wages and increase corporate profits. Workers are pushed harder but don't gain from their extra efforts. As we saw, the average worker has seen little gain from their greater productivity since large cuts in marginal tax rates were passed during the Reagan era. Most gains have gone to the top 1%.

Piketty and Saez (2013) show that those countries lowering their top marginal tax rates the most tended to have the largest increase in the share of total income going to the top 1%. They contend that this relationship is causal. First, they argue that income stems from bargaining power rather than marginal productivity. Second, they contend that incentives matter. When marginal tax rates are very high it is not worth it for CEOs to fight compensation committees for a little more income since most of it will go to the government. With low marginal tax rates, CEOs keep a large fraction of any extra income and have great incentives to fight for higher pay. We can add a third factor. Since the 1980s CEO compensation has increasingly come to depend on stock performance and comes in the form of stock options. Economists argued that this would solve principal-agent problems by aligning the incentives of CEOs and the incentives of investors (Jensen and Meckling 1976). However, this is true only in the short run. A focus on stock prices creates incentives to cut costs, and labor constitutes the largest cost for firms. As a result, senior executives sought to reduce wages and benefits. Although this might reduce demand and harm long-run firm performance, CEOs cared more about their current pay; their successor would have to deal with any long-run problems. It is for this reason that tax cuts for the rich have not helped the middle class in the past. What Trump proposes will increase pressure for wage cuts.

A related problem is how to pay for large tax cuts geared to the wealthy. While Trump claims that deregulation and tax cuts will generate faster growth, and while Congressional Republicans can force the Congressional Budget Office to use "dynamic forecasting" and conclude that economic growth and tax revenues will both increase, based on past experience and what we know about economic relationships this won't happen.

One possible solution is Trump's suggested 10% "repatriation rate", which would encourage corporations to bring profits earned abroad back into the US. With $2.6 trillion parked abroad, this will provide some money to fund a large tax cut (Huang, 2016). Other revenue may come from people selling assets now in the belief that low marginal tax rates will not last and they should benefit while the going is good.

Once these temporary revenue streams dry up, tax cuts will have to be paid for by some other means. Trump has blamed government waste and fraud for the US budget deficit, but the amounts involved are far too low to close an annual budget gap of $600 billion plus another $500 billion if Trump's tax cut plan passes (Cole, 2016). Popular measures among many Trump supporters, such as defunding the Corporation for Public Broadcasting and ending all foreign aid, won't significantly reduce a deficit exceeding $1 trillion. Hiring freezes and pay cuts for government employees won't do much better. The bottom line is that if you exclude military spending (which Trump wants to increase) and non-discretionary spending (Social Security, Medicare, interest on the debt) only $600 billion in government spending remains. If cut by half, this would not eliminate the current deficit and cannot finance Trump's tax cuts. While Trump has suggested negotiating down US debt, this "haircut" would lead investors to flee US government securities and raise government borrowing costs. So the only way to keep the Federal budget deficit from soaring due to Trump's tax cut plan is to cut Medicare, Social Security, and other programs that benefit middle-class households.

The big losers in this process will be Trump supporters, who get miniscule tax breaks, and Trump himself, who will have to explain why the budget deficit exploded under his watch. Additional borrowing by the US Treasury, plus news reports of massive deficits and record debt, will be hard to rebuff as "fake news". It will also put upward pressure on interest rates, raising borrowing costs for Trump supporters living hand-to-mouth and in debt. This too will be difficult to deny or dismiss.

Protectionism may save a few jobs, but tariffs and other trade restrictions will also push up prices and lower US living standards.

Trump is right that the US trade deficit reduces jobs and lowers incomes. Workers are hurt when production goes abroad and they must try to find new employment, possibly at a much lower wage. The big flaw in his argument is that manufacturing jobs comprise a small fraction of US employment and they do not require employers pay decent wages and benefits.

Manufacturing firms producing in China and Mexico do not pay their workers well, and service jobs in the US actually pay production and non-supervisory workers more (on average) than manufacturing jobs do (Wolff, 2017).

Coal mining provides a good example of what is wrong with trying to save production jobs. In the US and elsewhere these jobs have paid good wages for many years. But this has not always been the case. Émile Zola's novel *Germinal* (and the excellent movie starring Gérard Depardieu) makes it clear that these were awful jobs paying bare subsistence wages. They became better only when French workers organized, demanded better wages and working conditions, and the French government supported their right to unionize. US manufacturing jobs have paid well historically because US workers unionized and they used their power to counter the power of large business firms and obtain higher wages, generous benefits and better working conditions. Something similar can take place in the service sector today – if we had a government willing to support unions and increase the minimum wage.

Another problem is that even if high-paying manufacturing jobs return to the US, they will not go to Trump supporters. These jobs require education and computer skills to run the actual production process. At some point, despite Trump's assertions that he has made America great again, Trump's supporters will come to realize that they don't have better jobs or bigger paychecks.

Finally, there is Obamacare. After taking office, President Obama saw affordable health care as one way to help middle-class and working-class households priced out of insurance markets. To the detriment of Democrats and the benefit of Trump, Obamacare insurance premiums rose sharply right before the 2016 election. And, as noted earlier, Obamacare did not result in any economic gains to make the required insurance more affordable.

Repealing Obamacare will help some young and healthy workers who can get by without health insurance. If these people don't buy insurance, the cost of providing insurance to everyone else increases and companies will raise rates. This will drive others from the insurance pool, mainly those less expensive to insure because they are healthier. Again, rates will rise. The end result will be extremely costly insurance for those who need it most and many people without health insurance.

Trump promised to replace Obamacare with something better, but this will not be easy. Repealing any aspect of Obamacare will cause the whole thing to collapse. Ending the insurance mandate will lead to problems described in the paragraph above. Ending the requirements that insurance companies cover pre-existing conditions and pool risks to determine rates will either increase rates or leave important health care needs uncovered. Low-income individuals lacking a college degree (strong Trump supporters) will be hurt the most. They are less likely to have health insurance through work, and more likely to require health care given the relationships between education level, income, and health.

After criticizing Obamacare vehemently while campaigning, Trump will have to do something to replace it. As this was being was written (in mid-February), the solution seemed to be tax credits to purchase insurance for those without health insurance through work or the government. This won't do any good for those with some pre-existing condition. Worse yet, the tax credits will increase with age rather than decline with rising income, as under Obamacare (Sanger-Katz 2017). The likely result is that many middle-class households will find themselves priced out of the health insurance market. We can count on gruesome news stories about people denied health care as a result of these changes, and we can expect similar results from any other Republican plan for replacing Obamacare. Trump can Tweet that these horror stories are lies, but when many people know someone that this has happened to, and when real people appear on TV to speak about their problems, many will long for the good old days when we had Obamacare to kick around.

In sum, Trump's main policy proposals will not help the people who voted him into power. The losers (to use one of Trump's favorite expressions) will be working-class voters without a college degree who were recently pushed out of the middle class or are struggling hard to remain there.

5.   Where do we go from here?

It is not enough to point out that Trump's policies won't revive the US middle class. Policy failure should open the door for practical alternatives. Here are a few suggestions.

First, there needs to be a focus on creating good jobs. The US has a long tradition of building a middle class through education (Lindert, 2004). Germany uses apprenticeship programs that prepare people for high-paying jobs (Nortdurft, 1989). Either approach would help. Strengthening unions and raising the minimum wage are also crucial. Union jobs helped build the US middle class after World War II. France grew its middle class, in part, because the government supported unions and a high minimum wage (Piketty, 2014).

On the demand side, standard fiscal policy is needed for job creation. Well-paid, public-sector employment should be *an automatic response* to economic stagnation or falling real wages. I strongly prefer infrastructure spending, but if this is not possible for political reasons, we need a contemporary equivalent of burying money in abandoned coal mines (Keynes, 1936, p. 129) – perhaps building a wall along the US border with Mexico.

Second, the US lacks many of the programs in advanced economies that bolster the middle class. This helps explain why the US middle class is smaller than the middle class of other developed countries. Paid parental leave helps parents around the birth of a child by providing an income replacement for lost wages. Child allowances, strongly supported by Keynes, assist larger families having greater economic needs (Pressman, 2014b). These policies each reduce child poverty and increase the percentage of families with children that are middle class – by around 10 percentage points (Pressman, 2014a).

Third, we need more generous unemployment insurance, disability insurance and old-age pensions. The US has the weakest such programs in the developed world. This is one more reason the US has the smallest middle class among major developed nations. Governments are supposed to protect their citizens from risk; social insurance programs are designed to do this. They enable families to continue to live a middle-class existence following some unexpected setback (Hacker, 2006).

Donald Trump was elected president because he understood the fear and anger growing in America. But governing requires accomplishments that make good on campaign promises. The problem is that Trump's campaign promises will not make America great again, if this means bringing the US middle class back up to around 60 percent of all households. At some point his supporters will recognize they have been had. The real danger we face is what might come next.

References

Cole, A. (2016) *Details and Analysis of Donald Trump's Tax Plan* (Washington, DC: Tax Foundation).

Frank, M. (2014) A New State-Level Panel of Annual Inequality Measures over the Period 1916-2005, *Journal of Business Strategies* 31, pp. 241-263.

Giannarelli, L. & Barsimantov, J. (2000) *Child Care Expenses of America's Families* (Washington, DC: Urban Institute).

Hacker, J. (2006) *The Great Risk Shift: The New Economic Insecurity and the Decline of the American Dream* (New York: Oxford University Press).

Horrigan, M. & Haugen, S. (1988) The Declining Middle-Class Thesis: A Sensitivity Analysis, *Monthly Labor Review* 111, pp. 3-13.

Huang, C.-C. (2016) Three Types of "Repatriation Tax" on Overseas Profits: Understanding the Differences, Center on Budget and Policy Priorities Report, October 7, http://www.cbpp.org/research/federal-tax/three-types-of-repatriation-tax-on-overseas-profits-understanding-the.

Jensen, M. & Meckling, W. (1976) Theory of the Firm: Managerial Behavior, Agency Costs and Ownership Structure, Journal of Financial Economics 3, pp. 305–360.

Keynes, J.M. (1936) *The General Theory of Employment, Interest, and Money* (London: Macmillan).

Kolko, J. (2016) Trump was Stronger Where the Economy is Weaker, FiveThirtyEight blog, November 10, https://fivethirtyeight.com/features/trump-was-stronger-where-the-economy-is-weaker/.

Lindert, P. (2004) *Growing Public* (Cambridge: Cambridge University Press).

Malthus, T.R. ([1803]2008) *An Essay on the Principle of Population,* 2nd ed. (New York: Oxford University Press).

Marshall, A. (1920) *Principles of Economics,* 8th ed. (London: Macmillan).

Nothdurft, W. (1989) *School Works: Reinventing Public Schools to Create the Workforce of the Future* (Washington, DC: Brookings Institution).

Orshansky, M. (1965) Counting the Poor: Another Look at the Poverty Profile, *Social Security Bulletin* 25, pp. 3-29.

Orshansky, M. (1969) How Poverty is Measured, *Monthly Labor Review* 92, pp. 26-41.

Pew Research Center (2012) *The Lost Decade of the Middle Class,* available at http://www.pewsocialtrends.org/2012/08/22/the-lost-decade-of-the-middle-class/.

Piketty, T. (2014) *Capital in the Twenty-First Century* (Cambridge, MA: Harvard University Press).

Piketty, T. & Saez, E. (2013) Top Incomes and the Great Recession: Recent Evolutions and Policy Implications, *IMF Economic Review* 61, pp. 456-477.

Pressman, S. (2010) The Middle Class Throughout the World in the Mid 2000s, *Journal of Economic Issues* 44, pp. 243-262.

Pressman, S. (2013) Cross-National Comparisons of Poverty and Income Inequality, in R. Rycroft (Ed.) *The Economics of Inequality, Poverty and Discrimination in the 21st Century* (Santa Barbara, CA: Praeger), pp. 17-37.

Pressman, S. (2014a) Beast of Burden: The Weight of Inequality and the Second Obama Administration, in C. Harrington (Ed.) *Obama's Washington: Political Leadership in a Partisan Era* (London: University of London), pp. 89-112.

Pressman, S. (2014b) Keynes, Family Allowances, and Keynesian Economic Policy, *Review of Keynesian Economics* 2, pp. 508-526.

Pressman, S. (2015) *Understanding Piketty's Capital in the Twenty-First Century* (London & New York: Routledge).

Rothstein, B. & Uslaner, E. (2005) All for All: Equality, Corruption, and Social Trust, *World Politics* 58, pp. 41-72.

Sanger-Katz, M. (2017) Republican Health Proposal Would Redirect Money from Poor to Rich, *New York Times,* February 16.

Scott, R. & Pressman, S. (2013) Household Debt and Income Distribution, *Journal of Economic Issues* 47, pp. 323-332.

Silver, N. (2016) Education, Not Income, Predicted Who Would Vote for Trump, Fivethirtyeight blog, November 22. Available at https://fivethirtyeight.com/features/trump-was-stronger-where-the-economy-is-weaker/.

Wider Opportunities for Women (2010) *The Basic Economic Security Tables for the United States, 2010* (Washington, DC: Wider Opportunities for Women).

Wolff, G. (2017) Will Trump's Strategy Repatriate Highly-Paid Manufacturing Jobs?, available at http://bruegel.org/2017/01/manufacturing-in-the-us-will-trumps-strategy-repatriate-highly-paid-jobs/.

Zucman, G. (2015) *The Hidden Wealth of Nations: The Scourge of Tax Havens* (Chicago: University of Chicago Press).

Mourning in America: Trump and the traumas of the twenty-first century[1]

Neva Goodwin [Tufts University, MA, USA]

Trauma is the word of the year. It may also be the word of the century.

The trauma of finding our country led by a vindictive president who appears to have little empathy for the people, especially for those with fewest resources, is a knife that has opened our hearts to the larger traumas that have been building around us.

What do we know about trauma? There is a relatively new body of good research and understanding on the subject of Posttraumatic Stress Disorder, or PTSD. Individuals who are diagnosed with PTSD are described thus:

> PTSD negatively impacts a person's daily life, resulting in fractured relationships, depression, inability to maintain employment, diminished cognitive and psychosocial functioning, substance abuse, high-cost healthcare utilization ($34.9 billion in inflation-adjusted charges for hospitalizations (2002–2011)), and increased suicide risk due to experiencing symptoms of PTSD... Insufficiently treated PTSD becomes chronic and is associated with serious suicidal ideation and behavior. Approximately 7% of the U.S. population, and 11.2–17.1% of veterans, will have PTSD sometime in their life... As of June 30, 2016, more than 868,000 veterans with PTSD received disability compensation, with an estimated cost of $17 billion/year. In

[1] This paper is dedicated to the memory of Dr Richard Rockefeller, who alerted me and many others to the prevalence and implications of PTSD, and trauma in general, in the modern world.
I thank Edgar Cahn, Dick Chasin, Rick Doblin and Anne St Goar for their very helpful comments on the paper.

the general population, 27% of suicides are associated with PTSD.[2]

The trauma that I am talking about includes the trauma that in some groups partially accounts for Trump's election, and in other groups is an immediate reaction to it; but it goes well beyond this political scene, to be more generalized and more widespread. I will go on to discuss an historical background, and an alarming global future, but first let me say a little about the groups that voted for Trump.

The largest group among Trump supporters were white males at the lower end of educational attainment. Arlie Hochschild, in *Strangers in their Own Land,* has done a brilliant job of describing many of these people, and why they belong to the Tea Party, hate government, and deride environmental protection – even though none of this appears, to most observers, to be in their self-interest. Hochschild differentiates between economic and emotional self-interest. The latter has to do with feelings about fairness. As virtually all other groups (women, minorities, immigrants, disabled, endangered species, etc.) appear to be "getting in line ahead of them" to receive support ("handouts") from government, the under-educated white male, especially in the American South and in the Rust Belt, feels that his lifetime of hard work is belittled and overlooked in favor of the objects of bleeding-heart liberal sympathy. Tea Party members have made a choice between government, which they see as on the side of everyone else, and the free market, which they feel is impersonally fair and gives them a chance. As I will note below, this choice, and the beliefs behind it, have been carefully nurtured.[3]

---

[2] Document submitted by the Multidisciplinary Association for Psychedelic Studies (MAPS) to the U.S. Food and Drug Administration, 18 October 2016, to request permission to submit a full application for Breakthrough Therapy Designation.

[3] Many people have described how this happened. A relatively early summary may be quoted from economist Susan George: "Starting from a tiny embryo at the University of Chicago with the philosopher-economist Friedrich von Hayek and his students like Milton Friedman at its nucleus, the neo-liberals and their funders have created a huge international network of foundations, institutes, research centers, publications, scholars, writers and public relations hacks to develop, package and push their ideas and doctrine relentlessly." *A Short History of Neo-liberalism: Twenty Years of Elite Economics and Emerging Opportunities for Structural Change*

As important, the people in Louisiana whom Hochschild came to know intimately have been, in her words, "in mourning for a lost way of life". It isn't only the jobs that have been lost to globalized cost-cutting and automation; it is the fishing-hunting way of life that depended on pine forests, and healthy waters that have been polluted by vast industrial complexes. Those industrial complexes are accepted because they appear to offer the possibility of jobs, through which to regain a sense of pride and honor. It is easy to keep returning to the economic irrationality of believing in jobs that are largely a mirage; Governor Bobby Jindall impoverished Louisiana to lure in oil companies with "the lowest business taxes in the entire country". Oil companies provide something like one tenth of all jobs in the state even as they have decimated the seafood and tourism industries, and even as big corporations have squeezed out so many small businesses.

At both state and county levels across the U.S., right-wing, anti-environmentalist beliefs – and votes for Trump – tend also to be found in areas of high exposure to toxic pollution. But these logical paradoxes are less powerful than feelings; and the feeling among Tea Party members is a combination of indignation that they have somehow been tricked out of their piece of the American Dream, and deep, continual anxiety about loss of jobs and status, and of familiar cultural and natural landscapes.

This deep anxiety and resentment feeds into a state of trauma – not usually as intense as what is called PTSD, but a state that is, I believe, becoming more widespread around the world. Studies of PTSD, leading the way to increased knowledge and understanding of trauma in human life generally, have been undertaken in countries such as Israel and Bosnia- Herzegovina, where the experience of trauma can be traced back for centuries. There it appears that genetic markers for trauma have carried some symptoms over multiple generations,[4] at the same time as devastating events have

---

(Conference on Economic Sovereignty in a Globalising World, Bangkok, 24-26 March 1999)

[4] The new field of epigenetics explores what kinds of life experiences may be physically carried across generations, in the germ plasm, or possibly elsewhere. The extent of this possibility – separate from the "nurture" effects that traumatized persons may have on their offspring – is not yet clear; certainly less than Lamarck supposed, but probably more than is allowed for in Mendelian genetics.

repeatedly reinforced the PTDS-like characteristics that are held in mind, body and spirit.

As more has been learned about trauma, more has also been learned about resilience. Here is a brief summary of what is now known about why, when different adults are exposed to the same traumatic experiences, some develop the symptoms of PTSD, and others do not:

- There is some genetic factor such that some people are born with more resilience than others
- An individual who has in her or his life someone who can be trusted to be loving and supportive will have more resilience than one who has no such support
- Children who live in severe poverty and deprivation are likely to be less resilient than those who have been able to feel more secure about having their physical needs met
- A child suffering poverty and deprivation will be less likely to suffer reduced resilience to PTSD if he or she has grown up in a stable community of supportive people, whether or not they are blood relations

As I go on I will mention a variety of reasons for believing that trauma is widespread in the 21st century. The last bullet-point about resilience may be relevant if we ask ourselves whether this century is really different from others. Acute poverty and physical deprivation are notably less than they have been for much of human experience; what may be new is the extent to which children in many parts of today's world grow up without a stable community of supportive people.

As humanity moves into the huge, perhaps overwhelming, challenges of the 21st century, we carry with us a build-up of trauma from the events of the 20th century. Consider the horrors of the Holocaust; the suffering in large parts of Europe and Asia during and after the two world wars; or the massacres directed by despots like Stalin, Pol Pot and the rulers of North Korea. Colonial rule in Africa was followed by conflict, disease and government oppression – that continent now has an enormous contingent of orphans who have lived through rape, violence and destitution. China also emerged from colonial status, experiencing the world's largest famine, the madness of the Cultural Revolution, and now a new economic revolution that has lifted millions from poverty but tossed them into a market economy that pursues profit while trampling on human health and other rights, as well as on the health of the environment. In India the world's second largest famine occurred while food was being exported from the hardest-hit regions – the result of a market operating without regard to human need. India has now caught up with China in the extent of pollution, and of pollution-caused illness and death. In Latin America, as in Africa, giant multinational corporations, supported by governments (including, significantly, that of the U.S.) have caused violent deaths along with severe environmental abuse.

The 20th was not the only century of human history marked by violence and famine, but it was unique in combining these with two other vast changes. One was the extent of population growth, which has multiplied the number of people on the planet by about seven times over the last hundred years. Some places have thrived with more workers, but in other parts of the world, especially where population growth was most rapid, local systems were overwhelmed by the numbers of people to feed, house, and provide sanitation for. Demographic shock may also be related to cultural and social changes. In Japan, China, Italy, Russia and other countries where the birth rate has now dropped *below* the level needed to maintain the size of the population, there is a new struggle to find ways to care for a bulging population of elderly. In other places social turmoil occurs when intra- or international migration is a cause of rapid population growth – as in parts of Europe. In the U.S. the search for explanations for the present political climate has noted that those who shifted from previous support for Obama to vote for Trump are disproportionately found in counties where there has been rapid rise in non-white populations.[5]

---

[5] "Immigrant Shock: Can California Predict the Nation's Future?" Emily Badger, Feb. 1, 2017 *New York Times*. For a poignant metaphor on the effects of population growth, here is an image put forth by Isaac Asimov, in an interview with Bill Moyers. Imagine two people living in an apartment where there are two bathrooms; each one can use a bathroom whenever she wants, for as long as she wants. But then suppose the population is multiplied by 7: now there are 14 people living there – but still only two bathrooms. Now there are lines, bangings on doors, arguments – it is much harder to maintain freedom and democracy. (The bathrooms, in this image, may be seen as standing in for our finite Earth, with its source and sink functions.)

The other exceptional trend over the last three generations was the rapidity and the reach of technological change. Medical and sanitary advances were the major cause of the population explosion, as they allowed a much greater proportion of infants to live into adulthood. Technology has, of course, also been a major force for economic growth; over the last 70 or so years there has been a substantial shrinking of the percentage – and, by some measures, the absolute numbers – of people living in desperate poverty around the world. But economic growth itself has become increasingly toxic. The form it has taken in recent decades has greatly increased inequality, as information technology, robotics, and other innovations work through the market to amplify the rewards, or lack thereof, to winners and losers in the system. It has also contributed to prospects for ecological disasters that may turn back much of what we have known as progress in civilization. People are feeling this intuitively, if not consciously.

One of the outstanding features of the time in which we live is the terrifying prospect of global climate change, regarding which it has been said that contemporary humankind is suffering from *"Pre*-Traumatic Stress Disorder".[6] Whether we squarely face what this will likely mean for the coming years, or whether we simply can't bear to look at the facts, it is getting ever harder to avoid the gut-knowledge that the world is rapidly becoming markedly less beautiful, rich and generous to its human inhabitants. Tens of thousands of species disappear forever every year. Large coastal land areas will be submerged; diseases will multiply and spread; food from the oceans and the climate-stressed fields will be scarce; fresh water will be expensive or unobtainable for ever more millions of people; environmental refugees will swell the ranks of unwelcome migrants; and armed conflicts will reach many people who had assumed they were safe.

Armed fortress living will be increasingly common among the rich, and will doubtless create some areas of relative security, but the people inside will be their own prisoners. They will find it difficult to visit the beautiful natural areas in the United States, or the cultural jewels of other continents. Many of these cultural jewels are already being sacked in the raging conflicts of the Middle East and elsewhere; many of the world's natural beauties are already

---

[6] I first heard this term from Thomas Homer Dixon and Carolyn Raffensperger, separately.

eroding under pressure from climate change – as well as from actors in the market economy. The rich are not immune to pre-traumatic stress, as this century heads for various forms of catastrophe; their awareness and response will be important for any hope we may have for a constructive response to the threats we face. An indicator of awareness is a comment by the investor, Seth Klarman, warning that the Trump administration could lead to a major stock market correction and "global angst" among the investor class.[7] But some of that angst is already translating into escapist survivalism among those who can afford to buy land in New Zealand, or build bunkers out of former missile sites in the U.S.. The work of Dr Richard Rockefeller, to whom this piece is dedicated, is an example of a more responsible kind of reaction among the one percent.

Next to climate change, the other most outstanding source of widespread 21st-century trauma is the growing feeling that at least 99% of the people are largely helpless before the power of the giant corporations. Government in the United States is, to a terrifying extent (the ascension of President Trump only makes this more obvious), controlled by Big Ag., Big Pharma., and Big Petrochemicals. Slightly less obvious, because they don't produce anything tangible, are their enablers – the global consulting firms – and the final skimmers of profits, in the financial industry. These, in various combinations, continue to be major forces in toppling or raising up various governments around the world – never to the benefit of the people.[8]

When we speak of the forces that have, to a greater or lesser extent, taken over and degraded the public realm, we cannot leave out the roles of the intelligentsia and the media. The economics profession has played a large role in defining the "free market" as the great bulwark against the kinds of overweening government that were to be found in the Soviet Union – or in the United States. These disparate government types were bizarrely lumped together as Milton Friedman and his allies, with support by the Koch brothers

---

[7] "A Quiet Giant of Investing Weighs in on Trump", Andrew Ross Sorkin, Feb 6, 2017, *New York Times*
[8] A useful source on this is *The New Confessions of an Economic Hitman*, by John Perkins. Obviously not all individuals in these parts of our economy are bad people. In each of these industries one can find companies that are doing more to solve problems than to create them, and that are only tangentially involved in the starkly widening gap between the fortunate and the unfortunate people of the world.

and other beneficiaries of petrochemical money, fed the market solutions message to the public via Fox News, right-wing radio, and the like.

A little example of how this message permeated and echoed was an absurd debate I heard in the late 1980s, between an ecological economist and a speaker from the libertarian Cato Institute. It was absurd because each spoke as if one of these institutions was entirely to be trusted, and the other was the enemy. As though the market can operate "freely", let alone to the benefit of the people, without being nudged and regulated by government – as if government could do everything markets can do, as well or better! And as if "the market" was just one thing, while in fact, those markets that come closest to the "free" ideal preached by Friedman and his popularizers are dominated by small businesses, not by giant corporations. Yet this debate continues in the same absurd, polarized and simplified form.

Naomi Oreskes and Erik M. Conway, in their 2010 book, *Merchants of Doubt*, do an excellent job of describing how the public was given a false picture of science, especially that of climate change. The petrochemical industry has used bad science and clever marketing to cast doubt on the need for urgent action against climate change. Many of these writers and spokespeople were ready and willing to fight *for* the market, *against* government, because they felt they were upholding capitalism in the Cold War. Industry continues to benefit from an anti-science, anti-government atmosphere fanning hatred of all regulations – even those intended to protect the environment and provide safety nets for people who are suffering in a rapidly changing economy.

Early in this paper I cited some reasons to believe that white, Christian, male supporters of Trump feel themselves to be a discriminated-against minority. This is noteworthy because until fairly recently this was the demographic that had least reason to feel this way – and that, indeed, enjoyed a belief system which allowed them to discriminate against other minorities (as well as females, who are rarely in the minority). It is important to add, to the reasons for widespread trauma in the modern world, the experience of discrimination, which is liable to create and perpetuate a lifelong trauma for those who suffer it. This includes Blacks in much of the world; Jews, over a long history; native peoples, wherever their lands have been taken over by a more powerful set of newcomers; and women and girls in those places where their inferior status leaves them subject to violence, without recourse.

The above does not exhaust the topic of trauma in the 21st century, but it may make it easier to understand its scope.

Included in a feeling of trauma is often a wish to find an enemy. There is indeed an enemy of all humankind – a cluster of enemies; and they can be identified. They are not the quarter of the American electorate who voted for Trump. Their voting decision was fueled by their distress; and it is a distress that is widely shared, though different groups understand the causes very differently. Humanity's real enemies today – those who stand against addressing the huge difficulties that face the world – include "experts" that insist you have to choose between governments and markets, as well as governments that are hostage to a cluster of powerful, very rich actors. Humanity's enemies today are the giant corporations that profit in the short term from business as usual while diverting attention from the huge difficulties that face the world – most of all, climate change, inequality, discrimination, and corruption of democracy.

Much of humankind shares the traumatizing knowledge that large forces are doing great harm to our livelihoods, our families, and our beloved places. The mourning is not only taking place in America, and it is interpreted and acted on in a wide variety of ways. Some of the ways are violent, including what we call terrorism; some are beautiful, such as the marches of January 21 of this year, around the world; and some are designed (as I believe the Trump vote was) to create disruptive change. There are grounds for finding common cause among many of those who feel a crying need for a fairer, kinder, safer world.

Can we imagine such a better world?

In order to address the great social and ecological challenges we face, we need, for sure, better, more effective government, freed from the chokehold of money. In the U.S. this requires campaign finance reform, along with voter registration and education efforts, to overcome the suppression of voting by the underprivileged. Perhaps even more critical is to get control over the contracting-out system whereby private contractors, hidden from public view, now outnumber the federal civilian workforce by 3 or 4 to 1.[9] This is enormously lucrative for the corporations that have the contracts – and that keep hold of them, in part, through a cozy relationship greased by campaign contributions.

We also need a very different, very lively market sector, dominated by small businesses, many of them locally grounded, including various socially responsible modifications of profit-maximizing capitalism, such as cooperatives and Benefit Corporations. Large corporations could again (as was the case in the 19th century) be held to charters that spell out their contract with the people. A re-chartering movement is probably as important in this realm as campaign finance reform is for the restoration of responsive government.

Reforms to markets and governments are necessary so that both institutions can work on behalf of the vast number of people who are economically insecure, increasingly left out of the existing systems. While technology is filtering away ever more of the jobs of the past, fewer and fewer people can be funneled into the specialties of the future. What will be needed, however, is more of the care work that for most of human history has been underappreciated and underpaid – when paid at all. Societies will need to address how the fruits of technology-enhanced productivity can be apportioned among all the people, while acknowledging the critical work of the core economies of households and communities.

Such a market, such a government, such a society would need to work together in recognition of planetary limits. In order to more equitably share the Earth's finite resources, cultural shifts are required, to elevate the values of cooperation and compassion over competition and greed-defined success.

---

[9] See June A. Sekera, *The Public Economy in Crisis, A Call for a New Public Economics* Springer, 2016. Contrary to public opinion, the federal government workforce is essentially the same size now as it was in the 1950s, under Eisenhower; it has, in fact been shrinking, so that there are now fewer government employees than there were under Reagan. The Freedom of Information Act does not cover government contractors; they are paid by the government, but not accountable to the public.

Right now, in opposition to any such possibilities, the forces that are determined to reap short-term profits, regardless of long-term harm, have strong allies in President Trump and his team; but it is not just this president who is the cause of so much harm and loss, in this century of loss. The votes for Trump, and for others like him, in other countries, have their seeds in the trauma of a past and a future of loss. As we address the threats we face – threats to livelihoods, to democracy, and to our ecological surroundings – we must also be mindful of a widespread need for emotional healing.

Honest Abe was a co-op dude: how the Donald can save America from capital despotism

Stephen T. Ziliak [Roosevelt University, Chicago, USA and University of Newcastle, Australia]

> "Labor is prior to and independent of capital. Capital is only the fruit of labor, and could never have existed if labor had not first existed. Labor is the superior of capital, and deserves much the higher consideration" (Abraham Lincoln, 1861).

Greetings, America, and good luck. Now more than ever the world stands to gain by cooperating with each other.

Good day in particular to Republicans, and congratulations. This is a new day. And, in a very real sense, it is your day. Republicans' Day. Abe Lincoln's Day. The people have voted. Ordinary workers – or, more exactly, a small number of extraordinary delegates – have had their say. And the whole nation – or anyway, the part of the nation that is voting and paying attention to "things that are trending" such as political elections – we need for you to succeed. To keep your word. You're hired.

Now we need from you some sort of contract with America, like the one you tried in the Nineties, only seriously this time. Regular folks have been shoved aside for too long. The well-being of honest workers continues to sink with debt and despair. The economy is badly broken; wages are depressed or disappearing altogether; productive folks are still being sacked and pensions have been badly looted; meantime, overpaid bosses, supervisors, and "protective service" workers (a euphemism for police) have multiplied disproportionately in the ranks of the average firm while vacation and sick days vanish or can't be used without fear of loss. Something's gotta give.

America voted you into office, based on what you said you'd do differently. Now we need you to make good on your promise to "bring back the great state" of Illinois, as that state's newly elected Governor Bruce Rauner has promised. Make good on your promise, Republicans and Democrats alike, by cooperating with America to bring back family and wealth – bring back the freedom, the jobs, the manufacturing and democracy-first-philosophy we all want and need in every state of this great union.

You may not realize it but America voted for Republicans like you because you represent the party of Honest Abe, Abraham Lincoln, the first Republican President and Co-op Dude. Labor before capital, people over profits, that kind of thing.

That's what Honest Abe believed, he told Congress time and again. You heard that right: Lincoln was a co-op guy, *sans* Birkenstocks and vegan diet, true. Still, there it is.

Let's get the facts straight.

Economists in the know have acknowledged that the worker owned cooperative firm is the most perfect model of economic democracy and rational business organization dreamed up so far. That is true around the world, from Springfield all the way back to Shelbyville, economists who've examined such co-ops agree. Co-ops are more productive. And every worker is an owner.

From the Dutch blossoming of commerce in the 1600s to the Asian Spring of the 2000s, socialists and capitalists alike have not produced, it seems, a better, more efficient and democratic form of economic production and distribution. Co-ops win.

Not everyone is convinced.

If co-ops are so great, why don't they dominate the economy? Negligence and ignorance, more than any other possible cause, it would seem.

For example, the infamous "socialist calculation debate" in economics dragged on for two decades before a single word was said by either side, from Lange and Lerner to Mises and Hayek, about the nature of the firm. Nary a peep from economists about how or even why firms choose to organize into production units of a certain scale, large or small. Ronald Coase's article on "The Nature of the Firm" (1937) was good enough to fetch him a Nobel Prize. But Coase did not bring as much clarity to the debate as most economists believe.

Coase was vague and conventional to point of embarrassment. He made straw man assumptions about the firm being a hierarchical-capitalistic entity. Coase's firm, though more "tractable" and "realistic" than previous notions, is assumed to be run by a "master" or "masters," by capitalists who seek to maximize profit by bossing around "servants" – that is, wage earners possessing little autonomy, little or no ownership, and no voting rights on capital, their sole purpose being assumed to serve the "masters" of capital.

Said Coase, "If a workman moves from department Y to department X, he does not go because of a change in relative prices, but because he is ordered to do so." But if Coase (himself a lovely man in person) would have taken a closer look at the real world, he could have found cooperative firms succeeding in stark contrast to the anti-democratic firms of his imagination.

The paucity of the co-op form in America is costly to more than pocketbooks. Worker owned co-operatives have been designed by people from all walks of life sharing Republican values of ownership, democratic decision making, autonomy, security, and voluntary cooperation. The surest defense against despotism is the immediate extension of universal economic democracy. That is the nature of the just firm.

If co-ops sound scary, or left wing, or creepy in that church-based or high school way, it's not your fault: with few exceptions, most people – economists included – make it all the way through graduate school never even hearing about the cooperative form of business.

Few are aware that Abraham Lincoln, the first Republican President of the United States, was a pro-labor, pro-democratic, Co-op Dude who put people first, "prior to and independent of capital," as Honest Abe put it. And as nature, democracy, and common sense dictate.

Oui, oui, Madame, yes Sir, he was: Honest Abe was a Co-up kind of guy. He had a hip looking neck beard, too. Wore a flannel shirt sometimes; rolled up his sleeves, worked hard (and at various types of jobs), read difficult books, made difficult decisions, made deadline, and drank beer – all in cooperation with others. As Lincoln said elsewhere: "I am a firm believer in the people. If given the truth, they can be depended upon to meet any national crisis. The great point is to bring them the real facts, and beer."

Cheers, a toast to Abraham Lincoln!

So far as we know Honest Abe did not himself belong to a worker owned co-op. But his theory of labor and capital imply that co-ops are prior to, and superior to, Corporate America and other forms of economic despotism on the road to serfdom, such as Kmart.

Republicans should be among the first to grasp this elementary principle of economics and democracy. Labor is us; thus we, labor, have the first, most valid claim to output, and we have the first say about its means and modes of production, whatever the ratio of capital to labor might be, small or large, capital intensive or labor intensive.

Let's remind our newly elected officials of the actual, not mythical, Republican philosophy of labor, as originally articulated by President Lincoln in his "First Annual Message" to members of the U.S. House and Senate (December 3rd 1861):

> "Labor is prior to and independent of capital. Capital is only the fruit of labor, and could never have existed if labor had not first existed. Labor is the superior of capital, and deserves much the higher consideration."

There it is, there's the writ, from the Patriarch of the Republican Party to the Industrial Workers of the World. It wasn't Marx and Engels who drunkenly scribbled (though the thought arises). The sober author of the quoted passage was the first Republican President of the United States, speaking truth to power – and power to truth – of labor's priority over capital.

So you don't have to be Karl Marx or George Carlin or a lunatic in the night to believe that economic democracy – and the priority of labor over capital – is as American and Midwestern Republican as corn dogs and kale.

> "Capital has its rights, which are as worthy of protection as any other rights," Lincoln noted. "Nor is it denied that there is, and probably always will be, a relation between labor and capital producing mutual benefits."

But the primary emphasis on labor, and not on speculative finance or maximization of shareholder value, "is the just and generous and prosperous system which opens the way to all, gives hope to all, and consequent energy and progress and improvement of condition to all," said Lincoln. He added:

> "No men living are more worthy to be trusted than those who toil up from poverty; none less inclined to take or touch aught which they have not honestly earned."

And finally:

> "Let them [labor, that is, you and me] beware of surrendering a political power [to abstract capital] which they [that is, we human laborers, not mere machines or money] already possess, and which if surrendered will surely be used to close the door of advancement against such as they and to fix new disabilities and burdens upon them till all of liberty shall be lost".

> "Till all of liberty shall be lost," Lincoln said, in his noble address against capital "despotism".

In other words, the worker-owned cooperative model for doing business and earning a living is not as hippie-commie as it sounds. It was good enough for John Stuart Mill, too – the great English economist and philosopher. Even

Trumponomics: Causes And Consequences

Friedrich Hayek, the Nobel laureate and free market muse of both Thatcher and Reagan, himself belonged to a co-op, back when he was on the faculty of the University of Chicago: The Seminary Bookstore Co-op, in Hyde Park, Chicago. (Full disclosure: I've been a member for many years.) Father Jose Maria Arizmendiarrieta (1915-1976), the Spanish Catholic philosopher, educator, and founder of the Mondragon cooperative community, might be canonized for the humanity and jobs his work has brought to the Basque region of Spain and beyond.

The worker owned co-operative firm turns out to be as American as plywood and taxi cabs, too. In fact, those industries and many others have been partially produced by cooperatively owned and managed firms, though co-op industry share remains puzzlingly low in the U.S. and most other countries, Spain and Italy included. Even in the co-op friendly plywood industry of the Pacific Northwest co-op industry share peaked in the 20th century at less than one-half of total industry output.

The lack of co-ops in America appears to come less from economic incentive and more from sheer ignorance. Put plainly, most people don't know what a co-op is or does. (I reached 19 years of age before I heard the very words, "cooperative grocery store", and 21 years before I first joined one.) People just don't know about co-ops, nor of how successful they've been from the cooperative milk and cheese makers of Jura, in early medieval France, to today's taxi drivers and electrical engineers organized cooperatively in Madison, Wisconsin or Mondragon, Spain.

"One worker-owner, one equal vote" on all business matters. That is the foundation of ownership and democracy at the democratically and self-managed cooperative firm. Co-ops require six to seven times fewer supervisors and managers – the overpaid numbskulls we currently cope with. And everyone takes a turn supervising, just like safety patrols at school or in the management of common pool resources, such as timberland in mountainous regions of various nations.

Maximization of income per worker, democratic decision making, and employment stability are three of the other main inputs to the cooperative objective function. Worldwide that's typical co-op practice, from Rome to Rio.

Thus the objective of the cooperatively owned and managed firm is to maximize the material, sociological, and psychological well-being of labor, minus the cost of capital and reinvestment for rational expansion or change in the mix of inputs and outputs. And get this: most co-ops allow the resigning, retiring, or perishing co-op member to transfer his or her asset and right to work to a family member – a way of keeping jobs for a stable community and healthy families that one does not find in the despotic firm.

Co-ops promote family values.

That's because people are credits, not debits. Labor is us, labor is people. Lincoln, the first Republican President, understood that. Too many people today do not understand. They understand that co-ops are for hippies, reds, and other neck beards. That is not true. "We the people are not machines" is a line that Jefferson forgot to add to the Declaration of Independence. (To satisfy skeptics I concede that most humans are not machines, despite Fox News, iPhone 6+, and Obama's polished voice.)

In his 1861 address to Congress, President Lincoln extended to the economic democracy what Senator Lincoln had summoned at least two years prior. In his "Annual Address" before the Wisconsin State Agricultural Society, in Milwaukee, Wisconsin, September 30th 1859, Lincoln told an assembly of farmers and brewers: "The world is agreed that labor is the source from which human wants are mainly supplied. There is no dispute upon this point."

So, ye newly elected Republicans: summon your inner Abe. Stay true to Republican philosophy.

Start by injecting capital into the National Cooperative Bank, the still promising cooperative bank of the United States that the Reagan administration all but killed in 1981, less than two years after the necessary bank was first established by Congress. The Cooperative Bank – and other banks like it – can help to fulfill the promise of economic democracy, by supplying loanable funds and grants to build and to grow cooperative enterprise.

Pass legislation making it easier to establish a cooperative firm, corporation, and village or town, not unlike the successful producer and consumer models already found in the plywood cooperatives of the Pacific Northwest, the home appliance and solar panel and other small manufactories of Mondragon, Spain (which currently boasts over 100,000 worker-owners), and the giant grocery store co-op of Switzerland, called simply "Co-op", which claims over 2.5 million current members. Pass legislation authorizing Congress to support cooperative education, conferences, and other institutions in aid of cooperative banks and firms.

We are destined to fulfill the promise of economic democracy in America. We owe it to ourselves, and to Honest Abe.

Besides the attack on the National Cooperative Bank, additional attempts to kick-start cooperatives have been resisted by Republicans and Democrats alike. *The 1994 Economic Report of the President* stated that "the Administration aims to increase the productivity of the work force by helping employers make better use of their workers through increased worker participation" (p. 128). The Report noted:

> "Numerous studies have now demonstrated that cooperative techniques increase productivity substantially in a wide range of enterprises. By helping to disseminate information on what successful firms have been able to accomplish, the Administration hopes to speed the adoption of these practices throughout the economy."

We are still waiting for the information dissemination and speedy adoption.

The United Nations called the year 2012 "The International Year of Cooperatives", and sponsored a number of conferences and workshops worldwide to help to disseminate information and support for co-ops as promised by the Clinton Administration back in 1994. Unfortunately, few business and political leaders are aware of the U.N.'s recent initiative to boost the co-op sector.

Co-ops have existed in the United States since the days of Ben Franklin but today they represent less than 1 percent of the American economy. Back in the 70s, 80s, and as even recently as the 90s, however, worker-owned co-operatives saw a surge in empirical economic research and fare – in most regards – incredibly well when compared to today's conventional firm.

Economists, not all of them known for holding democratic-cooperative ideals, have put co-ops to the test of statistical and economic proof. Jaroslav Vanek, David Ellerman, Katerina Berman, Ben Craig, John Pencavel, Alan Krueger (Obama's Chief Economist), Louis Putterman, Christopher Gunn and many others have conducted rigorous empirical studies comparing and contrasting the economic performance of worker owned cooperatives.

What did they conclude? In their 1992 *American Economic Review* econometric study of veneer and plywood producers, for example, Craig and Pencavel (both at the time of Stanford University) found that co-op share prices are highly undervalued. Craig and Pencavel demonstrated empirically that there are $1 million dollar bills (in the form of missed opportunities for investments in co-ops) waiting to be picked up on the street. Holding equal net discounted present value of joining and working in a co-op versus working in a conventional unionized firm, the share prices on offer for each firm type should be roughly equal. They're not, the economists found. Co-op share price could rise by a factor of three in some firms and still make a profit for the worker-owner whose opportunity cost is a job at a unionized plant.

Employment stability and fairness in pay are better too. Much, much better. In the cooperative firm, economic democratic virtues are used to guide its policy for distributing rewards and punishments, unlike in the conventional firm, where vast inequality of income, autonomy, and surplus prevails.

Worker-owned co-ops are found to be more productive, holding input levels constant, economists such as Alan Krueger and Henry Farber agree; co-op workers have more job satisfaction; they have lots more say about the process and mission, and equality of status too; employment levels are far more stable (virtually no one loses their job); and income differentials are

2-or-3-or-4-to-1 at maximum versus the 500-or-550-to-one ratios of today's neoclassical firm.

In a disturbing (but hilarious) book, *Get Rich Cheating: The Crooked Path to Easy Street* (2009), Jeff Kreisler reports (pp. 76-81) on the incomes of CEOs. Kreisler names a dozen executives who took home as much as $50,000 U.S. per hour on average, hour after hour, year after year, as the company they lorded over, including Merck and Fannie Mae, lost billions. Kicking in the head an already dead President Lincoln.

Cooperation at work, at the shopping center, and even in our housing and communities, is not what it could be. Not even close to what economists call the "production possibilities" of output and happiness.

The biggest problem of democracy is not the failure to fully extend political rights, however important. The promise of political and human rights is not perfectly fulfilled, true, though many gains have been made.

The bigger problem is economic in nature. The threat today is from a lack of economic democracy – a lack of ownership, of self-reliance, of autonomy, and of justice in the distribution of rewards and punishments at work – from the appropriation of company revenue to the lack of protection against pension raids and unfair taxes, capital despotism is rife.

"The road to serfdom" has many paths to choose from, Hayek warned in his important book of 1944, but too many Americans – including most economists and politicians – have forgotten the economic path, the road to serfdom caused by a lack of *economic* democracy. Unlike Lincoln.

The average American has failed to notice – or is so far unwilling to act upon – the fact that they themselves spend six or more hours per day working in or with an anti-democratic, speculatively financed, and capital-first firm or government or bank. Your bank and government and firm, for example.

Political activists frequently complain (we should be grateful) about one violation or another of political or human rights, forgetting about the oftentimes much, much larger and more devastating lack: economic rights.

The Republican Party could now be poised to make great strides for economics, democracy, and family values. The fight against despotism, against unwarranted loss of wages and wealth and democratic control; the fight against the alienating feelings induced by an increasingly antagonistic, speculative, overleveraged, and hierarchical-narcissistic capitalism must be priority number one.

We can learn from the successes and struggles of the 70-year-old Mondragon experiment: we learn that good American manufacturing jobs can be won back by restoring the proper relation between labor and capital. Ordinary American workers can rediscover the virtues of full employment, self-reliance, self-governance, and of earnings and pensions being paid to the rightful producers of them.

What would a Whitman or Tubman do? How about Adam Smith's "impartial spectator" – what would she or he say about the lack of economic democracy?

On the co-op question they would agree with Lincoln and Marx, not Hayek. If America fails to cope with the fact that capital is the fruit of previous labor, economic despotism and the road to serfdom will be knocking at the front door of the whole society; already we sense their presence.

Well more than 230 years ago, Mr Adam Smith himself would heed the moral side of the call out, in *The Theory of Moral Sentiments*. In a chapter of the great tome he titled "On the Corruption of our Moral Sentiments," the eminent economist Mr Smith (1790 [2009], p. 73) observed:

> "This disposition to admire, and almost to worship, the rich and the powerful, and to despise, or, at least, to neglect persons of poor and mean condition, ... is, ... the great and most universal cause of the corruption of our moral sentiments."

You can't change a light bulb without the assistance of a new light bulb, not to mention a socket, some electricity, possibly a ladder and other capital inputs, that's true. Capital has partial rights. Economic units have to grow to efficient scale (holding justice constant) and people need to save and invest for their uncertain wealth of the future.

But capital efficiency is not the definition of economic justice. Capital is a subtraction from labor, not the reverse. We mustn't ever forget again what Lincoln told Congress not long after the start of the Civil War, when the capital relation was on many people's minds: "The error," Lincoln warned, the corruption, "is in assuming that the whole labor of community exists within that relation."

Thus begins the art of the just deal.

Further reading

Akerlof G., P. Romer, R. E. Hall, N.G. Mankiw. 1993. "Looting: The Economic Underworld of Bankruptcy for Profit." *Brookings Papers on Economic Activity*, Vol. 1993, No. 2 (1993), pp. 1-73

Craig, B., J. Pencavel. 1992. ""The Behavior of Worker Cooperatives: The Plywood Companies of the Pacific Northwest," *The American Economic Review*, Vol. 82, No. 5 (Dec., 1992): 1083-1105

Craig, B., J. Pencavel [Comments by H. Farber and A. Krueger]. 1995. "Participation and Productivity: A Comparison of Worker Cooperatives and Conventional Firms in the Plywood Industry," *Brookings Papers on Economic Activity*. Washington DC: Brookings.

Ellerman, D. 1992. *Property and Contract in Economics: The Case for Economic Democracy.* Cambridge, MA: Blackwell Publishers.

Gunn, C. 1984. *Workers' Self-Management in the United States.* Ithaca: Cornell University Press.

Lazonick, W., M. O'Sullivan. 2000. "Maximizing Shareholder Value: A New Ideology for Corporate Governance," *Economy and Society* 29 (1, Feb.): 13-35

McElwee, S. 2014. "When Workers Own Their Companies, Everyone Wins: How a Very Old Economic Model Could Help the New Economy," *The New Republic* (August 1). http://www.newrepublic.com/article/118933/economic-benefits-coop.

Ruccio, D. 2014. "Abraham Lincoln and the Road to Despotism," Anticap, Nov. 14th. https://rwer.wordpress.com/2014/11/14/abraham-lincoln-and-the-road-to-despotism/

Smith, A. 1790 [2009]. *The Theory of Moral Sentiments.* Sixth revised edition, with an introduction by A. Sen. New York: Penguin.

Stephen T. Ziliak

Vanek, J. 1975. *Self-Management: Economic Liberation of Man*. New York: Penguin

Wolff, R. 2012. *Democracy at Work: A Cure for Capitalism*. Haymarket Books.

Ziliak, S. and S. Barbour. 2016. "Smith's Wedge: The Invisible Mishandling of Context in Robert Frank's *The Darwin Economy*," Schmoller's Jahrbuch 136 (1): 87-108.

Prolegomenon to a defense of the City of Gold

David A. Westbrook[1] [University at Buffalo School of Law, State University of New York, USA]

In 1992, Democratic Party strategist James Carville posted a sign in the campaign staff's "War Room", that included the message "The Economy, Stupid", which quickly morphed into "It's the Economy, Stupid" and became a *de facto* slogan for Bill Clinton's successful bid for U.S. President. The slogan reflected a widespread belief that American votes are usually decided by pocketbook issues, a view that bears some kinship to the Marxian position that economic reality is somehow more fundamental (base) than ideology and the rest of culture (superstructure), a thought not unrelated to the economists' traditional prejudice in favor of materialism. Whatever the genealogies of such collective imaginaries, it seems fair to say that lazy materialism has continued to suffuse Democratic Party ideology, and indeed the positions of mainstream center left parties in many high income societies.

This simplistic epistemology – often risibly presented as a hardheaded lack of sentimental idealism – left Democrats unprepared to understand or engage the populist rhetoric of recent years, which uses economic language in far more complex ways. More generally, in contests between "populists" and "the establishment" or "elites" in the United States and other high income societies, the vocabulary of economics has served psychological and so political purposes far beyond ordinary pocketbook concerns. "The economy" has gone from being understood as knowable, fundamental, factual, the basis of argument, to a field of discourse, opaque, emotional, intensely subjective, a mode of disputation and, most importantly, identification.

---

[1] Louis Del Cotto Professor, University at Buffalo School of Law, State University of New York, and author of *City of Gold: An Apology for Global Capitalism in a Time of Discontent*.

Before proceeding further, it may be worthwhile to emphasize an analytical complexity, especially for readers from outside of the United States. The divide between Republicans and Democrats is not congruent with the divide between populists and the establishment. In fact, throughout the 20th century the Republican Party positioned itself as the party of the establishment, especially the business establishment. Many Republicans, including of course the mainstream candidates, were literally incredulous at the decisive power of Trump's populist appeal. Conversely, many populists supported the insurgent Bernie Sanders against the Democrat's longstanding heiress apparent, Hillary Clinton. A significant number of populists who voted for the Democrat Obama, hoping for change, went on to vote for the Republican Trump, for the same reason.

Those things said, during the Obama presidency, i.e., when the Democrats held the White House, Republicans naturally tended to position themselves as outsiders, and railed against Washington generally and the Affordable Care Act ("Obamacare") especially. Republicans summoned radical populism and radical populism came, to the delight of some people and the consternation of others, in the form of a reality show President who communicates directly to the people via Twitter. (From time to time one must pause to contemplate the raw newness of the present situation.) Trump thus appears to be the populist extreme of a more moderately populist party.

It should also be emphasized that the Republican Party has been very successful in recent years. It is true that the Democrats held the White House from 2008–2016, in large part due to the appeal of President Obama. In the meantime, however, and despite greater membership and presumptively better demographics, the Democratic Party became in many ways the minority party in the United States. As of February 2017, Republicans control not only the Presidency, but both houses of Congress. Thirty-three State governors are Republican (16 are Democrats, and one is independent). In 32 states, Republicans control the legislature; Democrats control 13 states; and the rest are split. In sum, Republican Party power is both broader and more representative, and somewhat less populist, than a narrow focus on the very close Trump election might suggest.

Nonetheless, national political discourse has polarized, and this polarization has included economics. Far from being somehow objective, the language of economics has been pressed into partisan service. The tropes have become familiar:

1. Populists vote against establishment parties, professing to worry about jobs taken by immigrants, legal or not, or lost to international trade. Nativist rhetoric flourishes; ugly things are said about those seen as outsiders.

2. Elites scratch their heads and wonder about populist discontent, since ordinary people are awash in the cheap goods offered by globalized production. Even gasoline is cheap, global warming be damned. Moreover, ordinary people benefit from the subsidies provided by a benevolent state, run by right thinking mandarins for the good of all.

3. Populists decry the growing privilege and entrenchment of elites. Meanwhile they and their spouses work harder than ever and get nowhere, or do not work and fall behind.

4. Elites call populists losers, unable to succeed in the modern era.

5. Populists call elites unpatriotic, godless hypocrites, and the like.

6. Elites call populists morally unacceptable, deplorable, xenophobic, racist, etc.

Politics is rarely gentle, and this is hardly the first time in U.S. history that the nation has been polarized. That said, the *ad hominem* quality and lack of decorum of contemporary politics are largely unprecedented, at least in living memory. This charged atmosphere raises problems for political thought. In a polarized milieu, where "you are either for us or against us", it is difficult to say much without being understood to adopt one of the familiar attacks or counter-attacks. And so political discourse in the United States in recent months has been especially repetitive, along the lines sketched above. How to get out of this loop, without being coopted by the agonistic structure of contemporary politics?

David A. Westbrook

From an American perspective, the polarized character of contemporary politics is rather sad. In the U.S. political tradition, which lies near the heart of the national identity, politics has been idealized as a rational and collective enterprise. A nicety of history: in 1776, the same year as the Declaration of Independence, Adam Smith published *The Wealth of Nations*, arguing that national prosperity resulted more from sound institutions and wise policies than from natural favor or battlefield success. The United States was founded, made rather than inherited, and so both its political institutions and its economy were from the start in question. What sort of institutions, laws, economy would the new nation have? Consider, in this regard, not just the *Federalist Papers*, but the tensions between a more agrarian republic associated with Jefferson as opposed to Hamilton's more mercantile and industrial vision; the debates over the First and Second National Bank (the central bank); and of course the existence and expansion of slavery and the economy founded thereon. It would be easy enough to carry the theme through the Civil War and up until the present, but the point here is that arguments over how to answer such questions, how to construct the nation, have been not just the substance but also the practice of American politics, the warp and the woof. What else did these immigrants share?

The traditional fora for such arguments have been broadly circulated newspapers, black and white and read all over, as an old children's riddle has it. Consider Benjamin Franklin, newspaperman, or Watergate and the *Washington Post*. None of which is to deny that there have been lapses in the quality of argument, times when argument was less than principled and appeals were venal, but it is a tradition of virtue that makes a lapse possible. Now the practice of rational and collective argument, and the broad fora in which such arguments are held, to say nothing of the manners, seem at risk of passing from the scene.

Aristotle's claim that man is a political animal is often taken as a sort of preface to constitutional thought, discussion of different forms of political life, their strengths and vulnerabilities, different understandings of citizenship, and so forth. But the famous claim also lends itself to a simpler and darker reading that seems particularly pertinent nowadays: men (and women) will form political associations, tribes of one sort or another, with whatever materials fall to hand. Politics, the ties that bind, can be based upon any number of things: descent from a hero or a god, common birth in a location, shared history or religion, or race, or national chauvinism, or sports, or even policy, including of course economic policy. Indeed, in vast polities like the United States or the European Union, policy – the state of being *bien pensant* – is an especially attractive foundation for political life, because it requires only agreement, not personal knowledge. One can make common cause with absolute strangers, indeed must in order to elect a president. Conversely, one can use political abstractions to assess whether strangers are otherwise our kind of people. So political identities and even marriages are formed on notional assent to abstract ideas. Is this not the stuff of talk radio, or slightly more subtly, the congratulatory pieties of the liberal media? From this perspective, the very American idea that policy talk is about what is to be done seems naive, and the notion that "economics" forms some sort of objective ground for political discourse – "it's the economy, stupid" – begins to seem tragicomic.

The better question is why this economic language, now, for these people? What sort of political identity does this language constitute? To begin with the heart of populism in the contemporary United States, working class white males: contemporary society has little use for such men. Some of this dislocation is sexual and racial – to be a white male is no longer automatically a position of privilege. Much of this dislocation, however, is economic. Decently paying high skill labor is becoming scarce, and even middle class wages have been relatively stagnant for years and years. But "economic" is hardly objective. When Americans meet for the first time, they frequently ask, "what do you do?" that is, what is your job? In a vast commercial republic, a great many people found their personal identities and their social roles on their employment – their jobs make them who they are. The stagnation and uncertainty of the contemporary job market have thus raised existential issues, even for those not threatened with poverty.

Economic precariousness, even poverty, need not be completely disabling. Members of other ethnicities and genders often tell stories of heroically overcoming historic injustice. Civil society abounds with "women in law" and "Black History Month" and so forth. Such forms of association and such stories are by and large unavailable to straight working class white men, because they are straight, white, and male, that is, members of the oppressor class against which other identities are founded. Not everybody can be a subaltern. Public discourse effectively prohibits such men from portraying themselves as victims, and so they had better be successful, or they will have no narrative with which to explain their lives to themselves or to their fellow citizens. As already suggested, in the event of failure or even mediocrity, such men are likely to be scorned as losers, failures. Some such men turn (have always turned) to blaming others, in familiar patterns of isms – antisemitism, racism, xenophobia, various forms of sexism – but perhaps mostly just bitterness looking for a target. Such men may be called "deplorable" by establishment presidential candidates. Recent studies indicate catastrophic levels of substance abuse and suicide among this population in the United States.

Turning to the establishment, and especially the overwhelmingly liberal elites: contemporary U.S. society is in fact quite unequal and that inequality is entrenched by the professions. American inequality is not just a matter of the very wealthy, or the historically underprivileged. A mandarin class (well-trained symbol manipulators, often bureaucrats) both runs and benefits from the academy, the civil service, much of finance, law and medicine, the press and media generally, various high tech industries, and other established institutions that require prestigious educational credentials in order to participate. Their position is conservative for the traditional and structural reasons that they are highly privileged by the status quo, and increasingly able to pass along such privilege to their children through meritocratic institutions of higher education, "meritocratic", that is, for those with the proper backgrounds.

Liberal elites in the US seem, however, to be an *haute bourgeoisie* that dare not speak its name. Certainly people have been more honest about their status in other times and places. The Democratic Party led by Hillary Clinton, centered on professionals rather than labor or even ethnic minorities, is dominated by Whigs masquerading as progressives. There is much to be said about claims to progress, but for now it bears remembering that comfort with sexual variation is quite compatible with hierarchy – de Sade was a Marquis. Interestingly, contemporary professionals are relatively staid in their personal lives. Dual income professional couples not only are more likely to stay married, their double incomes create surplus capital for investment purposes, not to mention a stable platform from which to get their children into elite schools. Nor is it obvious how people who received their positions through a lifetime of brutal zero sum competition, often in Ivy League institutions, somehow come to think of themselves as egalitarian. Indeed, contemporary American elites have intensely uncharitable feelings about swathes of life in the United States, ranging from entire states to cuisines to amusements to music, to say nothing of political positions... There is much more to be said, but in short, this generation of mandarins may well be remembered as far more hypocritical than the Victorians, or perhaps simply unreflective.

Hypocrisy is fairly minor as sins go, in places bordering on good manners. The real problem, intellectually, is that none of the foregoing amounts to a *defense* of the status quo. Members of the establishment, by definition somewhat conservative even if blissfully unaware of the fact, should be able to articulate what they feel worth preserving about the society with which they are entrusted, besides their own privilege. As suggested above, saying "the peasants are revolting" i.e., ignorant, racist, homophobic, etc. simply does not suffice. (Apologies to Parker and Hart's *The Wizard of Id*.) It is better, but not much better, to be sympathetic and say that the peasants have had a really rough time, what with globalization and automation, and are acting out. Sometimes poor uneducated white men, like children, say terrible things (can one imagine saying anything similar about any other group?). Nor is it enough for members of the establishment to say that while we may be privileged, one must look at the alternatives. Perhaps abandoning the status quo means that populists will do terrible things, by which it is usually meant that various populations will lose various rights. This evidently was the argument of the Women's March on Washington and elsewhere on January 21, 2017. But this is an essentially negative argument for any establishment: support us because you fear them. And the argument comes at the cost of demonizing a large part of the population that the establishment claims to govern, to represent, and on which it ultimately relies, even in the absence of democratic sentiment among the governing elite. After all, who takes the "people" in "populist" seriously?

David A. Westbrook

Negative arguments in support of the establishment are unlikely to be enough, or at least have not been enough recently in the U.S., in the U.K. and on the Continent. Fears evidently can be allayed, or subordinated to a more profound discontent with the status quo. What is needed are positive arguments. With both the British and the Belgian empires in mind, Joseph Conrad wrote "What redeems it is the idea only. An idea at the back of it; not a sentimental pretense but an idea; and an unselfish belief in the idea – something you can set up, and bow down before, and offer a sacrifice to..." Unfortunately, the establishment on both sides of the Atlantic has been woefully short of positive ideas in recent years.

What Conrad calls an idea might in some circumstances be called a narrative, a story that people tell to one another and themselves, perhaps the United States as an opportunity and a succession of frontiers, or the unfolding history of a self-governing people. But sometimes the idea is more of an aesthetic, perhaps a city on a hill, or the peacefully cosmopolitan Europe imagined by a cognac merchant. For Conrad it was a complex of associations, being British. But the important point, here, is that it was "the idea that redeems it" – not that there was no sin in colonialism, but that the sin was in service to a larger vision, worthy of allegiance.

The indispensable function of shared beliefs for large polities is that they bridge physical and temporal differences. They make us one, even if only in our heads (how else could we be one?). So, since Rousseau is correct that the citizens of large republics cannot all participate in the general will because it is not directly familiar, such republics require large scale shared beliefs. Rephrased, belief makes collective participation possible, i.e., a polity exists because people believe it exists, and that they belong.

The danger in both the United States and Europe and indeed globally is that people may cease to believe collectively in important aspects of the ideas or narratives that have constituted their polities. Such polities risk polarization, indeed have experienced great polarization, which history warns threatens outright fragmentation, and that often ends badly. In the absence of shared narrative, things fall apart. To be blunt, there seems to be a substantial risk of the fragmentation of the liberal order in the United States, in Europe, and established internationally after World War Two, largely under American leadership. In each context, one may ask, what are the shared narratives, and are they still shared?

Perhaps most consequentially, and the focus of the remainder of this essay, the Trump administration has put the liberal international order at issue. Trump may not succeed in fundamentally changing the course of U.S. foreign policy; inertia is an awesome force. Nonetheless, the administration has signaled its desire for an essentially bilateral basis for U.S. trade policy, and foreign policy generally. Not just NAFTA but the United Nations and NATO have been called into question. Immigration policy became radically more restrictive overnight. In saying such things and taking such actions, Trump appears to be willing to reverse U.S. policy running through both Republican and Democratic administrations back to World War II.

This is not just a matter of U.S. policy and its effects on other states. The world that was born after WWII (globalization, the integration of Europe, and the multilateral liberal international order generally) may be understood to constitute a polity, which I have elsewhere called the City of Gold. The essence of the City is that economic integration can be used to create human connections that span spaces in complicated ways not reducible to the nation state; the organizational expressions of this thought are the Bretton Woods institutions and the European project. In establishing these institutions and thereby constructing the City, the founders sought to replace the nationalism most perfectly represented by Hitler's Germany, in which borders, political identity, economic power and military organization are all coterminous, and available for warfare. In the nation's stead, it was hoped, new forms of social and political life would emerge, forms that have come to be called globalization, or more intensely, Europe, and perhaps less obviously or completely, the multicultural contemporary United States, with its over 320 million souls. As a matter of political philosophy (including political economy) globalization represents a shift in the dominant grammar: a turn from the politics of the modern nation-state, more or less Enlightened, toward a supra-national and post-Enlightened politics largely based on market participation. From this perspective, of Keynes and Monnet, economics is essentially aspirational, a way of constructing politics and a hope, rather than a foundational form of knowledge.

David A. Westbrook

As the rise of global populism makes clear, the survival of the City cannot be taken for granted. Nor should it be. Again, polities need animating ideas, grounds for solidarity. Why should the world be organized in this fashion? What are the ideas that animate the City? What are its weaknesses? *City of Gold* was, of course, an effort to answer to such questions, to articulate the idea that provided a *raison d'etre* for globalization and indeed the contemporary modernity under attack by Trump and other populists.

Many of the center-left parties of the world do not understand that they are playing defense, and therefore should be able to call the contemporary order into question and justify it nonetheless. That kind of thing is for conservatives, and, as already noted, the Democratic Party at least does not understand its conservative commitments. Consonantly, since the fall of Marxism, Davos man has had few critical traditions with which to question his own moral legitimacy. There has been some concern about jobs, and for a while there were protests at WTO meetings. None of that made much difference to center-left thought. Apart from the sheer difficulty of thinking about the contemporary, for those who have done well, as with most elites throughout history, the regime that rewards them needs no justification. The world in which I am privileged is the best of all possible worlds, the order of nature, probably divinely ordained. So, suddenly under pressure from populists, contemporary elites have few intellectual resources on which to draw and little of substance to say, and therefore indulge in name-calling. Hardly edifying, even if sometimes accurate.

But name-calling is besides the deeper point, which is articulating why *this* is a meaningful way to construct political order nationally and internationally. There are indeed alternatives, some of which are articulated by Trump and other populists, some of which are expressed by Islamists, and no doubt others besides. More deeply, the City of Gold, like any form of political life, has shortcomings that must either be changed (leading to a different sort of polity, with shortcomings of its own), or with which some sort of peace must be made. Any civilization has its discontents, and they are not entirely wrong. From this perspective, it is tempting to see the intellectual situation of liberal elites as an updated version of Marie Antoinette playing shepherdess: the fact that elites have a hard time even conceptualizing different politics, much less justifying their own politics, indicates a lack of imagination or

461

critical equipment, perhaps a certain laziness, no doubt the distraction of big wall diving off Belize. Forgivable, even expected, as a human matter, but not responsive to the demands of the day, as Weber urged sociology to be.

A serious establishment confronts the failings of the order it seeks to defend, even as it articulates shared ideas, aesthetics, narratives to which its people subscribe, and which constitute far-flung individuals as a people. On February 18th, 2017, the *New York Times* online ran an article, "Trump's 'Winter White House': A Peek at the Exclusive Members' List at Mar-a-Lago." The same article appeared above the fold on the front page of the New York print edition the next day, under the slightly less breathless headline "For $200,000, a Chance to Whisper in Trump's Ear". A couple of headlines are only snapshots, but at this juncture it is difficult to argue that the Democratic Party or the liberal establishment generally in the U.S. is serious. Hope springs eternal, but it is also difficult to be sanguine about this establishment's capacity to ensure the national and global political orders that it has inherited and that suddenly seem at risk of dissolution.

Trump's bait and switch: job creation in the midst of welfare state sabotage

Pavlina R. Tcherneva [Levy Economics Institute, Bard College, NY, USA]

When President Trump announced his Cabinet members, the chair of the Council of Economic Advisers was conspicuously missing. Two months later, Kevin Hassett (conservative economist and author of the 1999 book *Dow 36,000)* was tapped for the post, which notably is no longer a cabinet-level position.

Economists, it seems, have been demoted. And it was only a matter of time. The malaise over the last half century that produced long term unemployment, acute inequality, and low economic growth is largely the result of trickledown mainstream economic theory and policy and the assault on the welfare state and key government macroeconomic functions.

The rise of Trump was the result. Policy improvisation and experimentation is now the order of the day. In the words of Trump's Chief Strategist Steve Bannon, we should expect a new type of economic populism:

> "…we're going to build an entirely new political movement… *It's everything related to jobs*. The conservatives are going to go crazy. I'm the guy pushing a trillion-dollar infrastructure plan. With negative interest rates throughout the world, it's the greatest opportunity to rebuild everything. Shipyards, ironworks, get them all jacked up. *We're just going to throw it up against the wall and see if it sticks*. It will be as exciting as the 1930s, greater than the Reagan revolution – conservatives, plus populists, in an economic nationalist movement" (Bannon, Nov. 18, 2016, emphasis added).[1]

---

[1] http://www.cnbc.com/2016/11/18/the-conservatives-are-going-to-go-crazy--trumps-top-advisor-lays-out-his-vision-for-shaking-up-america.html

If "it's everything related to jobs," the task herein is to unpack the job creation promise.

Trump's job creation promise

In the fifty days since inauguration, we have yet to see a specific economic plan,[2] but two figures have been repeated over and again: 25 million new jobs and $1 trillion in infrastructure investment.[3]

The White House issues page "Bringing Back Jobs and Growth" shows that the plan is to create those 25 million jobs *over ten years*. Assuming for a moment that there will be no recession during that time (an unlikely scenario), this plan essentially promises an average of 208,333 jobs per month. This is a tepid goal by historical standards and almost identical to the monthly job growth we saw during President Obama's recovery, which was the most anemic in postwar history. Note that 145,000 jobs per month is the minimum necessary to keep up with population growth. In other words, to tackle unemployment, President Trump is promising only 63,333 additional jobs/mo (i.e. 208,333/mo–145,000/mo) for ten years for a total of 7,720,000 jobs.

According to the narrow official BLS definition of unemployment, there are 7,635,000 unemployed people today who want to work but are unable to find employment. That is, we need those 7.7million jobs *now*, not in ten years. And if we look at the broader and more accurate definition of the total number of people who are seeking but unable to find stable, well-paid, full time work, we see a deficit of 19million full time jobs today (njfac.org).

---

[2] As this article went into publication, President Trump unveiled his first proposed budget, which did not include funding for infrastructure investment.
[3] Compare that to president Obama's promise of creating or saving 3-4 million jobs in the midst of the worst post-war recession.

Table 1

Trump's job creation promise in context

Jobs needed **today** (full count/NJFAC measure)	19,000,000
Jobs needed **today** (narrow BLS U-3 measure)	7,635,000
Jobs promised by Trump in **10 years** (adjusted for population growth)	7,720,000

The promise of 7.7million jobs over the next decade is of little consolation to the unemployed. To paraphrase FDR's advisor Harry Hopkins, the unemployed *do not eat* in the *long run,* they *eat* every day.

The above estimates are based on a big assumption – that the economy will not enter a recession, nor will it experience net job losses at any point during the next ten years. If that were to happen (including the past six years of post-Great Recession recovery), we would have lived through the longest expansion in postwar history – a total of 17 years. The average expansion in the US is six years, and the longest was 11.5 years, which means that we are due for another recession in the not-too-distant future. Note that key indicators such as commercial lending activity, median household income, durable goods orders, among others, are already decelerating.

The upside potential

Whereas Trump's job creation promise may be tepid, there is upside potential for actually creating significant employment growth, depending on the specific policies put in place. That unemployment has fallen to pre-recession levels (in the context of an anemic recovery) is largely due to the mass exodus of workers from the labor market, and the increase in the number of people who are discouraged, marginally attached, or trapped in long term unemployment. If a Trump policy manages to tighten labor markets sufficiently to bring those invisible unemployed workers back into paid work, GDP growth could easily reach and even exceed his 4% target. And in his first address to Congress, he emphasized the depressed labor force participation as a key problem in need of a solution.

What is the solution that Trump offers? Apart from the general refrain "everything that relates to jobs", the specifics thus far center almost exclusively on 1) restoring manufacturing, 2) large infrastructure investment, 3) tax cuts and subsidies, and 4) reactionary public policy.

The next sections will argue that the first of these measures (a focus on manufacturing) will be largely ineffective, the second and third (tax cuts and infrastructure investment) have significant upside potential, and the last (reactionary public policy) is of greatest concern with severe long term consequences for the health of the economy. Trump's reactionary public policy largely centers on a) the intent to dismantle the existing administrative state, b) the continued assault on the safety-net, c) neo-nationalist protectionist policies, and d) an aggressive anti-immigrant and civil liberties approach.

I. Manufacturing folly

To claim that unemployment can be significantly reduced by "bringing manufacturing jobs back" is akin to saying that it can be done by "bringing agricultural jobs back." In the early 20th century, the idea that agriculture would no longer be a source of job growth was an anathema, much like it is with manufacturing today. Still, it is technically impossible to address the looming unemployment problem outlined above by focusing on the manufacturing sector.

The transformation of developed nations into service-based economies has led to the precipitous decline in the employment content in manufacturing. In the US, only 8% of total employment was in manufacturing in 2014 (www.bls.gov). Similar trends can be found in many former manufacturing powerhouses like the UK and Japan, and current manufacturing leaders like Germany, Korea, and China.

Manufacturing jobs are disappearing globally in part because of automation, but largely because the sector cannot support itself with internal demand in any country. It seems that there is a limit to the amount of manufacturing goods households and firms in the developed world can or want to consume, much like there was a limit to their demand for agricultural production.[4] Thus, countries that are considered manufacturing "success stories" have largely relied on external demand (exports) for their products. In a world of global export-led competition in manufacturing, the United States has traditionally been the net importer. This trade position will be very difficult to reverse, precisely because other countries are supporting their dying manufacturing sectors via aggressive net exporting strategy.

Even if the US were able to bring some manufacturing production "back" to its shores via high tariffs and aggressive protectionist trade policies, it will not be able to bring back manufacturing *jobs* due to falling share of employment in manufacturing across the globe (Figure 1). The share of employment in manufacturing in most developed countries has collapsed anywhere between 40% (e.g., Japan) to 70% (e.g., US and U.K.) since the 70s, when manufacturing employment was around its peak.

Figure 1 Percent employment in manufacturing, various countries, 1970-2012

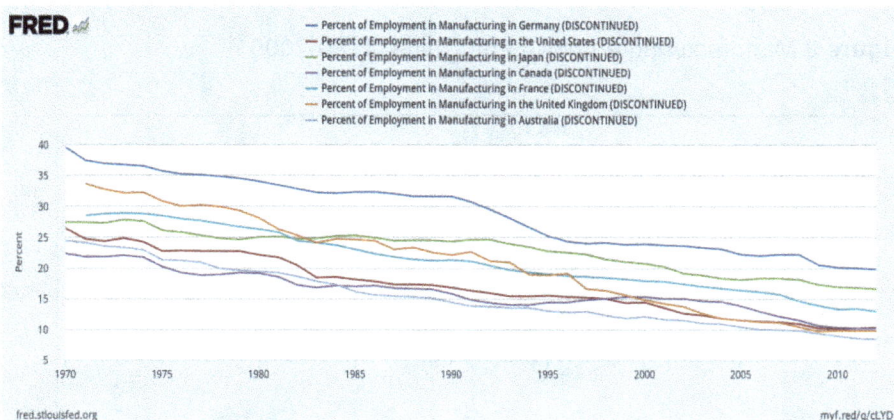

Even in countries like Korea and China, the manufacturing sector is no longer a source of employment growth (Figures 2 and 3). Manufacturing employment in China collapsed approximately 20% (or 26 million jobs) after

---

[4] Greenwald, Bruce, 2016. "The Death of Manufacturing", Levy Economics Institute, 25th Annual Hyman Minsky Conference, April 13. Annandale-on-Hudson, NY.

its 1996 peak. It managed to recover about half of those job losses by 2006, but the trend is flat-lining. The sector is no longer a reliable source of job growth for these countries' increasing population.

This manufacturing-centric vision of job growth is not exclusively Trump's folly. Many economists both on the right and left seem to share it.

Figure 2 Manufacturing employment, Korea, 1990-2014

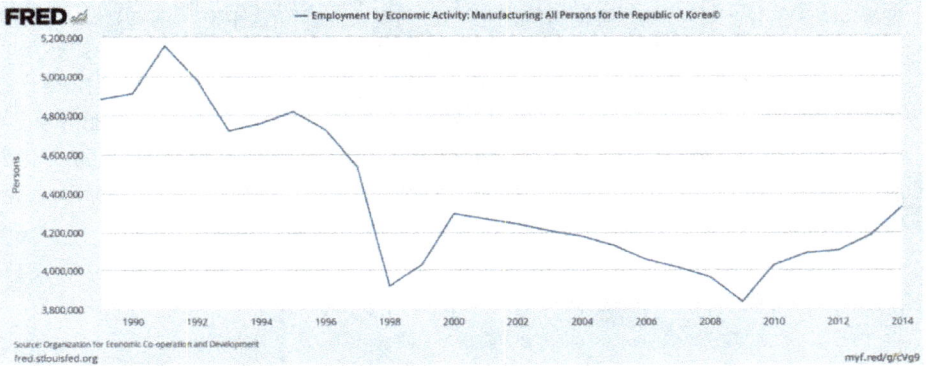

Figure 3 Manufacturing employment, China, 1990-2006[5]

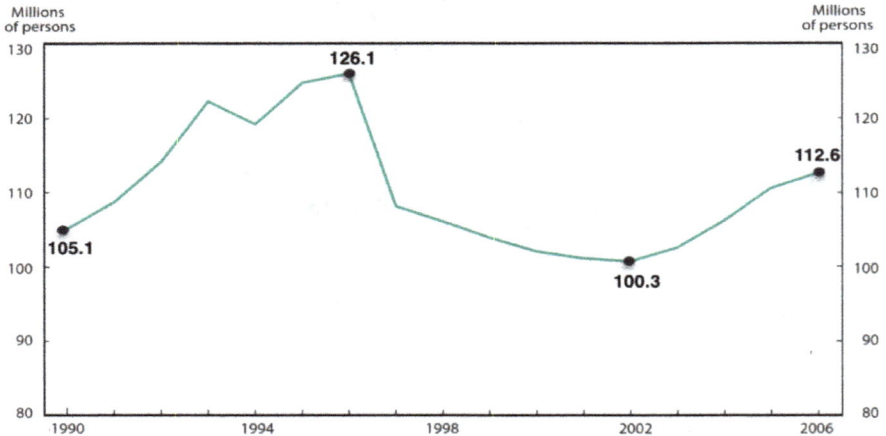

SOURCE: Table 1. Based on and updated from Judith Banister, "China trend report: How many manufacturing employees are there in China?"The Conference Board, China Center for Economics and Business Monthly Member Briefing, October 2007, p. 4.

---

[5] Yearend manufacturing employment in urban units and in village enterprises, China, 1990-2006.

Pavlina R. Tcherneva

An unstable manufacturing-to-services economic transition

When the US transitioned from an agricultural to industrial economy, it was with the help of a long lasting and robust industrial policy that began with Alexander Hamilton's 1791 *Report on the Subject of Manufacturers* and culminated in Roosevelt's National Industrial Recovery Act.

By contrast, as the economy steadily became service-based in the postwar era, there has been no equivalent strategy to support the service sector as a source of stable and strong employment growth.

What we need today is a policy that makes service sector work less precarious, much like we did with manufacturing early in the 20th century. Before manufacturing was able to offer a safe working environment and decent family wages, employment in that sector was insecure and hazardous. Child labor, 10-16 hour working days, and dangerous working conditions were common. It took a series of laws to transform jobs in the industry into the good jobs for which the Rust Belt population now longs. For example, the standard of an eight-hour work day was globally accepted only in 1919.[6] The first federal minimum wage law in the US was introduced much later (in 1938), though some states had such laws on the books earlier. Other labor laws helped improve the physical working conditions of manufacturing work and make it relatively safe. And while today's nostalgia is in part for the lost factory jobs, it is essentially nostalgia for the stable life and prosperous communities they engendered. There is no technical reason why service sector work cannot deliver a good standard of living.

The vast majority of jobs in the US today are directed to the reproduction of labor, i.e., to the care, education, health, feeding, entertaining, etc. of people. Today, 80% of all jobs in the US are in the service sector, compared to only 12% in goods-producing industries (ex-agriculture). It is these service sector jobs that continue to be poorly paid and unstable. The task today is to design a comprehensive policy strategy to remedy the precarious nature of service sector work. To do so a two-prong strategy is needed that includes

---

[6] ILO's Hours of Work Convention calling for eight-hour working days was ratified by 52 countries in 1919.

securing tight full employment over the long run and strengthening the social wage.

II. Infrastructure investment, tax cuts, and the social wage

If Congress passes a $1trillion infrastructure investment program, which Republicans have opposed in the past, there will be a significant upside potential on growth and job creation. Any impact on improving the pay and working conditions of service sector jobs however will be indirect.

Can we expect robust job growth, despite the tepid goals and focus on manufacturing discussed above, from a bold infrastructure plan? Maybe. Much will depend on the execution and financing of these projects.

If the $1 trillion is spent in a manner that directly employs the unemployed, the program could create 20 million living wage jobs over the very short run,[7] though it is doubtful that the construction industry alone can absorb all 20 million people. Considering that CEA chair Hassett is on record strongly advocating for direct job creation, perhaps this is the intention of the administration:

> "It is clear that something terrible happens to individuals as they stay unemployed longer, but that this negative effect is not responsive to normal policy interventions. Accordingly, it is imperative that we think outside the box and explore policies that reconnect individuals to the workforce. As our knowledge of what works is so spotty, this is an area that is crying out for policy experiments that can be rigorously evaluated" (Hassett, 2013 Congressional testimony).[8]

Hassett here echoes Bannon's call for experimentation. At the same time Trump has talked about financing such infrastructure projects by providing

---

[7] Tcherneva, Pavlina R. 2009. "Obama's Job Creation Promise", *Policy Note 2009/1*, Levy Economics Institute, Annandale-on-Hudson, January 2009.
[8] http://www.aei.org/publication/long-term-unemployment-consequences-and-solutions/

tax incentives and subsidies to private equity firms. In that case, it is reasonable to expect that the employment creation effect will be considerably smaller. And the administration will likely subsidize only those projects that can quickly generate a cash flow for the private equity firms. In other words, we could see a lot more toll roads and bridges. This would also mean that investments without an obvious steady cash flow stream may not be prioritized, e.g., levees, dams, inland waterways, hazardous waste, drinking water, schools (all of which are judged to be in "poor" or "near failing" condition by the American Society of Civil Engineers).[9]

While aggressive infrastructure upgrades and investment are long overdue, they are not the best strategy for ensuring tight labor markets and full employment over the long run. Fluctuating infrastructure with the business cycle is not always possible, especially since unemployment in the US accelerates quite rapidly in recessions and decelerates much more slowly during recoveries. To tackle joblessness over all phases of the business cycle, something close to an Employer of Last Resort will be necessary, i.e., a program that directly employs the unemployed in good times and bad, in projects that can quickly absorb them on as needed basis. That means projects in the service sector as well, not just in construction._Nevertheless, a bold infrastructure plan has the potential for delivering significant immediate benefits to the labor market.

In addition to tightening the labor market, a second strategy to making modern work less precarious is to strengthen the social wage. This can be accomplished by expanding existing programs that socialize basic living expenses, such as those for retirement, healthcare, education, etc.

Strengthening the social wage, however, is not what informs this administration's jobs and benefits policies (quite the opposite, see below). So far, only paid family leave has the potential to make a material impact on working families, but the current conversation in the administration has turned away from paid *family* leave to paid *maternity* leave, which is an

---

[9] The current executive action to rollback President Obama's provisions to the Clean Water Act (aiming to protect inland waterways and streams from pollution) means that some of these fundamental infrastructure problems may not ever be addressed under the current administration.

improvement over the current situation, but leaves out fathers and other caregivers.

The likelihood that infrastructure and paid leave can deliver some boost to the economy and working families hinges on sufficient Congressional support from Republicans who have traditionally vocally opposed both.

The rest of Trump's policy agenda (by all indications, the vast majority) is outright reactionary, focusing on dismantling an already weak New Deal institutional architecture, an onslaught on civil liberties, and the advocacy of an American brand of neo-nationalism.

III. Reactionary public policy and the sabotage of the welfare state

At the 2017 Conservative Political Action Conference, chief Trump strategist Steve Bannon succinctly summarized the philosophy behind this administration's public policy. It rests on three pillars: national security, economic nationalism, and the deconstruction of the administrative state.[10] By far the most aggressive changes have begun on the latter. The first proposed budget by the President indicates a wholesale attack in essential public institutions, and while the actual budgeting process is decided by Congress, it speaks to the policy priorities of the President. Additionally, the recent government agency appointments point to an internal sabotage strategy of the public sector.

Consider this partial list:

1. Scott Pruitt, a long-time foe of the Environmental Protection Agency (EPA), now leads it. Apart from calling climate change a "hoax" and "fraud", he has a long track record of bringing up lawsuits against various EPA programs and provisions.[11]
2. Businesswoman Betsy DeVos will lead the Department of Education after a very contentious confirmation process. DeVos is well known for

---

[10] http://www.cnn.com/2017/02/23/politics/steve-bannon-world-view/
[11] https://www.theatlantic.com/science/archive/2016/12/trumps-epa-pick-is-skeptical-of-more-than-just-climate-change/509960/

her ties to the privatization movement and her funding and advocacy of charter schools and voucher programs. In her own words, "my family is the largest single contributor of soft money to the Republican party... and we expect results".[12] When asked about candidate Trump's support for eliminating the Department of Education, she said "It would be fine with me to have myself worked out of a job", though she didn't think that there was a "champion movement in Congress to do that".[13]

3. Incoming Office of Management and Budget (OMB) director Mick Mulvaney has called Social Security a "Ponzi scheme" and reaffirmed his commitment to cutting the program along with Medicare during his confirmation hearing.[14]

4. Tom Price, the new Secretary of Health and Human Services, has supported strictly capping Medicare block grants to states and converting them into voucher programs.[15]

While enemies of the public sector have comfortably walked the halls of Congress at least since Reagan famously said "Government is not the solution to our problems, government is the problem", the current appointments represent a deliberate strategy of rupturing the very agencies and programs these directors are supposed to manage. The traditional Republican approach to governing can be summarized as "devolve, defund, and destroy". Devolve essential federal functions to the states, provide increasingly smaller or strictly capped grants-in-aid, and eventually shrink, privatize, or eliminate programs altogether.

Trump's administration offers a radical extension of this approach – a *welfare sabotage strategy* that aims to subvert core institutions from within. While Trump himself has promised to preserve Social Security and Medicare, his appointments indicate that the assault on these programs is

---

[12] http://www.newyorker.com/news/news-desk/betsy-devos-trumps-big-donor-education-secretary

[13] https://www.washingtonpost.com/news/answer-sheet/wp/2017/02/22/so-far-education-secretary-betsy-devos-is-just-what-her-critics-feared/?utm_term=.026c60b3fcc9

[14] https://www.theatlantic.com/politics/archive/2017/01/will-trump-cut-medicare-and-social-security/514298

[15] https://www.nytimes.com/2017/02/23/us/politics/social-security-safety-net-trump.html

not over. The fate of the Affordable Care Act is also uncertain. One path to "repealing and replacing" Obamacare, while preserving (what Trump called) the good features of the program (i.e., pre-existing condition and dependent care coverage), is to extend Medicare to all citizens. Given Republicans' hostility to all public assurance programs, the likely reform will include some mix of private sector subsidies, rebates, and vouchers, which are fundamentally at odds with the goal of guaranteeing access to all.

Trump has also announced a federal hiring freeze. Despite the uproar over this executive order, it is nothing new. Federal government employment has been declining since the late 80s, but is essentially flat since the 70s. State employment experienced a significant increase in the postwar era, but stopped growing over the last 15 years (Figure 4) and is outside the purview of the presidency.

Notably, during the last recovery, public sector employment was a drag on total employment growth. Precisely when the private sector was finally beginning to rehire the unemployed, the public sectors (federal and state) either decelerated hiring or slashed jobs altogether (Figure 5).

Figure 4 Federal and state government employment, 1940-2016

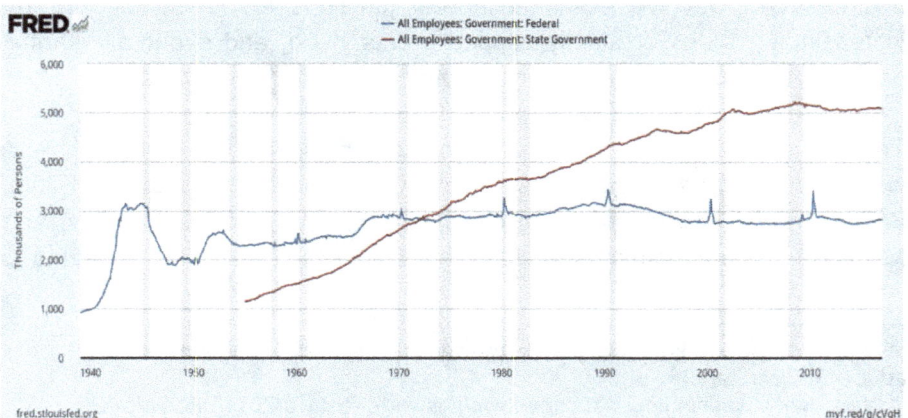

Figure 5 Government and private sector employment, percent change, 2008-2015, year over year

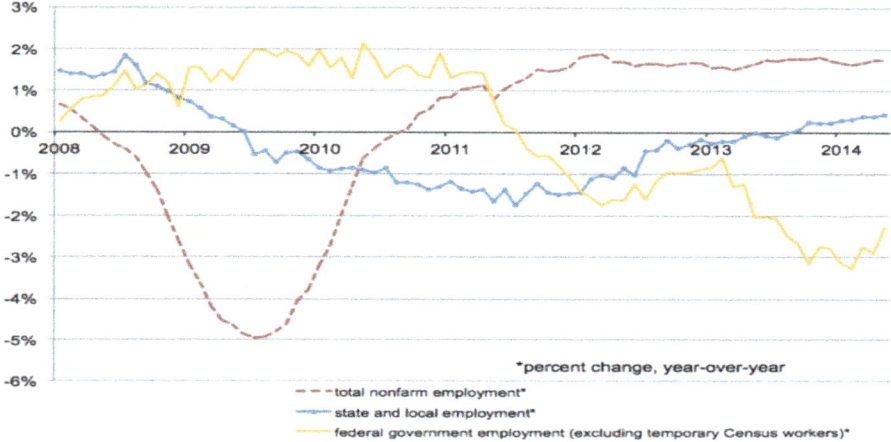

While there will be no visible change in the overall federal government labor force from the hiring freeze, it will likely cause additional disruptions in the daily operations of various government agencies, heightening the administrative sabotage strategy.

IV. Bait and switch: jobs today, insecurity tomorrow?

If the administration hopes to deliver the jobs it had promised over a decade by focusing on manufacturing, it will fail. The way to think about the actual employment effect of Trump's policies is to consider three key factors: 1) the expected net deficit position of the government, 2) the manner in which spending will be targeted, and 3) the success of the Welfare State Sabotage strategy.

Significant deficit spending ahead

Much like it was under Reagan's administration, a Trump presidency will likely generate large government deficits. At the macroeconomic level, they will be a net positive for the economy, considering that the deficit had been shrinking rapidly since 2012. Since the economy is already weakening (as above, orders, incomes and credit conditions are worsening), federal government receipts will continue to decelerate, widening the deficit further. If Trump's policy manages to shrink net imports further, the real terms of trade may deteriorate but government deficit spending will have a positive impact on private sector surpluses. The question is, whose coffers will fill up – those of financial firms, nonfinancial firms, or households, and, if the latter, will they be at the bottom or top of the income distribution.

How will government spending be targeted?

Not all deficits are created equal. If the manner of spending (even if it is more aggressive) produces little shift from the policies of the past five decades, then it may not reverse the critical levels of inequality. It is likely that incomes at the top of the distribution will continue to grow. Trump has proposed deregulating financial markets, cutting income taxes, and changing the income brackets to make taxation less progressive. He has also proposed $54 billion in additional military spending next year (a 10% increase). The federal hiring freeze notwithstanding, Trump has also called for employing 10,000 Immigration and Customs Enforcement and 5,000 border patrol agents. While the impact on employment will negligible, the policy priority indicates a likely boost in spending for national security and criminal justice. Any additional subsidies that may be directed to private equity or other firms will be a welcome windfall for them, boosting profits and the capital share of income. In other words, this could be Reaganomics on steroids – a mix of Military and Penal Keynesianism with aggressive trickledown policies centered on firm incentives, tax cuts, and subsidies.

By design, these policies improve incomes of those at the top of the income distribution and the owners of capital. Furthermore, the current labor market structure improves job prospects and incomes of workers who are high-wage, high-skill, and already employed. The question is whether these policies will manage to create enough jobs for people who are at the bottom and in the middle of the income distribution. Since manufacturing will not return an adequate number of jobs back to our shores, it is unlikely that the hollowed out middle class will find stable well-paying jobs in that sector. A

Pavlina R. Tcherneva

bold and targeted infrastructure policy that directly hires the unemployed has the potential to help in that respect. Finally, let us consider those workers who are at the very bottom of the income distribution, who are first fired and last hired, and who have the greatest trouble finding stable, full-time employment at above-poverty wages. It is unclear that any of Trump's proposed policies are aimed to directly raise the floor and help those workers.

Sabotage of the welfare state

Finally, while deficit spending and infrastructure investment have the potential of tightening labor markets over the short run (even as they continue to disproportionately favor incomes at the top through subsidies and tax cuts), the greatest downside risk to the economy is the strategic assault on the welfare state as we know it. Trump will be a big deficit spender, but conservatives will use the myth of sound finance and revenue neutrality to defund key public programs. For example, the proposed increase in military spending was "offset" by proposed cuts of the same amount in other nondefense programs and agencies (e.g., 25% reduction in the EPA's budget).

More importantly, however, the possible systematic destruction of the already weak safety-net and New Deal institutions means that, structurally, the economy will be more fragile as we reach the next recession. If the attack on the EPA, education, Medicare and Social Security is successful, it will also mean that the quality of life for many will deteriorate one poisonous drop of water, one deteriorating public school, and one medical-related bankruptcy at a time.

In sum, the negative effect of the long-term assault on the administrative and welfare state may be temporarily masked by short-term improvements from economic growth, which could prove sufficient to give Trump another term and more time to institutionalize the destruction of the welfare state.

The social reformers of the 20th century put in place an important (albeit incomplete) safety-net that made economic depressions a thing of the past. That included guaranteed and directly provided housing, education, health insurance (for the elderly and children), retirement income, and many other programs and policies. Instead of strengthening the safety-net, the current philosophy is on a radical deconstruction of the administrative state. All of the above indicates intent to devolve these functions not simply to states, but to corporations (e.g., the privatization movement of public education, healthcare, and social security). If the Trump/Bannon vision is to convert the Welfare State into a Corporate Welfare State, and if it comes to fruition, it will represent an entirely new world order, one that ushers in a new Dickensian world of modern robber barons, precarious labor, and social and economic insecurity and injustice.

Can "Trumponomics" extend the recovery?
Stephanie Kelton [University of Missouri, Kansas City, USA]

Donald Trump was elected President of the United States as the U.S. economy headed into its eighth year of expansion following the deepest and most protracted recession of the post-WWII era.[1] Since the start of the recovery in June 2009, real GDP growth has averaged a reliable 2.1 percent, and the labor market has clawed back all of the 8.7 million jobs that were lost in the aftermath of the financial crisis. Inflation has remained low, and the official unemployment rate had fallen to just 4.6 percent in November 2016. Goldilocks might have declared the porridge to be just right.[2]

To some observers, this looked like a pretty decent backdrop against which to make the case for a continuation of the Obama-era policies that many credited with finally healing the wounds of the Great Recession. While not blazing hot, the American economy was growing and creating jobs, and many believed that Hillary Clinton could best her opponent by pledging to build on the achievements of the past with a fiscally responsible, steady-as-she-goes agenda.[3] Yuge changes were unnecessary, she insisted. America was already great.

Many voters had other opinions, along with vastly different lived experiences. The tailwinds that were supposed to propel the first woman into

---

[1] http://www.cbpp.org/research/economy/chart-book-the-legacy-of-the-great-recession

[2] Consistent with this reading of the overall health of the U.S. economy, the Federal Reserve made good on its long-awaited promise to boost a key interest rate in December 2016.

[3] Although she embraced some progressive elements of the Sanders' agenda (e.g. making public colleges and universities tuition-free for up to 83 percent of America's families), readers will recall that she vowed that her policies, "not add a penny to the debt". A bold, progressive agenda it was not.
https://www.theatlantic.com/politics/archive/2016/10/hillary-clinton-national-debt-presidency/504905/

the Oval Office met their fiercest resistance in the so-called Rust Belt states, where people who had seen their lives and their communities transformed by decades of disinvestment and disenfranchisement decided to roll the dice on a foul-mouthed reality TV star with no experience in public office.

I'm not going to spend time diagnosing the decades-long forces that gave rise to Donald Trump. For that, I recommend Thomas Frank's excellent book, *Listen, Liberal* or Matthew Stoller's outstanding piece in *The Atlantic*, "How Democrats Killed Their Populist Soul". What I am interested in pursuing here is a different question altogether – now that we have President Trump, what will he and his Republican colleagues do? Which constituencies will Trump fight for, and can the GOP hold together to deliver any substantive legislative victories for the new president?

Some argue that Trump's policies pose major downside risks to the U.S. economy. Others see the potential for an upside surprise, at least in the near term. What will President Trump do, and will his policies work as advertised? No one can say for sure. What we do know is that the voters who delivered the White House to Mr Trump[4] are counting on him to deliver real improvements in their lives. This means that simply extending the recovery may not be enough to hang on to the Obama voter who crossed over to give her vote to Donald Trump. To retain the support of these voters, Trump's policies must go beyond simply prolonging the recovery. They must promote the kind of growth that raises the living standards of millions of struggling Americans, lessens the share of total income going to profits and reverses the yawning gaps in the distribution of wealth and income. Unfortunately, these are not the stated goals of the Trump administration, so the remainder of this essay will focus on the narrower question: can "Trumponomics" extend the recovery?

Where are we today?

At 93 months of age, the U.S. economy is in the midst of its fourth-longest expansion since 1850. If we can extend the recovery for another two-and-a-

---

[4] Specifically, those in Michigan, Pennsylvania and Wisconsin, which all flipped in favor of Trump, giving him the razor-thin margin he needed to win the electoral vote.

half years, we will break the all-time record.[5] For that to happen, the economy's tailwinds must remain stronger than its headwinds. The broad consensus today is that the economy is very close to its full employment potential. And while few see a downturn in the near future, Goldman Sachs puts the risk of recession at about 1-in-4 through 2018Q3.[6]

Whereas Janet Yellen recently gave the economy "a little more room to run[7]," she now argues that it is close to its potential, and she is preparing markets for a series of rate hikes beginning in March.[8] Such a tightening cycle is consistent with the belief that the Fed's dual-mandate has been broadly achieved and that there is little room for an acceleration of growth. Goldman's Hatzius and Pandl (2016) agree:

> "While expansions do not die of old age, history shows that they are at greater risk when spare capacity is exhausted, as it probably is now. So it is especially important to monitor whether growth may be running out of steam."

Before we move to an analysis of "Trumponomics", we should pause and ask two important questions. First, are we really near our full employment potential? Second, is there room for "Trumponomics" to extend the recovery?

It is probably safe to say that the consensus opinion among Fed economists and academic economists alike is that the economy has essentially returned to its full employment potential. That belief is consistent with the data reported in Figure 1, which shows that the gap between actual and potential GDP has been nearly eliminated.

But there is a problem here, at least in my view. The data depict an economy that is close to bumping up against its long-run ceiling, a constraint that many believe will frustrate Trump's effort to get things running much hotter.

---

[5] The longest expansion on record, which lasted 120 months, occurred 1991-2001.
[6] http://www.zerohedge.com/news/2016-12-31/goldmans-10-most-important-questions-2017
[7] https://www.federalreserve.gov/mediacenter/files/FOMCpresconf20160921.pdf
[8] Morgan Stanley is forecasting seven rate hikes by the end of 2018, three this year, beginning in March, and four next year.

However, there is something more we should know about the position of this ceiling.

Figure 1

Gross domestic product

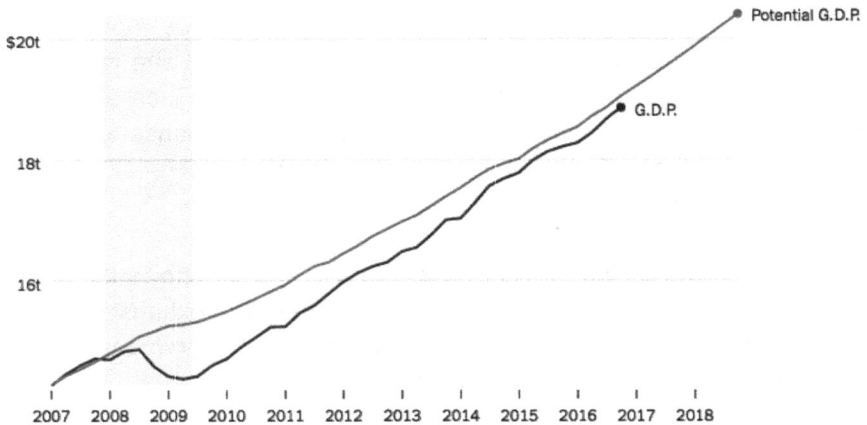

Shaded area indicates recession

Sources: Congressional Budget Office; Bureau of Economic Analysis

As Larry Summers has shown, the bulk of the progress that was made in closing the output gap came, "not through the economy's growth but through downward revisions in its potential" (2014, p. 66). In other words, as Figure 2 shows, output is near its full employment ceiling not because the economy rose to its potential but because we lowered the definition of what we believe our nation's productive capacity to be. It's a bit like giving up on the idea that your child is capable of achieving straight As, relaxing the goal to a 2.0 GPA, and then celebrating when he presents you with across-the-board Cs. Junior is now a high achiever!

Figure 2

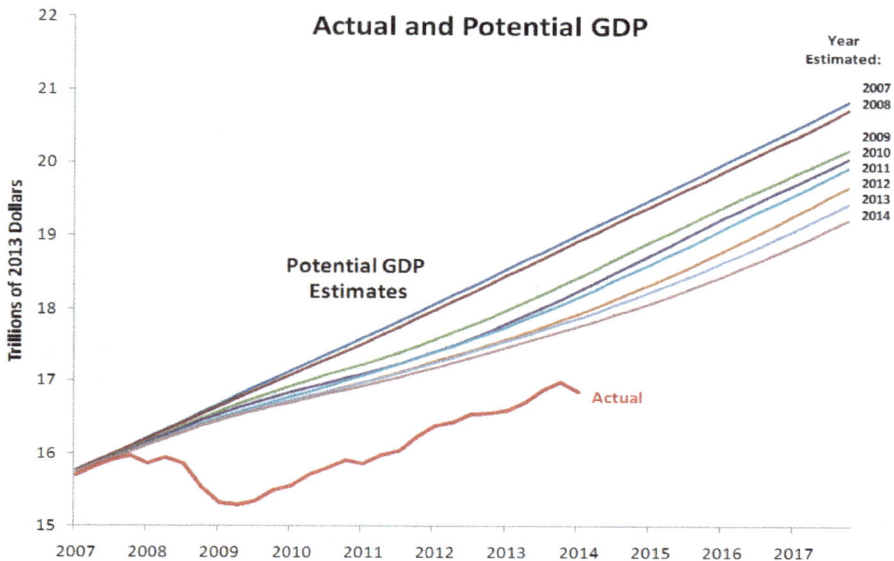

Figure 2: Actual and Potential GDP

Sources: CBO and BEA

To see what a difference these downward revisions make, consider what it would look like if today's output gap was measured using the 2007 estimate of potential GDP (shown in Figure 2) rather than the revised estimate shown in Figure 1. Instead of full employment, we would be looking at a GDP gap of roughly 14 percent, or nearly $2 trillion.

Why did potential GDP get revised downward in the first place, and how much of that lost potential could be clawed back? The short answer to the first question is that the failure to bring about a swift recovery from the Great Recession imposed lasting harm on the economy. The answer to the second question may be among the most important of our time. And while I cannot offer a rigorous empirical estimate here, both history and theory suggest that there are ways to reverse at least some of the damage.[9] Investments in

---

[9] This is similar to what happens to the human body when you give up your exercise regimen for a more sedentary lifestyle. Your muscles begin to atrophy and your long-term physical capacities become impaired. By restarting the exercise routine, some

infrastructure, education, R&D, etc., should help the U.S. reclaim some of the lost potential by boosting long-run productivity.

Even without the kinds of investments that would help nudge potential GDP northward, it still may be possible to safely accelerate growth. Whereas Goldman and Yellen[10] see little slack left in the economy, new research from Dantas and Wray (2017) suggests that the U.S. labor market is still far from full employment. In their view, "we are not even close" to full employment, and "reaching full employment would require, on average, gains in payroll employment of 420,000 jobs per month for the next four years". Nick Buffie (2016) agrees, arguing that, despite the low official unemployment rate, the labor market remains quite weak. If these assessments are correct, then it should be possible to squeeze more growth out of the economy in the short term. It also means that "Trumponomics" could surprise on the upside.

What is Trumponomics?

Less than three months into the Trump presidency, there is no formal budget and no precise blueprint that describes the full range of policies and programs that the administration intends to pursue. "Trumponomics", therefore, is still very much a moving target, although we are beginning to see the broad contours of an economic agenda taking shape. Harvard economist and former U.S. Treasury Secretary, Larry Summers, sees "enormous uncertainty" ahead, adding:

> "This is probably the largest transition ideologically and in terms of substantive policy in the last three quarters of a century."

---

of the damage can be reversed. As Jared Bernstein (2014) has argued, something similar is possible in the economy.

[10] Asked whether additional stimulus was needed at a Dec. 2016 press conference, Yellen pointed to the "solid labor market," adding that additional fiscal stimulus was "not obviously needed".

https://www.nytimes.com/2016/08/01/business/economy/clinton-trump-either-way-count-on-deficit-spending-to-rise.html

What is the ideological philosophy behind "Trumponomics" and how does it represent a break from the guiding principles of the last 75 years? As a presidential candidate, Donald Trump explained his thinking in this way:

> "It's called priming the pump. Sometimes you have to do that a little bit to get things going. We have no choice – otherwise, we are going to die on the vine…The economy would be crushed under Hillary. But no matter who it is, the debt is going to go up."[11]

To some economists, Trump's economic approach sounded downright Keynesian.[12] Channeling Bernie Sanders, he called for a trillion-dollar boost to infrastructure spending, along with (the usual Republican call for) deregulation and massive tax cuts. He was unapologetic about running budget deficits and adding to the national debt. But he combined the more Keynesian-inspired fiscal maneuvers with a protectionist trade agenda and a nationalist pledge to seal the borders and deport millions of undocumented people. On Social Security and Medicare, he sounded a more compassionate tone, vowing no cuts, and he even talked about bringing the U.S. into the 20th century by supporting paid family leave. As Figure 3 shows, this blend of policy positions makes it difficult to situate "Trumponomics" within a conventional ideological matrix.

So, what exactly *is* "Trumponomics"? The short answer is that it is too early to put concrete numbers the full range of proposals that will be coming down the pike. Mick Mulvaney, director of the Office of Management and Budget (OMG) is working on those numbers now, promising that "[a] full budget will contain the entire spectrum of what the president has proposed".[13] An early look at the numbers could come mid-March, when the Trump administration is expected to release a sneak preview of its plans in the form of a "skinny budget".

---

[11] These remarks were made during a phone interview with the *New York Times*. Quoted in Schwartz (2016). https://www.nytimes.com/2016/08/01/business/economy/clinton-trump-either-way-count-on-deficit-spending-to-rise.html
[12] See Noah Smith (2016).
[13] For more details, see Phillip and Snell (2017).

Figure 3

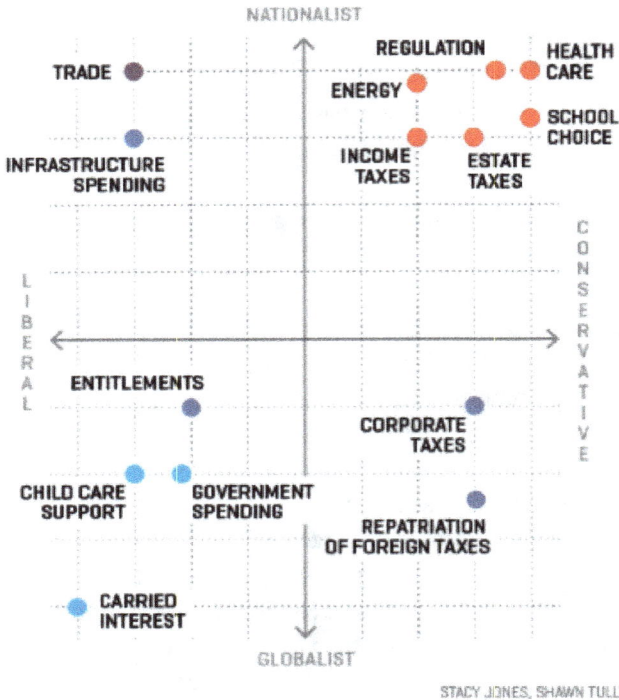

Source: http://fortune.com/2016/08/11/trumponomics-chart/

For now, we know that the President's FY18 Budget will call for a 10 percent increase in defense spending, along with equivalent ($54B) offsetting cuts to other federal agencies. The president has also pledged to make long-overdue investments in our nation's infrastructure, promising, "we're going to start spending on infrastructure – big". Democrats have balked at both proposals, preferring traditional government-funded infrastructure investment to the widely-anticipated public-private schemes that are expected to form the basis of the Trump model.[14] And they oppose the cannibalizing of the non-defense, discretionary budget as a means of allocating more resources to the military. As House Minority Leader Nancy Pelosi (D-CA) put it:

---

[14] Reports indicate that the plan will rely on some $167 billion in private financing. Investors, who will require roughly a 10 percent rate of return, will receive tax credits in exchange for financing. Democrats worry that this will mean toll roads and other user fees and that it will leave projects in low-income areas out.

"A $54 billion cut will do far-reaching and long-lasting damage to our ability to meet the needs of the American people and win the jobs of the future. The President is surrendering America's leadership in innovation, education, science and clean energy."[15]

Thus, Democrats are bracing for massive cuts that could more than offset any stimulus that might result from higher spending on infrastructure and defense. Just how big could these cuts be?

Some (Bolton, 2017) have suggested that Trump's budget will closely track the Heritage Foundation's Blueprint for Balance,[16] which calls for $10.5 trillion in cuts over the next 10 years. The already-tiny amounts spent on the Corporation for Public Broadcasting (CPB), the National Endowment for the Arts (NEA) and the National Endowment for the Humanities (NEH) would be eliminated completely, and the departments of Justice, State, and Transportation would suffer deep cuts.

As all good Keynesians know, one person's spending is another person's income. So how is cutting $10.5 trillion in spending supposed to help to extend the recovery?

Ronald Reagan to the rescue?

During their first presidential debate, Hillary Clinton criticized Donald Trump's approach to growing the economy, labeling it "Trumped up trickle down" economics. It was an obvious jab at the kind of supply-side policies that characterized the Reagan years. Rather than fight the comparison, Trump focused on the bigness of his agenda:

> "By the way, my tax cut is the biggest since Ronald Reagan
> – I'm very proud of it."

---

[15] http://www.democraticleader.gov/newsroom/22717/
[16] http://www.heritage.org/conservatism/report/blueprint-new-administration-priorities-the-president

Hillary maintained that she and Trump had different economic philosophies, adding that giving the biggest tax cuts to the top percent "is not how we grow the economy."

Nobel laureate Paul Krugman also compared Trump's agenda with Reagan's, predicting Trump's policies "won't actually do much to boost growth because [interest] rates will rise and there will be lots of crowding out. Also a strong dollar and bigger trade deficit, like Reagan's morning after Morning in America." And while it is true that interest rates rose sharply and America's trade deficits ballooned under Reagan, it is also true (as Figure 4 shows) that the economy grew at a good clip during much of the Reagan era. Remember, Reagan was reelected in a landslide.

Figure 4

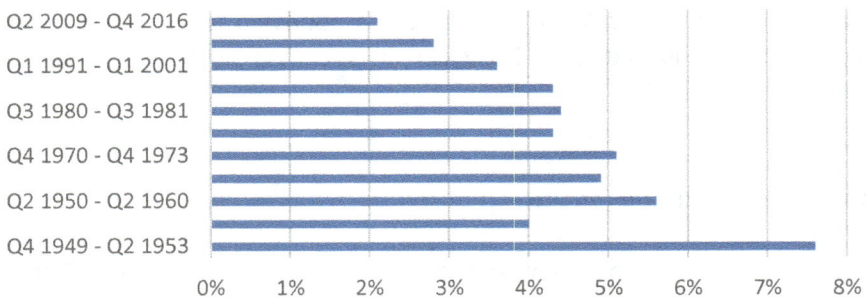

Average Annual Change in Real GDP, by expansion

According to Harvard's Ken Rogoff (2016), "Trumponomics" has the potential to really juice the American economy. "Even if you oppose Trump's policies," he says, "you've got to admit they are staunchly pro-business."[17] For this reason, Rogoff has cautioned against the kind of doomsday scenario described by Krugman, warning, "[b]eware of pundits who believe Trump will bring economic catastrophe".

---

[17] https://www.project-syndicate.org/commentary/trump-business-confidence-growth-boom-by-kenneth-rogoff-2016-12?barrier=accessreg

What Rogoff doesn't say, however, is that the benefits of the Reagan expansions went overwhelmingly to those at the top of the income distribution. Tax cuts for the wealthy, attacks on unions, cuts to programs aimed at helping the poor and an obsession with deregulation and "free markets" shifted the balance of power toward owners of capital and ushered in an era of increasing insecurity and growing inequality for the working class. Figure 5 shows the remarkable shift in the distribution of income that began under Reagan.[18]

Figure 5

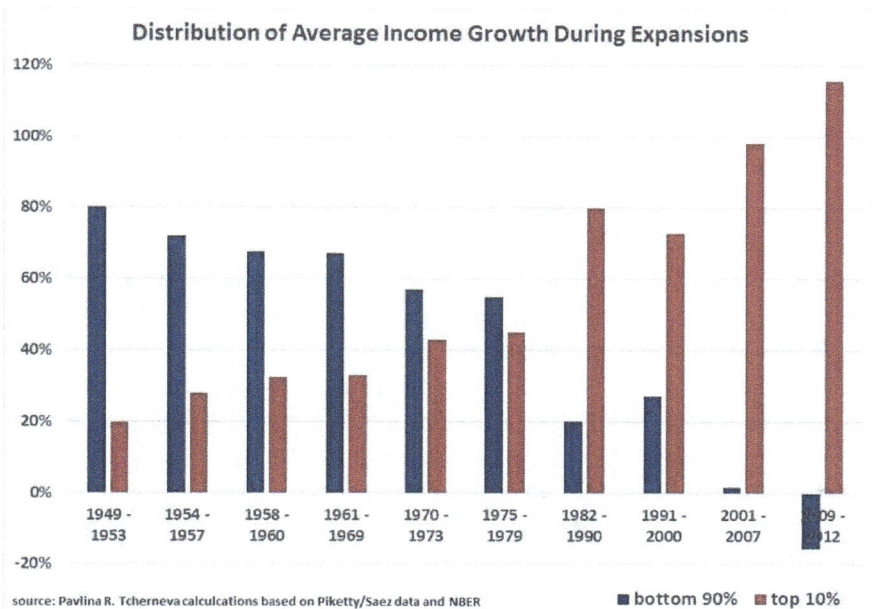

Distribution of Average Income Growth During Expansions

source: Pavlina R. Tcherneva calculcations based on Piketty/Saez data and NBER   ■ bottom 90% ■ top 10%

Prior to the election of Ronald Reagan in 1980, the vast majority of Americans – the bottom 90 percent – received the lion's share of the income generated in a growing economy. It wasn't a utopia – there were still periods of high unemployment and maldistribution that left millions impoverished –

---

[18] This incredible graph from Tcherneva (2014) can be found here: http://www.levyinstitute.org/pubs/op_47.pdf

but the bulk of the income produced during an economic expansion went to the vast majority of the population. After "Reaganomics," however, things changed. The benefits of a growing economy were no longer broadly shared, as the top 10 percent began hauling in more than the bottom 90 percent. It's a trend that has not only continued but one that has generally worsened over time.[19]

Donald Trump isn't promising to reverse these trends, though he is claiming that his policies will substantially boost the economy and improve life for millions of "forgotten" Americans. Specifically, the president has championed an agenda that the he says will deliver 3.5-4.0% growth, something the U.S. hasn't experienced on any kind of sustained basis since the "Clinton Boom".[20] Judging from the details we have thus far, "Trumponomics" appears to be just what Hillary Clinton called it, a Trumped-up version of Reagan's trickle-down recipe, with an added ingredient or two.

What do we know about Trump's recipe for the economy? First, we know that the Trump administration has embraced the House Republican proposal to reduce the number of tax brackets from seven to three and to lower the marginal tax rate on the highest income earners from 39.6 percent to 33 percent. We also know that the president is proposing to eliminate the estate tax, cut the corporate income tax rate from 35% to 20%, and allow businesses to repatriate offshore profits at 10%.[21] Finally, we know that even his health care plan is really just a massive tax cut for the rich. According the Center on Budget and Policy Priorities (2017), the 400 highest income earners in America would see an *average* tax cut of about $7 million a year if the Republicans succeed in repealing the Affordable Care Act. And while Trump says that his policies will improve life for the "forgotten Man", the Tax Policy Foundation (TPF) has shown that the little guy isn't getting much of anything when it comes to the proposed tax reforms. Indeed, TPF estimates

---

[19] According to research published by the Washington Center for Equitable Growth, the top 1 percent of Americans captured 52 percent of the total real income gains from 2009-2015.

[20] For more on the drivers of the Clinton economic expansion, see Baker (2012).

[21] Goldman Sachs estimates that repatriation could allow as much as 75 percent of the $2 trillion currently stashed offshore to return home only to be used for share buybacks, which will mainly benefit wealthy individuals who comprise the bulk of investors in the stock market.

that after-tax incomes for the top 1 percent of earners could surge by as much as 16 percent, while the bottom 80 percent could see an after-tax lift of just 1.9 percent. Meanwhile, the bottom quintile would end up with a paltry 0.8 percent boost in their take-home pay.

And then there's Trump's proposal for a regressive Border-Adjustment Tax (BAT).

> "Like any tax, the tariff burden does not fall uniformly across goods, but falls more heavily on particular goods and the populations that purchase them" (Furman, et al. 2017).

Hence, the tariff burden is essentially a regressive tax. Furman, et al. estimate the distributional impacts of current US tariffs, which amount to $33 billion per year or around 0.2 percent of GDP. They find that tariffs cost the bottom 10-20 percent of households about $95 per month, while middle-income households pay about double that amount ($190 per month) and the richest 10% pay about $500 per month. While the rich pay more in absolute terms, Figure 6 shows that the tax is substantially regressive when you consider the burden relative to income. Taken together, Trumponomics includes a hefty serving of Reagan-inspired trickle-down economics along with a side of protectionism, a dash of military Keynesianism and a social agenda that is anti-worker and anti-immigrant.

Figure 6

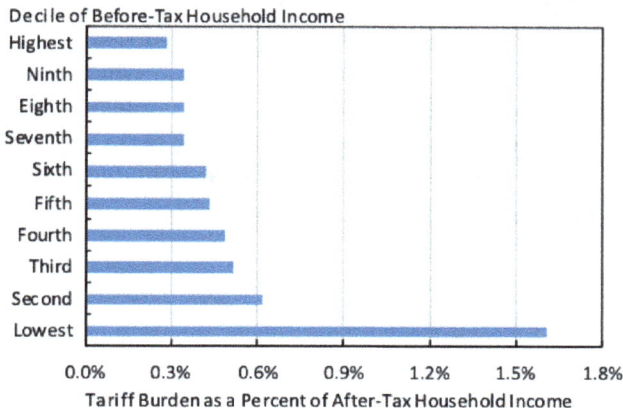

Decile of Before-Tax Household Income

Tariff Burden as a Percent of After-Tax Household Income

While the CEOs of some of America's retail giants have taken aim at the proposed border tax, Wall Street appears to love where Trump is trying to take the economy. For example, Jamie Dimon, chairman and CEO of JPMorgan Chase & Co., says that Trump's proposed tax cuts, deregulation and infrastructure investment have reawakened animal spirits. "If he gets it done, even part of it, it will be good for growth, good for jobs, good for Americans."

Is it possible? Can Trump's supply-side tax cuts and deregulation unleash a current of tailwinds strong enough to propel the economy forward even as they're coupled with massive cuts in other programs (not to mention mass deportation and a possible trade war)? Most experts find it unlikely.

Can "Trumponomics" extend the recovery? No consensus among experts

For the most part, what follows is a brief overview of the macroeconomic consequences of "Trumponomics" as analyzed by the research staffs at Moody's Analytics and Goldman Sachs. Both have produced forecasts for a range of macro variables – including real GDP, unemployment, inflation, interest rates, etc. – using different assumptions about what might ultimately come to pass as "Trumponomics".

Over at Moody's, Zandi, et al. (2016), looked at three scenarios. The first hews most closely to the agenda espoused by Donald Trump in speeches, interviews, tweets, etc. This scenario is referred to as the "Full Monty Trump" in Figure 7. A toned-down version is also examined, one in which Trump succeeds in getting his basic agenda adopted, though on a smaller scale.[22] This is the "Trump Lite" scenario below. Finally, the Moody's team simulates a "Washington Reality" scenario that assumes the kind of budget neutral program that Congress could actually pass.

---

[22] Tax cuts are smaller, "only" 6 million undocumented immigrants are expelled, and there is no trade war.

Figure 7

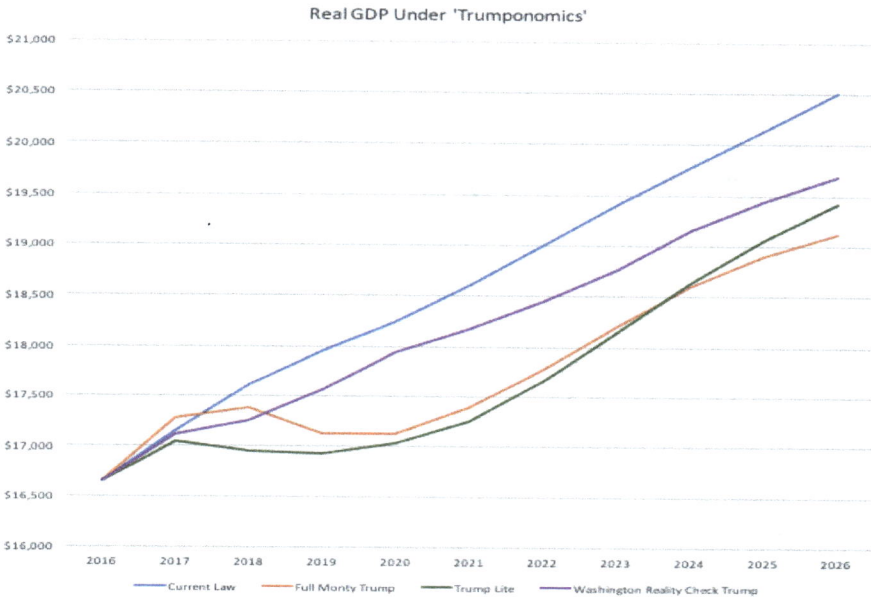

Real GDP Under 'Trumponomics'

In all three cases, Trump's policies produce outcomes that are worse (over the full forecast horizon) than the baseline scenario, which assumes no change in current policy. Even in the best-case scenario (Washington Reality) where a recession is avoided, the economy averages just 1.7 percent annual growth over 10 years, well below the promise land of 3.5-4.0 percent. Under the worst-case scenario, the one that assumes all of Trump's proposed policies become law, including tariffs and the deportation of millions of undocumented people, the economy enjoys a year or two of improved growth, but "a lengthy recession" follows, with 3.5 million fewer jobs and an unemployment as high as 7% by the end of his first term. The economy also does more poorly under the "Trump Lite" scenario, with Moody's predicting a deep recession beginning in 2018 as unemployment climbs to 8.9% by 2020.

You might wonder whether Moody's is uniquely pessimistic about the prospects for growth under a Trump administration. That's a fair question, so let's look at the analysis done by Goldman Sachs. Over at Goldman, Haztius and Stehn (2017) ran their own simulations, using the Federal Reserve's economic forecasting model. Their results are shown in Figure 8.

Figure 8

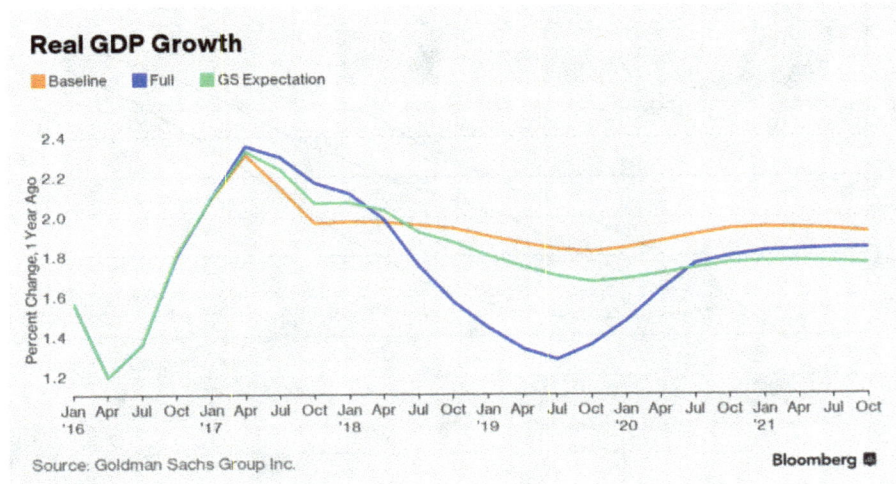

Source: Goldman Sachs Group Inc.

Like Moody's, the Goldman team found that Trump's policies are a net negative for growth relative to the baseline (*status quo*). To get the extreme case, Goldman ran a "Full" Trump scenario that included $450 billion in fiscal stimulus (a combination of infrastructure investment and tax cuts), some reciprocal tariffs, and immigration restrictions that reduce the size of the labor force by 2.5 million compared with the Fed's baseline projection. As Figure 9 shows, the Full Trump scenario juices the economy in the near term, but the effects of the stimulus quickly diminish, as the model assumes that limits on labor force growth begin to bind, slowing overall growth. As with Moody's, Goldman doesn't expect Trump to get everything he wants, so they also simulated a more realistic agenda (GS Expectation), which extends the economy's growth rate above 2 percent for about an additional year. "Our simulations suggest that Mr Trump's policies could boost growth slightly in 2017 and 2018, but are likely to weigh on growth thereafter if trade and immigration restrictions are enacted," wrote Hatzius and Stehn.

Goldman differs from Moody's in that "Trumponomics" *does* manage to extend the recovery through 2020, however growth doesn't approach anything like the 3.5-4.0%. The bottom line is that, compared with the *status quo* scenario, both Goldman and Moody's predict a smaller economy at the end of Trump's first term.

It's an astonishingly gloomy outlook that is shared by a number of high-profile academic economists. For example, Joseph Stiglitz, speaking at the ASSA meetings in Chicago, said, "There is a broad consensus that the kind of policies that [President Trump] has proposed are among the policies that will not work." Harvard Professor and former U.S. Treasury Secretary, Larry Summers, believes financial markets are overly enthusiastic about "Trumponomics", comparing their zeal to a "sugar high" that will dissipate as reality sets in. That reality includes the harmful effects of Trump's immigration policies and his protectionist impulses, which many believe could drive up prices (of labor and imports), fueling higher inflation and causing the Fed to hike rates more aggressively. Finally, Paul Krugman notes that "Trumponomics" ultimately relies on a burst of supply-side tailwinds, powered by huge tax cuts, which, in his view, are unlikely to propel the economy through the gale force headwinds that will result from trillions in spending cuts:

> "But the tax cuts will go to the wealthy, who won't spend much of their windfall, while the spending cuts will fall on the poor and struggling workers, who will be forced into sharp cutbacks in spending. The overall effect on demand is therefore likely to be negative, not positive."

Not everyone shares this glum perspective on "Trumpnomics". As I noted above, Harvard's Ken Rogoff remains optimistic. While he believes that "inflation is a near certainty", he sees the potential for a doubling of growth, at least temporarily, cautioning against "pundits who believe Trump will bring economic catastrophe".

Conclusion

President Trump has promised to "Make America Great Again". Part of this pledge involves getting the U.S. economy growing at rates it hasn't experienced in almost two decades. Many economists are skeptical of "Trumponomics" and doubt that his policies can extend the recovery, much less deliver the 3.5-4.0% growth he has crowed about.

My own view is that economists have probably displayed too much pessimism when it comes to the potential for higher economic growth. But that does not mean that I side with Rogoff entirely. As I see it, both Rogoff outcomes are possible. That is, "Trumponomics" – especially tax cuts and deregulation – could produce windfall gains that energize asset prices (stocks and even real estate), generating a strong – if temporary – wealth effect that leads to a surge in aggregate spending. If there is more slack in the economy than Moody's or Goldman imagine, it seems reasonable to think that growth could surprise to the upside – 3.5 percent does not strike me as inconceivable.

But, as Figure 6 reminds us, growth alone does not prevent economic catastrophe. In other words, both outcomes – higher growth with catastrophic consequences – are possible. And the just-released "skinny budget" from the Office of Management and Budget (2017) certainly looks like a catastrophe for the sick, the poor, the middle-class and the planet. It includes a Reaganesque beefing up of the defense budget, along with massive cuts in non-defense discretionary spending. Couple this with the yet-to-be-announced cuts to non-discretionary spending (Social Security and Medicare) plus Trump's proposed tax cuts, and you have Reagan on steroids, a full-throated trickle-up program designed to lock in gains for those already at the top of the income distribution. It may elevate growth, for a time, but it will be a catastrophe nonetheless.

References

Baker, Dean. 2012. "There is No Santa Claus and Bill Clinton Was Not an Economic Savior," *Truthout*, December 25. http://www.truth-out.org/opinion/item/13526-no-santa-claus-and-bill-clinton-was-not-an-economic-savior

Bernstein, Jared. 2014. "Undoing the Damage to Potential Growth," *The New York Times*, Economix Blog, March 3.
https://economix.blogs.nytimes.com/2014/03/03/undoing-the-structural-damage-to-potential-growth/

Bolton, Alexander. 2017. "Trump Team Prepares Dramatic Cuts," *The Hill*, January 1.
http://thehill.com/policy/finance/314991-trump-team-prepares-dramatic-cuts

Buffie, Nick. 2016. "The Case for a Weak Labor Market," *Center for Economic Policy Research*, September. http://cepr.net/images/stories/reports/weak-labor-market-2016-09.pdf

Debot, Brandon, Chye-Ching Huang and Chuck Marr. 2017. "ACA Repeal Would Lavish Medicare Tax Cuts on 400 Highest-Income Households," *Center on Budget and Policy Priorities*, January 12. http://www.cbpp.org/research/federal-tax/aca-repeal-would-lavish-medicare-tax-cuts-on-400-highest-income-households

Dantas, Flavia and L. Randall Wray. 2017. "Full Employment: Are We There Yet?" *Public Policy Brief*, No. 142, Levy Economics Institute of Bard College.
http://www.levyinstitute.org/pubs/ppb_142.pdf

Frank, Thomas. 2016. *Listen, Liberal: Or, Whatever Happened to the Party of the People?* Metropolitan Books/Henry Holt & Co.

Furman, Jason, Katheryn Russ, and Jay Shambaugh (2017), "US tariffs are an arbitrary and regressive tax." *VOX: CEPR's Policy Portal*, 12 January.
http://voxeu.org/article/us-tariffs-are-arbitrary-and-regressive-tax

Furman, Jason. "Inequality: Facts, Explanations, and Policies," October 17. *City College of New York (CUNY)*.
https://obamawhitehouse.archives.gov/sites/default/files/page/files/20161017_furman_ccny_inequality_cea.pdf

Hatzius, Jan and Pandl. 2016. "US Economic Analyst: 10 Questions for 2017," *Goldman Sachs Economics Research*, December 30.

Hatzius, Jan and Jari Stehn. 2017. https://www.bloomberg.com/news/articles/2017-02-13/trump-looks-like-a-net-negative-when-it-comes-to-growth-goldman

Heritage Foundation. 2016. *Blueprint for a New Administration: Priorities for the President*, November 1. http://www.heritage.org/conservatism/report/blueprint-new-administration-priorities-the-president

Irwin, Neil. 2017. "The Big Question for the U.S. Economy: How Much Room Is There to Grow?" Upshot, New York Times, February 24.
https://www.nytimes.com/2017/02/24/upshot/the-big-question-for-the-us-economy-how-much-room-is-there-to-grow.html?_r=1

Leubsdorf, Ben. 2017. "US Economy Returns to Lackluster Growth," *Wall Street Journal*, Jan 27. https://www.wsj.com/articles/u-s-gdp-grew-1-9-in-fourth-quarter-1485524015?utm_content=buffer39bab&utm_medium=social&utm_source=twitter.com&utm_campaign=buffer

Mester, Loretta. 2017. "Transcript: Wall Street Journal Interview with Cleveland Fed's Loretta Mester," *Wall Street Journal*, January 6.

https://www.wsj.com/articles/transcript-wsj-interview-with-cleveland-feds-loretta-mester-1483732612?tesla=y

Office of Management and Budget. 2017. "America First: A Budget Blueprint to Make America Great Again," https://www.whitehouse.gov/sites/whitehouse.gov/files/omb/budget/fy2018/2018_blueprint.pdf

Phillip, Abby and Kelsey Snell. 2017. "Trump to Propose 10 Percent Spike in Defense Spending, Major Cuts to Other Agencies," The Washington Post, February 27. https://www.washingtonpost.com/powerpost/trump-to-propose-10-percent-spike-in-defense-spending-massive-cuts-to-other-agencies/2017/02/27/867f9690-fcf2-11e6-99b4-9e613afeb09f_story.html?hpid=hp_hp-top-table-main_budget-1115a%3Ahomepage%2Fstory&tid=a_inl&utm_term=.f201ba4126b3

Rogoff, Kenneth. 2016. "The Trump Boom?", Project Syndicate, December 7. https://www.project-syndicate.org/commentary/trump-business-confidence-growth-boom-by-kenneth-rogoff-2016-12?barrier=accessreg

Schwartz, Nelson D. "Clinton? Trump? Either Way, Count on Deficit Spending to Rise," The New York Times, July 31, https://www.nytimes.com/2016/08/01/business/economy/clinton-trump-either-way-count-on-deficit-spending-to-rise.html

Smith, Noah. 2016. "Even Trump is a Keynesian." Bloomberg View, November 18. https://www.bloomberg.com/view/articles/2016-11-18/even-trump-is-a-keynesian

Stoller, Matthew. 2016. "How Democrats Killed Their Populist Soul," The Atlantic, October 24. https://www.theatlantic.com/author/matt-stoller/

Summers, Lawrence H. 2014. "U.S. Economic Prospects: Secular Stagnation, Hysteresis, and the Zero Lower Bound," Business Economics, Vol. 49, No. 2. http://larrysummers.com/wp-content/uploads/2014/06/NABE-speech-Lawrence-H.-Summers1.pdf

Summers, Larry. 2017. "U.S. Tax Reform is Vital, But Donald Trump's Plan is Flawed," Financial Times, January 8. https://www.ft.com/content/7e5900ec-d401-11e6-b06b-680c49b4b4c0

Tcherneva, Pavlina. 2014. "Growth for Whom?" One-Pager, No. 47, Levy Economics Institute of Bard College, October 6. http://www.levyinstitute.org/pubs/op_47.pdf

Tully, Shawn. 2016. "All You Need to Know About 'Trumponomics' in One Chart," Fortune, August 11. http://fortune.com/2016/08/11/trumponomics-chart/

Yellen, Janet. 2016. "Transcript of Chair Yellen's Press Conference," September 21. https://www.federalreserve.gov/mediacenter/files/FOMCpresconf20160921.pdf

Zandi, Mark, Chris Lafakis, Dan White and Adam Ozimek. 2016. "The Macroeconomic Consequences of Mr. Trum's Economic Policies," Moody's Analytics, June. https://www.economy.com/mark-zandi/documents/2016-06-17-Trumps-Economic-Policies.pdf